An Introduction to

Bibliography

for Literary Students

RONALD B. McKERROW

Introduction by David McKitterick

An Introduction to

Bibliography

for Literary Students

RONALD B. McKERROW

Introduction by David McKitterick

ST PAUL'S BIBLIOGRAPHIES · WINCHESTER

OAK KNOLL PRESS · NEW CASTLE · DELAWARE

1994

The Clarendon Press, Oxford, published the first edition of
An Introduction to Bibliography for Literary Students
in 1927 and the 2nd impression, with corrections, in 1928.
St Paul's Bibliographies,
1 Step Terrace, Winchester, SO22 5BW, UK,
reissued the 1928 text with an Introduction by
David McKitterick in 1994.
This was published in North and South America in 1994 by Oak
Knoll Press, 414 Delaware Street, New Castle,
DE 19720, USA.
Distributed in the USA by Lyons & Burford, Publishers,
31 West 21 Street, New York, NY 10010

A CIP catalogue record for this book is available from the British
Library.

Library of Congress Cataloging-in-Publication Data
McKerrow, Ronald Brunlees, 1872-1940.
An introduction to bibliography for literary students/
by Ronald B. McKerrow.
    p.   cm.
Originally published: Oxford : Clarendon Press, 1927.
Includes bibliographical references and index.
ISBN 1-884718-01-9
    1. Bibliography, Critical.   2. Bibliography – England – Early
printed books – 16th century.   3. Bibliography – England – Early
printed books – 17th century.   I. Title.
    Z1001.M16 1994
010'.42- -dc20   94-7048

(UK) ISBN 1-873040-07-5   (USA) ISBN 1-884718-01-9

Printed in Great Britain by St Edmundsbury Press,
Bury St Edmunds

CONTENTS

CONTENTS

vi

CONTENTS

APPENDIX

LIST OF ILLUSTRATIONS

INTRODUCTION

David McKitterick

'I RATHER disapprove of the title: for one thing I wanted it myself; for another his book is a pretty thorough survey of the particular field he has chosen.' These words, by McKerrow's friend, ally and constant critic, W.W. Greg, were spoken in the course of a lecture on 'The present position of bibliography' delivered to the Bibliographical Society in London in October 1930. The circumstances of their delivery, quite apart from their content, are a reminder of how a small group of people transformed textual scholarship with respect to English literature, and thereby set in train a course of critical reflection whose effects are still very much to be seen today. *An Introduction to Bibliography for Literary Students* is, as a title, not only disarmingly modest. It is also one charged with specific references at a time when the study of English literature itself was in transition. McKerrow was acutely aware of the need for such a book, and was aware also that each word of his title carried its own frame of meaning and allusion.[1]

Ronald Brunlees McKerrow was one of a remarkable trio who between them were most responsible for the founding principles of modern bibliographical studies.[2] The three men had much in common, both in their work and, remarkably, in their backgrounds. The oldest was A.W. Pollard (1859-1944), a member of the British Museum staff since 1883. Pollard had been brought up in London, and was educated at King's College School. He had then gone up to St John's College, Oxford, where he formed a firm friendship with A.E. Housman, an exact contemporary. McKerrow, born in 1872, was brought up beside Wimbledon Common, and after Harrow proceeded first to King's College, London, and then in 1894 to Trinity College, Cambridge. W.W. Greg, the youngest of the three, was born in 1875. Like McKerrow, he too grew up by the Common, following McKerrow first to Harrow and then in 1894 joining him at Trinity College. In due course Pollard was to move with his family also to a house near Wimbledon Common, following the move of his old school to

Wimbledon from the Strand. The three were by no means always in accord; but in their regular meetings and discussions, joined intermittently by others, they established the principles that they believed should underlie bibliographical and textual study. In great measure, these principles, and the practices on which they are based, remain in place today.

These ideas were disseminated partly in publications; but also, no less importantly, in the societies to which all three men were deeply committed. First there was the Bibliographical Society, founded in 1892, which McKerrow joined in 1902 – four years after Greg. From 1912 to 1940 McKerrow served as Secretary of the society, until 1934 in conjunction with Pollard, and from 1938 with F.C. Francis. He edited the society's journal, *The Library*, briefly, and he contributed to the society's surveys of early English printers. But his most important work to be published by the society on this subject lay in two illustrated monographs: *Printers' & publishers' devices in England & Scotland, 1485-1640* (1913), and, with F.S. Ferguson, *Title-page borders used in England & Scotland, 1485-1640* (1932). In 1929 he was among the first recipients of the Society's gold medal. Apart from the Bibliographical Society, there was the Malone Society, founded in 1906 at the suggestion of A.W. Pollard, and dedicated to the publication of English plays and dramatic documents before 1640. Pollard became the first treasurer. Other founding members included E.K. Chambers as president, and Greg as honorary general editor; McKerrow was among its first council members.[3] In three successive years, 1907-09, under the scrutiny of Greg, McKerrow produced books for this society, but he seems to have been as much attracted to an older series, *Materialen zur Kunde des älteren Englischen Dramas*, edited by W. Bang, and published in Louvain until brought to an end by the First World War.

Originally, McKerrow had been intended for his family engineering firm. He trained for this in London, and throughout his life kept abreast of many of the principal scientific developments in his generation. But after modern languages at Cambridge he spent three years in Tokyo, as Professor of English, before returning to London and, eventually, to a career in publishing.

But by far the most important work of McKerrow's early years was his edition of Thomas Nashe, published in five volumes between 1904 and 1910. Together with his several editions of Elizabethan and Jacobean literature that appeared at much the same period, they formed the basis of all his subsequent bibliographical work; they remain unsuperseded to this day. It was by the experience and knowledge gained in the course of editing and annotating Nashe that McKerrow was moved to write, in the opening words of a paper in 1913 which was to prove a turning-point, 'that modern editorial methods demand some bibliographical knowledge'. Such words seem today to be hardly revolutionary; but McKerrow had been obliged to read widely for his editions of Nashe and his contemporaries, and neither he nor Greg had been impressed by recent work. Less succinctly, he developed his theme:

> Those who have had occasion to examine somewhat minutely any large quantity of work done at the present day upon English writers of the sixteenth and seventeenth century, and more particularly editions of their writings, must, if they have even rudimentary bibliographical knowledge, have been struck by the curious ignorance of the most elementary facts of the mechanical side of book-production during the Tudor and Jacobean period which is sometimes shown even by scholars in other respects well equipped.

This charge opened a paper (published in the Bibliographical Society's *Transactions* for 1912-13) entitled cumbersomely but accurately, 'Notes on bibliographical evidence for literary students and editors of English works of the sixteenth and seventeenth centuries'.[4] These 'notes' formed the last hundred pages or so of the volume, and in 1914 were issued as a separate booklet. They were to be the basis of *An introduction to bibliography*.

It was at once a broadside against ignorance and incompetence, and a means to rectify a situation that did little credit to English scholarship. Both the Oxford and the Cambridge University Presses had been responsible for editions of English dramatists that had earned Greg's scorn. Years later, in his presidential address to the Bibliographical Society in 1930, Greg recalled one of the more notorious occasions concerning Oxford:

INTRODUCTION

There was a time when the belief there prevailed that any one with a good classical education on the broad lines of the Oxford tradition was sufficiently equipped to undertake the editing of any English author. Of course, this simple faith was bound sooner or later to lead to disaster, and one day a book appeared that was a real disgrace, and which received well-merited castigation.[5]

In February 1912 Greg took his criticisms from the review columns to the lecturer's podium, and made similar points as he addressed the Bibliographical Society on the question, 'What is bibliography?'[6] He was most concerned to establish what he termed 'critical bibliography' (as distinct, for example, from descriptive, or systematic, bibliography); and he attempted a summary:

What is constant as a requirement, what every editor, what every textual investigator needs, what may therefore be truly called the grammar of literature, is critical bibliography. Critical bibliography is the science of the material transmission of literary texts, the investigation of the textual tradition as it is called, in so far as that investigation is possible without extraneous aids. It aims at the construction of a calculus for the determination of textual problems.[7]

It is not altogether clear what Greg meant by investigation without extraneous aids; and his attachment to the term 'calculus' in determining literary texts, followed up in his celebrated paper *The calculus of variants* (Oxford, 1927) has since been questioned.[8] But the central point could scarcely be denied. As for his lament that so far there had been no attempt to systematise such a discipline and framework of knowledge, he must have known even as he spoke that McKerrow, with whom he was in almost daily contact, had such a scheme in preparation. So, too, may A.W. Pollard, who likewise pointed out the need for such a book in his summary of Greg's paper published in the Society's *News-sheet* for March 1912.

So the way was prepared for McKerrow's paper, more a small book than an article. Its focus was on the period and the literature with which he and Greg were most concerned. It also addressed primarily English literature, the subject which, in Greg's opinion, the Bibliographical Society ought most to consider. Thus it was at once expansionist, in claiming that some knowledge of bibliographical method based on the experiences of earlier printers was an essential skill in the editing of texts, and parochial, in its silence with respect to those concerned with texts of other literatures or times. Greg had written the manifesto; McKerrow now drafted the legislation. Both men had a programme that was limited in its scope, if not necessarily in its applications.

For its first half century, Pollard's devotion to the causes and interests of the Bibliographical Society had a greater effect on its fortunes than that of any other single individual. His strong sense of collegiality was to be seen most obviously in the *News-sheet*, written almost entirely by himself, and circulated to all members between 1894 and 1914, though it informed all his other writings in relation to the society. In his hands, and particularly in the hands of Greg, McKerrow and others of their generation, bibliography was given a new meaning and new purposes. In particular, it was to be applied not only to the listing of books (essential as this was, as in Pollard and Redgrave's *Short-title catalogue* of English books down to 1640, published in 1926), but also to the application of the information thus made available, coupled with analysis and understanding of the ways by which authors' manuscripts were turned into printed books, to the critical editing of literary texts. Thanks to the interests of Greg and McKerrow, attention was given first, and primarily, to Elizabethan and Jacobean literature.

Such concentration on a single area of literature, by a series of principles worked out within a circle of dedicated scholars, helped, usually for the first time, to produce publications that provided a series of reliably based texts of principal English authors from this period. In the hands of others, most notably perhaps R.W. Chapman of the Oxford University Press, some of the principles explored for earlier literature were extended to the eighteenth century: that is, for the remainder of the time that the hand press, and hand-made paper were the normal ways of printing books.

But the sense of collegiality remained; and it was to this sense of collegiality in the kindred subject of English studies that McKerrow addressed himself when in 1925 he used the resources of his publishing firm, Sidgwick and Jackson, to launch a new quarterly journal, the *Review of English Studies*. Its advisory panel was drawn from people having experience in some of the principal centres of English studies in British universities at that time. While on the one hand this group included figureheads such as A.C. Bradley and Sir Henry Newbolt, on the other it included many of those who could be said to have some proven sympathy with the bibliographical and editorial work of McKerrow. Among this latter group were C.H. Herford, then at work on a new edition of Ben Jonson, and Percy Simpson (both from Oxford), A.W. Reed and John Dover Wilson (both from King's College, London, where McKerrow lectured on historical bibliography at this time[9]), R.W. Chambers (University College London), and Greg himself. Others, such as R.W. Chapman and Ernest de Selincourt, also from Oxford, represented later though cognate interests.[10] Instead of the kind of forum for critical discussion of the kind encouraged in the next few years by *Criterion* or *Scrutiny*, the *Review* offered the chance for new bibliographical method to engage with the editorial and historical – and hence literary and critical – concerns of modern literaty and linguistic discussion. And, not least, the new periodical was to serve as a centre:

> English studies have in the past suffered greatly from want of co-ordination. Many of the best researchers have worked in ignorance of what others were doing in the same field, and much time has been wasted by duplication. It is our hope that this review may serve as a centre for all such workers, that they may report in it what they themselves are doing, seek through its means the aid of others in their difficulties, and by its help be brought into touch with other workers in their own and neighbouring fields.

Even at the time it must have seemed an optimistic view. But the collegiate nature of English studies, as McKerrow saw them, was epitomised during the first years of the *Review of English Studies* in the lists provided of university examination results in the subject, from Belfast, Birmingham, Bristol, Cambridge, Durham, Leeds, Liverpool, London, Manchester, Oxford and Sheffield, as well as Wales, Aberdeen and Edinburgh. By far the largest numbers were at Cambridge, London and Oxford. Needless to say, while there was much support for the position taken up by McKerrow's venture, it was not appreciated with equal enthusiasm in every university. The obvious absentee was Cambridge. Although both were members of Trinity, neither Greg nor

McKerrow had any connection with teaching, and contributions to the new journal from Cambridge were noticeably thin in its early years. More encouragingly, the list of subscribers in America grew with unexpected speed. In many respects, while the advance of approaches propounded by McKerrow or Greg could not easily be denied, it was quite easy to ignore or marginalise them. By 1937, Stephen Potter, in the University of London, was to write in a widely read book, *The muse in chains* – lighthearted in manner but serious in purpose – of 'this concentration on such more tangible subjects as palaeography, bibliography and printing (there is a Press at University College),' and linking these to attempts to bring science to bear on the study of literature and language. 'The question remains,' he concluded, 'is the scientific attitude, still so urgently needed in such subjects as politics or penology, the right attitude with which to approach the great English writers? And do these new improvements bring about the radical change in the subject which is necessary? Or is it merely a less superficial treatment of externals?'[11]

Potter's chance to influence English studies in universities further ended soon afterwards when he joined the BBC. But articulation of his question revealed that despite commanding attention, in its implications for the study and criticism of English literature more generally, the work of Pollard, McKerrow and Greg was misunderstood. The *Review of English Studies* remained a central voice, edited by McKerrow almost until his death; but it became one voice among many, as approaches to the subject diversified.

The manifesto of a new magazine is not the most reliable prophet for its future contents. But those who launched the *Review of English Studies* were clear in their beliefs: that 'research as they understand it is the life-blood of literary theory', and something rather different from research in the natural sciences: 'We have less to do with that which has never previously been known, and more with that which has never been rightly interpreted.' 'It is our task as researchers to discover not only the facts, the dry minutiae, but the relations between them, their reactions upon one another, those slower changes and developments to which the most clear-sighted of contemporaries must be ever blind. This knowledge, if we can attain it, is new knowledge, and as well deserves the name of discovery as any secret wrested from nature by the astronomer or physicist.'

INTRODUCTION

It was characteristic of McKerrow that in launching the *Review of English Studies* he should have written of its practical purpose in saving time. 'One of the chief aims of this review,' he wrote to A.F. Pollard, Professor of History in University College London, 'is to help students in English Literary History by publishing articles on methods of research.'[12] So, too, he took advantage of the stiff wrappers of the journal to print on them a calendar made of two sliding parts, which enabled those interested to discover on what day of the week any date fell between 1558 and 1623 – his own particular period. The same awareness of the need for practical help was plain in the review of A.W. Pollard and G.R. Redgrave's *Short-title catalogue of books printed in England, Scotland and Ireland, and of English books printed abroad, 1475-1640* (soon to be abbreviated by everyone to *STC*), which McKerrow himself contributed to the issue of October 1927. He began with the words, 'As I grow older I feel increasingly certain that there is no man of letters who deserves better of the community than the compiler of a good index. A man has but a certain number of hours during which to work, and whoever saves some of those hours by the abridgment of mechanical labour prolongs his effective life and enables him to make more and better use of his acquired knowledge and experience.'

The first year of the journal opened with R.W. Chambers on the *Ancrene Riwle*, and included substantial articles on Byron and Wordsworth. But by far the greatest attention was allocated to drama, particularly of the sixteenth and seventeenth centuries. In these first issues, McKerrow also began to fulfil his promise to examine the 'relations' between 'facts', in publishing a survey of Elizabethan handwriting. For it was by understanding handwriting that more would be discovered not only in archives and contemporary manuscripts, but also of Elizabethan and Jacobean printing. So an article by Muriel St Clair Byrne on 'Elizabethan handwriting for beginners' appeared in the second issue. Also in this volume, C.J. Sisson contributed a paper on 'Bibliographical aspects of some Stuart dramatic manuscripts'. In the second volume, Hilary Jenkinson, then currently collaborating with Greg on *English literary autographs*, but also engaged on his own study of later English court-hands, wrote briefly on English punctuation in the sixteenth century. A.W. Reed offered hints for those engaged on research in London's libraries. And in the third, McKerrow himself supplemented Byrne's article with one of his own on capital letters in Elizabethan handwriting. More revealing still, perhaps, was the review by Robin Flower, of the Department of Manuscripts at the British Museum, of the first part of Greg's (and others') *English literary autographs, 1550-1650*, in January 1926. Flower took up not only the obvious, autograph, application of the fascicules, as references for authenticity; he also suggested that here was the kind of evidence that could be brought to bear on questions respecting the relationship of written to printed copy. Again, here were practical evidences for application to literary questions. These various essays and reviews, interspersed among historical and critical matter, were supplemented by surveys of periodical literature and, for several issues, by a guide to the opening arrangements of the country's major research libraries. In all this, there was much in common with the work of the Institute of Historical Research in London, whose combination of research with practical advice and instructions similarly served the historical community.

The location at 44 Museum Street of McKerrow's firm, Sidgwick and Jackson, which published the *Review of English Studies*, was conveniently close to the British Museum, and hence frequent contact with Pollard. Indeed, the editorial relationship between the two men, McKerrow as editor of the *Review of English Studies* and Pollard as editor of *The Library*, became so close that on occasion it confused even themselves.[13] Sidgwick and Jackson were already committed to the cause of bibliographical scholarship, including in their list not only Greg's editions of the Henslowe diaries and the Henslowe papers, but also McKerrow's own edition of Thomas Nashe, and the catalogue of the library of Samuel Pepys. But Chapman was at Oxford University Press; and perhaps there was some wry satisfaction to be had from McKerrow's being published by the very firm whose books Greg in particular had repeatedly castigated.

When therefore he came to revise his paper of 1913, McKerrow's purposes had become yet more clear: to explore the relationship between what an author wrote, and what was printed on the page confronting the critical reader; and to offer guidance not only to the beginner in the subject, but also (as he well realised) to those who considered themselves, sometimes mistakenly, to have advanced beyond the elementary. His preface to the aptly titled *An introduction to bibliography for literary students* spoke of the book's still retaining 'the original idea of a help-book for literary students'. Moreover, by 1927 he was able to draw on his experience as teacher of the subject at King's College, London. His express aim was 'to keep before me throughout the problem of the relation of the printed book to the written word of the author'. In other words, on the one hand he was most concerned with questions respecting the editing of literary texts; and on the other he assumed that by understanding this primary relationship – primary in the sense that it assumed a direct link between author, printer and reader – it was possible to understand an author's intentions more clearly. Reviewing the book in *The Library*, Charles Sisson remarked somewhat drily, 'there are still those who distinguish sharply between the book as a material object and the book as a thing of the spirit'.[14] In the obituary of his friend written after McKerrow's death in 1940, Greg returned to the same theme: 'the whole significance of his teaching lies in the importance he attached to the derivation of the text.'[15] In his edition of Thomas Nashe, it had been McKerrow who had coined the term 'copy-text', a concept that he was to reconsider in his later work on Shakespeare. Neither Greg nor McKerrow was content to leave his early opinions and conclusions unexamined later.[16]

But as they each also realized, their work was both revolutionary and timely. In a highly critical review of a work by Leon Kellner, *Restoring Shakespeare; a critical analysis of the misreadings in Shakespeare's works* (Leipzig: Tauchnitz, 1925), Greg had made explicit the point of which none of his readers can have been unaware: that in the previous decade there had been laid the foundations of 'a new method in the emendations of his [Shakespeare's] text'.[17] Thanks in particular to Sir Edward Maunde Thompson (especially on *The play of Sir Thomas More*[18]), A.W. Pollard, and John Dover Wilson (whose *New Cambridge Shakespeare*, the comedies edited in conjunction with Sir Arthur Quiller-Couch, had begun to appear in 1921), the study of the text of Shakespeare had advanced as never before. *An introduction to bibliography* was designed to take stock of this work, to set it beside what had also been done on literature of much the same period, and to provide training and inspiration for the next generation.

The book was published in October 1927, in a first printing of 1750 copies.[19] Among reviews in the ordinary press, the *Times Literary Supplement* was first, with over twenty-five column inches; and by the end of December there had also been reviews in *The Nation and the Athenaeum* by Edmund Blunden (who treated it as an addendum to Iolo Williams's *The elements of book-collecting*), and by Michael Sadleir in the *Observer*, as well as in the *London Mercury*.[20] But perhaps Falconer Madan summed it up best: 'a standard work from the day of publication', he wrote to McKerrow in January 1928.[21]

Bis dat qui cito dat. In 1913 McKerrow had written deliberately of the period which most interested him, and with which he was most familiar: the reigns of Elizabeth I and James I. In 1927, thanks principally to R.W. Chapman, whose interests lay primarily in the eighteenth century, he extended his range, to write more generally of the period down to 1800. Nonetheless, the concentration on McKerrow's first interests remained. It was at once a strength and (since the book has inevitably been sought out by, and rightly recommended to, those interested in other periods) a limitation. The title itself did nothing to discourage a wider readership. On the whole, the first two parts are an expansion, revision and reconsideration of the paper of 1913. As a consequence, his book is unusual in that the footnotes are as essential as the main text, and contain some of his best observations. But it remains best of all on the sixteenth and seventeenth centuries.

The very brief third part approached the heart of the book's justification. 'All that has been written hitherto in this book has been, or should have been, directed, immediately or remotely, to the elucidation of the single problem of the relations between the text of a printed book and the original MS. of its author' (p.239). But now he turned to the question of how nearly a printed book might be expected to reproduce an author's manuscript, and what might be the chief causes of any failure or compromise. The brevity of this part is curious, in view of its express importance to McKerrow's argument and to so much in scholarship that had immediately preceded his book. Indeed, one reviewer identified these pages accurately as the 'kernel'.[22] But it touched questions that McKerrow was already working on in order to take advantage of another opportunity to extend his investigations. In 1928 he gave the Sandars Lectures at Cambridge, and he chose as his topic 'The relationship of English printed books to authors' manuscripts in the sixteenth and seventeenth centuries' – closely akin to that which he had treated so summarily in his recent book.[23] In the course of three lectures, he surveyed questions of compositors' spellings, of the relationship (as he saw it) of authors' manuscripts to licensed and printers' copy, of proofing, and in the final lecture he challenged the commonly held belief that Elizabethan compositors were necessarily worse than their nineteenth-century counterparts. Again, his emphasis was on Elizabethan and Jacobean printers and authors.

McKerrow's need to lend to his longer study something of the range of a textbook led him into areas of knowledge with which he was less familiar from his everyday research. Close as he was to Pollard (and therefore to the work even then going forward on the British Museum's catalogue of incunabula), in some respects it seems strange that he did not also seek to take his study further back, into – or at least towards – the fifteenth century. The few pages that he devoted to matters before 1500 are noticeably dull when compared with the obvious enthusiasm and familiarity with which he approached his strongest period. They are manifestly written from secondary sources (relying heavily on D.B. Updike's *Printing types*, published in 1922), and show little appreciation of the ways in which early printing methods were changed and adapted, or the often experimental or hybrid practices of even well-known printers long into the sixteenth century. In these pages, it was perhaps a mistake to venture into the practice and history of printing on the continent, without taking cognisance of recent work in German in particular.

The eighteenth century is less puzzling, in that even while McKerrow was drawing together his materials, Chapman was regularly publishing observations on books of the period (and not least in the pages of the *Review of English Studies*). Nonetheless, there was much less systematic work in train. Chapman, too, seems to have read the entire book in proof, making further suggestions as he did so. But it remained to later generations, for example, to establish the nature of press figures (discussed very briefly on pp.81-2), and to supplement McKerrow's observations on the sizes of editions (pp.130-3, 214) by the cautionary but documented figures to be found in the archives of later establishments such as the Cambridge University Press, or the Bowyer printing house.[24] He did not venture far into the nineteenth century, though both for this period and even for the sixteenth and seventeenth centuries he could not resist drawing occasionally – if not always very usefully – on his experience as a publisher in the 1920s. The short passage on stereotyping and electrotyping (pp.71-2) is especially noticeable, in that it deals unsatisfactorily even with the few aspects that are alluded to so briefly here, quite apart from giving little guidance on nineteenth-century bibliography. It was not his purpose to concern himself much with developments after 1800, and the great strengths of his book lie well within the previous period. It is both a measure of McKerrow's commitment to earlier centuries, and a reminder of how much bibliographical practice and application have since changed, that he was able to open a brief chapter (seven pages long) on 'The forms in which books have been issued to the public' with the remark that 'Binding as an art or craft lies outside our subject'.[25] In a study that sought to explain why books look as they do – and thus to begin with the reader – such an attitude seems oddly restrictive. The sentence may have seemed determined and clear at the time; today it seems contentious, even at best. As for nineteenth-century binding, in the absence of his own knowledge (quite apart from enthusiasm, conviction or purposes) he could in 1927 refer at that date only to an early paper by a fellow-publisher Michael Sadleir, published in the *Bookman's Journal* in 1924 (p.127).

Within his own period, and especially on England (for, not surprisingly, the book still had little to say of foreign books) he was widely informed, and could be formidable. For an account of the process and principles of printing, from hand composition to the hand-press, in the sixteenth, seventeenth and eighteenth centuries, there is no-one who is at once more approachable and more clear. The best way to learn about such matters is by practical experience, from setting type to imposition, inking and printing, through to the finished folded sheets. Many a student has come to understand the principles of bibliographical practice by the joint lessons offered on the one hand by McKerrow, and on the other by a hand-press and its associated equipment. In this respect, his omissions and failures are few indeed, though one might note a failure to associate the sizes of sheets of paper with the means by which they were printed in the fifteenth century. But it is important now to recall that when McKerrow was writing it was possible to walk into almost any small, or even quite large, jobbing printer, and see an iron hand-press in everyday use, its principles of operation not so very different from the wooden presses with which McKerrow was most concerned. As for manuscript copy, though in his Sandars Lectures of 1928 he was to return at greater length than he allowed himself here (pp.239ff.), in the end much of his work was to be overtaken by that of Percy Simpson, teaching at Oxford, whose study of *Proof-reading in the sixteenth, seventeenth and eighteenth centuries* appeared in 1935.[26] Some of this work was also to emerge in McKerrow's own paper on 'The Elizabethan printer and dramatic manuscripts' in 1931.[27]

The first impression of *An introduction to bibliography* was soon sold out, and McKerrow therefore had the opportunity to make some minor alterations. Just as sales of the *Review of English Studies* had proved especially strong in America, so the same was true of *An introduction to bibliography*, which rapidly found a place in departments of English. G.P. Winship was among those who drew attention to the mistaken arrangements for imposition of type-pages for a sheet in octavo (p.35), which McKerrow corrected for the revised second impression of 1928.

In retrospect it seems a little surprising that it took so long for two aspects of the processes of printing to engage the serious attention of bibliographers. McKerrow's remark (p.130) that shared printing required 'fuller investigation' was taken as a proper warning. But it was not until the 1970s, with the work of Katharine Pantzer, on the revised edition of the *STC*, and of Peter Blayney, on the London trade in the first decade of the seventeenth century, that evidence was produced to demonstrate it to have been so common as to be almost usual.[28] As for compositors' spelling habits and the practices in their copy, McKerrow was scarcely encouraging in his remark that such an investigation 'would be a tedious one' (p.248). It remained to Charlton Hinman to attempt the greatest challenge of all in this respect, and to publish his results in the two volumes of his account of *The printing and proof-*

reading of the first folio of Shakespeare (1963). McKerrow's own approach to questions respecting, and to be sought from, the study of individual printing houses are to be seen in his 1929 paper on Edward Allde.[29] On some other topics that have since proved to be of significance in understanding the medium by which words are placed before readers, he could be summarily dismissive, as for example of typography. 'It is not of any importance to our subject that we should try to follow the course of type-designing or type-founding in England' (p.298). Such an attitude was to be overturned for many bibliographers with the exposure of the forgeries described in John Carter and Graham Pollard's *An enquiry into the nature of certain nineteenth century pamphlets* (1934). On the more general question, McKerrow refused to entertain questions of design or appearance. While in some degree this was a natural reaction against bibliophily, it obscured a critical point. In a perceptive review, Gustav Binz, philologist and University Librarian at Basel, questioned whether such exclusivity did in fact properly represent the purposes of bibliography, the elucidation of texts.[30] But it remained partly to Stanley Morison, and in this context perhaps most to Harry Carter, to demonstrate how the typographic appearance of a page may affect its meaning, and bear witness to the assumptions – quite apart from the equipment – of the printer.[31] Of authors and their opinions as to how their work should be presented, McKerrow likewise had little to say. Certainly he was himself no printer, for his remark (p.307) to the effect that a pica em equals exactly one-sixth of an inch conceals much that was at issue in the printing trade even as he wrote – as reference to a current printers' manual such as Southward's *Modern printing* would have told him.[32] Insofar as he discussed types at all, his remarks are peculiarly balanced, with an emphasis on foreign, earlier, examples; little on his central period of the sixteenth and seventeenth centuries other than on John Day and John Fell; and a tendency to lapse into the kind of aesthetic judgements that he professed to avoid. On the types of Fell, Baskerville and Caslon, right through to the revivals and recuttings of the nineteenth century (many of them, still, in 1927, easily available), we hear not the voice of the bibliographer but of the twentieth-century publisher. It was, after all, McKerrow who reported the occasion when the Bibliographical Society experimented briefly in 1924-7 with the formal exhibition and judging of modern book design and production.[33]

But while he frequently showed the way, in inspiring or suggesting where next investigation would be fruitful, on other occasions his work has proved to have serious lacunae even within his chosen period. The advent of the beta-radiograph, and its exploitation by Allan Stevenson, for bibliographical studies with respect to paper stocks, marked a major advance, not least in harnessing scientific equipment to the service of historical scholarship.[34] But most of all, perhaps, and with respect to the sixteenth and seventeenth centuries, his understanding of how independent documents might be brought to bear on the management and practice of printing and the other book trades was bounded by the most obvious. The section on this aspect of London printing and publishing is all too brief. In his British Academy obituary of McKerrow, Greg, again, made the point, with respect to McKerrow's dictionary of members of the book trade in the British Isles working between 1557 and 1640. The volume followed on the heels of H.R. Plomer for the subsequent period, 1641 to 1667, and it suffers by comparison. Plomer was familiar with the Public Record Office in ways that McKerrow and his companion authors never attempted. It remained to Greg to exploit the records of the Stationers' Company, taking the investigation beyond Edward Arber's transcripts of the registers – magnificent as they were – and with which McKerrow had tended to rest content. In a similar way, his remarks about copyright and censorship (pp.142ff.) have now been overtaken, on the one hand by Greg in his Lyell Lectures in 1956,[35] and on the other by the still more recent work of Sheila Lambert in particular.[36]

On foreign printing McKerrow was also on unfamiliar ground. To dismiss the practice of including a printed register of sheets as 'at no time universal or even very common' (p.87) was to ignore much early Italian printing, for a start. But his unfamiliarity is also to be seen, for example, in the rarity with which he uses the evidence of the Plantin printing house (much of it already available in print in 1927), and in his simplified accounts of signatures and catchwords. Binz, again, pointed out the shortcomings of the discussion of the use of roman and black-letter type in German-speaking Europe.[37] *An introduction to bibliography* was emphatically, if not in its title, a book for students of English, not for students of the bibliography of continental-printed books. It was to be some years before the implications of the practical, personal and trading connections between printers and booksellers on each side of the English Channel and North Sea were to be seen in the context of the study of specifically English (and English-language) books.

McKerrow's book was widely welcomed, not only in reviews but also in correspondence. After the first printing in 1927, reprints have all been from the slightly corrected version of 1928. Readable, concisely written and drawn from not only his own work on Elizabethan and Jacobean literature, but also innumerable conversations with Greg and Pollard as well as from the knowledge of Chapman, Simpson and others, it remains essential for any student of printing or bibliography. No book has been more influential in the subject, and in many ways it is still the best to put into the beginner's hands. Few textbooks have stood the test of time so well. As McKerrow intended, and in accordance with his constant tendency to suggest or opine, rather than to legislate over-rigorously, many have since explored subjects of which he was the first to gather examples and to seek out their meanings and implications for the route from author to reader. Most substantially, in 1949 Fredson Bowers' monograph *Principles of bibliographical description* (dedicated to Greg) not only expanded on McKerrow's pages on the subject, making clear the significance of some aspects that McKerrow had been content to pass as unrewarding, and tidying up some of the less satisfactory aspects of his work with collational formulae; he also began to explore in more detail questions respecting the centuries preceding or following those that McKerrow had most emphasised.

Then in 1972 Philip Gaskell's *New introduction to bibliography* offered not so much a thorough revision as an extension. Its aim was the same, even if its method was different: 'to elucidate the transmission of texts by explaining the processes of book production' – and no longer for literature alone.[38] Most obviously, and as we have seen, McKerrow had been especially weak in his discussion of practices after about 1800, with the advent of machine presses, machine-made paper, edition and cloth binding, stereotyping, and new patterns of publication.

INTRODUCTION

They fell not so much outside his professional competence – for as a publisher he can hardly have been unaware of them – as outside his interests. Gaskell's work established itself immediately as the essential guide on such matters, while his survey of questions in the earlier period, and in particular his remarks on the eighteenth century, were now greatly strengthened by a generation of detailed research. But Gaskell was explicit: his was 'a new book, not a revision of McKerrow'.[39] McKerrow's work, humane, alert to many an unresolved question, remains an inspiration – to the beginner and the more advanced 'student' alike. Despite almost three-quarters of a century of work since, it is still endlessly suggestive. Like Pollard and Greg, McKerrow wrote with a sense of discovery and excitement, distilling several decades' work into a book that would be useful to those who came after. *Tolle, lege.* Take up, and read.

1 In preparing the following, I am particularly grateful to Dr Malcolm B. McKerrow, who made available his father's papers, and who gave me permission to quote from them; and to W.H. Bond for his generosity in sharing his annotated copy of *An introduction to bibliography*, fruit of many years' use in teaching the subject. The fundamental account of McKerrow's work remains the obituary notice by W.W. Greg in the *Proceedings of the British Academy* 26 (1940), pp.489-515, repr. in *Ronald Brunlees McKerrow: a selection of his essays*, ed. John Philip Imroth (Metuchen, N.J., 1974). Imroth also prints, with some minor revisions, the survey by F.C. Francis, 'A list of the writings of Ronald Brunlees McKerrow', *The Library* 4th ser. 21 (1940), pp.229-63.

2 See, in general, F.P. Wilson, 'Shakespeare and the "new bibliography"', in *The Bibliographical Society, 1892-1942; studies in retrospect* (1949), pp.76-135; also published separately, rev. and ed. Helen Gardner (Oxford, 1970).

3 See Greg's account of the society in the *Jahrbuch der Deutschen Shakespeare-Gesellschaft* 43 (1907), pp.227-30.

4 *Trans. Bibliographical Soc.* 12 (1911-14), pp.211-318.

5 W.W. Greg, 'The present position of bibliography', *The Library* 4th ser. 11 (1930), pp.241-62, at p.244; repr. in his *Collected papers*, pp.207-25. Dover Wilson believed the occasion to have been Greg's review of Churton Collins' edition of Robert Greene, printed in the *Modern Language Review*, 1906: see his memoir of Greg in *The Library* 5th ser. 14 (1959), pp.153-7, at pp.153-4.

6 W.W. Greg, 'What is bibliography?', *Trans. Bibliographical Soc.* 12 (1914), pp.39-53; repr. in his *Collected papers*, pp.75-88.

7 'What is bibliography?', p.48. In the version printed in his *Collected papers*, 'the grammar of literature' was altered to 'the grammar of literary investigation'.

8 McKerrow himself found Greg's work in this respect to be over-prescriptive. He tried, in vain, to persuade Sir Karl Pearson to review it in the *Review of English*

Studies, and finally wrote, 'I am very sorry that you cannot undertake a review as it will, I fear, be difficult or impossible to find anyone else with the requisite knowledge. The truth is, I think, the book is rather theoretical, and that when dealing with actual MSS, its usefulness might often be overshadowed by practical considerations. After all, one never has anything like a complete series of MSS, and the relationships of those that one has must generally be most easily determined by a detailed consideration of selected variants. It is difficult to see wherein the advantage of a purely formal method consists.' (McKerrow to Pearson, 9 August 1927, Bodleian Library, MS Sidgwick and Jackson 292, f.10.)

9   For a brief comment on English studies at King's at this time, see Sir Ernest Barker, *Age and youth; memories of three universities* (Oxford, 1953), p.123; for Dover Wilson, see his autobiography, *Milestones on the Dover Road* (1969).

10   The painful birth of English studies at Cambridge has been often described, but see in particular E.M.W. Tillyard, *The muse unchained; an intimate account of the revolution in English studies at Cambridge* (1958); Basil Willey, *Cambridge and other memories, 1920-1953* (1968); and Hugh Carey, *Mansfield Forbes and his Cambridge* (Cambridge, 1984). For Chapman and the Oxford University Press, see Peter Sutcliffe, *The Oxford University Press; an informal history* (Oxford, 1978).

11   Stephen Potter, *The muse enchained; a study in education* (1937), p.250. The bibliographical teaching press at University College London, to which Potter refers, was founded by Hugh Smith in 1933 – the first of its kind at a British university.

12   McKerrow to A.F. Pollard, 19 July 1926 (Bodleian Library, MS Sidgwick and Jackson 291, f.223).

13   Copies of McKerrow's out-correspondence as editor of the *Review of English Studies*, 1924-37, are in the Bodleian Library, MSS Sidgwick and Jackson 290-95.

14   Charles Sisson in *The Library* 4 ser. 8 (1928), pp.478-82.

15   W.W. Greg, 'Ronald Brunlees McKerrow', *Proc. British Academy* 26 (1940), pp.489-515, at p.508.

16   Most obviously in this context R.B. McKerrow, *Prolegomena for the Oxford Shakespeare; a study in editorial method* (Oxford, 1939); W.W. Greg, *The editorial problem in Shakespeare; a survey of the foundations of the text* (Oxford, 1942; 3rd ed. 1954); W.W. Greg, 'The rationale of copy-text', *Studies in Bibliography* 3 (1950-1) pp.19-36. Some of the subsequent debate may be followed in G. Thomas Tanselle, *Textual criticism since Greg; a chronicle, 1950-1985* (Charlottesville, 1987).

17   W.W. Greg in *R.E.S.* 1 (1925), pp.463-78, at p.463. This substantial review was not included in his *Collected papers*.

18   A.W. Pollard, W.W. Greg, E. Maunde Thompson, J. Dover Wilson, R.W. Chambers, *Shakespeare's hand in the play of Sir Thomas More* (Cambridge, 1923).

19   Kenneth Sisam to McKerrow, 23 September 1927 (private papers).

20   *Times Literary Supplement* 3 November 1927; *Nation and Athenaeum* 8 December 1927; *Observer* 18 December 1927; *London Mercury* December 1927.

21   Madan to McKerrow, 7 January 1928 (private papers).

22   Alfred T. Byles, of Exeter, in *Modern Language Review* 23 (1928), pp.223-6.

23   These lectures remain unpublished. Copies are in the British Library (MS Add.41998), Cambridge University Library (860.b.87) and Trinity College, Cambridge (MS Add.b.111).

24   In the first (1927) impression, p.131, McKerrow forgot H.R. Plomer's evidence

of edition quantities in Pynson's printing house ('Two lawsuits of Richard Pynson', *The Library* New ser. 10 (1909), pp.115-33), but he inserted it in 1928.

25 For recent observations on the importance of this aspect of the subject, see for example M.M. Foot, 'Bookbinding and the history of books' in her *Studies in the history of bookbinding* (Aldershot, 1993), pp.2-14.

26 Simpson published part of this work (having read it as a paper to the Oxford Bibliographical Society in February 1926) in the *Proceedings and Papers of the Oxford Bibliographical Society* in 1928 – the year after McKerrow's *Introduction* was published. But see now also W.G. Hellinga, *Copy and print in the Netherlands; an atlas of historical bibliography* (Amsterdam, 1962), and for Britain, J.K. Moore, *Primary materials relating to copy and print in English books of the sixteenth and seventeenth centuries* (Oxford Bibliographical Soc., 1992).

27 R.B. McKerrow, 'The Elizabethan printer and dramatic manuscripts', *The Library* 4th ser. 12 (1931), pp.253-75.

28 P.W.M. Blayney, 'The prevalence of shared printing', *Papers of the Bibliographical Soc. of America* 67 (1973), pp.437-42.

29 R.B. McKerrow, 'Edward Allde as a typical trade printer', *The Library* 4th ser. 10 (1929), pp.121-62.

30 Binz's review appeared in *Beiblatt zur Anglia* 11 (1929), pp.353-60.

31 For Morison, see Nicolas Barker, *Stanley Morison* (1972); his *Selected essays*, ed. D. McKitterick 2 vols (Cambridge, 1981); and Tony Appleton, *The writings of Stanley Morison* (Brighton, 1976). His Lyell Lectures were instrumental in demonstrating over a wide range of media – inscribed, written and printed – how the medium and shape of letters may affect reading: see *Politics and script; aspects of authority and freedom in the development of Graeco-Latin script from the sixth century B.C. to the twentieth century A.D.* (Oxford, 1972). But see also, from a more specialist viewpoint and more immediately applicable within the context of McKerrow's work, Harry Carter, *A view of early typography up to about 1600* (Oxford, 1969).

32 John Southward, *Modern printing* 5th ed. (1924), 1 pp.105-10.

33 R.B. McKerrow, 'English printing of to-day', *Gutenberg Festschrift* (Mainz, 1925), pp.33-7. A further similar exhibition was organised for books published in 1925-6.

34 Allan Stevenson, *The problem of the Missale speciale* (Bibliographical Soc., 1967); idem, 'Watermarks are twins', *Studies in Bibliography* 4 (1951-2) pp.57-91. See also Stevenson's introduction to C.M. Briquet, *Les filigranes*, facsimile of 1907 edition. 4 vols (Amsterdam, 1968).

35 W.W. Greg, *Some aspects and problems of London publishing between 1550 and 1650* (Oxford, 1956).

36 For example, Sheila Lambert, 'The printers and the government, 1604-1637', in R. Myers and M. Harris (eds), *Aspects of printing from 1600* (Oxford, 1987), pp.36-68.

37 See note 30.

38 Philip Gaskell, *A new introduction to bibliography* (Oxford, 1972), preface.

39 Not surprisingly, reviewers of Gaskell were quick to make comparisons with his predecessor, for his title invited them. Some of the strains inevitable in a subject that had grown so vastly since 1927 now made their appearance. See for example the

reviews by Fredson Bowers, 'McKerrow revisited', *Papers of the Bibliographical Soc. of America* 67 (1973), pp.109-24 (and a rejoinder by Peter Blayney, ib., pp.437-42); by G. Thomas Tanselle (*Costerus* n.s.1 (1974), pp.129-50, and by Albert H. Smith (*The Library*, 5th ser. 28 (1973), pp.341-4).

PREFACE

IN the autumn of 1913 I put together certain ' Notes on Bibliographical Evidence for Literary Students and Editors of English Works of the Sixteenth and Seventeenth Centuries ', and these were printed as part of the twelfth volume of the *Transactions* of the Bibliographical Society, a certain number of copies being made up separately as a pamphlet of 102 pages. The purpose of these notes was to give to students of the literature of the period in which I was myself most interested such elementary knowledge of the mechanical side of book-production as might enable them to make better use than many of them seemed at the time able to do, of the evidence as to a book's history which can be gathered from its material form and make-up.

That paper has, if I may judge from the friendly letters which I have received concerning it, during the thirteen years which have elapsed since its publication, proved of real use to many, and perhaps I may say without undue vanity that it does indeed seem to me to include a good deal of material which was, at the time when it appeared, only to be obtained elsewhere by the expenditure of considerable time and trouble.

It was, I think, no small part of such merit as it possessed that it was limited in its scope to a particular period in which our knowledge of the processes of printing is fairly exact and when they were at the same time sufficiently primitive for an understanding of them to throw light on the earlier period and sufficiently settled for it to throw light on the period which followed. I thought then, and still think, that a student who is familiar with the methods of book-production in England in the years during which Shakespeare was writing will only need a little experience with the books themselves to understand the methods of any other period up to the middle of the nineteenth century.

I have, however, been repeatedly asked to reissue the pamphlet (now out of print) in a more comprehensive form, and at a cost, I fear, of somewhat damaging the original unity of the scheme, I have rewritten and much enlarged it so that in some measure it deals with English book-production in general up to about the year 1800, though it is still, for the reason that I have stated above, centred, so to speak, in the Shakespearian period.

But it still retains the original idea of a help-book for literary students. I wish there to be no misunderstanding about this. It is not a hand-book for students of printing or of general bibliography. Still less is it intended for book-collectors. I have not concerned myself in the least with the rarity or beauty or commercial value of the products of the printing-press, but have kept before me throughout the problem of the relation of the printed book to the written word of the author. So far as was in my power I have dealt with everything which seemed to me to bear on this relation or which could throw any light on the processes involved in the transition from MS. to printed book, for one never knows at what point the transmission may be affected by these processes; but I have not attempted to do more. If here and there something may be found which seems to be rather remotely connected with my proper subject, such as the brief general sketch of the rise and spread of printing in the Appendix, I can only plead that it seems to me to be material of legitimate interest to literary students and which cannot very readily be found elsewhere in the books to which they ordinarily have access. Lastly I have here and there put in something for no better reason than that it interested me and because I should have been glad to have it myself in a book of this kind when I first tried to find my way about among Elizabethan bibliography.

There remains only the pleasant task of thanking those friends who have helped me in the preparation of this book. I must place first Dr. W. W. Greg and Professor A. W. Pollard who I fear I must frequently have wearied by innumerable questions and appeals for their advice on points of difficulty, and who have very kindly read the book either in MS. or proof. To Mr. R. W. Chapman I am also very greatly indebted not only for the help which I have derived from what he has written on eighteenth-century bibliography but for setting me right on several points of book-production during that period, of which I confess that my first-hand knowledge is by no means all that I could wish. My thanks are also due to Miss Lauraine Field, who read the whole book in proof from what I may term the student's point of view and made a number of valuable suggestions as to matters which called for further discussion or explanation. My debts to others who have helped me with respect to particular points are, I think, so far as possible, recorded in their places; but in such a subject as bibliography so large a part of what knowledge one has is necessarily, and often unconsciously, derived from friends and fellow workers that all acknowledgement must fall very far short of what is rightly due.

NOTE TO THE SECOND IMPRESSION

A reprint being required, I have taken the opportunity to make a few corrections and small additions.

R. B. McK.

June, 1928.

A SHORT LIST OF SOME BOOKS OF ESPECIAL UTILITY TO STUDENTS

ALBRIGHT, EVELYN MAY. Dramatic Publication in England, 1580–1640. (Modern Language Association of America.) New York and London, 1927.
> Especially Chapter VI : ' Printing and Publishing Conditions affecting the State of the Text.' With a useful bibliography.

AMES, JOSEPH. Typographical Antiquities; or an Historical Account of the Origin and Progress of Printing in Great Britain and Ireland. Begun by . . . Joseph Ames . . . considerably augmented by William Herbert. London, 1785–90.

ARBER, EDWARD. A Transcript of the Register of the Company of Stationers of London, 1554–1640. 5 vols. London, 1875–94.

—— The Term Catalogues, 1668–1709 (1711). 3 vols. London, 1903–6.

BIBLIOGRAPHICA. Papers on Books, their History and Art. [Edited by A. W. Pollard.] 3 vols. London, 1895–7.

BIBLIOGRAPHICAL SOCIETY, THE. Transactions of the Bibliographical Society. 15 vols. London, 1893–1920.
> For continuation see *The Library*, Fourth Series.

BLADES, WILLIAM. The Biography and Typography of William Caxton. Second edition. London, 1882.

BRITISH MUSEUM, THE. Facsimiles from Early Printed Books in the British Museum. Printed by order of the Trustees. London, 1897.

—— A Guide to the Exhibition in the King's Library, illustrating the History of Printing, Music-printing, and Bookbinding. Printed by order of the Trustees. London, 1926.

DUFF, E. GORDON. Early Printed Books. (A volume of ' Books about Books ', edited by A. W. Pollard.) London, 1893.

—— Early English Printing, a series of Facsimiles of all the types used in England during the fifteenth century, &c., with an Introduction. London, 1896.

—— Fifteenth Century English Books. A Bibliography of Books and Documents printed in England and of Books for the English Market printed abroad. (The Bibliographical Society, Illustrated Monograph XVIII.) London, 1917.

SOME USEFUL BOOKS

DUFF, E. GORDON. The Printers, Stationers, and Bookbinders of Westminster and London from 1476 to 1535. Cambridge, 1906.

HAEBLER, KONRAD. Handbuch der Inkunabelkunde. Leipzig, 1925.

JOHNSON, JOHN. Typographia or the Printer's Instructor. 2 vols. London, 1824.

LIBRARY, THE. A Quarterly Review of Bibliography and Library Lore. Edited by J. Y. W. MacAlister and Alfred W. Pollard. New (Second) Series. 10 vols. London, 1900–9. Third Series, 10 vols., 1910–19.

LIBRARY, THE. A Quarterly Review of Bibliography. Edited by A. W. Pollard. Fourth Series. London, 1920, &c.

> The Fourth Series of the *Library* incorporates the Second Series of the *Transactions* of the Bibliographical Society.

MADAN, FALCONER. Books in Manuscript: a short Introduction to their Study and Use. (A volume of 'Books about Books', edited by A. W. Pollard.) London, 1893, second edition, revised and corrected, 1920.

MOMORO, ANT.-FRANÇ. Traité élémentaire de l'Imprimerie, ou le Manuel de l'Imprimeur. Paris, 1793.

MOXON, JOSEPH. Mechanick Exercises: or, the Doctrine of Handyworks. Applied to the Art of Printing. The Second Volume. London, 1683.

> The first volume of the *Mechanick Exercises* is concerned with other 'Handy-works', not with printing.

POLLARD, ALFRED W. Shakespeare Folios and Quartos, a Study in the Bibliography of Shakespeare's Plays, 1594–1685. London, 1909.

—— Fine Books. London, 1912.

POLLARD, A. W. and REDGRAVE, G. R. A Short-Title Catalogue of Books printed in England, Scotland, and Ireland, and of English Books Printed Abroad, 1475–1640. (The Bibliographical Society.) London, 1926.

REED, TALBOT BAINES. A History of the Old English Letter Foundries. London, 1887.

SOUTHWARD, JOHN. Modern Printing, a Handbook of the Principles and Practice of Typography and the Auxiliary Arts. London, 1898.

UPDIKE, DANIEL BERKELEY. Printing Types, their History, Forms, and Use, a Study in Survivals. 2 vols. Cambridge, Harvard University Press, 1922.

PART ONE

Chapter One

FOURTEEN years ago, when I put together the
'Notes on Bibliographical Evidence', out of
which the present book has grown, it seemed to me
necessary to begin by a short introduction in which I
tried to make plain the importance to all who were
engaged in the editing or the minuter study of those
authors whose work has been transmitted to us through
the medium of printed books, of a certain amount of
'bibliographical' knowledge. I pointed out that in
all work so transmitted there has intervened between
the mind and pen of the original author and the printed
text as we now have it a whole series of processes, often
carried out by persons of no literary knowledge or
interests, almost any one of which may in one way or
another affect the transmission of the text, and that
a thorough understanding of these processes was a
necessary preliminary to any attempt to reconstruct
from the printed book the text as originally conceived
by its author. And I pointed out that even apart from
the question of the text itself, it is often possible to
derive very valuable information as to the literary history of a printed work from the material form or forms
in which it has come down to us, saying that

> 'bibliographical' evidence will often help us to settle such
> questions as that of the order and relative value of different
> editions of a book ; whether certain sections of a book were
> originally intended to form part of it or were added afterwards;
> whether a later edition was printed from an earlier one, and
> from which ; whether it was printed from a copy that had
> been corrected in manuscript, or whether such corrections as

it contains were made in the proof, and a number of other problems of a similar kind, which may often have a highly important literary bearing. It will indeed sometimes enable us to solve questions which to one entirely without bibliographical knowledge would appear quite incapable of solution.

No such insistence on the importance of bibliographical knowledge is necessary now, for the facts are acknowledged by all, or almost all, who concern themselves with our early literature. At no time have the methods by which students approach literary problems, especially those of the Shakespearian period, undergone so remarkable a change as in the last few years. We are all now for 'bibliographical' methods, keenly on the watch for every least indication of disturbance in the accurate transmission of a text, sorting out by many subtle and ingenious methods the first, second, or third stage of the composition, the original draft, the first completed form, the revision for this, that, and the other purpose, and so on. But there is much more in these modern methods of research than used to be understood by 'bibliography', and I am not sure that the recent extensions of the term have been altogether justifiable. The virtue of bibliography as we used to count it was its definiteness, that it gave little scope for differences of opinion, that two persons of reasonable intelligence following the same line of bibliographical argument would inevitably arrive at the same conclusion, and that it therefore offered a very pleasant relief from critical investigations of the more 'literary' kind.

There is a great group of questions concerning the transmission of texts, questions often of the highest interest and importance, which are indeed bibliographical in that without one step in the transmission having been by the medium of written or printed books they could not have arisen, but which, from the large amount of conjecture that must necessarily enter into any solution of them, differ entirely from the purely bibliographical problems to which we have been accustomed in the past. A theory, for example, which should seek to explain evident disturbances or inconsistencies in the text of a play by postulating a corrected manuscript in which, owing to lack of space, later additions had been so placed that the point where they should be inserted had been misunderstood by the copyist or printer, may be both ingenious and plausible, and such a theory is certainly in a sense bibliographical.[1] If, however, it involves, as it very often does, at some point or another, the theorist's literary judgement of stylistic differences in the passages claimed to be additions from those claimed to be original text, it is of a very different degree of what may be called material certainty from such evidence of insertion in proof as may be derived from a disturbance of the regular practice of a compositor, such as an increase in the number of lines to the page.

There will in the future be much to say about these newer kinds of bibliographical investigation, but they belong rather to the sphere of textual criticism than to formal bibliography and I do not propose to touch upon them here. At the same time it may be said that for work of this kind, even more than for the simpler problems concerning order of editions and the like, an exact knowledge of the way in which books are produced is necessary, for we must know not only what *may* be done but what is likely to be done.

In the 'Notes' to which I have referred I suggested that the best way of obtaining a clear and lively comprehension of the processes by which books of Shakespeare's time were produced would be by actually composing a sheet or two in as exact facsimile as possible of an Elizabethan quarto or octavo, and

---

[1] As would be, I suppose, a theory explaining the ambiguity of a telegram by the sender's desire to get it into twelve words—unless such an explanation should be classed rather as ' economic ' than ' bibliographical '.

printing it on a press constructed on the model—so far as is ascertainable—of those used in the early seventeenth century. But though a little practical experience of this kind would probably be much the easiest and quickest way of putting oneself in a position to appreciate the evidence which a book may contain as to its own history, it is by no means essential. The numerous processes through which all books pass are perfectly simple, and very little trouble will suffice for the understanding of them. What is needed is that they shall be grasped so clearly as to be constantly present to the mind of the student as he handles a book, so that he sees this not only from the point of view of the reader interested in it as literature, but also from the points of view of those who composed, corrected, printed, folded, and bound it; in short, so that he sees it not only as a unit but as an assemblage of parts, each of which is the result of a clearly apprehended series of processes. Once he does this he will find that the material book, apart altogether from its literary content, can be a thing of surprising interest.

A few words may be said as to the plan adopted in the following pages. For many reasons the material is not easy to present in logical sequence, for the various processes to be discussed are to such a degree interdependent that no one process can be completely understood without some knowledge of the others. At the cost, I fear, of a certain amount of repetition, I have done my best to clear up difficulties as I went along, but I am conscious that readers may find in the early chapters certain matters dealt with, the importance of which may not be at once apparent. Such passages may, however, be passed over on a first reading and returned to later.

In the first part I have considered the production of the book mainly from the point of view of the *producers*, the compositor and the pressman. In the second part I have taken the *completed book* and, so to say, worked backwards from this, explaining its structure

4

and peculiarities in the light of the processes already discussed. In the third part I have discussed, but very briefly, the relation of the text as it finally appears to the author's MS., especially dealing with the errors which may be introduced by the processes through which it has passed. For the student for whom the book is intended the third part therefore, though the shortest, contains the kernel of the matter, but it cannot be properly understood without the second, nor the second without the first. In an appendix I have collected together a certain amount of matter which it seemed to me desirable to include, for reference at least, but which could not be placed in the body of the book without causing tedious digressions.

One thing I would say in conclusion, that nowhere have I attempted to lay down any rules for bibliographical investigation, for none are possible. There is no general course of inquiry to be followed. Every book presents its own problems and has to be investigated by methods suited to its particular case. And it is just this fact, that there is always a chance of lighting on new problems and new methods of demonstration, that with almost every new book we take up we are in new country, unexplored and trackless, and that yet such discoveries as we may make are real discoveries, not mere matters of opinion, provable things that no amount of after-investigation can shake, that lends such a fascination to bibliographical research.

Chapter Two

SUCH knowledge of the mechanical side of book-production as is possessed by the majority of students of literature has as a rule been picked up bit by bit as chance decreed, and this makes it difficult to know where to start in attempting a cursory account of the subject as a whole. It is dangerous to assume that any one fact will be known to all possible readers and to pass it over in silence, and even at the risk of offending some by telling them things with which they have long been familiar, it seems safest to begin at the very beginning—and for this I shall make no further apology.

We will begin then by passing very briefly in review the whole series of processes which go to make the completed book. But, it will be asked, what sort of book and when produced? for the craft of printing, like every other craft, has undergone changes and developments, and a description of the methods followed at one period would not be correct in detail of any other period. This is true enough, but fortunately, so far at least as the purpose of the present study is concerned, the development of the art of printing has been somewhat peculiar. After a comparatively short period of experiment, methods were evolved which remained extraordinarily constant for centuries, so that we can say that in all essentials of book production there was little difference between the methods of 1500 and those of 1800. Indeed, until within the last thirty years the methods of composition, imposition, folding of paper, and so on, were in ordinary book-work very much the same as in the sixteenth century, though there had of course been innumerable improvements in detail, in regularity and finish of the

6

type and of the other materials used in printing, in quality of ink, in methods of inking, and in the efficiency of the press. It is, I think, not too much to say that if the staff of John Day's printing-house could have revisited the world of 1850 and been set down in the house of some jobbing printer of that date, they would have found very little that they did not understand at sight, and would have been capable of taking it over and running it without further instruction—except perhaps in the use of the ink-roller and in certain details of the adjustment of the press.

It results from this that we can, without inconvenience, base our study on the books of the end of the sixteenth century, the period in which bibliographical knowledge is generally most important for students of literature. If we understand how books were produced in 1600, we shall have very little difficulty in understanding the methods of any other period, and it will be easy with this as the point of reference to complete the story backward or forward.

We will therefore begin by considering the production of a book in the year 1600 or thereabouts, and to avoid confusion we will in the first instance confine our attention to the ordinary 'quarto' book, as this format is especially common in those dramatic and poetical tracts with which the student of literature is generally most concerned. Other sizes will be considered later, when we shall also consider certain processes in somewhat more detail and the modifications made in them at various times.

Let us suppose that a printer has a manuscript to print, and that all such details as the size of the type, length of lines, and number of lines to the page are settled, and that he is about to begin the actual composition of the matter ; and let us follow the compositor at his work.

He takes in his left hand a composing-stick which is so adjusted that it will exactly hold lines of type of

7

the length required. He then picks up with his right hand, one by one, the types required to form the first word from the case [1] in which they lie, and as he does so, inserts them in the stick, beginning from the left side and holding them in place with his left thumb, as shown in figure 3.[2] The types are of course put

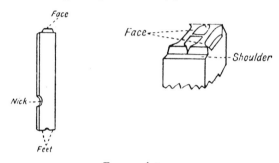

FIG. 1. A type.

[1] The ' case ' is the receptacle in which type is kept. A pair of cases are always used together; the ' upper case ' contains the capitals, numerals, and certain other characters, the ' lower case ' containing the ' small ' letters and the spaces. Each case is a sort of shallow tray, about 2' 9" long by 1' 4½" broad and about 1¼" deep, divided by cross-partitions into ' boxes ' for the different types, there being 98 boxes in the upper case and 53 to 56 in the lower. The divisions in the upper case are all of the same size, while those in the lower case vary according to the frequency of the type which they hold, the e-box being, for example, about five times the size of those for the capitals in the upper case, the o-box three and a half times, and so on. The arrangement of the lower case is not alphabetical, those types in most frequent use being towards the centre where they are handiest for the compositor. The seventeenth-century ' lay of the case ' is given in figure 2. It remained much the same until quite recent times. The two cases were propped on a stand before the compositor, the lower case only slightly tilted, the upper resting above the lower one at a greater angle. At an earlier date, if we may trust the pictures which have come down to us, only a single case was probably used, or if there were two they were placed one above the other at the same slope. See figures 11 and 14.

[2] The figure is based, by kind permission of the publishers, on one in J. Southward's *Modern Printing*, Raithby, Lawrence & Co., London, 1898, pt. i, p. 164, and of course represents a modern composing-

8

in the stick with the face upside-down, so that when printed the letters will be in their proper order. After each word the compositor puts a space, which is merely a short type without any letter on it.

A	B	C	D	E	F	G	â	ê	î	ô	û	♂	Δ
H	I	K	L	M	N	O	ä	ë	ï	ö	ü	*	♂⁰
P	Q	R	S	T	V	W	á	é	í	ó	ú	□	
X	Y	Z	Æ	J	U		à	è	ì	ò	ù	♌	†
♄	♃	♂	☉	♀	☿	☽	♈	♉	II	♋	♌	♍	*
1	2	3	4	5	6	7	♎	♏	♐	♑	♒	♓	
8	9	0			ſt	k	ffi	ffl	ffi	ffl	℞	⊕	§

j			æ	œ		s					fl	fi
' / &	b	c	d	e		i	ſ	f	g	fh	ff / fi	ff / fi
ct / ;	l	m	n	h		o	y	p	q	w	?	
z / x	v	u	t	‡‡		a	r	, / .	: / -		⊠	

Fɪɢ. 2. The arrangement of the type ('lay of the case') in the upper and lower case in 1683, from Moxon's *Mechanick Exercises*.

stick, made of metal and furnished with a sliding-piece that can be set to the length of line required. Such adjustable composing-sticks were in regular use towards the end of the seventeenth century. They were in general principle exactly similar to the one here illustrated, but had the additional complication of a second sliding-piece which could be adjusted to the width of a column of marginal notes, so that these could be composed simultaneously with the body of the text (see Moxon, *Mechanick Exercises*, 1683, p. 32 and plate 2). The earliest composing-sticks were probably of wood and of fixed length, and such wooden composing-sticks seem to have always remained in use for special purposes, such as the setting of exceptionally wide measures.

When he comes to the end of his first line he may find that he has also come to the end of a word. If so, well and good ; he proceeds to set the next line. The chances are, however, that he finds that there is not in the stick exactly room for a complete word. He may find that he has room for the first syllable of a word, with a hyphen. If so, he inserts this ; if not, he must exactly fill the line in some other way. If his line is a letter or two short, he must fill it out with spaces. These cannot, of course, be added at the end of the line, as all the lines of type must end evenly,[1] so the

FIG. 3. A modern composing-stick. The size of the type is, of course, greatly exaggerated in order to show the faces.

additional space must be distributed over the spaces already standing between the words in the line. To do this he will take out the spaces already inserted, or some of them, and replace them by thicker ones. Or if he can nearly get another word or syllable in, he may take out the existing spaces and insert thinner ones. By this process, which is called ' justifying ', he will eventually get his line of exactly the right length.

A modern printer generally has three spaces of varying thickness which can be used without the space between the words looking excessive or too small,[2] but it seems doubtful whether the Elizabethan printers used more than two in ordinary work.[3] They had, however, a means of justifying the lines of type which

[1] Assuming that the book is prose.

[2] A very thick space can be used between two upright letters, as in the words ' tall house ', or a very thin one between round letters, as in ' more open ', without in the one case the words looking too far apart or in the other too close together.

[3] It is impossible to be certain of this on account of the irregular casting of the type, the face of which (i. e. the top part which prints as a letter) was often not central on the shank, or ' body ' as it is called.

is denied to modern compositors, namely, by varying the spelling of words.[1]   If when nearing the end of a line the workman saw that he was going to have space to fill up, he could add an e to the end of some of the words, or could spell such terminations as -nes and -les as -neffe and -leffe, or could give ' dance ' as ' daunce ', or ' many ' as ' manie '.   If on the other hand he wished to save space, he could omit final e's or use a vowel with a line over it to indicate a following n, or in some founts[2] could use the y^e and y^t contractions for ' the ' and ' that ' and other similar ones.[3]

[1] Or when printing Latin or Greek by varying the number of contracted forms which they used.

[2] A ' fount ' of type was originally the whole assortment of letters of the same style, or ' face ', and body which were cast at one time. In ordinary use, however, the word has now no relation to the time of casting, but merely to the style of the letter and size of the body. Thus the roman type in which the text of this book is printed is all one fount, the italic another. If type of these faces were cast on bodies of a different size, so that the spaces between the lines of print or between the letters were different, these would be other ' founts '.

[3] It is not possible to say exactly to what extent the printers relied on variations in spelling as a means of justification ; it seems, however, not unlikely that it was their chief expedient. In a review of this book in its original form in the *Jahrbuch der Shakespeare-Gesellschaft*, 1916, p. 211, Professor Max Förster cited a most interesting passage from the grammarian W. Salusbury, which shows that variation of spelling for this purpose was quite well recognized. The passage (quoted by Ellis, *E. E. Pronunciation*, iii. 752) is to be found in Salusbury's *Plain . . . Introduction teaching how to pronounce . . . Welch*, 1567.   He is complaining that people unnecessarily write (in English) ' manne, worshippe, Godde ', &c., and advising a change to ' mann, worshipp, Godd ', &c.   A marginal note adds ' An obseruation for wryting of English whych in pryntyng cānot so well be kept ', and Salusbury continues, ' And though thys principle be most true *Frustra id fit per plura, quod fieri potest per pauciora*, that is done in vayne by the more, that maye be done by the lesse : yet the Printers in consideration for iustifying of the lynes, as it is sayde of the makers to make vp the ryme, must be borne wythall '.   It may further be noted that when in one copy of a sheet we find that a correction involving a change in the number of letters has been made in a particular line, we commonly find that the spelling of other words in the line has been varied to compensate for it. Lastly, the great difference in spelling (apart from

Having now got one line of type in his ' stick ' the compositor would, providing the work was not to be ' leaded ', proceed to set the next line, laying the types above those already in position.[1] If, however, it was to be ' leaded ', that is to say, if there were to be blank spaces between the lines of type, he would insert a strip of type-metal, or possibly of wood, above his first line of type, and lay the second upon that.[2]

' Leading ' (it is convenient to keep the term ' leading ' whether the actual ' leads ' were metal or wood, though strips of wood used in this way are properly called ' reglets ') is, of course, a very common practice nowadays ; the great majority of books in which there is no special desire to save space are leaded, as it is thought to make a book more readable.   In Elizabethan times the practice seems, however, to have been unusual, if not non-existent.   I do not indeed know of a single English book of the sixteenth century which is consistently leaded throughout ; though leads may have been in occasional use for special purposes, e. g. to place between stanzas of poetry.[3]   Generally, how-

modernization) often found in reprints of different length of line or fount of type is most naturally thus accounted for.

[1] Actually before laying down the first line of type the compositor places in the stick a thin strip of brass, called a setting-rule, the length of a line of type and provided with a small projection at one end by which it can be lifted. As each line is completed the setting-rule is removed from below it and placed on the top of it, the next line being set on the rule, and so on. The purpose is to afford a smooth surface on which the types can be laid and on which they can more easily slide into place. The setting-rule was used in Moxon's day (cf. *Mech. Ex.*, p. 214), and though there is no direct evidence of its use by the earlier printers, it is such an obvious device and, as Blades points out (see p. 56 below), would be so especially needed with imperfectly cast type, that we can, I think, assume the existence of something of the sort whether in wood or metal.

[2] It is, of course, possible that leads, when and if these were used, were inserted after and not during composition.

[3] Berthelet may occasionally have used leads, cf. Greg in *Transactions of the Bibliographical Society*, viii. 194, type 13. In this, however, as in some other cases of a similar kind, it is impossible to be sure that

COMPOSITION

ever, 'quads' seem to have been employed, i.e. pieces
of metal similar to spaces, but much broader, so that
a few—say half a dozen or eight—would fill an ordinary
line.[1] Whenever the blank space is found to be of the
same depth as an ordinary line (or two or three ordinary lines) of type, it is probable that the space has
been made by inserting a line or lines of quads.[2]

When he had got some six or eight lines of type in
his composing-stick, the compositor would transfer the
mass to something corresponding to what is now termed
a 'galley', i.e. a sort of shallow tray with edges on three
sides somewhat lower than the height of the type. He

the type was not cast on a larger body than was usual for the size of
face (a so-called ' bastard ' fount). The earliest example of apparent
leading known to me in English printing is in the Cicero *Pro Milone*
printed at Oxford, *c.* 1482. It may be noted that Caxton seems never
to have used any form of leading (Blades, *Caxton*, p. 123), but this
occurs in the *Siege of Rhodes*, printed by an unidentified printer probably
before Caxton's death. The leading here must have been either of
thin and soft wood or very flexible metal, as crooked lines influence
those above and below. Duff considered that leading was well understood by the early printers, and Professor Pollard tells me that leads
were used in the fifteenth century in school books to permit interlinear
glosses, but certainly in some such cases we may suspect the use of lines
of quads. In Italian printing they are said to occur in the second
quarter of the sixteenth century. How much earlier I do not know.

[1] Quads were no doubt originally square spaces, as broad as the height
of a line. From the fact that the letter m (or M) used to be cast on
a square body, such a square space is called an em-quad. It is difficult
to prove that broader ones were in general use, but this may be inferred
as highly probable from the fact that ornaments and rules of several
ems in length were quite common, and from their obvious convenience.
The sticking up of spaces so that they print as a black oblong—the
only conclusive evidence as to their dimensions—is curiously rare in
Elizabethan printing.

[2] The only certain proof of the use of a lead would be the sticking
up of one end of it, when it would print like a short piece of black
rule, the impression being much stronger at one end than the other.
It is also to be noticed that if leads are used an irregularity in any line,
such as an accidental space caused by letters falling apart, or any
considerable want of straightness in the line, will not, normally, be
continued in other lines up and down the page.

would then fill his stick again in the same way and again transfer the contents to the galley, and so on, until he had a sufficient number of lines of type to form a page. A modern printer uses long galleys, generally containing two or three pages of type, and does not as a rule divide up the matter into pages until proofs have been taken and at any rate the first corrections made. The reason of this is that the type can more easily be lifted for the purpose of correction when in a galley than when in the chase in which the pages are subsequently arranged ; further, if large corrections involving additions to or subtractions from the matter are made after this has been divided into pages, the work of measuring it up and dividing it has to be done all over again.

There is, however, so far as I am aware, no evidence of the practice of proofing matter in long galleys in the Elizabethan period, while on the other hand there is evidence of work being arranged directly in pages, the signature [1] (if any) at the foot of the page, and the catchword, being added directly the page was composed.[2]

Each page of type as completed would probably be tied round with string and put aside to wait until the rest of the pages required to form a sheet [3] of the book were ready. This in the case of an ordinary quarto book would be eight.

The requisite number of pages having been completed, the printer would next ' impose ' them on a flat table or stone in such a manner that when an impression was taken from them on a flat sheet and the paper afterwards folded to form part of a book, the pages would be in the proper order. A modern printer, who works with larger presses and larger sheets of paper

---

[1] See p. 25 below.   [2] See p. 65, note 1.

[3] Really a ' gathering ', as will appear later (see p. 31). For example, in a folio the compositor would often have to set twelve pages of type before it was possible to proceed with the printing. In a quarto, however, the ' gathering ' was usually a single sheet.

than the Elizabethans, will generally lay down the whole number of pages (let us suppose eight—for a quarto) at one time, and print them on one side of a sheet of paper of twice the size of the sheets forming the book (see p. 69 below). The Elizabethan would, however, arrange his eight pages of type in two separate groups, taking first the pages which are required to print one side of his sheet, namely, the 1st, 4th, 5th, and 8th page, or in the usual bibliographical notation,[1] pages 1, 2^v, 3, 4^v of the sheet. These he would arrange on the stone as in figure 4, the two upper ones being upside down. He would then place round them a bottomless frame called a 'chase' (indicated by the thick outer line of the figure),[2] and proceed to fill up the intervening spaces between the pages and between them and the chase with pieces of wood or metal below type-height called 'furniture'. It is to be noted that supposing AB, CD to be lines crossing the centre of the chase, the distance from AB to the top of the pages will give the height of the top margin of the page when the sheet is folded ; and that the distance from CD to the sides of the pages will similarly give the breadth of the inner margin.

The four pages thus arranged in the chase are called a 'forme', and because this forme contains the pages

[1] i. e. counting by leaves instead of pages, the first page being called ' 1 recto ' or simply ' 1 ', the second ' 1 verso ', the third ' 2 recto ' or 2, the fourth ' 2 verso ', and so on. Another notation, more general in dealing with very early books, uses 1^a for the recto of the first leaf, 1^b for the verso, and so on. This in certain respects is better, but has the disadvantage that some writers use the same notation to refer to columns of print when a page has more than one. In purely biblio-graphical work there is seldom or never any danger of confusion, but in literary work this may easily occur.

[2] Modern chases intended for book-work have cross-bars in the position of lines AB, CD (in chases for quartos), which greatly facilitate the arrangement of the pages and the locking-up of the type. It seems probable that the Elizabethan chases had at least one cross-bar, but the point is of no importance in the present connexion, and we therefore need not discuss it.

which, when the sheet is first folded, will be on the outside of the fold, namely, the 1st, 4th, 5th, and 8th

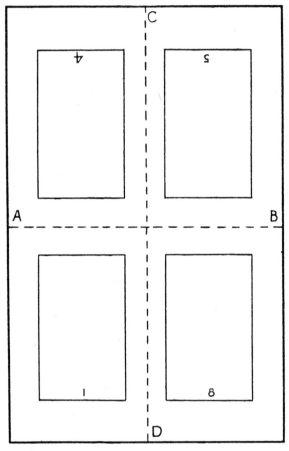

Fig. 4. Imposition of type-pages for a sheet in quarto (outer forme).

pages, it is called the outer forme, and pages 1, 4, 5, 8 (or 1, 2^v, 3, 4^v) are called pages of the outer forme.

The furniture employed to fill up the chase is ' locked up ' by the insertion and driving home of wedges or ' quoins ', so that the type is tightly jammed and the whole may safely be lifted as if all in one piece.

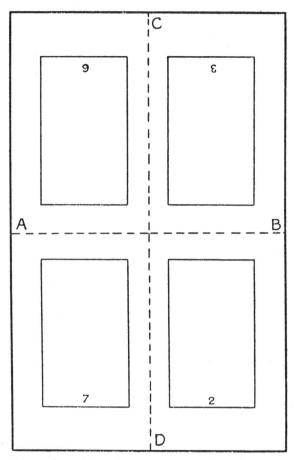

Fɪɢ. 5. Imposition of type-pages for a sheet in quarto
(inner forme.)

The printer would next take the other four pages belonging to the sheet and lock them up in another chase, arranging them as in figure 5. The distance of the top and sides of the pages from AB and CD must of course be the same as in the other forme. This forme contains the pages which in a folded sheet are within the fold, namely, 2, 3, 6, 7 (1^v, 2, 3^v, 4), and hence is called the 'inner forme'.

To make all clear, let the reader take a sheet of paper[1] and mark on it four oblongs on each side to represent the pages of type. Let him then number those on one side 1, 4, 5, 8, as if they had been printed on to this sheet from figure 4, i.e. 8 to the left and 1 to the right in the lower half of the paper, 5 (reversed) to the left and 4 (reversed) to the right in the upper part of the paper. Having done this, let him turn the paper over sideways (keeping the same edge to the top) and mark on the other side the numbers 2, 3, 6, 7, corresponding in a similar 'looking-glass' way to the numbers in figure 5.

If he now folds the paper into four by first bringing pages 2 and 3 and 6 and 7 together, and then by bringing 4 and 5 together, he will have a sheet folded as a sheet of a quarto book and will find that the pages are in the correct order from 1 to 8. It is therefore evident that if, having arranged the pages of type in the two formes in the manner indicated, the printer takes an impression from one forme on one side of the paper and from the other forme on the other side of the paper, laying the paper in such a way that page 2 falls on the back of page 1, the sheet when folded will have all the pages in the correct order.

Having thus imposed his pages correctly and locked them up in the two chases, the printer can proceed to the actual printing. One of the chases, probably first that containing the inner[2] forme, is placed on

---

[1] The ratio of the length to the breadth should be approximately as 4 to 3, in order that, when the paper is folded, the pages may be of usual proportions (see p. 103).

[2] According to Momoro, *Traité élémentaire de l'Imprimerie*, 1793, p. 147, there was in his day a strong, and in his view absurd, belief in some French printing-houses that the inner forme *must* be printed first.

the bed of the press and fixed there with wedges. The bed is so constructed that it will slide under the 'platen', a thick piece of beechen board perhaps reinforced with an iron plate, which, when brought down upon the type by means of a screw, presses the paper upon the type and so gives the impression.

The general form of the sixteenth-century press can be seen in the woodcuts reproduced on pages 39–47, and such description as seems needed for our purpose will be found in chapter v. For the present it must suffice to say that to the end of the wooden frame enclosing the bed of the press was hinged an iron frame covered with a sheet of parchment or thick paper. This frame, with or without the sheet of parchment attached thereto, was (and is) called the 'tympan'.[1] The hinges of the tympan allowed it to be turned back so that the sheet of paper to be printed could be laid on it. It was then turned over and brought down upon the type, which in the meantime had been inked

I know of no evidence as to any such notion among English printers. In most cases it would presumably be a matter of indifference which forme was laid on the press first, though, as pointed out on pp. 31–2, the inner forme must always be ready in advance of the outer one. Dr. Greg has been able to show that in one particular case, namely sheet K1 of the 1623 edition of the *Works of Samuel Daniel*, the inner forme was printed first (see *The Library*, 4th ser., vii. 216). In the First Folio of Shakespeare the printing of sig. D apparently began with the inner leaves of the gathering (see Pollard in *Sh. Folios and Quartos*, pp. 134–5), but as Dr. Greg has pointed out to me, an error in the head-line of *2 Hen. IV* shows that sig. 2 g was begun with the outer forme of the outside sheet. This, however, was an abnormal gathering (irregularly signed 'g g' between g and h, and 8 leaves instead of the usual 6). Similar evidence seems to show that in *Cymbeline* the outside sheet of sig. 3 a was printed last.

[1] In later times the tympan consisted of two sheets of parchment or other material, each stretched on a frame. One of these frames fitted within the other, and between the two sheets packing, consisting generally of a sheet of felt, was placed in order to soften and equalize the pressure of the platen. The arrangement was probably the same, or at least very similar, in Elizabethan times, but I am not aware of any evidence on the point.

by another workman.[1] The whole was then slid
under the platen, and this was brought down upon the
type by pulling the ' bar ' or lever in order to make
the impression. The lever was then released, raising
the platen; the forme was slid away from under it,
the tympan lifted, and the printed sheet removed and
placed on one side.

The inking of the type was done by what were called
' balls '. These were in general similar to those still in
use by etchers for spreading the ' ground ', and continued to be used by printers until the introduction
of the ink-roller, *c.* 1810. They were circular pads
of cotton or hair, covered with some material such as
leather, and provided with a stick or handle projecting
from the back at right angles (see figures 10 to 14,
pp. 39–47). The ink was first spread on a stone,
from which it was taken up by the ink-balls (always
used in pairs—one in each hand) and dabbed on the
type.

It is, however, evident that with such a method of
inking the forme there would be a great likelihood of
part of the ' furniture ' between the pages of type being
inked, with the result that when the paper was brought
down upon the forme it might come into contact with
these accidental patches of ink and be soiled. To
obviate the risk of this an attachment to the tympan,
called a ' frisket ', came into use.[2] This is a light frame
attached by a hinge to the free end of the tympan in
such a way that it can be folded down between the

---

[1] Two workmen must always have been necessary, or at least one
and a boy, as the same person could not ink the type and lay on the
paper. In most of the pictures of early presses it seems that one man
did the inking, the other laid on the paper and worked the machine.
In one or two, however, there is a boy in addition to lay on the paper,
and in one the man who inked the forme seems also to have worked the
press, a boy being employed to lay on the paper (*Bibliographica*, i,
pl. xii).

[2] The use of the frisket in early printing has been questioned, but
I think there is ample evidence of it, see pp. 46–8.

tympan and the forme. The frisket is covered with a sheet of paper in which holes are cut corresponding to the pages of type. After the sheet of paper to be printed is laid on the tympan, the frisket is folded down upon it, and thus all parts of the paper except those on which the impression is to fall are protected. The frisket and tympan together are then folded down upon the forme and the impression is taken.

Our printer has now a sheet printed on one side only and bearing the pages of one forme, say the inner. To complete it, the four pages of the other forme must be printed on the other side of the paper. Now if he has two presses, he may have placed the other forme on the second press ; but he cannot at once proceed to 'perfect' the sheet by laying it, printed side downwards, on the tympan of that press and printing it on the back ; for if he does so the result will be that the still wet ink of the first side printed will 'set off' on the tympan of the second press and thence will be transferred to the next sheet printed, and will spoil it. He must let the ink of the first printing dry before he attempts to print the sheet on the other side.[1] This necessary interval between the printing of the two sides of a sheet is, as we shall see later, of great importance in connexion with variations between copies of the same edition of a book.

As a matter of fact it is often evident from the occurrence of the same cut, ornament, or initial letter on both sides of a sheet, that the printer printed the whole number of impressions on one side before starting to perfect ; for it is unreasonable to suppose that he would first print, say, 100 impressions on one side, then transfer the initial to the other forme and, after waiting for the ink of the first printing to dry, proceed to perfect the 100 impressions ; then re-transfer his

[1] There are ways of avoiding this trouble by the use of 'setting-off sheets ', but it is unlikely that the sixteenth-century printers were often sufficiently pressed for time to make such expedients worth while.

initial to the first forme, and so on. Such a process would in all ordinary circumstances be an absurd and purposeless waste of time. Indeed, although it is possible that, when two presses were available and there was especial need of haste, a printer may occasionally have begun to perfect when a few copies of the first side printed were dry, there is no reason for doubting that the normal procedure at all periods has been to print all the copies of a sheet on one side before perfecting was begun.

We must pause to discuss a question which will probably already have occurred to the reader, namely, by what means it was arranged that the pages on one side of the sheet should correspond in position with those on the other, or in other words how they were made to 'register'. Evidently if all the sheets of paper used were exactly of the same size, and had straight edges, it would be possible to mark the tympan-sheet for the two printings in such a way that if the paper was laid to the marks the register would be correct. Even if the paper varied somewhat in size this would be possible (provided that the marks were towards the opposite edges of the tympan in the two cases [1]). Hand-made paper, however—and of course all early paper was made by hand—has uneven edges, and such a method would therefore prove, at best, unsatisfactory.

The method actually employed [2] seems to have been as follows. Two 'points', probably somewhat like ordinary drawing-pins, were attached to the tympan-sheet (by glue or otherwise [3]) so that when the tympan was folded down, the points would fall on the line equally

---

[1] So that the same edge of the paper, when it was turned over, would be laid to the marks.

[2] Essentially the same as that employed at present on hand-presses.

[3] In later forms of the press the points are at the ends of thin strips of metal which can be screwed to the sides of the tympan-frame so that the points project over the tympan-sheet.

distant from the top of the pages (line AB in figure 4). When the sheet of paper was placed on the tympan these pins would pierce holes in it ; and obviously if pins were similarly placed when the sheets came to be perfected, and the paper was so laid on the tympan that the pin-holes made when printing the first side fitted the pins, then, provided that the forme was correctly placed on the bed of the press, perfect register would be obtained. If a loosely bound folio book be examined, the pin-holes can usually be found in the fold, near the top and bottom of the leaves. In a quarto they would be in the top edge of the folded sheet and thus would generally have been cut off in binding. In an octavo they would be in the outer edge and are generally absent for the same reason.[1]

Some of the early cuts of printing-presses seem to show that as a guide for the correct placing of the sheet on the pins of the first press, the sheets, before printing was begun, were all folded so as to form a crease across the middle. What appears to be such a crease can be clearly seen in the pile of flat sheets about to be printed.[2] If the sheet were so placed on the tympan that the pins pierced the crease it would be rectangular to the pages.

The drying of the sheets between the printing of the first and second side, and after the second, was done by hanging them on strings or wooden battens across the room,[3] a process that was probably rendered easier by the crease already mentioned. When dry they were ready to be folded and sewn to form the book.

A few words must be added as to the disposal of the type after the forme had been printed from. The

---

[1] In very early printing many more points were used. In the 42-line Bible there were as many as ten ; later four were frequent (Duff, *Early Printed Books*, p. 49 ; Blades, *Caxton*, p. 130). In Caxton's early work they were placed at the four corners of the sheet (in all books printed with his type no. 1, but only once later).

[2] See figures 11 and 14.   [3] See p. 40 below.

forme was first washed down with an alkaline solution, called ' lye ', to remove the ink from the type, and then rinsed with clean water. It was then 'unlocked' by loosening the wooden wedges and removing the 'furniture'; the pages were separated and, unless distribution was to take place at once, they were tied round with string to prevent the type from falling apart and set aside in a safe place. Distribution was effected by taking a few lines of the type, supported on a setting-rule, in the left hand in such a way that the nick was outward, or away from the distributor, and the face of the letter consequently inverted (as it was in the composing-stick). The type would therefore read from left to right but upside down. The distributor next took a word at a time with the finger and thumb of his right hand, read it, and proceeded to drop the type letter by letter into the appropriate divisions of the case. It is probable that so far as possible each compositor would distribute the type which he had himself composed into the case from which it originally came, or at any rate into a case under his own charge, though we need not suppose this to have been a universal rule.

Chapter Three

THE PRINTED BOOK AND ITS PARTS. SOME
BIBLIOGRAPHICAL TERMS EXPLAINED

LET us now take in hand the completed quarto book and examine it. If it is a typical one we shall notice the following facts about it.

First as regards the general construction of the book. We shall see that it is made up of groups of four leaves, between the middle pair of which leaves the thread with which the book is sewn can generally be perceived.[1] Each group in an ordinary quarto consists of a single sheet of paper folded into four, and one may therefore speak of the groups as ' sheets '. It is, however, convenient when dealing with the bound or sewn book to call them ' gatherings '. In certain sizes, and even sometimes in quarto books, a ' gathering ' may consist of two or more sheets or of half a sheet.[2]

At the foot of the first page of each gathering will be found a letter or other mark, called the ' signature ', which is intended as a guide to the binder in placing the sheets in their correct order. On the second leaf will be found the same letter or mark with ' ij ' or ' 2 ', the third leaf generally and the fourth occasionally being also similarly ' signed ' with 3 and 4 in roman

---

[1] It is of course always there, but a book bound with a stiff back can sometimes not be opened sufficiently for the thread to be seen. Very thin books were sometimes sewn through sideways, as some magazines at present, though this is now done with wire or staples instead of thread. Books thus sewn are said to be ' stabbed '.

[2] ' Gatherings ' are sometimes called ' quires ', and the use of the word has good authority to commend it, but neither this nor ' gathering ' seems appropriate when a single sheet is in question. ' Section ' has also been suggested, but has the disadvantage that the word is commonly applied to divisions of a book's *literary* content. It would, I think, be better if some new word could be introduced such as 'consute' (i.e. what is sewed together), which has no other associations.

or arabic numerals. We shall recur later to several points of interest in connexion with signatures. It may, however, be noted here that the preliminary matter of a book, consisting of the title, dedication, preface, and, if there is one, list of contents, is often signed by an asterisk or other arbitrary mark, the signature 'A' being used for the commencement of the text itself.

At the foot of each page, below the end of the last line, we generally find the first word—or part of a word —of the following page. This is called the 'catch-word'. Its purpose was probably to aid the printer in imposing the pages correctly.

The lower part of the title-page, when it gives the place of printing, date, and information as to by or for whom the book was printed, or where it was to be sold, or any of these, is called the 'imprint'. Similar information given in a separate paragraph at the end of the book is generally called the 'colophon'.[1]

A list of the signature-letters of the various sheets placed (generally) at the end of the book as a guide to the binder is called a 'register'.

Large capital letters, woodcut or cast in metal, occurring at the beginning of a paragraph are generally called 'ornamental initials', or simply 'initials'. An ornamental block having a space in the centre for the insertion of a capital letter of an ordinary fount of type is called a 'factotum initial', or more properly a 'factotum'.

An ornament especially designed for the top of a page is called a 'head-ornament' or 'head-piece', and one for the foot of the page or the end of the matter occurring on it·is called a 'tail-ornament' or 'tail-piece'.

A line of type at the top of a page, above the text, is called a 'head-line'; or, if it consists of the title of

[1] This also is an imprint, but it seems more customary to keep the word for information given on the title-page. The practice is, however, not uniform.

the book (or of the section of the book) on every page or every ' opening ' (i. e. two pages facing one another), sometimes a ' running-title ' or ' running-head '.

The white margins of a page are called respectively the head, tail, outer, and inner margins, the inner being of course that nearest to the fold of the paper (or the back of the book). In almost all early printed books the inner margin is the smallest, then the head, and then the outer ; the tail-margin being the largest. The exact proportions seem, however, to have varied considerably, and indeed exact information on the point is not easy to obtain, as nearly all extant copies of early books have been at one time or another cut down by a binder.[1]

The folds at the outer margin or fore-edge of a sheet folded in octavo or smaller sizes are called ' bolts '. The word is also used, though less frequently in bibliographical work, of the folds at the top edge or (in those foldings in which they occur) at the foot. It seems to be a universal rule that pages were so imposed and sheets so folded that the bolts of the fore-edge occur in the *second* half of the sheet, though as the number of early books that have not been at some time or other cut by a binder is very small it is difficult to be certain that the rule has obtained at all periods.

Two leaves which ' belong to one another ', i.e. if traced into and out of the back of the book are found to form a single piece of paper, are said to be ' conjugate '.

If we hold a leaf of our quarto book up to the light we shall see some five or six lines crossing the page horizontally, where the paper appears to be thinner than elsewhere, these lines being crossed by others

[1] See, however, a paper by Prof. A. W. Pollard entitled ' Margins ' in *The Printing Art*, vol. x, pp. 17–24 (Sept. 1907), in which some very interesting figures are given as to the margins in certain fifteenth-century books and these are compared with the practice of some modern private presses.

much closer together which run vertically.[1] The former, those widely spaced, are called ' chain-lines '; the latter, those close together, the 'wire-lines'.[2] They are due to the wire bed of the mould in which the paper was made. On some leaves, on the inner margin of the page, about midway between the top and bottom, part of a design in similar semi-transparent lines will be noticed. This is the watermark. We shall have a good deal to say about this and the chain- and wire-lines later.

A book of which the ' gatherings ' consist each of four leaves is said to be ' in fours ', if of eight leaves ' in eights ', and so on. A quarto book such as we have been describing will therefore be a ' quarto in fours '. If, however, the gathering had consisted of eight leaves, two of the original sheets being sewn together, it would be described as ' a quarto in eights '. All these matters will have to be dealt with more particularly when we come to discuss the sizes of books.

[1] It is to be remembered that we are dealing with an early book. Almost all paper until towards the end of the eighteenth century shows these lines, though in some makes they are much less distinct than in others. Modern paper, on the other hand, when held up to the light often shows only a slightly mottled or grained appearance without any lines. Paper showing the lines is termed ' laid ', that which has none is ' wove '. See chapter viii below.

[2] Both the widely spaced and the narrow lines are sometimes called ' wire-lines ' or ' wire-marks ', but it is much more convenient to keep the distinction between them as above.

Chapter Four

WE have up to the present, for the sake of sim- plicity, taken as our typical book a quarto, one in which the original sheet of paper is folded into four —or as we were considering it from the printer's, not the binder's, point of view, we should perhaps rather say a book made up of sheets printed with four pages of text on each side. We have dealt already with the imposition, i. e. arrangement of type-pages in the forme, necessary to produce the quarto book. Let us now consider other possible kinds of imposition.

The simplest kind of imposition that is possible would obviously be if the whole of the matter to be placed on a sheet of paper were set up as two very large pages occupying the whole size of the sheet, one being printed on the front of the sheet and the other on the back. A book could certainly be made in this manner, but as there would be no fold through which to sew the sheets together, they could only be attached by some form of sewing through or ' stabbing ' along one edge, or by some such loose cornerwise attachment as one uses in fastening together a MS. of single leaves. While it would be hazardous to say that no book has ever been made in this manner, it is so obviously inconvenient that there can have been very few. Imposition as a single large page was, however, common enough in the case of proclamations and other things which were meant to be posted up and were therefore printed only on one side of the paper. Sheets so printed are called, as a rule, broadsides, or broad-sheets.[1]

In book-work the largest size ordinarily used was the folio, in which two pages were printed on each side of the sheet, this being then folded once parallel with the shorter side.

If each sheet were sewn separately, so that a gathering consisted of but two leaves, the imposition would be as in figure 6. In order, however, to avoid the enormous amount of sewing that would be involved

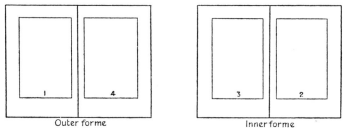

Outer forme   Inner forme

Fɪɢ. 6. Imposition of type-pages for a sheet in folio.

in binding a book in this fashion, and also the thickening of the back which would result from it, three or four sheets were frequently placed together in one gathering and sewn through at the same time.[2] Let

[1] This does not imply in ordinary usage that the print runs the broad way of the sheet, i. e. with the lines parallel with the longest side, though I believe that some bibliographers have used the terms in this sense. It may be remarked that the dictionaries define a broadside or broadsheet as being printed on one side of the paper only. I doubt, however, if this distinction is always observed in practice, and in any case there appears to be no name for a sheet similarly printed but on both sides. The usual abbreviation is ' b.s.' It would be convenient if one were permitted to use 1° (a graphic derivative of $4^o =$ quarto).

[2] My impression is that in the sixteenth century three sheets per folio gathering (folio in sixes) is the commonest arrangement, and that it is only exceptionally that we find sheets sewn singly (folio in twos). In the eighteenth century, however, as Mr. R. W. Chapman has pointed out to me, sewing ' in twos ' is quite common, even in the case of thick

us suppose three, as this is perhaps the commonest number. The gathering will then have six leaves and the book will be described as a folio in sixes. The appearance from above of a gathering set upright with the leaves partly opened will be as figure 7 ; the pages being indicated by the small numbers.

It will be at once clear that in order to print a book in this manner the printer must set up at least twelve pages of type to begin with,[1] as he will require page 12 to print at the same time as page 1. His six formes will be imposed as in figure 8.

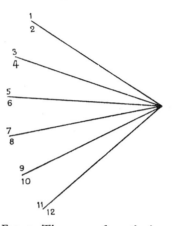

The point referred to in the last paragraph, namely, that a printer must set up the whole amount of matter which is necessary for one gathering, is so important in bibliographical work that we must devote a few lines to it before proceeding farther. To begin with, it is not absolutely

FIG. 7. The pages of a gathering of six leaves in folio.

true even when the gathering consists only of a single sheet, for the inner forme is always completed one page

books. In such cases the sewing is commonly so arranged that the threads do not traverse the same parts of the fold in adjacent sheets ; they are as it were ' stepped ', and thus excessive thickening of the back is avoided.

[1] Unless the book is a page-for-page reprint. In that case the pages could evidently be composed in whatever order was most convenient. There is good evidence that some reprints were set up forme by forme, which is, of course, the method requiring the smallest amount of type. In the case of a Bible printed by Barker in 1591, which is folio in sixes, it can be shown that the compositor set up the three outer, or possibly the three inner, formes of each gathering first. On an average four formes were in type at one time, including one in process of distribution

before the outer, and it is therefore possible to begin to print while the last page of a gathering is being set up.[1] In the case of gatherings consisting of two or more sheets, printing might begin much earlier. For example, in the case of a folio in sixes it will be seen from the diagram on p. 33 that

After setting page	7 the printer can work the inner forme of sheet 3,
,,	,,	8	,,	,,	,,	outer	,,	,,	3,
,,	,,	9	,,	,,	,,	inner	,,	,,	2,
,,	,,	10	,,	,,	,,	outer	,,	,,	2,
,,	,,	11	,,	,,	,,	inner	,,	,,	1.

He can thus save quite an appreciable time if he is in a hurry (and has presses at liberty) by starting to print as soon as 7 pages, out of the 12 forming the gathering, are composed, and this procedure will, if he distributes as he goes along, also serve to reduce the amount of type required, for he will never actually need more than seven pages in type at a time.

It would, however, be very inconvenient to work in this way, and a printer who attempted to compose a folio in sixes with only enough type for seven pages would undoubtedly soon find himself in difficulties owing to runs on particular characters. But without supposing such an extreme case as this we must recognize the possibility that, in primitive work and in certain special cases, our rule that at least a whole gathering must be in type at once may not always hold good.

and one being composed. We can tell this by observing the initial letters of the chapters, of which we frequently find the same block twice in one gathering, but almost invariably in opposite formes (i. e. in one of the three outer formes and in one of the three inner formes). Further, the especial frequency with which the same block occurs on both sides of a single leaf indicates that when a page was being, or had just been distributed, the compositor tended to be at work on the third forme farther on. See a note on this Bible in *The Library*, 4th ser., vol. v, pp. 357 ff.

[1] Hence probably the tradition which existed at one time in French printing-houses of always printing the inner forme of a sheet first. See p. 18, note 2.

In the smaller sizes, however, and in all cases where a gathering consists of not more than one sheet of paper we may take it as practically certain that, except in the case of page-for-page reprints, a whole gathering would be in type at the same time ; and, consequently, when we come across a clear case of the same material (initial letters, ornaments, &c.) [1] being used more than once in a gathering, we may infer, with little or no

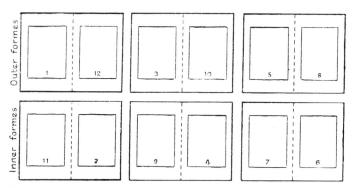

FIG. 8. Imposition of twelve type-pages (six formes) for a gathering of a folio in sixes.

risk of error, that we are dealing with a page-for-page reprint of an earlier edition.

Moxon's remarks on the point are worth quoting,

[1] It is important to observe that the repetition of borders or ornaments outside the text-page proves nothing, for these would, I think, normally be added at the time of imposition ; or of certain kinds of illustrations (e.g. necessary diagrams in astronomical books, &c.), which might *possibly* be so added, being transferred from one forme to another, space having been left for them during composition. Even so eminent a bibliographer as Henry Bradshaw seems to have overlooked this point ; see his paper on a fragment of the *Fifteen Oes* printed by Caxton, *c.* 1490–1 (*Collected Papers*, p. 342), where he argues from the repetition of the border-pieces, that in that book, a quarto in eights, the inner sheet of each gathering was set up after the outer sheet had been wholly worked off and the type distributed. This does not of course follow, and would indeed only be possible if the edition in question were set up page for page from an earlier one.

33

for they serve to illustrate it from the printer's point of view, a useful counterpart to that of the bibliographer :

> No wise *Compositer*, except he work on *Printed Copy* that runs *Sheet* for *Sheet*, will be willing to *Compose* more *Sheets* to a *Quire* than he shall have a *Fount* of *Letter* large enough to set out, unless he will take upon him the trouble of *Counting off* his *Copy*, because he cannot Impose till he has *Set* to the last *Page* of that *Quire*; all the other *Sheets* being *Quired* within the first *Sheet*, and the last *Page* of the *Quire* comes in the first *Sheet* (*Mechanick Exercises*, p. 219).

The next size of book, below the folio, will be obtained by printing four pages on each side of a sheet. This produces the quarto book, the imposition of which we have already discussed and of which nothing further need be said at present.

Below this again comes the octavo, in which eight pages are printed on each side of a sheet, the sheet being afterwards folded three times to make eight leaves. The imposition of a sheet in octavo will be as in figure 9.

Four other sizes of books were in occasional use during the Elizabethan period, those in which the sheet was folded respectively into twelve, sixteen, twenty-four, and thirty-two leaves (12mo, 16mo, 24mo, and 32mo).[1]

The imposition scheme of 16mo and 32mo can easily be inferred from that of octavo, or better by folding a sheet of paper for 16mo four times, or for 32mo five times, marking the pages on it and then opening it out;[2] and we need therefore say nothing further about these sizes. The 12mo and 24mo sizes, however, present some difficulty, as there are several ways in which the pages can be imposed for these sizes. To the bibliographer the important question is how to identify the resulting 'formats', and it seems therefore better to postpone discussion of them

---

[1] i. e. [in] duodecimo, sextodecimo, vicesimo-quarto, and tricesimo-secundo, but often called 'twelvemo', 'sixteenmo', 'twenty-fourmo', and 'thirty-twomo'.   [2] See Note IV on page 37.

IMPOSITION IN OCTAVO

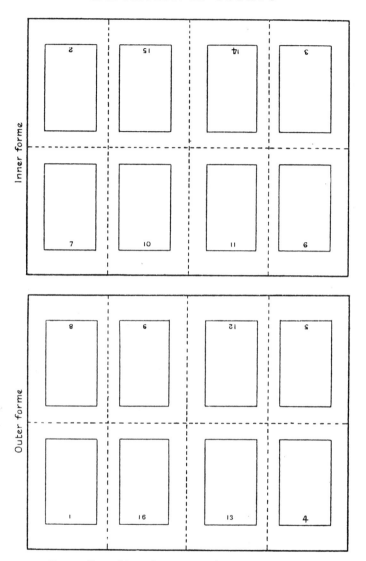

Fɪɢ. 9. Imposition of type-pages for a sheet in octavo.

until we come to deal with 'formats' in general in Part II, chapter ii.

Note I.

It is important to remember that in all sizes in ordinary use, other than in 12mo and 24mo,[1] every fold is made in the direction of (i.e. along or parallel to) what is at the moment the shorter diameter of the paper, and that the 'bolts' or folds on the outer edge are always in the second half of the sheet ; also that in *all* kinds of folding the final fold must be a simple doubling, for otherwise the sheet cannot be sewn. In case of any doubt proceed as follows : Place the sheet before you with the chain-lines running in the same direction as they run in the format to which it is desired to fold.[2] Then mark 1 on the lower right-hand corner of your sheet. Having done so, fold in the direction of the narrower diameter as often as you require, keeping page 1 always on the outside.

Note II.

On checking the correctness of an imposition. It may be noted that in *any* form of imposition if the first page is No. 1 the sum of the page numbers of each pair of pages standing side by side is always one more than the total number of pages in the gathering. Thus in the folio imposition (figure 8) the sums of 1 and 12, 3 and 10, 5 and 8, and so on are all 13, and in the octavo imposition (figure 9) the sums of 8 and 9, 12 and 5, and so on are all 17. If the sheet does not begin with page 1, then one less than the actual number with which it begins would of course have to be deducted from each number ; or which is simpler, we can see that each pair will add up to the *same* figure ; thus in a sheet of an octavo book beginning with page 17 every pair will add up to 49. A number of other numerical correspondences can be made out and some will be found in books on printing, but the above is sufficient for all practical purposes.

Note III.

The pages of the outer and inner forme. It is often useful to be able to ascertain without having a copy of a book before

---

[1] The rule *generally* applies to these also, but not to certain special methods of folding or to paper of unusual proportions.

[2] On the relation between chain-lines and format, see Part II, chap. ii.

one whether a particular pair of pages in a gathering belong to the same forme or not. This can be easily determined in the case of sizes below folio [1] by the following simple rule :

In the usual notation by signatures two rectos or two versos belong to the same forme if their numbers are either both even or both odd, e.g. A1 and A3, A2^v and A4^v. A recto and a verso belong to the same forme if the number of one is even and that of the other is odd, e.g. A1 and A2^v, A4 and A7^v

In notation by number of pages (provided that the pages are correctly numbered [2] and page 1 is the first page of a gathering), two pages belong to the same forme if both being even or both odd they differ by 4 or a multiple of 4 ; or if one being even and the other odd, the even one differs from *one less than the odd* by 0 or by 4 or by a multiple of 4.

I believe that these rules are of universal application at least for all usual foldings, but care must of course be taken that the pages one is investigating fall on the same *sheet of paper*. Otherwise of course they cannot be in the same forme. Thus in the case of a quarto in eights, one sheet being inserted within the other, A3^v (page 6) and A6 (page 11) will be on the same (inner) forme, but A1^v (page 2) and A8 (page 15) will be on another (though also an inner) forme.

Lastly it may be noted that in quarto and smaller sizes (not in folio) the odd rectos and even versos belong to the outer forme and even rectos and odd versos to the inner forme, or by pagination, counting the first page of a gathering as 1, all even numbers divisible by 4 or odd numbers which when divided by 4 leave a remainder of 1 are outer forme ; to the latter should be added page 1.

Note IV.

In working out imposition schemes by means of folded paper it is essential to remember always that the arrangement of pages in the printed sheet is a 'looking-glass image' of the arrangement of the type-pages in the forme itself (i. e. reversed from left to right *or* from top to bottom). If this point be overlooked, strange errors will result.

[1] The rules apply also in the case of folios provided that one has first ascertained that the pages fall on the same *sheet*.
[2] A dangerous assumption in the case of early books.

Chapter Five

THERE exist one fifteenth-century and several sixteenth-century woodcuts of the printing-press,[1] the earliest known being in an edition of the *Dance of Death*, printed in 1499.[2] In this the pressman is represented as standing to the right of the press, so that he would pull the bar with his left hand,[3] the inker facing him on the left. A compositor is also shown. He has a composing-stick and apparently a galley.

A somewhat more useful cut appears in the device of Badius Ascensius of Paris about 1507, but even here we find little detail, and it is not until we come to his later blocks in 1520 and *c.* 1529 (figure 10) that we have much to help us. From these, however, taken together with one in Johann Stumpf's *Swiss Chronicle*, printed by Froschouer at Zurich in 1548 [4] (figure 11), and a circular cut used by Enguilbert de Marnef at Poitiers in 1567 (figure 13) we can obtain a good idea of the construction and working of the early sixteenth-century

[1] See the article on ' Early Representations of the Printing Press ' by Mr. Falconer Madan in *Bibliographica*, i. 223–48, 499, and iii. 475, in which most of these woodcuts are reproduced. Unfortunately the evidential value of the cuts is not proportional to their number, as few of them give much detail and several go back to the same original. Mr. Madan has recently printed a fuller list of the representations of the press (1499–1600) in *The Bodleian Quarterly Record*, iv. 165–7. They now number thirty-five.

[2] *Bibliographica*, i. 225.

[3] A later cut of 1520–1 by L. Cranach shows the same position, which must, however, surely have been unusual. It may be remarked that, in the 1499 cut at least, this peculiarity cannot be due to failure to reverse the drawing when cutting the block, for a compositor who is also shown is correctly depicted holding the composing-stick in his left hand and picking up the type from the case with his right.

[4] On this is based Jost Amman's cut in Hartmann Schopper's Πανοπλία of Frankfurt, 1568, and the reversed cut in Bateman's *Doom*, see below, figure 14.

press, especially if we consider them in the light of the early presses still existing in the Musée Plantin-Moretus

FIG. 10. Device of Jodocus Badius Ascensius from the title-page of Cicero, *Pro M. Fonteio*, Paris, 1530.[1]

at Antwerp,[2] and Moxon's detailed description of a later press in his *Mechanick Exercises* of 1683. Unfortunately

[1] The press is wrongly drawn with a left-handed screw, which would cause the platen to rise when the bar was pulled.
[2] Photographs of these are given in Max Rooses' *Christophe Plantin*, 1896, and in the ' Album ' published by the Musée.

39

Moxon, though he gives a picture, very badly drawn, of an earlier type of press, bases his description on one of the newer Dutch presses which, designed by William Jansen Blaew of Antwerp fifty years before, were just coming into use in England when Moxon wrote, a curious sidelight on the enterprise of the seventeenth-century English printers. It is, however, evident that the improvements, and indeed all improvements in presses before the Stanhope press of 1800, were in matters of detail alone, and in no way affected the principles or general construction of the machine.

The two cuts reproduced below (figures 12 and 14) from the *Ordinary for all faithful Christians*, 1548, and Bateman's *Doom warning all men to the Judgement*, 1581, are the only ones known to me as occurring in English books before 1600.[1] With reference to the cut from the *Ordinary* it may be noted that the man at the extreme right of the picture is engaged in casting type, and that the signboard-like object leaning against the wall between the windows is intended for placing the damp printed sheets on lines [2] strung across the room from wall to wall just below the ceiling, which was the usual way of drying them. It was called a ' peel ', as is the somewhat similar contrivance used by bakers for getting loaves out of an oven.[3] The cut from Bateman's *Doom* is much superior in detail, but

---

[1] Not counting those in which a press is merely indicated without any details being shown, as the one in Day's *Book of Christian Prayers*. An interesting but unfortunately somewhat rough cut used by William Jones as his device in 1619–22 (see my *Printers' Devices*, no. 389) shows a press from the side, an unusual point of view. There is also, as Mr. H. R. Plomer has pointed out to me, an initial O (26 mm. square) depicting a printing-press in R. Bailie's *Ladensium Αὐτοκατά-κρισις*, 1640, sig. B 4, but it is too small to be of value.

[2] In Moxon's day the sheets were hung on wooden battens, $1'' \times 1\frac{1}{2}''$, placed ten inches apart, which were fixed below the ceiling. The upper edges of the battens were rounded so as not to mark the paper.

[3] I owe thanks to Mr. Henry L. Bullen of the Typographic Library and Museum of Jersey City, U.S.A., for the correction of a bad blunder which I made in the original edition of these notes, where

it has been reversed [1] in cutting and adds nothing save a beer jug to the 1548 cut from which it is ultimately derived.

The attempted description of the early press which follows is based principally on Moxon,[2] checked and sometimes interpreted, for Moxon was not a lucid

FIG. 11. From Johann Stumpf's *Gemeiner loblicher Eydgnosschaft Stetten . . . beschreybung*, C. Froschouer, Zurich, 1548, vol. i, fol. 23.

I explained this object as a copy-holder. Mr. Bullen tells me that he learnt printing before the practice of printing on damp paper was abandoned and that he has himself used a similar contrivance for hanging sheets on the lines.

[1] The screw should be right- not left-handed, and the pressman should stand on the left (i.e. here, nearer) side of the press and pull the handle towards him.

[2] *Mechanick Exercises*, the second volume (Printing), 1683.

writer, by reference to other later authorities, especially Momoro,[1] who has some good plates, though his text is of little value, and Johnson.[2]   It is, I believe, in general correct for the later part of the sixteenth century and the whole of the seventeenth, though there was no doubt variation in non-essential details.[3]   I have given many of Moxon's measurements, sometimes slightly modified where he is inconsistent, for although they can of course only be regarded as those of his own particular late seventeenth-century press, we may, I think, reasonably assume that they would apply with fair accuracy to the earlier presses as well.   After all, the dimensions of a machine of this sort are mainly dictated by convenience of working, and the stature and length of reach of the average pressman were, we may presume, fairly constant.

Essentially the press consisted of an upright frame standing about six feet high, the two side-pieces of which, called the 'cheeks', heavy posts $8'' \times 4\frac{1}{2}''$ in depth and thickness, were let into the front ends of two stout pieces of wood about $2'\ 9''$ long, which, being laid flat on the floor, served also as bases for the hind posts of the press, as will be seen later.   These cheeks stood about $1'\ 9''$ apart and were held together by a cross-piece at the top, called the 'cap', and a heavier one below, called the 'winter', the top of which was about $2'\ 6''$ from

[1] *Traité élémentaire de l'Imprimerie*, 1793.

[2] *Typographia*, 1824, vol. ii, especially cap. 15.

[3] It would hardly be too much to claim that the description applies in essentials to all presses in ordinary use until the introduction of the iron press at the beginning of the nineteenth century.   The important difference in these iron presses, beside the complete change in design necessitated by the different material of which they were constructed, was that some form of mechanical device, other than a plain screw, was introduced by which the rate of travel of the platen was caused to decrease, and the 'power' consequently to increase, as it descended, with the result that a much more powerful pressure on the forme (allowing the use of larger formes) was obtained by the same expenditure of effort on the part of the pressman, cf. p. 63 below.

the ground. Behind this frame was an extension supported by the two hind-posts, which fitted into the other ends of the two basal pieces or feet of the cheeks. These posts were rigidly attached to the cheeks by two side-rails and were joined together by two other rails, one at the top and a second, heavier one, set so that its upper surface was exactly level with that of the winter. This

FIG. 12. From the *Ordinary for all faithful Christians*, printed by Anthony Scoloker, London, *c.* 1548.

lower rail and the winter together served to support a horizontal frame which in Moxon's press was 4′ 5″ long by 1′ 11″ wide, the cheeks of the press being cut away on the inner sides to allow it to enter between them. The frame projected about 2′ 6″ in front of the cheeks, the near end being supported by a prop or stay resting on the ground.

Lengthwise of this frame and dividing it into three approximately equal portions ran two stout wooden ribs, bearing on their upper surfaces iron rails on which ran the plank of the carriage,[1] the part of the apparatus

[1] There seems to be some uncertainty as to the use of the term 'carriage', some writers, such as Johnson, understanding by it only

upon which was fastened the forme of type which was to be printed from. This ' plank ' was made of elm and measured $4' \times 1' 8\frac{3}{4}'' \times 1\frac{1}{2}''$; it was furnished on the under side with iron shoes sliding on the rails above mentioned.[1] The plank therefore could be slid in and out between the cheeks of the press on the rails, which, as we have seen, were ultimately supported by the winter. It was thus the winter which, when the platen was brought down upon the type, took the force of the impression.

The plank carried at its near end a rectangular frame about $2' 4''$ long by $1' 8''$ wide and $2\frac{1}{2}''$ deep, called the ' coffin ', in which was bedded a carefully smoothed stone of marble or Purbeck limestone about $2\frac{3}{8}''$ thick. Upon this, which was called the 'press-stone', the chase containing the forme to be printed was placed, a means being provided, by raised iron corners to the coffin, of wedging the chase firmly in position.

Below the frame carrying the iron rails on which the plank slid, and a little way in front of the cheeks of the press, was fixed a wooden roller which could be turned by a handle at the near (left) side of the press, convenient to the left hand of the pressman. Attached to this roller and wound round it in opposite directions were two leather straps or ' girts ' as Moxon calls them. These straps passed upward between the rails on which the plank slid, and their other ends were fastened to the two ends of the plank.[2] It is evident that turning the handle

the stationary frame on which the sliding part moved, others, including Moxon, both the stationary and moving parts, while still others use it for the sliding part alone.

[1] It would seem probable that in the earlier presses, instead of running on two iron ribs toward the centre of the frame, the plank slid in a kind of shallow trough formed by the raised sides of the frame. In any case, however, the centre of the frame must have been open to allow passage for the straps or girths by which, as will be explained later, the plank was moved in and out.

[2] In the more elaborate kinds of press the ends of these straps were not fastened directly to the plank but to two small rollers placed one

44

in one direction would cause the plank to run in between the cheeks of the press, and turning it in the other direction would cause it to run out again. The whole arrangement, and specifically the handle, was called the 'rounce'.

We must now return to the coffin and consider how the paper was held and brought down upon the type

FIG. 13. From the title-page of *La Fauconnerie de messire Arthelouche de Alagona* (part of *La Fauconnerie de F. Ian des Franchieres*), printed by Enguilbert de Marnef, et les Bouchetz, freres, Poitiers, 1567.

in order that the impression might be taken. Hinged to the near end of the coffin was a wooden or iron frame of dimensions slightly less than the outside of the latter and at such a height that when turned down horizontal upon a forme of type placed upon the press-stone it would lie exactly level with the faces of the type. Within this frame, which was called the outer

at the far end of the plank, the other at the near end of the coffin. These rollers were provided with ratchets and so arranged that by turning them any slack caused by the stretching of the straps in use could be taken up.

45

tympan, was fitted another frame, the inner tympan, just so much smaller that when a sheet of vellum, the tympan sheet, was pasted over the inner frame it could be pressed within the outer one and be held tightly by it. A rest rising from the plank was provided to hold the tympan, when turned back, at a convenient angle for laying the paper on it. To the free end of the outer tympan was hinged another lighter frame, called the frisket, so arranged that it could be turned down upon the paper lying on the tympan and then the two together turned down upon the forme. The frisket was covered with a sheet of paper in which holes were cut in order to allow the pages of type to print. Its purpose was to prevent the paper which was being printed from sagging down and so becoming soiled by ink from the furniture between the pages of type.

The use of the frisket in Elizabethan printing has been questioned ; but it is, I think, certain that it was used, at least, by many printers. A frisket is shown in those of the early cuts of printing-presses which show technical exactness in other respects.[1] It is true that most of these cuts are foreign, but there seems to have been a good deal of intercourse between English and foreign printing-houses, and it is hardly likely that an important improvement such as this would not be copied. One printer at any rate used friskets, Thomas Vautrollier, in whose will, dated 1587, they are especially mentioned among the printing material.[2] And indeed with the soft packing commonly used in the tympan, which frequently drove the paper

---

[1] See figures 11 and 14 and the 1568 cut in *Bibliographica*, i. 236, where both the tympan and the frisket are well shown. The three cuts cannot, however, be regarded as affording independent evidence, see p. 38, note 4.

[2] Plomer, *Wills of English Printers* (Bibliographical Society), p. 27. The ' appurtenances ' of a press which he bequeathed to his son Manases consisted, among other things, of ' fower Chassis, and three Friskets, two timpanes and a Copper plate '.

down to the shoulder of the type at the head and foot of a page, it is difficult to see how a clean impression could be obtained without a frisket of some sort. Lastly, in Elizabethan books we occasionally find that a letter or two at the beginning or end of several lines together has failed to print. This *might* of course be due to these letters not having been inked ; but this is unlikely, as there would generally be traces of ink

FIG. 14. From Stephen Bateman's *Doom warning all men to the Judgement*, R. Newbery, London, 1581.

from a former inking, while in the cases to which I refer there is no sign of ink at all. It would be a natural result of the hole in the frisket not being cut quite large enough, or having got slightly out of register, so that the edge of the paper was caught between the type and the sheet which was being printed, and it is not easy to see how it could come about in any other way. When the edge of a frisket sheet is caught between the type and the paper, the frisket is said to 'bite'. Blades (*Caxton*, p. 318) instances a case of a 'bite' in the *Speculum Vitae*

47

Christi [*c*. 1487], and also cases of small blocks of disused type-matter being used as bearers [1] and giving a blind impression (op. cit., p. 130). This implies the use of a frisket even at this early date. But I repeat, I do not see how it would have been possible at any period to produce clean press-work without something of the kind. Such ' bites ', however, are not common, and we may perhaps say that there is doubt whether the use of a frisket, however general, was universal.

It remains only to consider the means by which the impression was produced. Between the cheeks of the press, a little below the cap, was fitted a heavy piece of wood, the ' head ', bearing in the centre of its under side a brass nut (in Moxon's day) in which the main screw or spindle of the press worked. Tenons at the ends of the head fitted into mortises in the cheeks, and it was possible to raise or lower the head slightly and to fix it in any position by inserting packing in the ends of the mortises. This enabled the printer to ensure that when the bar of the press was fully pulled over, exactly the right amount of pressure was exerted on the forme of type.

The spindle of Moxon's press was $16\frac{1}{2}''$ long and was screwed for $3\frac{1}{4}''$ from the upper end, the diameter of the screw being $2\frac{1}{4}''$, with a pitch of $2\frac{1}{2}''$, there being generally in presses of his time either three or four

---

[1] When a page happens to consist of only a few lines at the top, the rest being blank, it is evident that unless something of a height equal to the type is placed in the lower part of the page the platen, when brought down on the type, will be subjected to a very unequal strain. To remedy this, blocks of wood of type-height called ' bearers ' were generally placed in blank pages. Occasionally, however, blocks of type which had been printed from and which were waiting for distribution were used for the same purpose. These naturally would be prevented from printing by the frisket through which they would give a faint ' blind ' impression. If no frisket was used such ' bearers ' of type would, if they were perfectly clean and were not accidentally inked, equally give a blind impression, but this would probably be sharper than those which we usually find.

threads or ' worms ' as Moxon called them. As the angle through which the bar of the press was turned in printing was about a quarter of a revolution, the travel of the platen would be about five-eighths of an inch, this being just sufficient to clear the frame of the tympan and to allow for the slight play or compression in all the parts of the press affected.

Below the screwed portion of the spindle was a cubical part pierced by a square hole to take the end of the ' bar '[1] or lever by which the press was worked, and below this again a cylindrical portion bearing at the end a blunt point, called the ' toe ', which worked in a depression on the upper surface of the platen. This cylindrical piece passed through a hole in a wooden cross-piece, called the ' till ', which was fitted between the cheeks of the press about half-way between the head and the printing surface. The ends of the till being dovetailed into the cheeks helped to hold them firmly together, and the hole in it apparently[2] served as a guide to keep the motion of the spindle exactly vertical and to prevent it from being dragged aside by the pull of the bar, which would inevitably have resulted in a slurred impression.

Above the till a kind of collar was fitted to the spindle having two projecting arms running sideways from it ; from the ends of these arms, rods, called the ' hose ', ran downwards parallel with the spindle and, passing through two holes in the till, supported below it a square plate of iron with a hole in the centre fitting

[1] The effective length of the bar is difficult to ascertain exactly, as it was curved. It seems to have been about three feet.

[2] I say ' apparently ' because I do not see that Moxon appreciated its use for this purpose. He seems to have regarded the hole simply as allowing the spindle to pass through, without implying that it must be a good fit. It is, however, surely inconceivable that the press should have worked without slurring in the absence of a guide of some sort, and there was certainly no other. The ' hose ' referred to in the next paragraph no doubt served to prevent the platen from turning, but could have had little effect in keeping its descent straight.

49

the spindle and with the corners turned up into four hooks called the hose-hooks. It will be seen that as the spindle turned in the collar and descended with a spiral motion, this apparatus descended with it at the same rate but without turning.

The important part of the press called the platen consisted in Moxon's press of a beechen plank, $2\frac{1}{2}''$ thick, its length being about $14''$ and its breadth about $9''$,[1] the under surface being of course planed exactly true and smooth. In the centre of the upper surface was an iron plate, called the platen-plate, bearing in its centre a stud in which was a hemispherical depression for the toe of the spindle to work in. Near the corners of the upper surface of the wooden platen, four hooks were inserted corresponding to the four turned-up corners of the plate which has been mentioned as moving up and down with the spindle. These hooks served to suspend the platen to the spindle, the method of attachment being to place a forme on the press-stone, lay the platen carefully in position upon it, pull the bar, so as to bring the spindle down, adjust the platen so that the toe of the spindle was in the stud on the top of it, then, keeping the bar firmly pulled, to lash tightly with many turns of strong whipcord each platen-hook to its corresponding hose-hook, finally whipping each lashing round and round to hold it firmly together. Once this was properly done the platen would of course always come down perfectly true and even on the face of the type and, so long as the bed of the press remained level, would not require readjustment.

One or two subsidiary points may be noticed. I cannot discover that the early presses had any special apparatus to cause the platen to rise again after the impression. It would seem that the pitch of the spindle-thread being very steep, the natural spring of

[1] These dimensions should be noted (see p. 61). Johnson's press, nearly 150 years later, had a platen $4'' \times 19'' \times 13''$.

the bar, aided by the compression of the packing in the tympan, caused it on release to fly back of its own accord and thus raise the platen to its normal position. The provision of a catch to hold the bar back as soon as it reached the cheek in its rebound seems to show that this natural spring was relied upon for the return of the platen, for had there been anything of the nature of a counterpoise this catch would have been unnecessary. It may be remarked that the extreme curvature of the bar away from the pressman in the later presses was in order that he might be able to start the pull by catching hold of the curved portion with his left hand, drawing the bar towards him until he was able to reach the handle itself with his right. This simple device gave him of course a different leverage for the idle and effective parts of the pull, and by making it possible to use a longer bar enabled him to exert a greater pressure on the forme without proportional increase of effort.

Inspection of the early cuts suggests a few possible differences in points of detail.

In most of the early pictures we see strong struts running upwards from the top of the press to the joists of the ceiling of the workshop. These may have been merely intended to prevent the press from rocking under the strain of pulling the bar, but in some cases (cf. figure 10), the struts appear to take the form of bloated nuts [1] working on screwed rods so as to be capable of extension. It is difficult to resist the idea that they were intended to hold the press *down*. This of course suggests that the table or carriage on which the plank and coffin ran was not attached to the press but simply placed below the platen, in which case the pulling of the bar would naturally cause the press to rise unless it was held down very firmly in some way or other.

[1] The black dots on these look like tommy-holes for turning them.

Some of the presses [1] apparently had a more cumbersome device than that described by Moxon for ensuring the straight descent of the platen, namely, a sort of square box which worked up and down in the till, to the corners of which the platen was lashed and through the bottom of which the toe of the spindle passed. This looks like being more effective in preventing slur than Moxon's ' hose '. It may be mentioned that it is in principle very much like the arrangement shown by Johnson in 1824.

[1] See the Froschouer cut of 1548, figure 11.

Chapter Six

AS has been often remarked, we are practically without external evidence as to the technique of early
printing, and such knowledge of this as we have has been
derived—with an admixture of conjecture—from a
study of the books themselves. I propose in this
chapter to discuss certain points in which the methods
of earlier or later printers differed or seem to have
differed from those of the printer of 1600 whose
methods we took as our standard in chapter ii.

We have already discussed the press itself, but there
is one subsidiary piece of apparatus of which a word
must be said, namely, the chase in which the pages of
type were fastened for the purpose of taking the
impression.

Modern chases consist essentially, as we have seen,
of a rectangular frame somewhat less than type-high,
large enough to contain all the pages which are to be
printed at one time, with the necessary spaces between
them to form the margins, and strong enough to with-
stand the pressure of the wedges by which the type is
'locked up'. As they have no bottom, the wedges
have to be driven in sufficiently firmly to render the
type practically a solid block, so that the whole mass
can be lifted from the bed of the press without any risk
of the type falling out, a catastrophe which would of
course involve re-setting the whole forme.

It has been suggested, however, that in the earliest
printing the chase instead of being merely a bottomless
frame was a shallow box only slightly larger than the

53

type page, with a firm bottom on which the type stood, and that instead of using a composing-stick, the compositor set up the type directly in these boxes. There were perhaps also screws at the foot of the box in order to tighten the page of type when composed.[1] I am not aware that there is any positive evidence as to this, but it may certainly be claimed that it would be the obvious way to make a first attempt. It would hardly occur to any one imposing pages for the first time to do it in a box without a bottom. Soon, however, it would become apparent that the bottom was not required and was indeed a disadvantage. If in the course of composition a thin type fell to the bottom of the box and other type were placed on it without its being noticed, it would be very troublesome to remove, and further, any liquid used to wash the type during printing [2] would lie in the bottom of the box, where it would probably soften the wood and corrode the feet of the type. Further, the adjusting of the height of any block or initial letter which was not quite of type-height and required packing-up from below would be much more difficult than if one could get at the back of the forme. A bottomless frame would tend soon to replace the shallow box. The screws also, if indeed they were ever used—which I take leave to doubt— would soon be replaced by the simpler and more convenient wedges. The next step would doubtless be to enlarge the frame to take two or more pages of type at a time.

If such shallow boxes were indeed used for holding the type, and the pages were merely kept together by pressure at right angles to the lines of type, it is evident that there would be no need for the careful justification of the lines which became necessary later in bottomless

[1] Blades, *Caxton*, p. 122.
[2] With primitive kinds of ink it might well be necessary to do this from time to time in order to clean the type during the course of printing.

chases. All that would be required would be some sort of small wooden pegs or wedges at the ends of the lines sufficient to hold the type from falling apart, and it is tempting to see in the slight irregularities of the line-endings in some early books evidence of some method such as this.

An examination of a few MSS. of the period immediately preceding the introduction of printing will show that in the more carefully written prose MSS. the scribes did their best, by the use of appropriate contractions and by dividing words when necessary, to fill out the lines to an even length. The early printers, basing their work on the best MS. practice, did exactly the same thing, and by employing a very large number of contracted forms were able in the earliest work to arrive at almost perfect uniformity in the line-endings.[1] Nevertheless, though this filling-out of lines could evidently be managed, by no means all the printers troubled about it and we find much early work in which it is neglected. Thus of two of the early *Indulgences* evidently printed at the same date but by different printers, one (that with 30 lines) has the lines filled out, the other (with 31 lines) not.[2] On the whole, however, there was a very definite and rapid progress from imperfect to perfect spacing-out of lines. Thus Caxton's earliest books are all irregular in line-endings, but from 1480 onwards he adopted the system of spacing out to an even length.[3] That it was not

---

[1] See, for example, the 42-line Bible. In this, as in some other early work, the hyphen and occasionally a full stop at the end of a line are outside the measure, which on the whole gives a more uniform appearance than the usual method.

[2] See the 30- and 31-line *Indulgences* of 1455, in *B.M. Facsimiles*, pls. 3 and 4. A curious case is noted by Bradshaw, *Collected Papers*, p. 150, in a group of books printed by the printer of the *Historia S. Albani*, some time before 1475, where the recto pages end evenly, the verso not, it being presumably regarded as more important that the outer margins should be even than the inner.

[3] See Blades, *Caxton*, pp. 44–7. It is perhaps worth noting that

a mere matter of careful or careless printing is evident from the fact that so excellent a printer as Jenson at Venice, *c.* 1470, freely allowed a small variation to the extent of an ordinary space at the ends of his lines, especially after a stop. Long before the end of the fifteenth century, however, complete regularity in line-endings seems to have been everywhere the rule.

Blades insists that when part of a printer's output is fully spaced out and part is not, the irregular must be taken to precede the regular. This is no doubt true in the main, but it is subject to exceptions. It is probable that much would depend on the habits of the particular compositor, and that at the time of the transition older men might be using irregular lining and younger men regular, in the same printing-house. Books are indeed known in different parts of which the different systems are followed. Further, one must beware of concluding that when a particular book is reprinted line for line the more irregular version must be the earlier. On general grounds the reverse of this is more probable : we might even go so far as to say that if in a book with irregular line-endings we find lines which would have admitted the first word of the following line, we can be practically certain that we have to do with a reprint.

Blades connects this irregular lining with the non-use of a setting-rule. He points out that if type is laid directly on other type, especially if the type is at all rough, the slight projections will make it very difficult to slide along. It is therefore much easier to insert all spaces necessary for the justification of the line *at*

when printing in the vernacular there must, owing to the lack of suitable contractions, have been special difficulty in ending the lines evenly until compositors hit on the device of varying the spelling of the words. Blades points out that this spacing-out to make the lines of print end evenly must not be confused with justification, which properly means the filling-out of the lines of type to an even length of metal. A line which in the printed book appears short may, so far as the type is concerned, be perfectly justified by having several spaces at the end.

the end. This is undoubtedly so, but I think it is hardly safe to infer from irregular line-endings that no setting-rule was used, as Updike does.[1]

Printing by Single Pages. We frequently find references in bibliographical literature to books having been printed one page at a time (in the case of folios or books printed as folios),[2] or two or four pages at a time (in the smaller sizes) instead of the normal full forme of four or eight ; and I am afraid that some of those responsible for these statements are not altogether clear as to what they mean.

Two absolutely different processes have been described as printing one page at a time, and it is most necessary that we should carefully distinguish them, as their results and the evidence concerning them are altogether different.

A. The genuine printing of one page at a time implies that having to print, say, a folio sheet of four pages the printer first printed all the required copies of, say, page 1, then removed the page of type from the bed of the press, put on a new page, say, page 4, and proceeded to print that, laying on each sheet of paper again, of course in a different position. The result of this process will obviously be that if every sheet is not laid on with perfect accuracy the relative positions of the pairs of pages will vary more or less in different copies ; they may not be parallel to one another, or the distances apart (the sum of the inner margins) may vary. On the other hand, the process will cause no special risk of slur or double impression.

This method, as we shall see later, was undoubtedly used in many early books.

B. The other kind of ' printing one page at a time '

---

[1] *Printing Types,* i. 94–7. Indeed the case quoted in note 2 on p. 55 seems sufficient to dispose of this inference.

[2] i. e. quartos in which the sheets were cut in half before printing, as was done by many of the early printers.

should rather be described as giving two pulls to the forme. By this method the whole forme is placed on the bed of the press at one time and the paper being placed on the tympan in the ordinary way, the carriage is first run under the platen to the distance of half its length ; the platen is then brought down and raised again ; the carriage is then run further in and the lever pulled a second time. Thus each page (in a folio) is actually printed separately, but as the pages of type are on the bed together and rigidly fixed with respect to one another, and as the paper does not (or should not) move between the two pulls, we ought to find no difference in register or in parallelism of the pages from what we should have if the whole forme had been printed by one pull of the lever.[1] On the other hand, if the packing of the tympan was soft there must have been some risk that the first descent of the platen would exercise a slight drag on the paper of the other half of the sheet, and as this would be lying on the inked type a certain amount of slur would be caused, or even in bad cases a double impression. Probably, however, the damp paper would give to some extent, for we do not find much evidence of slurring due to this cause.[2]

First, as regards the genuine ' one page at a time ' printing (A). The evidence which we may find of this is of several kinds. We may sometimes come across copies of early books in which while one page of a forme is printed, another page which should be part of the same forme is blank. This of course is positive proof that the pages were printed one by one. Equally positive

---

[1] I do not understand Horace Hart's remark in the Introduction to the Clarendon Press facsimile of the *First Folio* of Shakespeare, p. xxiv, that ' the faulty register ' seems to reveal that there were two pulls to each side of the sheet. Undoubtedly there were, but how does the register show it ? Dr. Greg, who had some correspondence with Hart on the subject, tells me that he believes that by ' faulty register ' Hart really meant slurring.

[2] But see Johnson's remark below.

would be the presence in two pages which would normally be printed together of the same ornament, initial letter, or block, but such cases, though I believe that they exist, are undoubtedly very rare. Almost equally good evidence may be found in the difference *in different copies of a book* in the relative positions of pages which would normally belong to the same forme and be printed together. Thus if in one copy a certain pair of pages is parallel and level with one another, while in other copies the pages make various angles or are at different heights, we must either suppose that the pages were printed separately or that they were in small separate chases (or shallow boxes), and being merely laid on the bed of the press without proper fixing, shifted during the course of printing, surely a much less probable supposition.[1]

Lastly, a case that was worked out by Professor A. W. Pollard some twenty years ago or more [2] affords a very pretty proof of this single-page printing, which depends on the order of distribution of the pages. The *Valerius Maximus*, printed by Schoeffer in 1471, has certain pages the setting of which differs in different copies, whereas the setting of other pages is always the same. These double settings occur in the early leaves of six gatherings scattered at approximately equal distances throughout the book. The natural inference is that the printing was carried out simultaneously on six presses,[3] each press having its own compositors working for it,[4] and that when the work

---

[1] Indeed an impossible one if a frisket was used, but perhaps just possible in the earliest period.

[2] See *The Book-Lover's Magazine*, vi, pp. 50–5.

[3] The 42-line Bible is also said to have been printed on six presses.

[4] The matter must of course have been previously divided into six portions. The division was not exactly equal, but the portions were made to meet properly by varying the number of leaves in the last gathering of each part. Incidentally we may infer that Schoeffer's fount of type must have been very large, enough to have a considerable part of the book in type at one time.

had progressed a certain distance, and some of the earlier pages of each group had been distributed, it was decided to increase the size of the edition. Those pages which had been already distributed had therefore to be reset, while of those which were still in type, or were composed later, only one setting was necessary. From our present point of view the interesting thing is that it is the *early* pages only of each portion which were reset. Now the first gathering of each of the six sections consists of ten leaves. By the ordinary methods pages 1 and 20 of each gathering would be printed together, pages 2 and 19, and so on, and it is natural to suppose that they would be distributed in the same order. We find, however, that it is the first seven or eight pages of the gatherings which were duplicated, implying that the pages were distributed approximately in the order in which they were composed. It is difficult to account for this except by supposing that they were *printed* in this order, in which case the printing must necessarily have been page by page.[1]

It seems, therefore, certain that some at least of the earliest books were printed one page at a time, and after all it is what we should naturally expect. There were at least two good reasons for it. In the first place, seeing that only one page of a MS. could be written at one time, the natural instinct of a beginner at print-

---

[1] To be quite honest, it seems just possible that such a result might be arrived at after ordinary forme imposition, provided that we assume that distribution was not begun until the whole of the first gathering of each portion had been printed off. In such a case it would of course be *possible* for the compositor to select the pages for distribution in their numerical order, if it was thought worth while to do so. It is conceivable that some such practice may have been followed in order to ensure that the type went back into the cases from which they came (a 20-page gathering would need several pairs of cases), with the idea of maintaining the correct proportions of the characters and preventing shortages of certain sorts. But Mr. Pollard's explanation is the obvious one.

ing would be to follow the same method. The convenience of printing pages 1 and 20 of a ten-leaf gathering together would hardly be perceived at once. Secondly, printing would be possible with a much smaller supply of type, indeed an impecunious printer could get on quite well with enough for two or three pages ; and though this consideration would not weigh with such a man as Schoeffer, who seems to have had ample supplies, it might well have had weight in establishing the normal procedure.

But enough of this primitive printing by single pages. Let us turn to B, the method of two pulls to the forme. And here I think that I may perhaps surprise some bibliographers by saying that *always until about 1800* a normal full-sized forme of type was printed by two pulls of the lever.[1] The fact is obvious. In the first place, if we examine the early cuts of the printing-press we shall see that in those which are most carefully drawn the platen is always much smaller than the tympan, so that evidently if these drawings are correct, in printing a forme which filled the carriage, it would be necessary to bring it down twice, moving the carriage between the two pulls. Secondly, we have the actual measurements of platen and tympan as given by Moxon and Johnson. The inside dimensions of Moxon's tympan were about $22'' \times 15''$, and of his platen $9'' \times 14''$. The inside of Johnson's tympan[2] was about $25'' \times 20''$, his platen $13'' \times 19''$. It is obvious that in each case the platen would only cover at one time half the forme suitable for the size of paper taken by the tympan.

But we have further and even more definite proof, for Johnson, writing in 1824, describes in detail the

---

[1] This has several times been pointed out, but seems not to have been generally appreciated.

[2] Actually the frisket, which in Johnson's press seems to have been a good deal smaller than the tympan. It is, of course, the frisket which determines the maximum area of the surface that could be printed.

whole process of pulling an impression as he himself knew it. He writes, apropos of the Wooden Press : [1]

> the build in this country (excepting those only upon the French plan) were [2] uniformly made with small plattins; consequently it was necessary to pull twice with every full form : it was difficult, and almost next to an impossibility, to prevent some of them from doubling in the impression, particularly in Twelves : but, notwithstanding the pressmen had to pull twice for each impression, they could get through equally as much, if not more work than the iron press with one pull.[3]

Elsewhere he describes in full the method used, telling us how the carriage is first to be run in to a certain mark, and the lever pulled ; then the lever is allowed to go back a certain distance, the handle of the rounce turned again to run the carriage in to the second mark and a second pull taken.[4] Lastly, in his list of technical terms, he explains ' vantage ' as what the pressmen call it ' when a form of one pull comes to the press '.[5] It is throughout perfectly clear that Johnson is speaking of the method actually employed in his own day, though it is clear also that larger platens were then coming into use.

There were probably two reasons for this practice of using a small platen and giving two impressions to each forme, one being that the larger wooden platens, even when backed with iron, were insufficiently rigid, tending to spring at the ends and thus give an uneven impression. This, however, one would think, might without difficulty have been got over by a different method of attaching the platen to the spindle so that the thrust was distributed over several points instead of being only at the centre. A more important reason

---

[1] In his day becoming old-fashioned, having been replaced from c. 1800 by the Stanhope and other presses constructed of iron.

[2] Johnson's English is not above criticism, but his meaning is generally clear. [3] *Typographia*, ii. 504.

[4] Ibid., pp. 525–6. [5] Ibid., p. 656.

was probably the difficulty of obtaining a sufficiently powerful impression to work a large forme by means of a single screw motion of even pitch.[1] In all forms of modern hand-press, from the Stanhope onwards, the amount of leverage increases as the platen descends. The first few inches of the pull cause the platen to descend perhaps nine-tenths of the whole distance that it has to go, the remaining much larger part of the motion of the lever producing a motion which is very small in range but exceedingly powerful. The result of this is of course that the energy of the pressman is far more economically expended and a much larger forme can be worked with the same labour.

The page 'galley'. In chapter ii I mentioned that the compositors of the Elizabethan period normally finished a page of work at a time, adding catchword and signature (if necessary) before proceeding to the next one, instead of setting up the matter in long columns and proofing and correcting these before dividing them up into pages as is customary at present. It is, however, necessary to say a little more about this.

We have already seen that at a very early stage in the development of printing, the type may have been set up directly in a shallow box which performed the function of a primitive chase. Very soon, however, we can be quite sure, some form of composing-stick would be evolved, for it would obviously be a great advantage to the compositor to set the type in a light ' stick ' which he could hold in his left hand rather than in a comparatively heavy box which would have to rest on a bench at his side or on the type-case. A moment's consideration of the amount of movement involved in the two processes will show the enormous gain in the use of the composing-stick. The early

[1] It may be mentioned that the length of the lever which could be employed and the angle through which it could be turned were, of course, limited by the reach of the workman's arm.

stick was doubtless made of wood and much more clumsy than the light adjustable affair of metal which is used nowadays, but the principle was the same, and it is probable that the drawing given by Blades represents it with fair accuracy.[1] It would of course be necessary to have a different stick for each different measure which was set.[2]

The depth of a composing-stick, i.e. the number of lines of type that it will hold, is of course limited by the weight that a compositor can conveniently hold in his hand. Ten lines of pica of a usual measure for a quarto book would weigh about 25 or 30 oz.,[3] and we may, I think, take this as the maximum weight which could be handled comfortably. After setting this number of lines, or of course less if the measure were wider, the compositor would have to transfer the block of type set to some other receptacle. A modern

[1] Blades, *Caxton*, p. 124. It does not appear on what the drawing is based, but it is much like the wooden composing-sticks which were used in much later times for setting large type for poster-work, &c.

[2] It might perhaps have been expected that non-adjustable composing-sticks would have led to standard lengths of line, but there seems not much evidence of this. Blades gives the line-length of almost all of Caxton's books, and it appears that, not counting a few exceptionally long measures for special purposes, he used at least fourteen different lengths of line varying from $2\frac{1}{2}''$ to $5\frac{5}{8}''$. It is, however, noteworthy that the identical measure is often used in a whole series of books printed about the same time. Thus eleven books have a measure of $4\frac{3}{4}''$, all except two dating from 1481–2 ; fifteen measure $4\frac{5}{8}''$, of which twelve date from 1487–91. In any case these wooden composing-sticks would have been quite cheap to make, and I do not think the great variety of measure that we find in early work is any argument against their use.

[3] The weight of modern type is given by Southward (*Modern Printing*, p. 127) as 5 oz. to the square inch, but Mr. C. T. Jacobi informs me that the figure that he has always taken is 4 oz., and that he has recently verified the correctness of this by experiment. The weight would of course depend on the length of the types or ' height to paper ' ; but we may assume this to have remained approximately the same from quite early times (see *The Library*, 4th Ser., ii. 98 note). The present standard height to paper is 0·92 of an inch.

compositor transfers the stickful of type to a long three-sided tray called a galley, which will hold enough type to form two or three pages of the book, proofs are taken from the galleys and, so far as possible, all corrections are made in the type before it is divided up into pages and imposed in the forme. The earlier printers, however, used short galleys containing the type of a single page. The type from the stick was transferred to a galley of this kind until there was enough for a page and the signature and catchword were then added before the composition of the next page was proceeded with.[1] This was the regular practice until early in the nineteenth century, and no other appears to have been known to any writer or printer up to and including Johnson ; indeed the first indica-

---

[1] I have discussed this question, so far as concerns the Elizabethan period of printing, in an article in *The Library*, 4th Ser., ii. 97–108, and need not repeat the arguments here. The most important proofs of direct making-up into pages are : (1) The fact that there are a good many instances of the last line or the last few words of one page being repeated at the beginning of the next. (See, among others, *Fulgens and Lucres*, n.d., a2–2ᵛ (two lines repeated) : *Tottel's Miscellany*, ed. Arber, p. 89 ; B. Googe, *Eclogues*, ed. Arber, p. 127 foot-note ; *Sir Giles Goosecap*, ed. Bang and Brotanek, ii. 1088–91 ; *Works of Beaumont and Fletcher*, 1647, 2K4ᵛ–2L1.) Such repetitions are easily explained by the compositor having forgotten, when he started the next page, exactly where he had left off. If the work had all been set up in galley, accidental repetitions would not appear at the beginning of a fresh page more often than elsewhere. (2) The comparative frequency with which we find a correct catchword in cases where the opening words of the next page are wrong, owing to the compositor having mistaken the point at which he left off and consequently omitted or repeated a word or two. The catchword must therefore have been taken from the MS., not, as would be the case if the matter had been first standing in galley, from the opening line of the next page. It seems clear that signatures were often, if not always, added immediately on the completion of the page, from the fact that they so often follow the type of the last few words of the page, when this happens to be in italics or of a larger face, or otherwise different from that generally used in the text of the book. Had the signatures all been added at the same time, after division of the matter into pages, it would have been natural for the printer to use the same type for them throughout.

tion of the long galley containing two or more pages of type seems to be in Savage's *Dictionary of Printing*, 1841.[1]

The question of page versus long-galley setting is, it may be remarked, by no means of purely theoretical importance, for it may in some cases have a bearing on our interpretation of a text. In the first place, it is clear that in all texts in which the pages were made up as the compositor went along, if the catchword differs from the opening word of the next page, the reading of the former may well be given the preference, for it was the earlier set up and is at least equally likely to be correct;[2] whereas a catchword inserted during making up into pages from long galleys can have no manuscript authority whatever. Another point is that when, as occasionally happens, we find a page too long or too short, we need not suspect an author's correction *at the last moment*, as we should if the work had been proofed in galley before being cut into pages. It may merely be that lines were omitted or repeated by the compositor in the original setting-up, for even if this were discovered immediately on proofing, it would probably not have been thought worth while to overrun later pages in order to remedy an irregularity caused by the correction.

Imposition by half-sheets. A variation from the normal method of arranging the pages in a forme, which came into use at a period not easy to determine, must be

[1] I am indebted to Mr. C. T. Jacobi for this reference, which is actually to slip proofs, not to long galleys, but the former of course imply the latter. Mr. Jacobi informs me that he believes that long galleys were first introduced in newspaper work, in order that articles might be proofed before the make-up of the paper was determined. He states that it was not until 1870 that the Chiswick Press sent out proof in galley form.

[2] It is also slightly more likely to preserve the spelling of the MS., as there can be no question of modifying this in order to aid in the justification.

mentioned here. We often find books of the smaller sizes, 16mo, 24mo, and 32mo, and somewhat less frequently 8vo,[1] sewn in gatherings of half the normal number of leaves, namely, 8, 12, 16, and 4 respectively. Now it would be quite possible, as any one can see by experimenting with folded paper, to impose the pages of two formes (outer and inner) in 16mo in such a way that when a sheet is printed from them it can be cut in the middle and will then form two consecutive gatherings of eight leaves each instead of one of sixteen leaves. There would, however, be little if any gain in doing this : a book in smaller sections indeed opens better and lies flatter when open than one in larger sections, but there is more labour in sewing, and if the book is at all thick the back may be inconveniently bulked out by the number of threads.

Suppose, however, that instead of imposing 32 pages at once in two formes, one containing 16 'outer' pages and the other 16 'inner' pages, we take only the first 16 pages and impose them together in one chase, the outer forme and the inner forme, of 8 pages each, side by side. If then, after printing one side of the sheet from this combined forme, we proceed to perfect from the same forme (the paper having of course been turned end to end) we shall on cutting the printed sheet in the middle, have two copies of one gathering of eight leaves. The press-work involved in producing any particular number of copies of a book by this method will of course be the same as by the usual method, but there will be a manifest saving in the amount of type required, for the printer need only have 16 pages in type at a time, instead of 32, and even if he is not short of type it will allow him to begin printing when he has only composed 16 pages and

[1] Mr. Chapman tells me that this arrangement in 8vo is common in the eighteenth century. It is, I think, comparatively rare in earlier times.

thus may facilitate the economical distribution of work between compositor and pressman. The fact that he can get the work read and corrected in smaller sections may also be of importance when speed is necessary. This method, resulting as it does in printing two copies of one half-sheet at a time, is generally known as imposition in half-sheets, and it is probable that it would generally be used in books that were intended to be *gathered* in half-sheets, though, as I have said, this is not strictly necessary.

Proof of the use of half-sheet imposition is not easy to obtain, for the only way in which it would show itself in a correctly printed book seems to be that any particular page would, in half the total number of copies of the impression, be printed on one side of the paper, and in half on the other. The simplest proof would be the discovery of a sheet which in perfecting has been laid the wrong way round, for this would give the pages duplicated, the ' inner-forme ' pages being replaced by ' outer-forme ' ones in a wrong order, e.g. 1, 4, 1, 4, 5, 8, 5, 8.[1]

That the alternative method of placing two outer formes on the press together and perfecting them from two inner formes was used is, however, I think, shown by an error of the same nature in a copy of the *Cosmographia* of Aethicus, printed by Guarin at Basle in 1575, and now in the British Museum. This is a 16mo sewn in eights and has in sheets f and g of the index a peculiar confusion of order whereby the first syllables of the first and last words of the pages run (from the beginning of f) ' op-ot, seg-ser, ser-sid, par-pei, pel-per, spi-suf ', and so on, while those from the beginning of g run ' scar-seg, ot-pan, pan-par, sid-sis, sit-spi, per-phœ ', &c., the strange confusion per-

---

[1] I do not think that I have ever come across an example of this, but it may be remarked that it would be a particularly easy error to detect in folding or binding, and that the chances of a sheet so misprinted being used are small.

sisting throughout the two gatherings. Investigation shows that the pages are really the following :

First gathering : f1, g1^v, g2, f2^v, f3, g3^v, etc.

Second gathering : g1, f1^v, f2, g2^v, g3, f3^v, etc.

We have therefore to do with nothing more than a simple interchange of the two inner formes, the outer forme of f being backed by the inner form of g, and vice versa. If the outer formes of f and g were on the bed together, and the sheets were backed from the two inner formes, this strange-seeming confusion would result from turning the paper the wrong way round when perfecting, and it is difficult to see how it could arise in any other way.

In later times, when it became possible to obtain sheets of paper double or four times the unit size [1] such as ' double crown ' (20″×30″) or ' quad crown ' (30″×40″), methods of imposition exactly similar to those which we have been describing were used. Thus when printing a ' double ' sheet, outer and inner formes of a gathering were often placed together on the press, so that the resulting printed sheet, perfected of course on the same forme, would give two complete copies of a full gathering. When, as is frequently the case nowadays, a quad sheet is used, which in octavo will of course give 64 pages, 32 on each side, it is usual to place the outer and inner formes of two consecutive sheets on the press together, so that the sheet when printed will comprise two copies of, say, sheets B and C.[2]

---

[1] The purpose of using larger sheets is of course to reduce the cost of printing, for though it takes twice the power, or nearly so, to print a double-sized sheet, the cost in labour of supervision is hardly increased, and the saving in total cost is therefore considerable.

[2] Note that this is still imposition ' in half-sheets ', though the result is two copies of a full sheet (or of two full sheets) of normal size ; for so far as imposition is concerned the ' sheet ' is simply the sheet of paper printed, whether it be of normal size, or double, or four times the normal one. Unless we recognize this it might seem more reasonable to regard the method as one of imposing in double (or quadruple sheets, rather than in half-sheets.

As we noted before, half the copies of any particular page will necessarily be on the right side (face) of the paper, and half on the wrong (back), a fact which may rather spoil the look of a decorated title-page in half the copies of an edition.[1]

A note on modern impositions. It may be useful to those bibliographers who carry their researches down to the present day to have a brief summary of present-day practice as regards imposition. We may divide books into three classes : (1) ' Éditions de luxe '; (2) ordinary books ; (3) very cheap books.

1. A very few expensive books printed on hand-made paper follow practically the original methods as regards imposition, i. e. if the book is a quarto the gathering is of four leaves and each gathering is printed separately with two pulls of the press on a single sheet of paper. There is nothing further to say about this.

2. Ordinary books. These are now very seldom, if ever, printed on less than ' double ' sheets of paper, and the great majority are printed on ' quad ' sheets of four times the normal size, the method in the former case being to have the two formes of one sheet, and in the latter case the two formes of two sheets, on the press together as already explained.

Books in quarto printed on double or quad paper are now generally sewn in gatherings of eight leaves, in order to save expense in sewing and to avoid the thickening of the back which too many gatherings cause. For similar reasons books in octavo on thin paper are often sewn in sixteens. In such cases quad

---

[1] If, in perfecting, a sheet is actually placed on the press the wrong way round we obtain of course a confusion of page-order similar to that noted in the 1575 Aethicus. Thus in a copy of a recent novel (1919) I have found pages running 241, 226, 227, 244, 245, 230, &c. (i. e. the outer forme of section 16 backed by the inner forme of section 15, or q1, p1ᵛ, p2, q2ᵛ, q3, p3ᵛ, &c.). Evidently sections 15 and 16 (p and q) were on the press together and a sheet got turned round in perfecting.

paper would generally be used and an outer and inner forme of 16 pages each would be imposed together, so that the sheet when perfected would comprise two copies of a single 32-page gathering.

3. Very cheap books. These are generally printed on 'double quad' paper (e. g. 40"×60" in crown), which gives 128 pages to the sheet, and are generally sewn in 32-page gatherings or even ·in 64's. It may be remarked that much binding is done nowadays by automatic machines. These carry out the whole process from the folding of the flat sheets onwards, but the pages of type for books intended to be bound by these machines are imposed according to quite a different scheme from those intended for hand-folding, and these schemes differ according to the machine employed. The future bibliographer who interests himself in the almanacs and railway-guides of the twentieth century will probably have to understand these matters, but I am glad to think that the time for this study is not yet.

Stereotyping and Electrotyping. Though printing from stereotype plates has only been used largely in comparatively recent times, a few words on the history of the process may not be out of place. As is generally known, it is as a rule only the first impression of a modern book that is printed directly from the type.[1] When that has been printed off, moulds are taken from the type in a kind of papier mâché produced by beating sheets of moistened paper down on the type. These are preserved and if a second impression is called for, type-metal plates are cast from them (somewhat sur-

[1] In the case of books of which the first edition is to be very large, it is usual to make electrotype or stereotype plates at once and not to print from the type at all. This seems to be the practice with all classes of books in America where, when the type has been corrected, electrotype plates are prepared and the book is printed from these. American printers seem to regard this process as economical, but the results of printing from plates are seldom quite so good as from the original type, though why this should be is far from evident.

prisingly, as many as six satisfactory plates can often be obtained from the same mould in spite of its only consisting of paper), and these plates, either mounted type-high on wooden blocks, or more commonly fastened down on the bed of the press, take the place of type in future impressions.

The invention is attributed to a certain goldsmith of Edinburgh, William Ged, who after experimenting with an old idea of producing a solid page of type by soldering together the feet of type set in the ordinary way, evolved, in or soon after 1725, a method not far removed from those of modern times. The invention proved, however, disastrous to him, owing to the opposition of both typefounders and printers, and although by 1739 he appears to have printed two Prayer Books and an edition of Sallust from stereotype plates, the attempt was regarded as having failed. Stereotyping was reinvented by A. Tilloch of Glasgow in 1781, but again abandoned, and it was not until 1800, when a London printer, Wilson, with the aid of Earl Stanhope, revived and perfected the method, that it at last attained success.[1]

A more recently introduced method of making plates is by electrotyping. Moulds of the type are taken in wax and the plates are produced by the electrical deposition of copper, the thin shell formed being backed up by pouring in molten type-metal. Electrotyping has the advantage of giving a somewhat more perfect facsimile of the type than stereotyping, and the finest line-blocks can be reproduced at the same time as the text of a book. The copper surface is also somewhat more durable than type-metal, though as stereotype plates can now be electrically faced with nickel, which is harder than copper, the advantage for ordinary work is not very great. At the same time the electrotype process is slower and more costly.

[1] See T. B. Reed's *Old English Letter Foundries*, pp. 218–20, and the authorities there cited.

Chapter Seven

WE have seen in chapter iii that the ' signature '
is the letter or other mark to be found at the
foot of the first leaf (and generally of one or more
following leaves) of a gathering, and that its purpose
is mainly to guide the binder in the arrangement of the
gatherings, and further in certain cases to tell him how
the sheet is to be folded and what sheets or portions of
sheets are to form a single gathering when the number
of these is not the same as the number of sheets, e.g.
in a folio, or in a quarto in eights. It may also serve,
when found on a cancel leaf, to indicate where this leaf
is to be placed, or for which original leaf it is to be
substituted, by the binder.

It might be objected that signatures are unnecessary
if the pages of a book are numbered, as the numbers
would tell the binder all that he need know. This is
true, but the information would not be nearly so easy
to obtain. In the first place, so far as the folding is
concerned, the number at the upper corner of a page is
inconveniently situated. It is not nearly so easily seen
as the letter at the foot. Secondly, the binder would
find it much more difficult to ascertain whether his
book was complete and the sheets all in the right order
if he had to note that the first pages of each gathering
were numbered 1, 9, 17, 25, &c., in a quarto, or
1, 17, 33, &c., in an octavo, than if he had simply to
see that they ran A, B, C, D, &c.; while if, as often
happens, page 1 was not the first page of a sheet, the
difficulty would be still further increased.

But seeing that signatures have been found so
necessary in printed books that they are still employed

73

at the present day, it is hardly necessary to insist on their usefulness. It may, however, be remarked that their practical importance resulted, in Elizabethan times at least, in their being as a rule far more accurate than the pagination. In the latter we very commonly find the grossest carelessness, numbers repeated or omitted, pages with no numbers at all, parts of a book in which leaves alone are numbered while elsewhere the numeration is by pages; but in the *essential* part of the signatures, the letter or other mark on the first page, and the number on the others,[1] mistakes are rare, even in the work of the inferior printing-houses. It is for this reason that many bibliographers in referring to a particular leaf or page of a book, do so in all cases by the signature and not by the pagination, even when this happens to be correct.

Signatures were not the invention of the printers, but are of frequent occurrence in medieval MSS. They seem, however, to have been by no means universal, being at best only a convenience and not a necessity, especially when the binding was carried out under the immediate control of the scriptorium. As they were generally placed at the extreme edge of the leaf, it is only in MSS. which have not been cut down by the binders that we can say with any certainty whether they were originally present or not.

The early printers would presumably try to follow this custom of signatures, but as it was naturally very troublesome for them to print a signature at a distance from the type-page, this appears in early books, when present, to have been generally added by hand.[2]

---

[1] It is not very uncommon to find a mistake in the letter on fols. 2, 3, &c., of a gathering (B1, D2, D3, &c.) : a misprint of this kind could only cause trouble to the binder if the book were a folio ; in other cases it would hardly be worth correcting. Sometimes, as I shall show later, these errors when occurring in a reprint afford evidence as to the edition from which the reprint was made.

[2] Either in manuscript or stamped in by hand as in some of Mentelin's books (Strassburg, *c.* 1460–78). In some cases the signatures run up

Blades mentions a copy of the ' Recuyell ' at Windsor Castle ' with manuscript signatures at the extreme foot of every sheet '.[1] It is, I think, impossible to say how general the custom of manuscript signatures in printed books really was, for as these were purposely so placed that they would be cut off by the binder, only a very small proportion of them would in any case be preserved.

The first recorded appearance of *printed* signatures dates from 1472, when they are found in the *Preceptorium divinae legis* of J. Nider, printed at Cologne by Johann Koelhoff. In England their first use in a dated book seems to be in the *Expositio in symbolum apostolorum*, printed at Oxford in 1478 (' 1468 ').[2]

The form of signatures varies, but the normal one consists of a letter, either standing alone or followed by the numeral 1 (roman or arabic), on the first leaf of a gathering ; the same letter followed by 2 on the second leaf, and so on, A or Ai, Aij, Aiij, or A1, A2, A3, &c. The letters i and j, and u and v, not being differentiated in early times, are not used separately in signatures, i.e. there is one gathering signed i or j, and one signed u or v. The letter w is also omitted

the outer margins. In spite of the obvious difficulty of *printing* signatures at the extreme edges of the leaves, Mr. Pollard tells me that the earliest Strassburg printed signatures were so placed.

[1] *Caxton*, p. 42, and *Bibliographical Miscellanies*, No. 1, p. 9. I suppose he means the French *Recueil*, but if so, this copy does not appear to be uncut. See de Ricci, *Census*, p. 7 (*Recueil*, No. 3).

[2] A very full account of fifteenth-century practice as regards signatures will be found in William Blades's *Bibliographical Miscellanies*, No. 1, 1890. He regarded signatures as universal—or almost so, from the earliest days of printing, but being first inserted in MS. and later stamped in at the extreme edge of the leaf, they were naturally in most cases cut off by the binder. Reference may also be made to the account of the printed signatures of the same period (1472–1500) given by Haebler, *Inkunabelkunde*, pp. 50–6, but for our present purpose it will suffice to say that almost every possible variation in position and in the form of the signature seems to have been tried by the early printers.

from signatures.[1] These practices have continued till the present day.

Sometimes, but rarely, z is omitted,[2] and we occasionally, especially in early books, find the contracted forms of *et*, *con*, and *rum* used at the end of the alphabet as in a horn-book, and even the tittle, 'est' and 'amen' which followed the contractions there.[3]

When the printer came to the end of the alphabet he generally began again, doubling the letter ; thus Z is followed by AA or Aa, ZZ (or Zz) by AAA or Aaa, and so on. Or he might go from upper case to lower, the latter method being especially common in books printed during the fifteenth century. There was no general rule, and even within a printing-house the practice seems not always to have been consistent, though some printing-houses seem to have had their own rules on the point.

Paragraph and punctuation marks of various sorts are commonly used in prefatory matter, and we may even sometimes find a whole book so signed, for example, the Εἰσοδια *Musarum Edinensium in Caroli ingressu in Scotiam*, printed by the heirs of Andrew Hart in 1633, after three unsigned leaves, continues with the following extraordinary collection of signatures §, §§, §§§, ℐ, †, ††, ¶, ℺, ( ), each signature comprising four leaves except §§§ which is two. It is difficult to see what can have been the purpose of this curious arrangement, which defeats the main purpose of signatures, namely, to show the binder in what

---

[1] Perhaps because w was not regarded as really a separate letter though it is found in English printing from the earliest times. In one case w is used as a signature instead of y (Ames, *Typog. Antiq.*, ed. Herbert, p. 362).

[2] Op. cit., pp. 693, 732, 1097 ; cf. also p. 227 below.

[3] Op. cit., pp. 136, 255 ; Duff, *Fifteenth Cent. English Books*, no. 27. A very remarkable method of continuing the alphabet of signatures is cited by Blades, *Bibliographical Miscellanies*, No. 1, pp. 14–15, from a copy of *Epistole Sancti Jeronimi de Libris Salomonis*, *c.* 1475, signed in MS., where the alphabet is followed by the words of the Lord's Prayer, thus p'ter j, p'ter ij, qui j, qui ij, es j, and so on.

order he is to place the gatherings, for in punctuation marks there is of course no order : unless perhaps it was specially desired to avoid any question of precedence among the sections, most of which are complete in themselves.

A peculiarity in the use of k as a signature may also be mentioned, though this does not seem to occur in English work. Certain French founts of the sixteenth century were without this lower-case letter, as it was not required in either French or Latin.[1] The upper-case K was, however, always present, perhaps as being used in Latin dates (a.d. VIII. Kal. Jan., &c.), and in certain proper names. Consequently K was included in the sequence of signatures, but when these happened to be lower-case a difficulty arose and various expedients were necessary. Thus we may find K used for k,[2] or the stranger device used by many French printers from early times down to and including the Estiennes, who replaced k and kk by lz and lzlz.[3] Other printers such as Simon de Colines had a roman K but no italic one, and we can find many books printed in italics at Paris in which a roman K interrupts the regular series of italic signatures. But once the cause and frequency of these irregularities is understood they are seen to have little importance.

A few more general peculiarities in the method of signing may here be noted :

Pynson signed certain quarto books according to a system which Duff states to have been common in

---

[1] Lower-case ' k ' has always been regarded as something of an outsider. Even in the type-case, it is in the older ' lay ' banished from the lower case, a home being found for it in an odd corner of the upper one.

[2] e. g. in the *Viridarium Illustrium Poetarum* printed by Denis Roce in 1513, where, text and (lower-case) signatures being italic, we find what should be *k* signed K.

[3] In the edition of ' Nizolius ' printed at Leyden by A. de Harsy in 1588, we find for k a small capital к, and for Kk on three leaves Kк, and on the fourth Klz.

books printed at Rouen.[1]   The first leaf is signed,
e.g. A1, the second has no signature, the third has A2.
I have not met with this curious and disturbing practice
in any other English books.

Robert Waldegrave had a method of his own which
has been of assistance in identifying books from his
press.   On the first page of a gathering he placed the
simple letter, the following pages having a number
alone.   Thus, the signatures of James VI's *Poetical
Exercises*, printed by him at Edinburgh [1591], run
B, 2, 3, [ ], C, 2, 3, [ ], and so on, the fourth leaf
of each gathering being unsigned.[2]

Generally speaking, one letter implies one gathering,
but there are occasional exceptions.   These may be
due either to reprinting from a book differently made
up, or to cancellation of matter, or change of arrangement while a book is in progress.   For example, the
1584 and 1587 editions of W. Baldwin's *Treatise of
Moral Philosophy* are ordinary octavos, but the first
gathering of eight leaves is signed with two letters,
the first four leaves being A1–4 and the second four
B1–4, the sewing coming after A4.   The reason is
clearly that Tottel's edition of 1575 had included the
Table among the preliminaries.   When East reprinted
the book in 1584 he started the text with C1, following
Tottel's edition.   He then found he had room for the
Table in the last gathering of the book and placed it
there, with the result that his preliminaries now only

---

[1] Duff, *Early English Printing*, p. 17.

[2] For the use of this peculiarity in attributing books to his press,
see Sinker's *English Books before MDCI. at T. C. C.*, p. 347; J. D.
Wilson in the *Library*, 2nd Ser., viii. 356–7; and for numerous
examples of the practice, Dickson and Edmond, pp. 410, 412, &c.
I have noted the same practice in an edition of the Psalms (Beza
and Tremellius) in 12mo, printed by R. Yardley and P. Short in 1590
(B.M. 3090. a. 17), both parts of which are signed in an unusual
fashion, the first part B. 1., b. 2., b. 3., b. 4., b. 5., C. 1., c. 2., &c., the
second (*A Paraphrastical Explanation of fourteen Psalms*), B. 1., 2, 3,
4, 5, C. 1., 2, 3, 4, 5.

needed eight leaves, though he had allowed two signatures for them. To omit either would have caused
trouble, so he used both in a single gathering. For other
examples of peculiar signatures due to cancellation, see
pp. 226–9.

In later times a curious and very misleading method
was sometimes used in 12mo, where the first two leaves
were signed, as usual, e.g. B1, B2, but B3 instead of
following directly appeared on the first leaf of the
inner four (i.e. on what is bibliographically B5).
Mr. R. W. Chapman in his paper in the *Library*,
4th Ser., iv. 168, to which I owe my knowledge of
the practice, quotes from Timperley's *Printers' Manual*
(1838), p. 18, to the effect that, ' To a sheet of twelves,
three signatures, which are placed to the first, third,
and ninth pages, in the following manner = B, B2,
B3 '.[1]

As to the *number* of leaves signed, there cannot be
said to have been in early times any definite practice.
We never, I think, in early times find only the first leaf
of a gathering signed,[2] but we may have anything from
the first two to every leaf.[3] In the case, however, of
a folio book in which an indefinite number of sheets
might be quired together, it was an obvious convenience
to continue the signatures until the first leaf of the
second half of a gathering, for if this were done the
binder could see at once whether or not his gathering
was complete. Thus suppose a folio in sixes. If we
sign only the first three leaves (and obviously all these

---

[1] He also cites a 12mo in twelves of 1815 of which the fifth leaf
is signed B2, and a 12mo in sixes of 1817 of which the third leaf is
signed B2 (*Library*, 4th Ser., iv. 180 note). It may be mentioned that
the rule which Mr. Chapman quotes from Timperley is still followed
when twelves are imposed, see Southward, *Modern Printing*, p. 219.

[2] But Mr. Chapman cites a case in 1782 in an octavo in fours
(*Library*, u.s., p. 170).

[3] Caxton signed each leaf in the first half of a gathering but no more,
so that his signed books have an equal number of signed and unsigned
leaves (Blades, *Caxton*, p. 131).

must be signed), the binder does not know for certain that there is not still another sheet to be placed in the centre of the gathering. If, however, we sign in addition the fourth leaf (so that the middle sheet has two signatures, e. g. B3, B4), it is obvious that nothing else is to be placed between them and that the gathering is complete. A custom thus grew up in the case of folio books of signing one more than half the leaves in the gathering, and this seems to have been extended to other sizes, where in fact it was of no real use. Thus, at any rate towards the end of the sixteenth century, we frequently find that three leaves of a quarto are signed and five leaves of an octavo (or of a quarto in eights). On the whole, this seems to me to be the commonest practice, but it would be folly to suggest that it is to be regarded as a definite rule, and I think it never applied to the smaller sizes such as 12mo and 16mo, of which we seldom find *more* and frequently less than half the leaves signed.

As time went on there was a tendency to get rid of the useless signatures. Mr. Chapman states that in the eighteenth century it was customary to sign the leaves of the first half of a gathering, two in a gathering of four leaves (whether folio, quarto, or octavo), four in a gathering of eight, and so on.[1] Later the number was still further reduced until it came down to the present practice of signing only the first two leaves of a gathering. Indeed many modern printers have dropped the old style of signature altogether and merely number the sheets with a single numeral on the first page of a gathering, using sometimes an asterisked number when a sheet has to be placed inside another.[2]

---

[1] *The Library,* 4th Ser., iv. 169 ; v. 251.

[2] In America, though not, so far as I have noticed, in England, some printers seem to have abandoned the use of signatures altogether. But America has produced what is surely one of the most curious systems of signature in the Furness Variorum *Shakespeare,* some volumes of which, e. g. *Romeo and Juliet,* 1871, and vol. i of *Hamlet,* 1877 (and

A kind of additional signature is often found in eighteenth- and nineteenth-century books, especially those which either were issued in parts or ran to several volumes. This which occurs normally only on the first leaf of a gathering generally consists of the number of the volume as ' Vol. I ', or simply ' I ', or a letter such as ' a ', ' b ', &c.[1] placed on the same line as the signature but towards the inner margin. In books printed abroad, but not, I think, often in English ones until quite recent times, an abbreviated form of the book's title was sometimes added.[2] The purpose of this was, of course, to prevent the sheets getting mixed by the binder with those of other books or volumes. Mr. R. W. Chapman tells me that these volume numbers, &c., are called ' catchwords ', at any rate at the Oxford Press, but I hope that no bibliographer will adopt this practice !

Press Numbers or 'Working with Figures'. Another sort of ' signature ' found in eighteenth-century books, to which attention has recently been called by Mr. R. W. Chapman,[3] deserves mention, though it is seldom of much bibliographical importance, as it relates solely to the organization of the printing-house.

later eds.), have two sets of signatures throughout, being signed by numbers in *sixes*, and by letters in *eights* ! They are sewn in eights. I presume that this peculiarity is due to a variation in the make-up of the volumes after the casting of plates, the signatures necessary for the new make-up being added without removing the original ones.

[1] I presume that such ' signatures ' as Numb. 1, Numb. 2, &c., which one sometimes finds (e. g. on a 1767 edition of l'Estrange's *Wars of the Jews*, where each ' Number ' occurs on two consecutive signatures), indicate publication in parts. An 1824 *Pilgrim's Progress*, also perhaps a part-publication, has a different system, sigs. D, E, F, G being numbered a2, b2, a3, b3, and so on.

[2] Dr. Greg points out to me that three of the editions (between 1508 and 1537) of *Everyman* have the title of the book (either as ' Euery man ' or ' The Som. ', i. e. Summoning) in the signature-line of all signed pages.

[3] *The Library*, 4th Ser., iii. 175–6.

This is a small figure which in books between 1680 and 1823[1] often appears at the foot of a page, sometimes twice in a gathering, once on a page of the outer forme and once on a page of the inner, the page on which it appears being apparently a matter of indifference, though there is some tendency to avoid a page bearing an ordinary signature. It seems that it was the custom when the compositor had finished his work on a forme and before it was handed over to the pressmen for it to be assigned to a particular printing-press and the number of the machine to be added. One may, I think, suppose that the purpose of this was to divide the work equitably between the different pressmen. It would also, no doubt, serve as a record of the work done by each machine and a check on the pressmen's claims for pay.[2]

Catchwords.[3] In medieval MSS. it was not uncommon for the scribe to add at the end of each section the first word of the next as a guide to the binder in arranging the sections correctly. Such catchwords thus served somewhat the same purpose as signatures in printed books. As used, however, in the latter, catchwords ordinarily appear at the foot of every page and are probably to be considered mainly as guides to the printer in imposing the pages.[4]

[1] Johnson (*Typographia*, ii. 489) notes that the custom of 'working with figures' had grown into disuse by 1824. In Brydges's *Censura Literaria*, printed by Thomas Bensley, figures are used occasionally up to the end of vol. iv (1807), but not in the later volumes.

[2] An interesting example, too intricate to be quoted here, of an inference derived from these 'figures' as to the order of printing of duplicate settings of a particular signature of the second part of Mandeville's *Fable of the Bees*, 1729, will be found in Mr. F. B. Kaye's edition of that book, vol. ii, pp. 394–5.

[3] It may be worth noting that the German for 'catchword' is *Kustode*, and the French *réclame*.

[4] If we could find a gathering in which two pages beginning with the same word had been accidentally interchanged this would amount almost to proof that the catchwords were relied on when imposing,

The earliest printed books had no catchwords. They seem first to be recorded as in use at Ferrara in July 1471,[1] and between that date and 1500 became fairly common in Italian printing, while occasional examples are to be found elsewhere. The early catchwords, however, occur as a rule only at the end of a gathering, as in MSS., or occasionally at the end of a pair of conjugate leaves, and it was not until the sixteenth century that it became usual to place them at the foot of every page. They were never used by Caxton, nor, I believe, by any other of the earliest English printers. Herbert stated that the first dated book in which he had noticed them was Thomas More's *Epistola ad Germanum Brixium*, printed by R. Pynson in 1520.[2]

From about 1530 catchwords were regularly used by English printers until about the end of the eighteenth century, when they began to disappear.[3] Johnson in 1824 says that catchwords or 'direction-words', as he calls them, 'are not now generally used'.[4] In English work between these dates they commonly appear at the foot of every page, though certain printers, e.g. Vautrollier, departed from this rule (see below).

On the Continent, however, there was great variety of usage as regards catchwords ; in many French books of the sixteenth century they do not appear at all and, though they seem to have been used fairly regularly in the seventeenth century, they went out of use earlier than in England.

The following are some of the chief varieties that I have noticed in the use of catchwords. I have added

but I have failed to find an instance of this though I have been on the watch for it for years.

[1] Duff, *Early Printed Books*, p. 72. According to Haebler, *Inkunabelkunde*, p. 59, their first use was by Wendelin of Speyer at Venice not later than this same year 1471.   [2] Ames, *Typog. Antiq.*, p. 267.

[3] The earliest eighteenth-century book which I have noticed without catchwords is Capell's *Prolusions*, 1760, a book which is typographically remarkable in other respects, see p. 309.

[4] *Typographia*, ii. 133.

in brackets a few names of printers and dates of books in which I have found them, but I have made no attempt whatever to trace them historically.

(*a*)   Catchwords are used on versos but not on rectos— a much-used method. (G. Giolito, Venice, 1562 (in octavo) ; Vautrollier, London, 1578 ; Claude Marin, Frankfurt, 1607 ; J. Stoer, Geneva, 1628.)

(*b*)   They are used on pages where there is no signature, but omitted where there is one. (G. Rouillius, Paris, 1556, 1557.)

(*c*)   They are used only at the end of each gathering, i. e. in octavo or 16mo in eights on 8^v. (H. de Marnef, Paris, 1560 ; J. Gryphius, Venice, 1567 ; Henry Estienne,[1] Geneva, 1569 ; Marcus Orry, Paris, 1603 ; F. Muguet, Paris, 1664.)

(*d*)   In quarto in eights there are catchwords only on the versos of leaves 2, 6, 8 (i. e. wherever a page of one sheet is followed by a page of another). This is the scientific method, for it gives all the guidance that can possibly be required by a binder,[2] and no more. (G. Giolito, Venice, 1554.)

(*e*)   The catchwords are in italic, though the text is in roman, an odd and troublesome practice which in the *Paradossi* of Ortensio Landi, printed at Lyons by ' Giouanni Pullon da Trino ' in 1543, is combined with (*b*) above.

(*f*)   In books with foot-notes a double series of catchwords is employed, the foot-notes having an independent catchword directing to the next note, whether this happens to be on the next page following or not. This will be found in the variorum editions of the classics printed by the Officina Hackiana at Leyden in the seventeenth century and in Dutch editions of the classics generally.

[1] Many (? most) of the Estienne books have no catchwords at all, and in the particular book referred to they are somewhat irregular.

[2] Though of course in practice he would simply follow the signatures.

Foliation and pagination. Little need be said here as to the numbering of the leaves (foliation) or pages (pagination) of printed books. It would seem to have been more or less usual to number the leaves of manuscripts, though there was no uniform practice in the matter, and one would have expected that the custom would be taken over by the early printers. This, however, was not the case and foliation is comparatively rare until the last quarter of the fifteenth century. When present the commonest form is the word ' folio ', or an abbreviation thereof, followed by a roman numeral. Arabic figures for the folio appear in Venice after 1475, but are rare outside Italy until after 1500. Occasionally columns of print are numbered instead of folios. When present the foliation is commonly placed at the head of the pages in approximately the same position as paging nowadays, but almost every variety of position can be found.[1]

In England Caxton foliated a few books from 1483 onwards, but foliation is quite unusual until the last five or six years of the fifteenth century. It seems to have been more frequent in Missals and other service books than elsewhere.

During the sixteenth century we find a gradual change of custom. The earliest method, that of printing ' folio ', ' fol. ' or ' fo. ' with a roman number, gradually gave place to the same with an arabic number. Later, in the neighbourhood of 1570–80, we commonly find the foliation represented by an arabic number standing alone. Lastly, towards the close of the century, foliation gives place to pagination after the modern method. These various systems, however, overlap to any extent, and at all periods there were many books in which neither leaves nor pages were numbered.

The first recorded use of *pagination* in an English

[1] For fifteenth-century practice in these matters see Haebler, *Inkunabelkunde*, pp. 56–8.

book seems to be in J. Sulpitius' *Opus grammatices*, Pynson, 1494, the pages of which are numbered ' Pagina prima ', ' pagina ii ', and so on.[1] According to Herbert,[2] the *Introductorium Linguae Latinae* printed by W. de Worde, *c.* 1499, is paged in a similar way, though according to Duff[3] this is foliated. After this I have been unable to find any record of an English book with pagination until Leland's Ἐγκώμιον τῆς εἰρήνης, R. Wolfe, 1546,[4] in which the page-numbers are arabic. For some considerable time longer pagination remained much rarer than foliation, but from about 1570[5] it becomes fairly frequent, and after a period in which foliation and pagination seem equally common, we find the latter gradually, towards 1590, getting the upper hand. After the close of the century foliation seems to be generally restricted to legal works printed in black letter and certain other books of a more or less antiquarian nature.

One can only suppose that the early printers regarded the numbering of leaves and pages as of little importance, for, as has already been noted, this is often most carelessly done, numbers being omitted or repeated in the most erratic fashion.

The Register is a list of the signatures which is often given at the end of early books, especially those printed in Italy.[6] Its purpose is, of course, to indicate to the binder the order and number of the gatherings in order that he may see that the book is perfect.

---

[1] Duff, *Fifteenth Cent. Books*, No. 388.   [2] *Typog. Antiq.*, p. 102.
[3] Duff, u.s., No. 232.   [4] *Typog. Antiq.*, p. 598.
[5] It may be noted that A. Marlorat's *Catholic exposition upon Matthew*, T. Marshe, 1570, is paginated, but the pages are called ' Fol. 1 ', ' Fol. 2 ', &c.
[6] The earliest example of the Register noted by Haebler is at Rome in 1469 or 1470 (*Inkunabelkunde*, p. 44). For the various forms which it takes in fifteenth-century printing readers must be referred to Dr. Haebler's detailed chapter on the subject.

This practice was, I believe, at no time universal or even very common, though we may find it here and there until the end of the sixteenth century. In England it seems decidedly rare. The earliest example known to me is in a book printed at Oxford by Theodoric Rood in 1483 (Duff, *Fifteenth Cent. Books*, no. 277), and between that date and 1500 there seem only to have been registers in four editions of Mirk's *Liber Festivalis*, printed by W. de Worde in 1493, 1495, 1496, and 1499, in the *Quatuor Sermones*, printed by the same in 1494 and 1496, and in one other book, the so-called *Cordiale* or treatise of the four last things, printed by him without date (Duff, u.s., no. 110). In the early part of the sixteenth century I have no doubt that one could find a good many examples of the register, but as the presence or absence of this is by no means always noted by bibliographers it is not easy to ascertain their frequency. In the case of later English books I know that one can look through quite a considerable number without finding a single register.

One or two points may be noted :

The 1483 Oxford book referred to above, a *Logic*, runs A–Z⁶, Aa–Cc⁶, Dd⁸, and the register, giving the first and second alphabet to Cc, states ' omnes isti sunt terni Dd vero est quaternus ', from which we may infer that Rood used ' ternus ' for a gathering of three double leaves [1] and 'quaternus' for one of four. Wynkyn de Worde, however, calls his register ' Registrum quaternorum ', even when part of the book is in sixes. He therefore used ' quaternus ' for quire or gathering irrespective of the number of sheets, and this indeed seems to have been a common practice.

A somewhat peculiar usage is found in the *De communibus omnium rerum naturalium principiis* of Benedictus Pererius, printed at Rome in 1585. This work

---

[1] The book is a quarto, but was presumably printed on half-sheets of paper, the sheets being cut in half beforehand as was done by Caxton (Blades, *Caxton*, pp. 62, 131).

is in quarto and runs A⁸, b², A–G⁴, H–Rr⁸, Ss². After a list of the signatures the note is added ' Omnes sunt duerniones. A B C D E F G sunt folia, b Ss vero media: quae omnia sunt folia 76.' It seems, therefore, that the printer used ' duernio ' for a gathering of two (original) sheets of paper folded together ; a usage which is exactly in accord with the manuscript use of quarternion for four sheets of parchment folded to make eight leaves, but appears to be quite uncommon. The more usual practice would be what is found, for example, in the *Discorsi* of G.-B. Giraldi Cinthio, printed by G. Giolito at Venice in 1554, which is also a quarto in eights. Here it is stated of the gatherings that 'tutti sono quaderni', they being regarded as four pairs of leaves (as if they were the four sheets of a manuscript quaternion), not, as was actually the case, two folded sheets.

The Title-page. If we define a title-page as a separate page setting forth in a conspicuous manner the title of the book which follows it, and not containing any part of the text of the book itself, we can, I think, say that title-pages were very seldom used in manuscripts before the date of their introduction in printed books. Nevertheless it would, as Professor Pollard has shown,[1] be quite incorrect to say that the idea of the title-page was unknown during the manuscript period. There is a manuscript of the Four Gospels in Latin (Brit. Mus., Harley MS. 2788), dating from about A.D. 800, which has a definite title-page, and a very elaborate one, to the Gospels, though its position on a verso page and on the twelfth leaf of the book is not quite in accordance with later practice. From 800 to the middle of the fifteenth century there seems to be a gap, though it is not impossible that there may be a connexion in descent between the Italian MS. title-pages of the fifteenth century and their predecessors of

[1] In an article on ' The Title-Pages in some Italian Manuscripts ' (*The Printing Art*, vol. xii, no. 2, October 1908).

the time of Charlemagne. However this may be, title-pages were certainly given to some of the more elaborate manuscripts produced at Florence round about the year 1460. Some of them are reproduced in Mr. Pollard's paper referred to above, and save that they also are generally on the back of a leaf (mostly of the first) instead of on the front, they have all the characteristics of the more elaborately designed and bordered title. We might perhaps also count as a difference, at least in intention, the fact that these manuscript title-pages were evidently designed so much more as an embellishment than as a label to say what the book contained.

The earliest known printed title-pages seem to be those in the Bull of Pope Pius II, printed by Fust and Schoeffer at Mainz in 1463, and the *Sermo ad Populum*, printed at Cologne by Arnold ther Hoernan in 1470,[1] but it was not till some ten years after this second date that they became at all usual.

The earliest book to be provided with a title-page in England appears to be an edition of the *Treatise of the Pestilence* by Canutus or Kamitus, printed by Machlinia at an unknown date but certainly before 1490. None of Caxton's books has a title-page, but one is found in the *Chastising of God's Children*, probably printed by Wynkyn de Worde soon after Caxton's death. This takes the form of a descriptive title printed in three lines in the middle of the first recto, which is otherwise blank, and is thus very different from the title-page as it became later. In the hands of Wynkyn de Worde, however, the title-page rapidly developed into a conspicuous feature of the book, and though one or two of his earlier contemporaries never used it, we find that by the beginning of the sixteenth century some sort of title-page is almost always present.

[1] Pollard in the article referred to, and Duff, *Early Printed Books*, p. 50. The *Sermo* also has the leaves numbered (in the centre of the right-hand margin), another innovation.

Both the matter and form of title-pages went through a series of changes and developments, which are not without interest, though the story is too complicated to be dealt with in any detail. In the *matter* of the title-page we may discern the following stages :

1. It gives merely the name or contents of the book, with or without the name of the author.

2. It begins to take over the function of the colophon, adding first the date of printing, then the name or sign of the printer or bookseller.

3. It becomes more definitely an advertisement of the book designed to attract purchasers. Laudatory phrases are added. The work is ' A pleasant Comedy ' or ' A proved practice ' or is ' intermixed with a variety of mirth ' or in it ' are more than a thousand several things rehearsed ; some set out in prose to the pleasure of the reader, and with such variety of verse for the beautifying of the Book, as no doubt shall delight thousands to understand ',[1] and so on. The author is given such titles as may serve to give authority or attractiveness to his book : he is called ' M.A. ', or ' Lutenist and Batchelor of Musick in both the Universities ' or ' Citizen of London ', as the case may be. A play is said to have been performed before the Queen, or by such and such a Company, and so on.

Care is also taken to make clear where the book may be bought, when there could be any doubt as to this point.

It seems clear that title-pages were actually posted up as advertisements,[2] and that with a view to this

[1] Churchyard's *Worthiness of Wales*, 1587.

[2] The following are some of the allusions to this practice : Nashe, *Terrors of the Night*, sig. A4 ; *Have with you*, R1v ; Hall, *Virgidemiae*, v. ii. 45–50 ; Jonson, *Epigrams*, 3 ; Guilpin, *Skialetheia*, no. 8, ' To Deloney ' ; Parrot, *The Mastive*, ' Ad Bibliopolam ' ; Davies of Here-ford, *Paper's Complaint*, l. 97. The practice continued until the eighteenth century ; cf. Pope's *Epistle to Doctor Arbuthnot*, ll. 215–16 ;

use of them they were sometimes kept standing in type after the rest of the book had been distributed.[1] This was no doubt one of the reasons for the care that was generally taken to specify where the book could be bought. During this period, which may be taken to include the last quarter of the sixteenth and the whole of the seventeenth century, we must, I think, regard the title-page not as part of the work to which it is prefixed, or as the production of its author, but rather as an explanatory label affixed to the book by the printer or publisher. Not only are some of the descriptions added to titles of plays so inappropriate that it seems impossible that they can have been supplied by the author,[2] but we have the definite statement of Wither in *The Scholar's Purgatory*, c. 1625, that some stationers having obtained a written copy likely to be vendible, ' contrive ' and name it according to their own pleasure, ' which is the reason so many good books come forth imperfect and with foolish titles '.[3]

There exist also a certain number of books in which the heading of the first page of the work itself and the running title differ from the title-page, and in such cases we may probably infer that this heading preserves the name that the author originally intended.[4] It is, of course, quite possible that he himself was responsible for the change,[5] but there are cases in which this seems

Dunciad, i. 40 (also Pope's note and Curll's comment on the passage quoted by Elwin and Courthope).

[1] See Dr. W. W. Greg in *The Library*, 2nd Ser., ix. 400–1.

[2] See the instances given by Creizenach, *The English Drama in the Age of Shakespeare*, p. 236 (*Geschichte*, iv. 269).

[3] See the whole passage in Prof. Dover Wilson's *Life in Shakespeare's England*, p. 153.

[4] As indeed the running title does in the case of certain modern novels, the title of which has been changed at the last moment owing to the discovery that it had been used before.

[5] For example, the original issue of L. Lloyd's *Pilgrimage of Princes* has on A2ᵛ–3 the running title ' The Paradice of princely Histories '. It is, however, clear from allusions in Lloyd's Dedication and in the

at least doubtful. Thus Thomas Nashe's work first published as *Strange News of the Intercepting certain Letters*, and afterwards as *The Apologie of Pierce Pennilesse* has, as head-title on the first page of the text *The four Letters Confuted* and so the running title throughout.[1] It seems probable that this last was the name chosen by the author, for it is as ' my *Foure Letters* '[2] that he generally refers to the book in a later work.

If this view is correct and the wording of title-pages of this period is, or at least may be, the work of the publisher, we may, on the one hand, more readily pardon the too laudatory terms which are often employed, and on the other hand we must exercise a certain amount of discretion in accepting statements on such title-pages. Thus when we find a play described as having been performed before the Queen, we are no more bound to accept the statement—if we have evidence to the contrary—than we are, for example, to believe that certain copies of the 1599 edition of *Soliman and Perseda* which bear the words ' newly corrected and amended ' differ from other copies of the same edition which do not. Definite repudiations on the part of authors, of statements made on the title-pages, are naturally somewhat rare, and we may suppose that as a rule the author, if he was available, would be consulted in the matter, at least in the case of the original edition. We have, however, Nashe's references to the title-pages of *Pierce Pennilesse* and *Strange News*, both printed while he was away from London, complaining that the first bore a ' tedious Mountebank's Oration to the Reader ', and that in

Epistle to the Reader, that he intended it to be called by the title actually given to it.

[1] Omitting ' The ' in the running title.

[2] In *Have with you to Saffron-Walden*. It is there twice referred to as ' my *Foure Letters* ', once as ' my 4. Letters cōfuted ', once as ' my *Foure Letters intercepted* ', and once as ' *Piers Penilesse* Apologie ' —a good example of Elizabethan indifference in such matters.

both the printer had added the word ' gentleman ' to his name.

After the Restoration, title-pages, at any rate of books of literary note, tended to greater sobriety. As a general rule the mere title, the author's name, and the printer's and publisher's, with the date, are given and not much besides ; or if there is anything more it is merely an explanatory sub-title of a kind which might well have been added by the author. We do indeed find *long* titles, but they differ from the puffing titles found in many Elizabethan books and are more definitely part of the work itself.

In the later eighteenth century, however, a new form of advertisement becomes frequent on the title-page, namely, the mention of an author's earlier work.[1] Mr. Michael Sadleir, who kindly looked through a number of volumes in his collection of early novels for me, tells me that the earliest instance of this in the collection is in the *School for Widows*, 1791, which is described as by Clara Reeve, ' author of " The Old English Baron " '. He has found examples in 1793, 1794, and 1797, and many between 1800 and 1805. The practice has, of course, continued.

Passing from the matter of title-pages to their form we may notice—so far as English practice is concerned —the following stages :

In quite early books we may get merely a title in type not much different, if at all, in size from that of the body of the book. In some cases this title may be above a large illustration occupying the rest of the page, in others it may have a border of ornaments.

The next stage is the introduction of the woodcut title-page border. Once introduced, this form of title-

---

[1] Scattered examples of this practice are found much earlier, e. g. in Bunyan's *Holy War*, 1682, R. Head's *Nugae Venales*, 1686, Wither's *Divine Poems*, 1688, and cf. Arber's *Term Cat.* i. 22, 39, 95, 122, 141, &c. &c., but it did not, I think, become usual until the period mentioned.

page became very popular and a considerable proportion of the books issued between 1520 and 1560 had either a woodcut border or a frame of heavy ornament.

In the next period, while woodcut borders are still frequent, we find an increasing use of a border made of type ornaments, the frame becoming lighter in proportion to its contents, together with a new fashion of borderless titles in which the type runs the whole width of the page, such embellishment as there is being limited to a printer's device or ornament in the centre or lower half. This change was accompanied by greater variety in the styles and sizes of type used and a more elaborate attempt at ' display '.

About the end of the sixteenth century we find a beginning of the use of plain horizontal rules across the title-page. Sometimes these were placed below the title itself, or above the imprint, or above and below the author's name or the device : occasionally they are used to divide the page into two or three panels.

In the early years of the seventeenth century we find this use of rules developing very frequently into a frame of rules surrounding the title-page, the rule-frame being, especially from about 1610, very often used throughout the whole of a book, especially in the case of books having side-notes, which were enclosed in a separate column of rules, or those which were printed in two columns.[1] In such books the headline is commonly enclosed between rules. The woodcut borders are still used until about the middle of the century, especially for the larger Bibles and for Prayer Books, but few new ones are being cut, such as there are being almost invariably of the arch-way type. In important books an engraved title is often found in addition to a plain type title.

[1] It must not be supposed that such rule-frames to the pages were never used in early times, for many scattered examples could be found, e. g. Thomas Marshe used them in 1570, but I do not think that they were at all general before the seventeenth century.

The later part of the seventeenth century presents few distinctive features. Woodcut borders have practically disappeared and the most common type seems to be a rule border, often double, and two or three transverse rules dividing the page into panels.

Eighteenth-century title-pages show a reversion to greater simplicity. Rules, when present, are often short and are merely used above and below an author's name or the number of the volume. They are sometimes heavy or double. There is not infrequently a small vignette in the centre of the page. The whole of the type is generally capitals, with the occasional exception of lower case in the imprint.

Of nineteenth-century title-pages there is, I think, nothing much to say, save that all kinds of experiments in arrangement seem to have been tried, including imitation of all earlier styles. The most noteworthy variation in general character is the frequent substitution, in the last thirty years or so, of the block arrangement of titles (several lines of the same length in type of the same size) for the ' hour-glass ' of earlier times, and the many experiments in uncentred titles in which balance is given by the artful distribution of typemasses sometimes aided by ornaments or rules.

The Colophon. In the early days of printing, the end of the book was the normal place for the printer's name and the place and date of printing to appear.[1] The history of the colophon is merely that of the gradual transference of this information to the title-page. When this was complete the colophon was as a rule of no use and it was abandoned.

At first the printer's name and the place of sale of a book was generally only given on the title-page for some special reason. For example, in 1506 the sign

[1] Occasionally a kind of double colophon is found, as in Bale's *Three Laws*, the first giving the name of the author, and the second that of the printer. Dr. Greg calls the first of these an ' explicit '.

of the Trinity in St. Paul's Churchyard is given as the place of sale of a *Provinciale* printed by W. Hopyl at Paris, a practice continued in later books from the same house, both those printed abroad and in England. On the other hand, Wynkyn de Worde and Pynson seldom, if ever, give their names except in their colophons. In Berthelet's and Grafton's books the colophon is still evidently the regular place for the imprint, but names and dates frequently appear also on the title-page. We can, I think, say that the change-over took place about 1530, between which date and 1570 the colophon gradually went out of use, though the more old-fashioned printers kept up the custom for a good many years later. Apart, however, from these instances of mere survival there are a good many colophons added for a special purpose, such as those which give a printer's name and a list of stationers for whom the book was printed, as in the second edition of Holinshed's *Chronicle* and the Second Folio of Shakespeare.[1] In such cases I suspect that the object was simply to put the arrangement on record. In the same way a colophon was sometimes added to a book of which the title-page had been printed with the first sheet, in order to indicate a change in the publishing arrangements, as in the case of the 1610 edition of *The Spanish Tragedy*,[2] or to correct an incomplete statement, as in the 1629 edition of George Wilkins's *Miseries of Inforst Mariage*, where the title states that the work was printed by Aug. Mathewes for Richard Thrale, and a colophon is added saying that it was printed by Aug. Mathewes for George Vincent and to be sold by Richard Thrale.

---

[1] For this book five different title-pages were printed each bearing the name of only one of the five stationers concerned in the venture.

[2] See Dr. Greg in *The Library*, 4th Ser., vi. 54–5.

Chapter Eight

A NOTE ON PAPER

A KNOWLEDGE of the processes by which paper is manufactured and of the substances of which it is composed has never, I think, been regarded as necessary to the bibliographer, however important it may be to the librarian, and it is no part of my intention to deal with such matters here.[1] Of late, however, in consequence partly of the prominence which has been given to watermarks in certain bibliographical arguments, the subject of paper has received a little more attention, and it will probably receive still more in future. It would undoubtedly be of use to us in the solution of many bibliographical problems if we had more exact knowledge of the different sizes, prices, and ' makes ' of paper of the fifteenth to seventeenth centuries, but much detailed work will be necessary before any connected view of the subject becomes obtainable. In the meantime the following desultory notes may be found better than nothing.

[1] So far as I am aware, there is no comprehensive work dealing with paper both from the historical and the technical side. There are numerous books on modern paper-making and on particular varieties of paper and their different uses, but such historical sketches as there are have as a rule little to say about the composition of the early papers or the process by which they were manufactured, while the modern technical treatise is generally wildly at fault if it attempts to touch on the historical side of the matter. On such subjects as the importation, method of sale, sizes, and prices of the early papers, little or no information seems to have been brought together. As regards English paper, the fullest account of the earlier period known to me is to be found in a series of papers by Mr. Rhys Jenkins in *The Library Association Record*, vols. ii and iii (1900–1). The first paper is entitled ' Early Attempts at Paper-making in England, 1495–1586 ' (*L. A. R.*, ii. 479–88), and others deal with paper-making in 1588–1680 (ii. 577–88), and in 1682–1714 (iii. 239 ff.). See also ' Some Notes on the History of Paper ', by Dr. P. Henderson Aitken in *Transactions of the Bibliographical Society*, xiii. 201 ff.

A NOTE ON PAPER

Paper made by similar methods to the European paper of the Middle Ages is said to have been manufactured in China in the second century A. D., and to have been in use among the Arabs in the eighth century. It does not seem, however, to have been introduced into Europe until about the twelfth century,[1] when the craft of paper-making began to be practised by the Moors at Valencia and Toledo. From Spain it spread to Italy, France, and Germany ; a mill is known to have existed at Fabriano, near Ancona, before 1278, and one was started at Nuremberg in 1390.[2] In England, and indeed in any civilized part of Europe, paper was evidently procurable without difficulty from the beginning of the fourteenth century.

The first English paper-mill of which any record is to be found was one kept by John Tate at or near Hertford. This mill is mentioned in a verse prologue to the *De Proprietatibus Rerum*, printed by Wynkyn de Worde in 1495 or 1496, as the source of the paper used in the book. Tate died in 1507 and the mill is referred to in his will as still existing, but there seems reason for thinking that the manufacture of paper had been abandoned. Indeed, as Mr. Jenkins points out, there is no actual evidence of paper being made there before 1495 or after 1498.

Half a century later, about 1549, we are told that no paper is being made in England on account of foreign competition.[3] About 1556, however, a paper-

[1] Various authorities date the introduction of paper into Europe from late in the eleventh to early in the thirteenth century. The earliest definite dates for the use of paper in Europe seem to be 1145 and 1154, see P. Henderson Aitken, u.s., p. 209.

[2] Jenkins, *L. A. R.*, ii. 481.

[3] *A Discourse of the Common Weal of this Realm of England* (by John Hales ?), ed. E. Lamond, pp. 65–6, quoted by Jenkins, u.s., p. 484. The passage is substantially unchanged in the refurbishment by W. S. under the title of *An Examination of Certain Complaints* in 1581, but need not be taken as true at the latter date also. Dr. Aitken notes that in the archives of the Drapers' Company of London, docu-

mill was started by Thomas Thirlby, a statesman and ecclesiastic of some importance in his day, with the help of a certain Remegius, whom be brought over from Germany. This mill is mentioned by Churchyard in his *Spark of Friendship*, 1588,[1] but he gives no details, not even the place at which the mill was situated, though this seems likely to have been at Fen Ditton, near Cambridge, where there is good evidence of the existence of a paper-mill in 1557.[2] There was also one at Bemerton, near Salisbury, which, according to different authorities, was established in 1554 or 1569.[3] Before 1565 Sir Thomas Gresham set up a mill at Osterley, Middlesex, but he lost money by it,[4] and it would seem that the experiment was soon abandoned.

After this failure we hear of no further attempt at manufacture for nearly twenty years. In or about 1585, however, the well-known printer and stationer Richard Tottel presented a petition to Burleigh, asking for the grant of a monopoly of paper-making in England, together with a prohibition of the export of rags, for thirty-one years,[5] which looks as if he at least did not regard it as a hopeless venture. Nothing seems to have come of Tottel's petition, but a few years later, in 1588/9, a ten years' licence for paper-making was granted by Elizabeth to her jeweller, a German named John Spilman.[6] He started a mill at Dartford in Kent and evidently at last made the business a success, for

ments of the early part of the fifteenth century are invariably on Italian paper, those from the end of the century always on French.

[1] See Nichols's *Progresses of Queen Elizabeth*, ii. 594.

[2] Jenkins, u.s., p. 485; cf. Ames, *Typog. Antiq.*, ed. Herbert, i. 201, where it is mentioned as existing in 1562.

[3] Jenkins, u.s., pp. 485–6; by a slip Jenkins has 1596 for 1569.

[4] Churchyard in Nichols, *Progresses of Queen Elizabeth*, ii. 597.

[5] Arber's *Transcript of the Stationers' Register*, i. 242. It appears from the petition that the chief difficulty was the cheapness of the French paper, the makers of which imported English rags.

[6] For a detailed account of Spilman, see G. H. Overend in *Proc. of Huguenot Soc. of London*, viii. 180–96.

his mill was visited by King James in 1605 and Spillman was knighted.[1] It remained in operation until late in the seventeenth century, by which time several other mills had been set up in various parts of the country and the making of paper was a well-established industry.

From its first invention, until the closing years of the eighteenth century, paper was made entirely by hand, though water-power was occasionally employed in crushing the pulp. The material used in the early days seems almost invariably to have been linen rags, which, after washing, were boiled for a long time and then beaten with hammers until they formed a smooth pulp. This pulp was stirred up with water in a vat to the consistency of cream. Shallow wooden frames were provided of the size of the paper to be made and furnished with a bottom of interwoven wires, those running longitudinally being fine and very close together, while those running crossways were thicker and from three-quarters of an inch to an inch apart. These frames or moulds were dipped by the workmen into the pulp, the water of which drained away as they were lifted out. During the lifting a peculiar horizontal shake was given to the mould, the result of which was to cause the fibres of the pulp, as they settled on the bottom of the mould, to cross or interlock together. As soon as the water had drained away, the wet sheet of paper was turned out to dry, generally on pieces of woollen material. It was then pressed, sized more or less according to the purpose for which it was intended, and dried.

It was customary from an early period in the European manufacture of paper, for the maker to introduce into all the better qualities, at least, his device or some distinguishing mark. This was done by interweaving the design in wire in the network of the bottom of the mould, the impression of these wires, as

[1] Nichols, *Progresses of King James I*, i. 515.

of the close and widely spaced wires of the bottom itself, appearing as semi-transparent lines in the paper when held up to the light. The devices, known as ' watermarks ', used in early papers are of the most varied kind, ranging from simple stars, crosses, initials of the maker, &c., to elaborate heraldic devices embodying the arms of the town or district of manufacture or of the maker's patron. Among the commoner watermarks of sixteenth- and seventeenth-century papers were hands or ' gloves ', various kinds of ewer or jug, pillars, and crowns. A very large number have been reproduced in the great work of C. M. Briquet, *Les Filigranes*, 1907, and it is sometimes possible with the help of this book to determine the place of origin and date of samples of paper with fair accuracy. Unfortunately, however, it is often most difficult to identify with any approach to certainty the watermark of paper used in a printed book of smaller size than a folio, on account of its position, in a quarto or octavo, in the back fold, or, in most other sizes, in the margin where most of it has usually been cut away by the binder. As a rule the utmost that we can do is to determine whether in a particular book or group of books the watermark is the same throughout or not, a point which indeed may be of great importance as indicating whether or not the whole was printed at or about the same time : [1] it is seldom that we can go

Cf. Dr. W. W. Greg's investigations into the ' 1619 ' Shakespeare quartos in *The Library*, 2nd Ser., vol. ix. Arguments from similarity or dissimilarity of watermark must, however, be used with extreme caution, for it seems quite clear that many printers bought their paper in job-lots, and it is common to find a number of different watermarks in a book about the printing of which there appears to have been nothing abnormal. At the same time, if we had reason for thinking that a certain part of a book had been inserted after the original printing, and we found that the paper of the rest of the book, both before and after this particular section, bore the same watermark whereas this section itself had a different one, we could certainly claim the fact as strongly supporting this view.

further and infer anything from the watermark as to the actual date of printing.

The watermark seems to have been normally placed in the centre of one half of the sheet, so that when the sheet was folded in two, as in a ' folio ' book, it appeared in the centre of a leaf. The question of how far we may regard this position as a standard one is of some importance in bibliographical work, for it is evident that if we could rely on its always occupying the same place in the sheet this would give us valuable information not only concerning the number of times a sheet had been folded, a point which determines the ' format ' of the book, but also, in the case of some foldings, its original size. Though, however, at least in the sixteenth and early seventeenth centuries, the *normal* place for the watermark was as I have stated, it is not by any means safe to regard this position as an invariable one : it is indeed far from infrequent to find the watermark somewhat nearer to the centre, and I should not like to declare that it was never placed quite centrally on the sheet. But the subject is one which, so far as I can learn, has not yet been fully investigated, though an excellent beginning has been made by Mr. Edward Heawood in a paper on ' The Position on the Sheet of Early Watermarks ' printed in *The Library*, 4th Series, ix. 38–47 (June, 1928).

Later papers, from about 1670 (?), often have a second watermark, termed a ' counter-mark ' and generally consisting of the maker's initials, in the centre of the opposite half of the sheet.[1]

The question of sizes of paper is also one which needs some investigation. From the early days of printing a number of different sizes seem to have been used. Blades states that Caxton used at least three

[1] Mr. R. W. Chapman tells me that during the eighteenth century the usual position for both watermarks was in or near the centre of the half-sheets, and that he has not met with abnormally placed marks until quite the end of the period.

sizes measuring respectively $15\frac{3}{4}'' \times 22''$, $13'' \times 18\frac{1}{2}''$, and $11'' \times 16''$. In the later sixteenth century we can recognize two sizes as especially frequent (forming respectively the 'large folio' and 'small folio' of certain booksellers' catalogues), the larger sheet measuring about $15'' \times 20''$ (the modern 'crown' sheet) and the smaller about $12'' \times 16''$. There seems, however, to have been much variation, and these sizes can only be taken as approximate. There are many books which, unless indeed they have been most extravagantly cut down, must have been printed on paper from $13''$ to $13\frac{1}{2}''$ by $17''$ or $18''$,[1] and the paper of a manuscript volume which I have measured, all of which is entirely uncut and has the whole of the deckle[2] preserved, is in two sizes measuring respectively $12\frac{1}{2}'' \times 15\frac{1}{2}''$ and $12\frac{1}{4}'' \times 15\frac{1}{4}''$. So far as I have been able to ascertain, the sizes had at this date no recognized names, the modern names when first introduced referring to the watermark and indicating the make or quality. Thus when Prynne complained that 'Shackspeers Plaies are printed in the best Crowne paper, far better than most Bibles ',[3] he is talking of the quality, not of the size of the paper. By 1674, however, as Mr. Chapman has shown,[4] such terms as 'pott', 'crown', &c., had passed from denoting the watermark to denoting the *size*, and all the modern names for sizes, with others now obsolete, were in use. The sizes were indeed not quite fixed, but the series was the same as to-day, *pot* being the smallest and *super-royal* the largest.

[1] The double leaf of the largest known copy of the First Folio of Shakespeare is said to measure $13\frac{3}{8}'' \times 17''$.

[2] The 'deckle' is the edge of a sheet of hand-made paper, which is always slightly uneven. This irregularity is regarded in modern times as an ornament, and 'deckle-edges' are artificially produced on many of the better qualities of machine-made paper.

[3] *Histrio-Mastix*, 1633, 'To the Christian Reader ', fol. 1, side-note.

[4] *The Library*, 4th Ser., iv. 175, vii. 402–8. In the second article a detailed inventory of a number of lots of paper offered in 1674 by two paper merchants is printed in full.

An important question which still awaits solution is at what date paper of double any of the normal sizes was introduced. Seeing that hand-made paper is now manufactured up to $22'' \times 30''$, there seems no reason why the sixteenth- and seventeenth-century workmen should not have been capable of turning out paper double their usual smaller size, say $16'' \times 24''$. Now if they did this and if they followed the usual rule of running the close wires lengthways of the frame, then a printer making use of imposition by half-sheets would produce a book in the ordinary sizes but with the chain-marks running in the wrong direction : his folio would have transverse chain-lines and his quarto vertical ones. The same result would, of course, follow if he used the ordinary imposition, but cut his sheets in two before printing. A practice of this kind would afford a simple explanation of those odd cases with which we sometimes meet, of books printed apparently partly in octavo and partly in quarto, with the leaves nevertheless all of the same size.[1]

From about the beginning of the nineteenth century, machine-made paper began to supplant hand-made for all the ordinary purposes of book-production. The principle of the paper-making machine was to replace the mould by a continuous travelling wire web which dipped into the vat of pulp. This web carried along the pulp raised by it for a sufficient distance to allow it to drain—the whole web being shaken to consolidate the fibres as a mould used to be shaken by hand—and become sufficiently firm to be passed to other heated rollers which dried it, the web of paper being then wound into a roll to be afterwards cut to the sizes required. The wire web which in these machines took the place of the bottom of the hand-moulds was closely woven and did not leave on the paper the impression of rectangular lines (chain-lines and wire-lines) which were usual in hand-made (laid) paper. Paper which has

[1] See p. 174 below.

104

an appearance of even granulation instead of these chain- and wire-lines is called ' wove '.

It would seem that in the early days of machine-made papers, 'wove' paper was normally machine-made and 'laid' paper generally hand-made ; but the two kinds cannot by any means always be so simply distinguished. There was wove paper before the days of the machines, a mesh of woven wire being presumably used to form the bottom of the frames instead of the old cross-wires ; and it was not long before the paper-makers discovered a method of giving a 'laid' appearance to the paper made by machinery. This was done by impressing the lines on the paper while still damp by running it between special rollers, and it is thus that the laid lines are produced in almost all papers, both machine-made and hand-made, at the present day, the watermark, when there is one, being produced by the same process.

Into the question of modern papers, their sizes and varieties, we need not enter beyond noting that very much larger sizes are now employed in printing than was formerly the case, papers double, four, or eight times the basic size being used, e. g. besides crown paper measuring $15'' \times 20''$, we have double crown $20'' \times 30''$, ' quad ' crown (i. e. quadruple), $30'' \times 40''$, and double quad crown $40'' \times 60''$; and that almost any required appearance can be produced by varying the ' finish '.

The sizes of paper commonly used in book-work with the size of an octavo page produced by them are as follows :

	Double.	Quad.	Page of 8vo.
Foolscap $13\frac{1}{2} \times 17$	17×27	27×34	$6\frac{3}{4} \times 4\frac{1}{4}$
Crown 15×20	20×30	30×40	$7\frac{1}{2} \times 5$
Demy $17\frac{1}{2} \times 22\frac{1}{2}$	$22\frac{1}{2} \times 35$	35×45	$8\frac{3}{4} \times 5\frac{5}{8}$
Royal 20×25	25×40	40×50	$10 \times 6\frac{1}{4}$

Several other sizes are in use for other kinds of paper such as ' medium ' ($19'' \times 24''$) for various kinds of cover or wrapping paper, 'post' (16"×20") for writing papers, &c.

The nominal 'measure' of paper is 24 sheets = 1 quire; 20 quires = 1 ream, but printing paper is, as a rule, sold in reams of 516 sheets (= 21½ quires), and occasionally in reams of 504 sheets (= 21 quires). The 516 sheet ream has the practical advantage of allowing about the right amount (in a short run) for printers' wastage, to give 500 perfect printed sheets per ream.

Hand-made and 'art' papers are usually sold in reams of 480 sheets.

The substance of paper is usually indicated by the number of pounds weight to the ream; hard paper, of course, on account of the closeness of the fibres, weighing more in proportion to its thickness than the softer varieties. Thus a quad crown (30"×40") paper such as is used in ordinary books may weigh anything from about 50 to about 120 lb. per ream. If it is a hard and dense paper it will probably weigh from 80 to 120 lb.; if a light and soft kind, such as is generally used in novels and books in which 'bulk' is regarded as more important than durability, from 50 to 90 lb. The so-called 'art' papers, the surface of which is coated with china-clay to make it perfectly smooth and thus able to take a clear impression of the minute dots (80 to 160 to the inch) of which a 'half-tone' print is made up, are much heavier for their thickness than ordinary printing papers. They are also much less durable as the surface tends to flake off.

It may be worth remembering that in the case of an octavo book and using 'quad' paper, the commonest size for ordinary work,

$$\frac{\text{number of pages of book}}{32} = \text{reams required per 1,000 copies.}[1]$$

If this be remembered it is easy to calculate the paper

[1] If the ream is not 516 a small allowance must be added for waste.

required when other sizes of either book or paper are under consideration. Thus :

(*a*) If either the book is in quarto or the paper is 'double' instead of 'quad', then in each case twice the number of reams will be required.

(*b*) If either the book is in 16mo or the paper is 'double quad', then in each case half the number of reams will be required.

Thus 1,000 copies of a book of 256 pages (including, of course, all preliminary pages, &c., which are generally paged separately), in 8vo printed on quad crown paper will take

$$\frac{256}{32} = 8 \text{ reams.}$$

2,500 copies of a book of 360 pages in 8vo printed on double quad crown paper will need

$$2 \cdot 5 \times \frac{360}{32} \times \tfrac{1}{2} = 14 \tfrac{1}{16} \text{ reams.}$$

500 copies of a book of 256 pages in quarto on double demy paper will need

$$\tfrac{1}{2} \times \frac{256}{32} \times 2 \times 2 = 16 \text{ reams}$$

Various well-meant proposals have been made for simplifying the apparent complexity of paper sizes and measures, such as that all papers should be sold by the 1,000 sheets,[1] or that the sizes should bear some definite proportions to each other, but most of such apparent simplifications would be bought at great loss of practical convenience. One ingenious proposal may,

---

[1] An agreement was reached in 1925 between paper-makers and printers that this new unit should be adopted, but we shall see ! Since printers' wastage cannot be eliminated, either the unit of paper must be irregular—a few sheets over even hundreds—or the number of perfect copies produced of anything printed must be irregular. It is more convenient to a publisher that his edition of a book should consist of 1,000 copies than, say, 983, and the person who pays the piper proverbially calls the tune.

however, be mentioned, that of Mr. Alfred Watkins [1] of Hereford, who has pointed out that if the sides of an original sheet are proportioned as $1 : \sqrt{2}$, then however often one folds it by doubling, the proportions of the resulting leaf are unchanged, and that this particular proportion is an excellent one for most kinds of book. He therefore suggests that all sheets should be so proportioned. The only objection to this proposal is that the power to vary the shape of page according to the particular matter which it is desired to set forth is of great practical value, and that it would be very foolish to forgo it for the sake of a theoretical uniformity.

[1] Well known to all photographers for his exposure-meters and other excellent devices.

Chapter Nine

THE DECORATION OF BOOKS

IT is no part of my purpose to attempt here an account of book-decoration from the aesthetic point of view. That is an interesting but intricate subject which in no way concerns us ; but a few notes on the more material side of the matter may be of use, though for the avoidance of complication they must be limited to English work.

It is necessary, in the first place, that we should distinguish between decoration and illustration. The former is intended primarily to beautify the book in which it is used, and it must therefore always be regarded in close association with the typography and general appearance of the work, and is more or less successful according as it harmonizes well or ill with this : the latter is intended primarily to elucidate the text or to place the reader in a better position for visualizing the events narrated, and is to be judged on its success in this aim and on its merits as an independent work of art. At the same time, however, it must be confessed that one cannot by any means always keep these two sorts of embellishment separate, for there are many things to be found in books which partake in some degree of the characteristics of both. Even here, however, one or other quality is generally predominant.

There is besides these, still a third variety of ornament to be found in printed books, those devices, coats of arms, &c., which are intended both to add beauty, or at least distinction, to the work and at the same time to identify it with a particular printing or publishing house, or sometimes in the case of coats of arms, &c., with a particular patron.

Like most other things in printed books, the idea of

109

decoration was borrowed from the manuscript tradition. The early printers were familiar with illuminated manuscripts which might contain : (1) decorative page-borders, or decorations at head or foot of the page, between columns of the writing, or between sections of the text ; and (2) miniatures in which the idea of decoration was mingled with that of illustration and perhaps even subordinate to it. As best they could, the printers imitated these things in their own productions, but there was one essential difference of which they soon found it necessary to take account. In a manuscript, work spent on a conventional decoration and on an illustration might equally enhance the value of the single copy of the book on which the illuminator worked, and hence be of equal economic advantage to his employer. A printer, however, who had a conventional border or ornament made for him had something which he could use over and over again until it was worn out, whereas a real illustration might prove to be of little value after it had once been used, for, however careless of suitability the Elizabethan printers were, and though *any* house might stand equally well for the Tower of London or for Constantinople, and *any* picture of people fighting for any battle, ancient or modern, yet even for them there were limits beyond which it was impossible to go. The economically-minded printer would therefore inevitably be more inclined to favour such forms of decoration and simple illustration as had no definite associations, a thing which, I believe, had in England at any rate a considerable influence on the art of wood-cutting, directing the artist more to conventional design and away from any attempt at realism. This does not mean that this country produced no genuinely illustrated books, as distinct from decorated ones, for there were a few which showed real merit, but on the whole it may be said without fear of contradiction, that the best efforts of the woodcutters and those who designed for them in the first two centuries or so of printing were directed to the production of conventional borders, printers' devices, initial letters, coats of arms, and the like—to decoration rather than to illustration.

Of illustration proper there is in the first century of printing not much to be said. The earliest known illustration in an English book appears to be two small woodcuts in an edition of the *Parvus et Magnus Cato* printed by Caxton about 1481.[1] From that date until the middle of the following century we find a certain number of woodcut illustrations and a somewhat larger number of little woodcuts of the kind which is intermediate between illustration and decoration, but most of them are very crude and a large proportion are directly copied from foreign work. For example, the little cuts of men and women that appear in *Horestes, Everyman, Youth, Jack Juggler,* and elsewhere and that have been claimed as of great importance for the light that they throw on the costumes of the early players, are now known to belong to a set of which the originals appeared in the *Therence en francoys* printed at Paris by Antoine Vérard about 1500, and which came to England through the medium of the *Kalender of Shepherdes*.[2] From about 1550, however, for some thirty years there was a small output of work of much better quality, most of it in books from the press of John Day.

Woodcut was, however, destined to give place to

[1] See ' Some notes on English Illustrated Books ', by A. W. Pollard in *Transactions of the Bibliographical Society*, vi. 29–61, the best short account of the subject with a most useful series of facsimiles.

[2] See A. W. Pollard in *Transactions of the Bibliographical Society*, vi. 38, and *Youth*, ed. Bang and McKerrow, pp. xvi-xviii. Some of the cuts seem also to occur in *Le Vergier d'honneur* by O. de Saint-Gelais, printed by J. Trepperel at Paris at about the same date as the *Therence*. Mr. Pollard's article on ' The Transference of Woodcuts in the Fifteenth and Sixteenth Centuries ' in *Bibliographica*, ii. 343–68, should also be consulted. Among other curious instances of the transfer of cuts it is here (p. 347) noted that the cut of a printing-press from the 1548 *Ordinary* (figure 12 above) was used in a ballad called *Solomon's Sacrifice* printed for Henry Gosson in 1630–40.

engraving on copper.[1]   One might hazard the conjecture that the inferiority of most of the press-work of the time, which was incapable of doing justice to good woodcutting, was not the least important factor in the change of fashion.   The earliest example of copper-engraving in English books was in *The Birth of Mankind* first printed in 1540.   For thirty years after this, advance was very gradual, but from about 1580 copperplates begin to take the place of woodcuts in all the more elaborate work.   The fashion was at its height in the earlier years of the seventeenth century, when engraved title-pages of the most elaborate design and often containing portraits of authors were frequent, especially in the larger books.   Such work is, of course, mainly decorative in intention, though the title-pages often include, as the well-known Coryat title, engraved by William Hole in 1611, or that by C. Le Blon to the 1628 *Anatomy of Melancholy*, small pictures which are genuine illustrations.   Illustrations in the *body* of a work, engraved or woodcut, are, however, rare, except in technical or semi-technical work where they cannot well be dispensed with.

After the Restoration, illustrations became fewer still.   One does indeed find a number of portraits, either engraved or woodcut, and there are several emblematic frontispieces, such as the owl and the ass laden with panniers before the 1728 and 1729 editions of the *Dunciad*, and a few engraved illustrations, especially in books of poetry, but in general and in spite of exceptions such as the early work of Hogarth, who between 1720 and 1745 produced several series

---

[1] Those who desire an explanation of the various processes used in illustrating books (other than the modern photographic methods) may be referred to *A Guide to the Processes and Schools of Engraving*, issued at 6*d*. by the Trustees of the British Museum.   This little book, so far as it goes, is excellent, though it would have gained enormously in value had it been accompanied by a carefully chosen series of reproduced examples of the processes described.

112

of book illustrations, it may, I think, fairly be said that from 1660 until after the middle of the eighteenth century there is little illustration worthy of note in English books. Then, however, there came a revival. Copper engraving began to be much more widely used in books, and at the same time the art of Thomas Bewick caused a revival in wood engraving, which had so degenerated as to be hardly employed at all save in the roughest and cheapest form for children's books, chap-books, almanacs, and the like.[1] The history of this revival is, however, of aesthetic rather than bibliographical interest and will be found fully dealt with in numerous works on book-illustration. It need only be said that in the early part of the nineteenth century the processes usually employed were steel and copper engraving, woodcut having again declined in importance as a serious artistic medium, though it continued to be very largely used in inferior work. It became in fact a matter for craftsmen rather than for artists, though at least twice in the century there were serious attempts at revival. Finally, towards the end of the century, photographic and photo-mechanical processes began to supersede all those which had depended on the manual skill of artist or engraver, until now even the few woodcuts which are made are, as a general rule, not themselves printed from, but are merely used as patterns from which far more durable electrotypes are made.

To the bibliographer the decorations of books are as a rule of much more importance than the illustrations on account of the greater amount of information which he can derive from them. As has been suggested above, ' decorations ' are as a rule far less limited in their use than illustrations, and the blocks were often used again and again for long periods, even sometimes for a hundred years or more. This fact may be very

[1] A curious experiment had indeed been made in woodcutting *c.* 1750 by the issue of a series of plates by Hogarth so executed, but it does not seem to have met with any success (see *D. N. B.*, art. Hogarth).

useful in helping us to trace the printers of books which bear no printer's name and to ascertain the date of printing of undated books, for on the one hand we may possess good evidence as to the ownership of the block at the particular time, and on the other, as the block gradually deteriorated by use we may be able to place the particular impression between two others the dates of which are known to us. Tracing printer or date by means of ornaments is, however, not always quite so simple a matter as might appear, and a few words of caution may be advisable.

'Decorations' may be roughly divided into ornaments, ornamental initials, printers' and other devices, and woodcut borders, and the value of these in bibliographical investigation differs considerably.

To take first the ornaments.[1] It is on the whole true to say that the worse, the rougher, and more insignificant an ornament is, the greater use is it likely to be to the bibliographer, for the reason that such rough and insignificant ornaments are (a) almost always woodcuts, (b) seldom closely copied by other craftsmen, and (c) unlikely to be borrowed and so used by another than their real owner. Their occurrence, therefore, in a book almost amounts to proof that the book was printed by the same printer as other books in which they occur about the same date. On the other hand, elaborate and better designed ornaments, especially after about 1570, seem often to have been not woodcuts but metal blocks, sometimes of foreign origin, produced apparently by casting from a matrix.

---

[1] We may omit altogether from consideration here what are called 'type ornaments', including not only such things as 'flowers', leaves, &c., cast on ordinary type-bodies, but the conventional designs cast on larger bodies and used to make up into 'lacework' and other frames for type-matter. These are produced in the same way as type, and for our present purpose may be regarded rather as part of the type-page than as 'ornament'. They are, as a rule, common to many printers of a period and are seldom of much help in a bibliographical inquiry.

114

Two ornaments apparently identical may occur on the same page,[1] showing that the printer had at least two blocks of the same design, and if there were two there were probably more, perhaps in the hands of other printers, and the evidential value of their appearance may then be little or nothing. And even when such ornaments were really woodcuts and not cast in metal, the better they were the more likely were they to be copied, and the greater care must therefore be taken to make sure that two impressions are really from the same block; while it is conceivable that a particularly striking ornament might be borrowed by one printer from another, so that even an undoubted print from the identical block might not be valid evidence of the printer. For all these reasons it is wise to pay the greatest attention to what may seem at first sight to be the least important of the ornaments which a book contains.

When instead of trying to trace a printer we attempt to fix a date, similar cautions are necessary. Here, however, the most important point apart from the identity of the block is whether it is of wood or of metal. A wood block will generally, as time goes on, become not only simply worn with use, but cracked, broken, and worm-eaten. Of the marks of age, worm-holes are by far the most important, for worm-holes almost always show unmistakably in any print, bad or good, lightly or heavily inked, and though it should

[1] Cf. the quarto edition of Sternhold and Hopkins's *Psalms*, printed by Day in 1583, which has the 'archers and dogs' ornament twice on the title-page. The 1587 Holinshed also affords instances of apparently identical ornaments twice on the same page, cf. the headings of Book 5 and (frames only) Books 4 and 8 of the 'History of England'. These cast blocks may have been finished with the graver, for we sometimes find a pair of blocks showing very minute differences here and there and yet on the whole so similar that we can hardly suppose one to be a simple copy of the other cut independently.

There seem also to have been blocks *cut* on metal instead of on wood (see p. 120 below), but for our present purpose these were, of course, as individual as woodcuts.

have been easy to obliterate them by means of a small wooden peg and a minute's work with a knife, I am not aware of any clear case in which this was done. An impression from a particular block which shows a worm-hole may therefore always be assumed to be later than one which does not show it.

One might suppose that cracks in the block would be of equal use in showing the order of impressions, but unfortunately this is not so : the only thing that they certainly prove is that the block was made of wood. Whether cracks in a block show in the prints from it seems to depend almost entirely on how tightly the block was locked up in the chase, and this, with wood furniture, must have depended a good deal on whether the furniture was dry or damp at the time of printing.[1] It is undoubtedly true that cracks which show plainly in certain prints from a block cannot be seen in other later prints.

Definite breaks in a block form much better evidence of age, but here again a caution is necessary. Only clear and sharp breaks are of use. It seems not uncommon for parts of lines to be slightly broken down, as by something having been dropped on the block, and such parts may print in heavy or much-inked impressions, but not in light ones. Care must also be taken that an apparent break is not due to a particle of paper or straw having been adherent to the sheet at the time of printing and having afterwards fallen off. ' Breaks ' due to this cause would of course only appear in a single copy of a book.

The apparent general wear of a block is of no importance at all in this connexion, as it depends almost

---

[1] As the paper was always printed damp, the furniture would probably get damper as the impression proceeded, even if it was not necessary, as might well be the case when using inferior ink, to wash the type down from time to time. Dampness or dryness of the weather might also have a considerable effect on the tightness of a forme which had been allowed to stand for a while after locking up.

entirely on the paper, inking, and skill of the printer. Blocks which appear in one book to be in the last stage of degeneration may often later give quite respectable prints in the hands of another and more skilful workman.

All these considerations apply of course equally to the other kinds of decorations mentioned above. Initial letters, being as a rule of little value or importance to their owners, afford quite as good evidence of the identity of the printer of books in which they appear as ornaments do, but in their case we have to be especially careful that we are dealing with woodcuts and not with metal blocks. A very large percentage of the initials after about 1570, and a good many earlier ones, were, I am convinced, metal, and their evidence must therefore be accepted with great caution. At the same time there are so many books in which the only decoration is the ornamental initials, that we often have to rely entirely upon these for the identification of the printer. Initials are seldom of use in fixing a date, as they are generally too small to show wear or damage sufficiently clearly.

Devices of printers and publishers have been more studied than any other form of decoration, and so far as English ones are concerned some attempt has been made to trace their history and ownership up to 1640. Many of them passed through the hands of a succession of printers, and their appearance in a book is often sufficient evidence of the house from which it came. It is, however, obvious that a printer who wished for any reason to conceal his connexion with one of the issues of his press, would not put his usual device upon it,[1] and it is precisely books of this class about which

[1] Nevertheless, as Professor Pollard points out to me, there are Marian Protestant books which are attributed to Singleton solely on the ground of his device! In later times, too, John Wolfe seems to have used on books which were more or less surreptitiously printed, or on which at least he did not think fit to put his name, devices which, though not his regular ones, had been used by him previously and which would therefore have betrayed his connexion with these books to any one who took the trouble to do a little detective work.

we most frequently desire information. Printers' devices are, however, sometimes of especial value in dating books, as many of them underwent alterations at various times—initials or mottoes were removed on change of ownership, portions were re-cut and the re-cutting inserted in the old block, borders or rules which had broken were cut away, and so on, and we can thus describe several ' states ', which if the date of the alterations are known may enable us to fix the year of printing of books in which these devices appear with some degree of precision.

Other devices, such as those of authors or of patrons, are of less value to the bibliographer in that they of course appear in works by the same author or dedicated to the same patron irrespective of the particular printer, and therefore are no evidence of the house of issue.

Woodcut title-borders offer a number of problems and it is difficult to say anything about them that is not subject to many exceptions. So far as the evidence that they afford as to printers is concerned it may, I think, generally be assumed that the simpler and inferior borders would remain in the same hands until their owner died or retired from business. The more elaborate ones, however, seem to have passed freely from one printer to another and therefore great caution must be used in drawing conclusions from their appearance in a particular book.[1] On the other hand, owing to the ease with which borders, and especially those with rules round them, were damaged during use, they can often give us valuable information as to the date of books in which they appear. Unfortunately, however, they occur comparatively seldom in the smaller and less carefully printed popular books in which we are most interested to-day.

[1] On the question of transference of borders from one printing-house to another, see an article in *The Library*, 4th Ser., v. 1 seq. on ' Border Pieces used by English Printers before 1641 ', esp. pp. 33–5.

It need hardly be said that most of the foregoing remarks as to the evidence derivable from wear and condition would apply equally to illustration blocks. Save, however, in the case of some of the early cuts used in such books as the *Kalender of Shepherdes*, I doubt if, in practice, illustrations are of much use in bibliographical inquiries. Such information as might be derivable from them is generally already discoverable in other ways.[1]

A few words may be said as to the manner in which woodcuts were produced. All the earliest woodcuts were executed by cutting with a sharp knife-like tool, the material being a piece of soft wood, such as pear, of which the grain ran parallel to the surface. The purpose of the cutter was to remove by clean cuts all the surface of the block except the lines which were to print, leaving these in as high relief as possible consistently with their being sufficiently strong to stand the impression. So far as English work is concerned, it seems to have been a general if not a universal rule that the grain of the blocks should run vertically,[2] and this rule was followed even in borders made up, as many were, of four separate pieces, in which we might have expected that, for the sake of obtaining greater strength in the top and bottom piece, the grain would there have been made to run horizontally. As time went on there seem to have been occasional experiments in the use of harder wood such as box, on which it would be possible to work with the

---

[1] Copper-plate engravings might also, of course, afford evidence as to the order of editions, when, as not infrequently happens, they are touched up or altered between the different impressions. In the case of several of the more important early copper-plates, and in particular the Droeshout portrait of Shakespeare a number of ' states ' have been described. Mr. M. H. Spielmann's essay on *The Title-page of the First Folio of Shakespeare's Plays*, 1924, may be usefully studied in this connexion.

[2] As is shown by the cracks in old blocks which almost always run up and down and not across the block.

' graver ', a more or less square-ended tool normally
used for engraving in metal, but which would have
been quite ineffective if used on soft woods. Towards
the end of the eighteenth century what amounted almost to a revolution in woodcutting was produced by
using box-wood cut on the end of the grain,[1] a method
of which one of the first exponents, in England at least,
is said to have been Thomas Bewick. When necessary,
the block was made up of a number of small pieces
fastened together. Blocks of this material can be cut
by the use of graving tools as cleanly as metal, with the
result that much of the technique of the metal engraver
was adopted by the woodcutter, and the old-fashioned
woodcuts were replaced in great measure by what are
properly called wood engravings.

Probably from the earliest times of the use of blocks
in printed books experiments were made in cutting in
soft metal as a substitute for wood. It is often difficult
to be quite certain whether a particular block was wood
or metal, but it is highly probable that any block of
which in the later prints the lines are found to have
bent without breaking, was of metal, and if in addition
we find that the lines, especially of shadings, are fine
and even, and that the block after several years of use
shows neither cracks nor worm-holes, we can be fairly
sure that this was the case. Probably some form of
pewter was used. It is, however, somewhat puzzling
that though at all periods we find occasional examples
of blocks which appear to have been cut in metal
(apart from the *cast* ones which I have already mentioned), and though cutting in pewter was still practised
in the middle of the nineteenth century for such things
as labels, of which many thousands were required to
be printed from one block, such ' metal ' blocks seem
at all times to have been the exception, and that wood,
in spite of its manifest inferiority from the point of
view of durability, seems always to have been preferred.

[1] i. e. as on a horizontal section of a standing tree.

120

Chapter Ten

THE FORMS IN WHICH BOOKS HAVE BEEN ISSUED
TO THE PUBLIC

BINDING as an art or craft lies outside our subject, but inasmuch as the form in which the book is delivered to the purchaser, whether as loose sheets, sewn or cased, often has a bearing on the state in which it has come down to us, it may be useful to consider briefly the custom as to this at different periods.

In the days of manuscripts, binding was of course quite a different art from that of the scribes and was presumably carried on by a different set of men, but it seems probable that the two were associated at least to the extent that a customer ordering a manuscript would generally at the same time give instructions for its binding, and would see it first in its bound state. The accounts for such work which have come down to us often, perhaps generally, include a charge for binding (cf. Madan, *Books in MS.*, pp. 43–4). This seems to indicate that the person who undertook the production of the book employed the binder, whose trade was thus a subordinate one, though it is of course possible that at all times there may have been binders of special note working on their own account and coming into direct touch with the customer.

Many of the early printers were also binders, or at any rate had special binders to work for them who used the printer's own ornament or initials on their books, for we must not assume that a binding bearing these marks necessarily emanated from the printer's own workshop. It has at all times been customary for a book printed *for* a particular person to bear his device, and there is no reason to deny the possibility of a similar practice in the case of binding. That some printers did however run a bindery of their own seems to be certain from the fact that the boards used are found to consist entirely of waste sheets from the press in question.

The point is however of little importance to us. So many of the early printers, including Caxton, de Worde, Pynson, Notary, Reynes, and Berthelet, seem to have had bindings of their own, easily to be identified by stamps or devices, that whether they were the actual binders or not it seems clear that they must have made a practice of selling their books ready bound. The price would probably be made up of a fixed price for the sheets and a variable one for the binding according to the kind selected, as American watches are sold at so much for the movement plus so much for the case. We find that when the price of a book was fixed by authority the binding was generally specified. Thus in 1541 the price of the Great Bible was fixed at 10s. in sheets or 12s. bound—' being trimmed with bullions ' (i. e. metal bosses),[1] and in 1543 the quarto edition of the *Necessary Doctrine*, ' bounde in paper boordes or claspes ', was not to be sold at more than xvi*d*., the octavo editions being priced at 2*d*. or 4*d*. less in the same binding (*Typ. Antiq.*, pp. 445, 572). In the case of the Book of Common Prayer, 1549, the price in sheets is indeed stated. The notice runs (*Typ. Antiq.*, p. 528):

> No maner of persone shall sell this present Booke vnbounde, aboue the price of two shillynges and two pence. And bounde in Forell for .ii.s. xd. and not aboue. And the same bound in Shepes Lether for iii.s. iiii. pence and not aboue. And the same bounde in paste or in boordes, in Calues Lether, not aboue the price of .iiii.s. the pece. God saue the Kyng.

If a purchaser had ordinarily bought the book unbound and the binding had been a separate transaction it would have been enough to specify the price in sheets. At the same time it is quite possible that by this date the increase in the number of booksellers had led to the binding trade being less closely allied

---

[1] See Gairdner and Brodie, *Letters and Papers of Henry VIII*, xvi, p. 365. The book consisted of 530 fols.

to the printing one. There is, at any rate, so far as I can learn, after 1550, no evidence of the association in England of a particular binding with a particular press, and it seems probable that after about this date the volumes were generally distributed in the form of sheets to the booksellers, who had them stitched or bound before selling them. Though the evidence is not all that might be desired, I think that we shall not be far wrong in assuming that in the neighbourhood of 1600 thin pamphlets were ordinarily sold merely stitched or stabbed [1] (i. e. sewn through sideways), in some cases a final blank leaf being folded back over the front to form a cover. A number of slightly thicker books seem to have been issued in a binding of limp parchment or forel, which is so uniform in style that it is difficult not to regard it as a sort of ' publisher's binding '. When such books happened to have a blank leaf at the beginning and end it is quite likely that these would be stuck down as endpapers.[2] When there was no such blank leaf the common method seems to have been to fold and sew a single-leaf end-paper round the first and last gathering, or else to use double end-papers, one to stick down and one as a fly-leaf; these might either be lapped round the end gatherings like the single ones or sewn as part of the book at the beginning and end of it.

Thus at the end of the sixteenth century I think that a person wishing to buy a new book would generally find at the booksellers copies of it ready bound, if it was large or thick in leather, if it was small or thin in

---

[1] Stabbing was prohibited in 1586 for books of more than 80 leaves in folio or 96 in octavo, presumably as interfering with work for the binders (H. G. Aldis in *Camb. Hist. E. Lit.*, iv. 404 ; I do not know the authority for the statement).

[2] A common practice nowadays, and one which gives rise to the bibliographical problem of whether we ought to consider a leaf originally and permanently stuck down to the binding as a leaf of the book or not, and if we do so consider it, whether the leaf consists of two pages or of only one !

forel. At the same time, if he wished, he would doubtless be able to buy the book in sheets and have it bound
in a binding according to his own taste or with others in
a single volume.[1] It seems, however, on the whole
likely that up to this point at least, and perhaps considerably later, the publisher would regard his task,
as a publisher, finished when he had produced the book
in sheets. If he was, as was normally the case, also
a bookseller, he would probably either himself undertake bookbinding or be in close touch with a binder,
and while selling the copies of his book in sheets to
other booksellers he would also bind up a certain
number of copies for sale in his own shop. In binding
these copies he would of course not be acting in his
capacity as publisher, but merely as a bookseller.
Copies of the book purchased from different shops
would be in as many different bindings. There is as
yet no question of a ' publisher's binding '.

Some time between 1600 and 1668 the date of the
first of the *Term Catalogues*, the ' publisher's binding '
seems to have begun, perhaps at first only for the smaller
and cheaper books. With the obvious purpose of
getting both the publisher's and binder's profits on the
works which they issued, those publishers who had
binderies began to bind their books before publication
and to sell them thus bound, instead of in sheets, to
the other booksellers. When the practice started is
not known, but it was evidently in full swing by 1668,
for in the *Term Catalogues* for this and the following

---

[1] There exists *A generall note of the prises for binding of all sorts of
bookes*, printed at London in 1619 (see R. Lemon's *Cat. of Broadsides
in the possession of the Soc. of Antiquaries*, 1866, No. 171). The prices
range from 15s. for a Church Bible in folio gilt, to 2d. for octavo
' grammers, or the like ' in sheep's leather. A quarto Bible cost from
5s. 6d. ' gilt over one way ' to 1s. 2d. ' in hard bords '. The *Book of
Martyrs* in two volumes cost from 12s. to 7s., according to style, and
Raleigh's *History* 3s. 6d. or 2s. 6d. Altogether about 140 different
items are priced. There is unfortunately no indication by whom the
list was issued.

124

eight or nine years we find a very considerable proportion of the larger books described as 'bound'. At
this period books seem seldom, if ever, to have been
offered in more than one form; we do not find alternative prices for 'stitcht' and 'bound' copies.[1]

I have been unable to ascertain how general this
system of publisher's binding was in the later years of
the seventeenth century. Certain considerations suggest that it soon ceased to be usual except for comparatively small and cheap books. From about 1680
we find in the *Term Catalogues* few large books with
prices stated, and hardly any of these are described as
bound. The 'bound' books are almost invariably
small volumes which might, had the binding not been
mentioned, have been supposed to be stitched. It is
possible that this apparent absence of a fixed price for
the larger books means that the cost depended on the
style of binding selected. It is in any case clear that
towards the end of the seventeenth century, owing no
doubt to the work of Samuel Mearne and other excellent
binders of the period, a good deal of attention was paid
to bindings. They had become a matter of individual
thought and taste, especially among those who prided
themselves on their libraries, and many book-buyers
preferred to have their books bound in a style of their
own by their usual binder or bookseller. It would
seem as if for those books regarded as worthy of a good
and permanent binding the normal form of the published volume had again become that of sheets. Cer-

---

[1] In *Term Cat.*, ii. 79 (1684), we find a book advertised as 20*s.*
unbound and 30*s.* bound. In later times alternative bindings were
sometimes offered. Mr. Chapman sends me, as showing the very great
variety that was possible, an advertisement of the publisher Stockdale
issued in 1785 concerning his recently published one-volume Shakespeare. This was offered at the following prices: boards, 15*s.*;
calf, 17*s.* 6*d.*; calf gilt, 18*s.*; russia, 19*s.*; vellum, 21*s.*; morocco
extra, 25*s.*; tortoiseshell, 63*s.* But Stockdale was a bookseller as well
as a publisher, and it was probably in the former capacity that he
prepared this long range of bindings.

tainly this appears to have been the case with works published, as so many were then, and throughout the eighteenth century, ' by subscription '. Subscriptions were, as a rule, for the book in sheets folded (or quires as they were commonly called), and the price of the book was the price in sheets or roughly sewn. An announcement of publication of any work of importance seems generally to take the form that it will be published on such and such a date when the book in quires will be delivered to subscribers at such and such an address.[1] The subscriber might of course, and, I think, generally did, arrange with his bookseller to collect the sheets and bind them for him before delivery to his own library, but this was a matter between customer and bookseller in which the publisher had no concern.

As time went on this way of issuing books either in loose folded sheets or at best roughly sewn within a flimsy cover merely intended to keep them from getting lost on the way to the binder, was naturally found to have disadvantages. It must have been obvious to any intelligent publisher that to be really successful a book should be read and discussed by a very large number of people simultaneously and immediately upon publication. The delay due to the book having to pass through the hands of the private binders before it could be read would inevitably mean a loss of interest. It would be to a certain extent already stale. If any one doubts this I would ask him how often he has read through after binding a work that he purchased in parts, even though he may have given the merest glance at the parts as they arrived. The remedy was of course for the publisher himself to provide some kind of temporary binding, which while naturally it would not render a leather binding unnecessary, would, without adding appreciably to the cost of the book,

[1] See, for example, the announcement of the publication of Theobald's *Shakespeare*, 1734, in Lounsbury's *First Editors of Shakespeare*, p. 444. And cf. *Term Cat.*, ii. 66, 174, 364, 496, &c.

enable it to be read at once by its purchaser. I think there can be little doubt that it was some such consideration as this which led to the general use towards the middle of the eighteenth century of grey or blue boards, with or without a printed label. In the case of non-fictional books these grey paper boards seem to have held the field until the introduction of cloth bindings in 1822.[1] The cloth bindings and the half-cloth ones which were introduced later had printed labels of paper until in 1832 a method was devised of lettering in gold directly on the cloth. After this date the use of printed labels seems gradually to have decreased, though they are found occasionally at all times, especially on books of an antiquarian nature and éditions de luxe which the purchaser was expected to have elaborately bound in leather. Nearer to our own day the possibilities of the paper label as an escape from the conventionality of the ordinary binder's lettering has of course led to a great revival in its use, in spite of its manifest inconvenience and the ease with which such labels are damaged or lost.

The development of the binding of novels was, however, somewhat different. As Mr. Sadleir shows, there arose between 1810 and 1825 a class of middlemen known as novel-distributors whose function was to buy novels in sheets from the publishers and bind them for sale to the booksellers. As each distributor cased the sheets which he had purchased according to his own fancy, it follows that we meet with copies of novels published in the second quarter of the century in what at first sight appear to be several different varieties of ' publishers' bindings ', the fact being of course that they are ' distributors' bindings ' and not those of the publisher at all.

[1] See Mr. Michael Sadleir's excellent article on ' Nineteenth-Century Binding Styles ' in *The Bookman's Journal*, ix. 153 (February 1924), which gives the only connected account of the development of ' publishers' bindings ' that is known to me.

Chapter Eleven

A MISCELLANY. ON DIVISION OF WORK BETWEEN DIF-
FERENT PRINTERS OR COMPOSITORS. THE SIZE OF
EDITIONS OF EARLY BOOKS. BOOK-PRICES. THE
STATIONERS' REGISTER, TERM CATALOGUES, ETC.,
AND DATES OF PUBLICATION. A NOTE ON CENSOR-
SHIP AND COPYRIGHT

On division of work between different Printers or Compositors

IN composing a new book from MS. the normal
course was to begin at the beginning of the text and
proceed straight on to the end, setting up the title-page
and preliminaries last. A single compositor might be
employed, or two, or more, but they would work in
succession, each taking up the composition at the point
at which his predecessor had left off. It is occasionally
possible to infer, from differences in spelling and in
minor details of style in different parts of a book, that
more than one compositor has been engaged upon it,
and this may be of importance if we are considering the
extent to which an author's spelling has been retained in
the printed text, but it does not concern us at present.

Occasionally, however, in the case of large books or
those in which especial haste was necessary, it appears
that the MS. was divided between different compositors
or even different printers, who would then work on
different parts of it simultaneously.[1] Three different
courses may have been followed. The whole execution
of the work, including the actual printing, may have
been divided between two or more printing-houses, the
completed sheets being delivered to the publisher ready
for binding, or the composition may have been done at

---

[1] Examples of books so divided in order to get out a new edition
as quickly as possible are the second quarto of *Every Man out of his
Humour*, cf. Greg in *The Library*, 4th Ser., i. 156–7, and, probably,
the second edition of Nashe's *Unfortunate Traveller*, cf. p. 195, n. 2.

different houses, the pages or formes being brought together at one house for printing, or, lastly, the whole work may have been executed at one printing-house but by two or more sets of compositors and press-men working simultaneously on different parts of the book.

The usual indication of such division of a book between different workmen is that the parts do not follow one another in the normal manner. In some cases the book is found to be made up of two or more incomplete series of signatures.[1] In others, while the series may in general be regular, we find certain signatures omitted, though the text follows on without a break, or extra signatures are inserted, or certain gatherings have a greater or smaller number of leaves than is normal for the book,[2] or we find a page or two of matter which has evidently been inserted as padding to fill up a blank.[3] Such irregularities are of course due to the fact that the amount of matter supplied to the various compositors has not filled exactly the space which was allowed for it. If in addition to such irregularities we find differences in the type or ornaments of the different parts, we may guess that the parts were composed and perhaps printed in different houses, while if the style is identical throughout it is natural to suppose that work on different portions of the book has been proceeding simultaneously at the same house.

There is, I think, no doubt that the first and third

[1] e. g. the Beaumont and Fletcher Folio of 1647. Dr. Greg's detailed investigation of the printing of this in *The Library*, 4th Ser., ii. 109–15, will repay careful study. He concludes that in this book ' we have to do with the work of at least eight compositors, and very probably that of at least eight printing-houses '.

[2] A well-known case is the First Folio of Shakespeare, where sig. g is followed by an eight-leaved gathering signed gg, the normal gathering being six leaves.

[3] As in John Smith's *General History of Virginia*, 1624, where there is no sig. O and the final pages of N contain verses which are quite out of place, see p. 195, note.

of the possible methods mentioned above were resorted to, but a few words must be said as to the second, namely, composition at different houses, the pages or formes being afterwards brought together for printing. It has not infrequently been maintained that jobbing compositors used to set up work in their own homes, bringing the formes to the master-printer to print them. Thus stated the theory is highly improbable,[1] but it does seem possible that composed pages were sometimes brought to other houses for printing. On the leaf following g 1 of the 1647 Folio of Beaumont & Fletcher is a note by the printer which contains the following passage :

> After the *Comedies* and *Tragedies* were wrought off, we were forced (for expedition) to send the *Gentlemens* Verses to severall Printers, which was the occasion of their different Character; but the *Worke* it selfe is one continued Letter . . .

Now when we look at the commendatory verses which precede this note, and to which reference is presumably made, we see that they are indeed in several different sizes of type and might well have been set up by different printers. Examination of the make-up, however, shows that these different types have no correspondence with the signatures. It seems clear therefore that in this case at least the composed matter must have been brought together at one printing-house, and there made up into formes. There is, I think, no evidence that such a practice, which has obvious inconveniences, was at all a common one, but the point— and indeed the whole question of the division of books between two or more printers—requires fuller investigation.

The size of editions of early books

A good deal more information seems to be available as to the size of the editions printed in quite early times than later. Dr. Haebler has collected facts which show

---

[1] Cf. Pollard, *Shakespeare Folios and Quartos*, pp. 131 (foot) to 132.

that before 1500 the number of copies printed ranged from as few as 100 in the earliest times [1] to 1,500, 2,000, and 2,300 in the case of certain service books or books used by the clergy towards the close of the century. He regards 400–500 as a fair average edition for an incunable of the middle period, say 1480–90.

We have no definite knowledge of the size of Caxton's editions, but of certain books printed by Pynson in 1493–4 the edition consisted of 600 copies, and of one, apparently, of 1,000 (cf. H. R. Plomer in *The Library*, 2nd Ser., x. 115–30). According to the Spanish theologian, Antonio Corranus (or de Corro), 300 copies at most had been printed of a tract of his in 1574.[2] Of John Dee's *General and Rare Memorials pertaining to the Art of Navigation*, 1577, as we know from a statement in the dedication, only 100 copies were printed. Of Ralph Brooke's *Catalogue of the Kings, Princes, etc.*, 1619, the edition was 500.[3] These are all the contemporary statements as to numbers printed which I have been able to discover regarding English printing up to 1640.[4] Sir Sidney Lee conjectures that the number printed of the First Folio of Shakespeare's Works was about 600. Professor Pollard thinks 500 more likely, but those are admittedly only guesses. Dr. Greg doubts on economic grounds whether an edition of less than 1,000 would

[1] *Incunabelkunde*, pp. 142–5. At Venice, John of Speyer printed 100 copies of his edition of Cicero, *Epistulae familiares*, in 1469. The editions of Sweynheym and Pannartz at Rome before 1472 averaged 275 copies. Generally speaking, the editions of classics would naturally be smaller than those of Bibles and service books, but an edition of Plato printed in Florence about 1495 reached 1,025 copies.

[2] *Zurich Letters* (Parker Soc.), 2nd Ser., p. 255 and Appendix 156. They were ' depravatissime excusa ' on account of the ignorance of the printer, who knew no Latin. This book must be the *Dialogus theologicus*, printed by T. Purfoot in 1574.   [3] See p. 206.

[4] There are in the *Stationers' Register* a few records of official orders or arrangements between printers in which the number of copies which *may* be printed of certain books are mentioned. In most cases, however, either the circumstances or the books were peculiar, and the entries throw little light on the normal practice.

have shown a profit.[1] As we shall see later,[2] a regulation of the Stationers' Company about 1587 forbade the printing of more than 1,250 or 1,500 copies of any book (with the exception of certain school-books), from one setting of type, the purpose of the regulation being to distribute the work fairly between compositors and printers. We may therefore probably take this as the maximum edition for the closing years of the sixteenth century, but we have no certain knowledge of how long, or how carefully, the rule was observed.[3] Further, in the *Stationers' Register*, we find occasional records [4] of arrangements by which in the case of certain books it would seem that any member of the Company might demand to have a ' reasonable ' number of copies printed for his own benefit, an arrangement which would seem likely to cause the limitation to be of no effect.

It is evident that it is only some such custom or rule as that which we have mentioned intended to distribute work fairly between compositors and pressmen that would set any maximum to the number of copies printed of a book, and that when such rules fell into disuse a printer or publisher would print as many copies from one setting-up of type as he could hope to sell within a reasonable time, weighing the initial outlay on paper or machinery, and the risk of destruction of stock by damp, rats, and fire, against the cost of re-setting. When, therefore, we come to later

---

[1] *Studies in the First Folio*, pp. 155–6.   [2] See p. 214 note.

[3] Miss Albright (*Dramatic Publication*, p. 373) notes that the [maximum] size of the ordinary impression was raised from 1,250 to 1,500 or 2,000 on 16 Nov. 1635 (*Stationers' Register*, iv. 22), and that ' larger editions were sometimes issued in piratical printing, as, for example, in the case of Wither's *Motto*, pirated in two issues of 3,000 copies each, in 1621 '.

[4] See, for example, *S. R.*, ii. 307 (1576), cf. 667 (1594). The whole business is rather mysterious. Those availing themselves of the arrangement presumably provided their own paper and pressmen, but did they pay nothing towards the composition ?

times, to the Restoration and the eighteenth century, we may assume the practice to have been similar to that of to-day. Books expected to have a popular sale would be printed in large editions, while expensive books would be produced in much smaller numbers. It is possible to put together a certain number of details of editions of particular books, but they tell us little save that, on the whole, considering the much smaller reading-public, the sale of good work by well-known writers seems to have been surprisingly large and rapid.

Book-prices

If we except the very earliest days of printing, when the fact that printed books had only to compete with the much more costly manuscripts would tend to high or at least variable prices (for the sellers would naturally ask whatever they thought they could get for them), it appears that, in England at least, the normal price of new books reckoned in terms of the cost of living has been remarkably constant, at least up to 1914.[1] From about 1580, perhaps a good deal earlier, the cost of a new play seems always to have been about the same as that of a good plain dinner.[2] At present the cost of books is relatively less, as the post-war increase in price has been less in books than in almost any other goods.

For the fifteenth [3] and early sixteenth centuries we have indeed little information as to the prices charged

[1] I should, perhaps, make it clear that I am only referring to new books purchased at the time of issue, and not to the vast number of cheap reprints, which, during the last two centuries, have made literature accessible to the widest public.

[2] The normal price of the Shakespearian quarto is said to have been 6d. sewn ; that of new plays in 1914 was generally 2s. 6d. in paper covers or 3s. 6d. bound. The ratio of the cost of living at 1600 and at 1914 is generally given as from 1 : 5 to 1 : 7.

[3] A good deal of information as to the price of foreign incunabula is collected in Haebler's *Inkunabelkunde*, pp. 149–57, but the prices even when accurately known in the currency of their own time and place are often difficult to convert into modern values.

for books to the public in this country, and such as we have is often difficult to interpret, for the occasional records of prices paid which we find in accounts or noted in the books themselves hardly ever tell us anything as to their condition at the time, whether new or second-hand, bound or unbound, and are therefore of little use. Towards the middle of the century we find prices fixed by authority for certain religious books,[1] but these were probably priced at a lower rate than secular works, so again we must be careful how we take them as a standard. When, however, we approach the end of the century we find a certain number of prices which seem to indicate that in the case of ordinary small books, pamphlets, and the like, a book of 10 or 12 sheets (80–96 pages in 4to, or 160 to 192 in 8vo) would normally be priced at a shilling ; one of 20 to 24 sheets at 2s.[2] Quartos of plays, however, though they often ran to 10 or 11 sheets, seem to have generally cost only 6d. We may suppose that, then as now, popular books of which a ready sale was expected would be cheaper than those of more restricted appeal.

The *Term Catalogues*[3] often state the prices of books. In the earlier part of the period (1668 onwards) the larger folios run from 8s. to 16s., generally ' bound '. Plays in quarto, sometimes specifically described as ' stitcht ', were 1s. By the end of the century, however, prices had risen somewhat and plays were usually 1s. 6d., operas and other entertainments remaining at 1s.

---

[1] See p. 122.

[2] These figures are derived from such notes as I have been able to collect and are at best no more than a rough approximation. The whole subject needs investigation. The prices at which Richard Robinson sold copies of certain of his religious works are given in his MS. *Eupolemia,* printed in full by G. McG. Vogt in *Studies in Philology,* xxi. 629–48. It may be noted that the price is in the neighbourhood of 1d. per sheet, which would suggest for the First Folio of Shakespeare (227 sheets) a price of 19s.

[3] See pp. 138 and 125.

During the first part of the eighteenth century book-prices seem to have remained stationary, a slight rise then occurred, and towards the end of the century the normal price for a play would seem to have been 2*s.* The subject of book-prices in the eighteenth century is, however, too complicated to be dealt with briefly, for on the one hand the formats in which books were issued were very various, and there were great differences in the quality of printing and paper, which led to a wide range of prices,[1] and on the other hand publishers had begun to realize the possibilities of large editions at popular prices and cheap reprints of successful books were becoming much more frequent. In fact conditions were approaching those of the present day.

In the late eighteenth and the early nineteenth century, books seem to have become somewhat dearer; novels were in general issued at a high price, and a good many elaborate and expensive editions were produced for wealthy patrons of literature. The custom of issuing novels in three volumes at from 18*s.* or 20*s.* in the first quarter of the century to 31*s.* 6*d.* in the third quarter was no doubt in the main the publishers' riposte to the growing habit of borrowing such books from the circulating libraries rather than buying them.

The Stationers' Register, Term Catalogues, &c., and dates of publication

The ' Registers ' of the Stationers' Company contain, among other documents of importance in the history of printing, lists of ' entries ' of books from the year 1557 onwards.[2] These entries of course give us most

---

[1] Comparison with earlier periods is also rendered difficult by the growing habit of issuing books in some form of binding, the style of which of course affected the price.

[2] With the exception of the years 1571-6, the entries for which seem to be lost. See *A Transcript of the Registers of the Company of Stationers of London, 1554-1640*, edited by Edward Arber, 1875-94,

valuable information as to the date of the original publication of books entered,[1] but there are a number of difficulties in regard to their exact interpretation—indeed the purpose and implications of the entry may have varied somewhat at different times—and they must be used with caution. Briefly it may be said that the entering of a book in the register was of the nature of the staking of a claim by a particular printer or publisher to the right of printing the book or of getting it printed. Presumably the entries were open for the inspection of the trade, and if they were not challenged the enterer had an absolute right in perpetuity to the printing of the book, and this right would in ordinary circumstances be upheld by the officers and Court of the Company. Exactly how much more was implied, whether in order for an entry to be accepted it was necessary for the enterer to exhibit the authorization of the official licensers (where this was needed), is an open question.[2] The important thing is that the entry was essentially a trade matter concerning the rights in the book entered of one member of the Company as against others, and had, primarily at least, no reference to the abstract right of any one to put the book into print. In other words, the force of the entry was really

5 volumes (vol. 5 containing indexes, &c.). This contains all the book-entries now extant for the period covered, together with most of the other matter from the Registers, the principal exception being certain decisions of the Court of the Company which Professor Arber was not permitted to print. Some of this omitted matter had already been printed by Herbert in his edition of Ames's *Typographical Antiquities*. The Book-Entries (only) are continued in *A Transcript of the Registers of the Worshipful Company of Stationers for 1640–1708*. Privately printed [for the Roxburghe Club], 1913–14, 3 vols. [Transcribed by H. R. Plomer.]

[1] 'Original publication' only, for later editions were normally not entered unless they involved a transfer of rights to another publisher and often not then. Many books were not entered at all.

[2] At certain periods we find entries being refused if the book had not been previously licensed, or stipulations that a licence should be obtained before printing; but there seems to be no general rule.

negative. No *other* member of the Company might print it (and in general no one not a member might print at all) ; the entry did not necessarily imply that the printing of the book was sanctioned by the Licensing Authorities, nor that the enterer had any legal right to the possession of the copy.

For our present purpose the chief point is the relation between the date of entry and the date of publication. We sometimes find it assumed that the two are identical. This is certainly an error, and so far as is known the two dates have no definite connexion. A number of entries seem never to have been followed by publication ; in other cases a year or more elapsed before the book came out. The most that they really tell us is that a book was in existence or at any rate seriously contemplated [1] at the date of entry.

All it is really possible to say is that, as a general rule, a book was entered *before* publication. Whether it was ever entered after publication,[2] and whether the entry was as a rule on receipt of the MS. from the author, or from the licensees, or on completion of printing, we do not know—or indeed whether there was any rule on the subject at all. The natural supposition would be that a book for the printing of which arrangements had already been made would be entered as soon as a licence had been obtained, but in one or two instances the entry would seem to have been immediately before publication.[3]

[1] Occasionally a book in Latin or a foreign language was entered as to be translated. In such cases several months' interval might elapse before the translation was ready for the press.

[2] The entry of *The Spanish Tragedy* on 6 October 1592 by a printer who seems to have already printed the play several months earlier (cf. Greg in *The Library*, 4th Ser., vi. 49–52) is a special case, for the entry appears to have been in anticipation of a future edition, and to prevent piracy by another printer, rather than in respect of the edition already produced.

[3] e. g. T. Nicholas's *Discovery and Conquest of Peru* was entered S. R. on 23 Jan. 1580/1, and the title-page is dated Feb. 6, 1581.

In the year 1668 began the issue of the so-called
'Term Catalogues ',[1] the first of which appeared under
the title of *Mercurius Librarius*,[2] or *A Catalogue of Books
Printed and Published in Michaelmas Term, 1668.* The
originator of the scheme was a bookseller named John
Starkey, who added at the end of the first issue a note
to the effect that 'A Catalogue, thus printed, is intended
to be continued and published at the end of every
Term, if this find encouragement; it being the First
Essay of this kind '. The original series was continued
until the eighth number (Mids. 1670), by which time,
in consequence of the publishers' ' unreasonable demands for inserting the Titles of Books ' and their
' imperfect Collecting, omitting many; and refusing
all under 1sh. Price ', a rival series had been started by
the ' Booksellers of London '. Starkey then seems to
have dropped out, and from this date the Catalogue
was continued regularly[3] by the Booksellers until
1709, with one or more later issues (one in 1711), four
times a year, appearing normally in February, May,
June, and November.[4] The entries are classified under
such headings as Divinity, History, Poems, Plays,
Reprints, &c., and give as a rule the full title, size, the
publisher's name, and often the price.[5] Advertisements
of forthcoming books are frequently added at the end.
The *Term Catalogues* are of great value in that they
apparently contain only books that were actually published, though in some cases the titles appeared in the
catalogue a short time before the actual date of

[1] Reprinted as *The Term Catalogues, 1668–1709 (1711)*, edited
by Professor Edward Arber, 1903–6, 3 vols.
 [2] ' Mercurius Librarius ' was dropped from the title after the first
series.
 [3] No issue for Michaelmas Term, 1695, is known, and it is possible
that none appeared.
 [4] There are varieties in the imprint and the whole range of issues
falls into six different series, but the plan remained in essentials unchanged.
 [5] The proportion of priced books varies much at different times.

publication.[1] On the other hand it is to be remembered that they were probably only intended to include books of more or less importance. Ephemeral and popular literature seems generally to have been ignored.

Information as to dates of issue may sometimes be derived from the habit of certain book-buyers of writing in their books the date of purchase. This at least gives a forward date for publication, but it may in certain cases afford more exact information than this, as in the well-known example of the great collection of Civil War tracts made between 1641 and 1662 by the bookseller George Thomason, and now in the British Museum. Thomason collected nearly 23,000 tracts and, to the great benefit of future historians, wrote on most of them the exact date of publication.[2] Other collectors at various times have followed the same practice but, there is, I believe, no other collection of ephemeral literature in which it has been carried out with anything like the same care or which contains anything like the same number of items.

For the eighteenth century from the year 1710 onwards there is no regular guide.[3] Monthly lists of new books were published from 1731 in *The Gentleman's Magazine*, but these were apparently in no way official and it is not clear how far they can be trusted. More or less exact information can often be obtained from advertisements in the press, especially the announcements of the publication of subscription books, though it must not be forgotten that announcements of works ' published this day ' are liable to be repeated in the same words at intervals extending over two or three weeks. There is also, of course, so much more literary

[1] *Term. Cat.*, ed. Arber, vol. i, p. xi.

[2] See F. Madan's notes on the Thomason Collection in *Bibliographica*, iii. 291 ff., and the *Catalogue of the Thomason Tracts* by G. K. Fortescue, 1908.

[3] For various short-lived attempts at book-catalogues see Arber's ' Contemporary Printed Lists of Books produced in England ' in *Bibliographica*, iii. 173–91.

gossip in letters, diaries, &c., of this period that in the case of any book of importance there is a great chance of discovering the date of publication from these.

For the nineteenth century we have the *English Catalogue of Books*, of which there exists a complete series beginning with the catalogue for the years 1835–63, published in 1864, the earlier years being included in a volume for 1800–36, compiled from various catalogues, the names of which will be found in the preface, and published in 1914. This last gives, when ascertainable, the month of publication as well as the year, as is done by volumes of more recent date ; that for 1835–63 gives the year alone. The series is continued to the present day by yearly volumes the contents of which are every few years rearranged into a single alphabet.

A note on Censorship and Copyright

Both these matters at times concern the bibliographer, but as neither is closely connected with my main subject, I must limit myself to a brief note.

A chapter on ' The Regulation of the Book Trade in the Sixteenth Century ', included by Professor A. W. Pollard in his *Shakespeare's Fight with the Pirates*, 1917 (2nd edition, 1920), gives the best short account of the official censorship during that period.[1] A few other details will be found in the introductions to Duff's *Century of the English Book-Trade* and to *A Dictionary of Printers, &c.*, 1558–1640, both issued by the Bibliographical Society. Most of the documents bearing on the history of the censorship up to 1640 are printed in Arber's *Stationers' Register*. So far as I am aware the story of the official regulation of printing during the Commonwealth period has not yet been fully worked out, but the post-Restoration time has

[1] See also Miss E. M. Albright's recently issued *Dramatic Publication in England, 1580–1640*, chapter ii of which brings together a great deal of information on the subject.

been dealt with by Professor Pollard in ' Some Notes on the History of Copyright in England, 1662–1774 ' in *The Library*, 4th Ser., iii. 97–114, which discusses the question of licensing and official control as well as that of copyright itself.

There is only one thing that I need say on the subject of censorship, and that is that students should beware of taking the numerous enactments concerning it too seriously. Had they been effective the control of printing throughout the whole period, from 1538, when what is apparently the first proclamation instituting a censorship was issued, down to the beginning of the Civil War, would have been indeed strict, but there is still much to be cleared up as regards the way in which the control actually worked and the extent to which the various orders were obeyed. Certainly they were not all effective, or so many of them would not have been needed. I think that study of the subject leaves one with the impression that while little attention was paid to the letter of the regulations, save in the period immediately following a new order, their spirit was on the whole fairly well observed. This observance was, no doubt, mainly due to the officials of the Stationers' Company, though we may guess that these were moved rather by their desire for a quiet life than by any particular sympathy with the regulations themselves. They had, I think, a shrewd notion of what books were likely to be offensive to the authorities, and also of which of the members of the Company were likely to print or publish such books, and perhaps without assuming any formal responsibility in the matter, put difficulties in the way of dangerous literature by insisting on seeing some authority before accepting entry in the Register and in other ways. In a close corporation like the Stationers' Company public opinion counts for a great deal, and there was always a possibility of further and more oppressive legislation which might not distinguish between the innocent and the guilty. It seems to me that on the whole the trade did its best to keep on good terms with the authorities ; but this is only a general impression : there was perhaps a good deal of difference in its attitude at different times.

Copyright and censorship have really nothing whatever to do with one another, but one kind of copyright, namely, the claim of the first person who has put into print and issued a work to the public to the sole right of producing further editions, is so much involved with the regulation of the trade through the medium of the Stationers' Company that almost all who have dealt with either subject have found it impossible to avoid dealing with the other at the same time. What we now term ' copyright ', namely, the *author's* right [1] in his work is quite another matter, entirely independent of official control.

The publisher's rights were, as we have already seen,[2] effectively safeguarded, so far as London printing was concerned, by the restriction of printing (with certain exceptions) to members of the Company and by the system of entry of publications to a particular member. There were of course occasional infringements and a certain number of disputes, but on the whole the system seems to have worked well and until towards the end of the seventeenth century there is little indication of piracy on a large scale.[3]

[1] Even if an author makes over his whole rights in a book to a publisher the rights are still, of course, derived from him. No person can now acquire a right in a work by *publishing* it. The essential difference between modern copyright and the sixteenth- to seventeenth-century reprinting rights, which, without being conferred by legislation, had arisen from the internal regulations of the Company, does not seem always to be fully appreciated by writers on the subject.

[2] See pp. 135-7.

[3] The troubles in which John Wolf and others were involved about 1581 were not, I think, an attempt to defraud other members of the Company by pirating their property, but a serious protest, with which many members were in sympathy, against the grants by the Queen of monopolies in certain classes of books.

The history of author's rights in England seems never to have been completely worked out. Most of the legal historians concern themselves little, if at all, with the position of affairs before the first Act establishing a limited copyright in the modern sense in 1710.[1] Previous to this there had been merely a vague common-law right[2] to the sole benefit of one's own intellectual productions, including the printing and publication of them, but it is very doubtful how far this was realized either by author or publisher, or whether either would have contemplated the possibility of an action at law for the maintenance of such rights. These seem in practice to have been completely overshadowed by the powers of the official censors and of the Privy Council. It is probable that in the event of any gross infringement, actual or proposed, of an author's rights, an appeal to the authorities would have resulted in pressure being brought to bear on the delinquent, which, even if not in strict accordance with legal forms, would have been difficult to resist.[3]

The net result, so far as we can judge by the absence of serious complaint, seems to have been that little injustice was done.[4] The selling value of ' rights ' in most kinds of literary work was small, but it is probable

[1] See, however, an article by W. F. Wyndham Brown on ' The Origin and Growth of Copyright ' in *The Law Magazine* for November 1908. Also Augustine Birrell's *Seven Lectures on the Law and History of Copyright in England*, 1899.

[2] In later times disputed. There seems to be singularly little discussion of rights in the matter before the eighteenth century.

[3] The classic instance is the stopping of the proposed publication of Sidney's *Arcadia* in 1586. See the letter of Fulke Greville, printed in Arber's *English Garner*, i. 488–9.

[4] There were, however, it seems, bitter complaints on the part of the theatrical companies against the publication of plays belonging to their repertory. But this was not quite on a par with an ordinary infringement of copyright. What really concerned them were the dramatic rights alone, and they apparently considered that these were reduced in value by publication in book form, a belief which still survives in the theatrical profession at the present day.

that, at any rate after about 1580, those authors who were not above such ways of making money were generally paid by the booksellers for the right to print their work. When an author complains of publication without his consent, the chief point of his grievance seems generally to have been that his work was printed from a faulty manuscript, not that he had not been paid for it. At the same time we must remember that in view of the feeling which evidently existed until towards the end of the sixteenth century, that it was not quite correct for a gentleman to sell the fruits of his literary invention, it is quite possible that some authors might prefer to pass over this aspect of the matter in silence.

It is not my intention here to touch upon the copyright disputes of the eighteenth century, which arose in great measure from the claim made by certain of the larger booksellers to perpetual copyright in Shakespeare, Milton, and other classical authors whose work dated from before the Act of 1710. The story is a complicated one and cannot be summarized briefly, while the questions at issue were mainly legal and concern the historian of the book-trade rather than the bibliographer. The main facts of the dispute have recently been well set forth in an article by Mr. A. S. Collins on ' Some Aspects of Copyright from 1700 to 1780 ', in *The Library*, 4th Ser., vii. 67–81.

PART TWO

Chapter One

SOME POINTS OF BIBLIOGRAPHICAL TECHNIQUE. THE
DESCRIPTION OF A BOOK. REFERENCES TO PASSAGES
IN EARLY BOOKS

WE must now pass from the study of books in
general to the question of how we are to describe
those books with which we have to deal—their material
form, I mean, for we have no concern with their literary
contents—and thence to what is the most important
part of our subject, namely the interpretation of the
evidence which their material make-up affords. I have
already in chapter iii of Part i briefly explained the
more common bibliographical terms, and we shall now
see how they are used in describing a book.

Firstly, let it be said that there is no such thing as
a standard bibliographical description applicable to
all cases, for the best form to use depends upon a
variety of circumstances. We must consider—

1. The purpose of the description. Are we describing the book as an example of the art of printing or
as the material form of a piece of literature? The points
which one must note will be very different in the two
cases.

2. The date of the book. An incunable (i. e. a book
printed during the fifteenth century, the cradle period
of printing) requires to be described in quite a different
way from a book printed in the seventeenth century,
and that again from a modern work. Any attempt to
treat books of all periods in the same fashion will
quickly be found to be impracticable and to lead only
to complications and inconsistencies.[1]

[1] The student would do well to read and ponder carefully the article
entitled 'Some Points in Bibliographical Description' by A. W.

If, however, we exclude modern books for the moment from our consideration we can perhaps discover a fairly satisfactory working formula, or at least one which will safeguard its user from the charge of bibliographical ignorance or insufficiency.

The usual bibliographical description of a book includes the following :

1. The title, copied from the title-page more or less minutely and fully according to the purpose of the description, but always giving the place of printing or issue, the name of the printer and publisher, and date, or as many of these particulars as are found there. To the transcript of the title may be added a note of any border, ornament or device (printer's or otherwise) which occurs on it.
2. The colophon, if any.
3. The format, as folio, quarto, &c.
4. The collation, i.e. a list of the signatures with indications of the number of leaves in the various gatherings.

To these four essential items certain other notes may, for various reasons, be added. Thus we may note the catchwords on certain selected pages. These may serve to identify the edition when there are two or more in the same year or undated. We may give a list of the principal contents, stating what the preliminary matter is and on what pages the various parts of this and the text itself begin. We may note the occurrence of ornaments or woodcuts of importance or of inserted plates or anything else of interest. In a few cases it may be necessary to describe the types used and identify them by reference to some standard classification, but this will seldom be wanted in ' literary ' work. Lastly we may, and as a rule should,

Pollard and W. W. Greg in the *Transactions of the Bibliographical Society*, ix. 31–52, with an appendix on ' Degressive Bibliography ' by F. Madan.

at any rate in the case of a rare book, note the whereabouts of the particular copy which we are describing, adding, if possible, the press-mark when it is in a public library.

Let us now take the four essential items in succession:

1. *The Title-page.* The young student may be advised to notice how the title-pages of works of the class with which he is dealing are transcribed in standard bibliographies of recent date and to follow the methods used, with such modifications as seem useful in view of his particular purpose. At the same time he should take care never to elaborate his work beyond need, for if he does he will almost certainly, sooner or later, land himself in difficulties ; and he should remember that a transcript of a title, however full and careful, is but a compromise. He cannot, whatever he does, give *all* the information that may be derived from an examination of the book itself ; nor can he foresee exactly what information may be needed by a worker who consults his book. Even a photographic facsimile will not satisfy a bibliographer who wants to know the watermark of the paper !

Transcripts of titles may be of many degrees of elaboration, but for our present purpose it will suffice to give two examples, one as full as is generally wanted, the other abbreviated, but so far as it goes correct. Let us take the title-page of the translation of Cornelius Agrippa's treatise, *De Incertitudine et Vanitate Scientiarum et Artium,* by James Sandford, 1569.[1] A complete transcript of the ordinary kind will run as follows :

[within a rule, within a border of type ornaments [2]] ¶ Henrie Cornelius A- | grippa, *of the Vanitie and* | vncertaintie of

[1] I take this book not as being of importance but because the title happens to include most of the points with which I wish to deal.

[2] By this I mean that the letterpress of the title is surrounded by a rule, and outside this rule there is a border of type ornaments. When, as here, two things are placed round the letterpress, bibliographers differ as to which should be mentioned first. Some work from without

Artes and | 𝔖𝔠𝔦𝔢𝔫𝔠𝔢𝔰, 𝔈𝔫𝔤𝔩𝔦𝔰𝔥𝔢𝔡 𝔟𝔶 | *Ia. San. Gent.* | *Eccle-*
ſiaſtes. 1. | All is but moſte vaine Vanitie : and | all is moſt
vaine, and but plaine | Vanitie. | ¶ *Seene and allowed according*
to | *the order appointed.* | ¶ *Imprinted at London, by* | *Henry*
Wykes dwelling in Fleete ſtreat, | at the ſigne of the blacke |
𝔈𝔩𝔢𝔭𝔥𝔞𝔫𝔱. | ANNO. 1569.

This is, I think, the fulleſt form of transcript (apart
from type-facsimile or photographic facsimile) which
is of any use. Attempts have been made to indicate
the spaces between lines when the type is not set solid
by describing it as equivalent to so many lines of text.[1]
This is obviously only possible when the whole title
is in type of the same size (only usual in quite early
work), for in what units shall we measure the space
occurring between, say, a line of english and a line
of long primer ?[2] If for any reason it is necessary in
a special case to indicate the disposal of the text on
a title-page it is best to give approximate measurements
(descender to ascender) in mm. But for various
reasons exact measurement in such cases is difficult.

The following points may be noted in this transcript :
(*a*) In the original several sizes of type are used. These
differences are ignored, as must be done in a transcript
of this kind. If one wishes to preserve the distinctions
of size the page must be set out as in the original, and
than this method a photographic facsimile would hardly
be more expensive. As a result the last word ' ANNO '
looks as if it were the most important on the page.
In the original it is in very small type and quite un-

inwards and would write ' [Border of type ornaments enclosing rule
enclosing title] ', others taking the actual title as the starting-point, as
I have done, work outwards from it. On the whole it seems to me
that if we place the description of the framework within brackets, the
latter is the more logical method.

[1] See p. 37 of the article on ' Bibliographical Description ', referred
to above (p 145, n.).

[2] Leads are of course *now* always described in terms of pica as a
unit (six to pica, ten to pica, &c.), but this is beside the point, as the
spaces in early times were generally lines of quads.

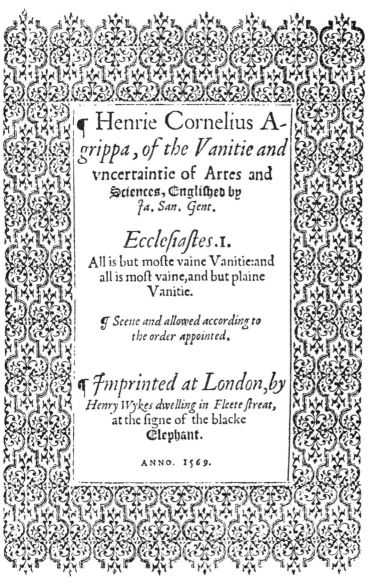

¶ Henrie Cornelius A-
grippa, *of the Vanitie and*
vncertaintie of Artes and
Sciences, Englished by
Ja. San. Gent.

*Ecclesiastes.*1.
All is but moste vaine Vanitie:and
all is moft vaine,and but plaine
Vanitie.

¶ *Scene and allowed according to*
the order appointed.

¶ *Imprinted at London,by*
Henry Wykes dwelling in Fleete ftreat,
at the figne of the blacke
Elephant.

ANNO. 1569.

FIG. 15. Title-page of James Sandford's translation of Agrippa's
De Incertitudine et Vanitate Scientiarum et Artium

obtrusive. The rule is that if the capitals in a line are all the same size (whatever that size may be) they are transcribed as capitals. If, however, *in one line* both capitals and small capitals (or two sizes of capitals) are used, the distinction is preserved.[1] Thus suppose that in this title-page the word ' Elephant ', instead of being in black letter were printed ' ELEPHANT ', all except the first letter being in the same type as the ANNO below, the transcript would run ' ELEPHANT. | ANNO. 1569 '.[2] This seems inconsistent, but there is really no inconsistency when we remember that in a transcript of this kind *each line of the original is considered as an independent unit.* In any case the inconsistency is unavoidable, for to try to preserve any relationship between the various lines of type would only lead to endless difficulties.

(*b*) Words in black letter in the original are represented by black letter in the transcript. Where black letter cannot be provided, a heavy-faced roman type is sometimes used, or a rule or a row of dots is printed below the words in black letter.[3]

(*c*) The sign | indicates the end of the original lines. A difficulty often arises in dealing with books of the late sixteenth and seventeenth centuries when it was very common for a number of rules, sometimes single, sometimes double or treble, to be run across the title-page (see p. 94). It is necessary to indicate these in a full form of transcript, and there is no simple or convenient way of doing it. Some indicate a single rule by doubling the |, some by printing a horizontal

---

[1] Provided that the use of two sizes seems to be intentional. Mere wrong-fount letters are generally ignored.

[2] An even more awkward result is produced when a word in small caps. with a capital is divided, e. g. ' LON- | DON ', for then if there are no full capitals in the second line we must transcribe as ' LON- | DON '. This looks very odd, but I do not see that we can avoid it.

[3] Both methods have their disadvantages ; the long ſ is generally not available in heavy-faced type (though the f can be adapted) ; while the second method can only be used if the type is leaded.

rule between two line division marks |—|, some by the words ' rule ' or ' double rule ' thus | [double rule] |. The first method is convenient if we have only single rules to deal with, but seems inconsistent as it omits the second line-division mark. One ought, I think, if one follows this method, to print ||| for one rule, |||| for two rules, and so on, which is cumbersome and ugly.

A fairly satisfactory system, if one had only to deal with books after about 1550, would be to use sloping lines throughout for the line divisions, and superior figures to indicate more than one rule. Thus in our collation above—*Ia. San. Gent.* / | / *Ecclefiaftes.* 1 . . . *Vanitie.* / |³ / ¶ *Seene* . . . would indicate one rule below the translator's name and three below the quotation. A half-length rule ı would indicate any rule shorter than one running right across the page (rare until post-Restoration times). In early books the sloping line cannot, however, be used as a division mark on account of its occurrence as a sign of punctuation.

A student will be well advised, if he is dealing with books of a period when these cross rules are rare, to indicate them by the word ' rule ' ; when dealing with books in which they are frequent, to work out the system which seems most convenient for his particular purpose rather than to follow any particular model.

(*d*) Ornaments, printer's devices, cuts, &c., are usually mentioned, and when possible described, thus ' [ornament: a mask with rings 23 × 18 mm.¹] '.

---

¹ When giving measurements of ornaments or devices of irregular outline, the measurements should be those of the smallest rectangular parallelogram which will contain them with its lines parallel to the edges of the type-page. The *vertical* measurement should be given first.

It may be worth while to warn beginners in bibliography that they must be prepared for considerable variations, amounting to 4 or 5 per cent. linear measurement, in the size of prints from the same block. Owing to the paper being printed damp, the print is when dry somewhat smaller than the block ; how much smaller depends on the dampness of the paper and on its quality. Further, as paper when damped is

If the device or ornament occurs in any standard collection a reference is advisable, thus : ' printer's device (Silvestre, 237) '.

(*e*) The odd signs such as paragraph marks, asterisks, &c., occurring on title-pages, are sometimes a difficulty as they often cannot be exactly reproduced in the fount of type used. In such cases it is perhaps best to normalize, using ¶ for *all* paragraph marks, whatever their exact form, * for *all* stars, and so on. The curious early paragraph mark like a reversed D with a solid centre can also be represented by ¶.

(*f*) A special difficulty occurs in connexion with italic *J*, as in the ' *Ja. San.*' and ' *Jmprinted*' on p. 149. In a book of this date these *J*'s are not *J*'s, but merely the ' swash ' form of *I*.[1] We can, if our type permits it, keep all ' swash ' forms occurring in the original. This is sometimes useful for distinction, and has the merit of simplicity. If we do this, distinguishing *M* and *M*, *T* and *T*, we may undoubtedly keep *J* when it occurs. If, however, we do not keep the swash letters, we logically ought not, I think, to keep *J*, but should substitute *I*, until we reach the period when the two letters came to be used separately. Whether, however, it is wise to bother about logic in the matter I am not at all sure. Some invariably transliterate this *J* by *J* at any period, regarding it perhaps as the simpler way, but ' *Jmprinted* ' (in spite of the modern Swiss practice in names like 'Jmhof') seems to me awkward and from every point of view indefensible.

(*g*) Two other difficulties are met with sufficiently often to deserve mention, though I must simply record them and can make no suggestion for dealing with them. One concerns the diphthong Œ, often used in COMŒDIE and TRAGŒDIE. Generally the

liable to expand unequally in the two directions, with and across the wire-marks, it follows that two prints from a block may have the same height but different widths, and vice versa, a fact which is somewhat disconcerting when one first comes across it.   [1] Cf. p. 295.

printer had no digraph, and if the words are set in the
ordinary manner one can transcribe with the separate
letters OE. When, however, as not infrequently
happens, especially in seventeenth-century titles, the
words are spaced out with hair spaces, the printer
sometimes puts no space between O and E, printing
'C O M OE D I E', thus showing that he *meant* a
digraph. Are we then to represent the word by
'COMOEDIE' or 'COMŒDIE'?

Another difficulty occurs in connexion with VV
used for W. Of course when the letters are just
ordinary separate V's one would transcribe them as
such, but sometimes a limb of one of the two V's was
evidently rubbed down, so that the two letters, though
actually separate, really form one. When we can be
certain of this, I think we should logically use W, but
we cannot always be certain whether we have a V that
is damaged or fails to print, or one purposely altered.

A simpler form of transcript would run

¶Henrie Cornelius Agrippa, of the Vanitie and vncertaintie
of Artes and Sciences, Englished by Ia. San. Gent. Ecclesiastes . 1 . [quotation]. . . Imprinted at London, by Henry
Wykes . . . Anno. 1569.

In this we do not give the line divisions, and when
these are not given it is inadvisable to show the differences of types (italic, roman, &c.), as if we do this we
have to give such forms as *Agrippa*, which look
absurd. In this form hyphens at ends of lines are
usually omitted, i. e. Agrippa, not A-grippa.[1]

Lines in capitals are, in such simplified transcripts,
represented by l.c., with caps where regarded as
necessary. This question of caps is a difficulty, for
suppose we have a line in caps such as ' OF THE

___

[1] Even in simplified forms of transcript it is always well, if space
can be allowed, to quote a printer's or publisher's address when this
is given. It is also, I think, safer to keep the punctuation of the original,
however awkward it may appear, though many bibliographers seem to
regard this as unnecessary. Omissions should always be shown by dots.

VANITIE AND VNCERTAINTIE', it would be natural in our transcription to capitalize 'Vanitie' and 'Vncertaintie' alone. But seeing that our capitals in such a case have no authority and merely mark the words which seem to us most important, should we not, in a transcript of this type, equally give a capital to 'vncertaintie' when transcribing the title given on page 149, though in the original it begins with a lower-case letter. The point must, I think, be left to the judgement of the transcriber. Personally I should be inclined in a simplified title to make the change from caps to small at will, but never to make the reverse change from a small letter to a capital; though I could not defend the rule as logical.

One important point to be observed is the use of v and u. As is mentioned elsewhere (Appendix 3), until the differentiation of the use of u and v according to sound, V was the normal capital of both u and v, lower-case u being used medially and v initially. Whenever, therefore, we replace a capital V other than an initial one by a lower-case letter we must use u. Thus the word 'VINVM' on a title may be transcribed as 'Vinum' or 'vinum', never as 'vinvm'. In the same way, if we ever have occasion to replace a l.c. spelling by an u.c. one we must follow the rule and transform such a word as 'Pasquil' to 'PASQVIL', not to 'PASQUIL'.

2. *The Colophon.* This is usually given in full after the title, specifying the page in which it occurs, thus:

> [Colophon on X7^v] *Imprinted* | *at London by Richard Graf-* | *ton, printer to the Kynges* | *Maiesty.* | Anno. | M.D.L.II.

or in a simpler form without indicating differences of type. A colophon should always be noticed, if there is one. It is also, I think, desirable to record the occurrence of a recognized printer's device (even without a verbal imprint) at the end of a book, as this often appears to take the place of a colophon.

3. *The Format.* For the method of determining the 'format' of a book, see chapter ii. The abbreviations in general use are :

Fol. = folio ; 4° or 4to or Q or Q° = quarto ; 8° or 8vo = octavo ; 12mo, 16mo, 32mo, 64mo, or 12°, etc. = duodecimo, sexto-decimo, tricesimo-secundo, and sexagesimo-quarto. For folio 2° has, I believe, sometimes been used. A broadside or single sheet is generally indicated by b.s. or s.s. We might perhaps, as I have suggested elsewhere, denote it by 1°.

4. *The Collation.* The collation of all but quite modern books is usually given in some such form as the following :

$$*^2, **^6, A-Z^6, Aa-Bb^6, Cc^4.$$

This signifies that the book described consists of two leaves of the signature * (probably if the first is the title, it is unsigned, the second being signed * 2), six leaves of signature ** (probably the first three or four are signed **, ** 2, ** 3, ** 4), then twenty-three gatherings of six leaves each signed with the letters of the alphabet, excluding J, U,[1] and W ; then two more gatherings of six leaves each signed Aa and Bb, then four leaves of signature Cc. The whole book consists of

$$2 + 6 + 23 \times 6 + 2 \times 6 + 4, \text{ i. e. } 162 \text{ leaves.}$$

We may note that—

(*a*) The number of leaves in a gathering is shown by the superior figure.

(*b*) When a series of alphabetical signatures run without other interruption than the normal omission of J, U, and W, and the number of leaves in each gathering is the same, we write merely the first letter and the last, thus $A-Z^6$, or $B-M^6$. In the case of irregularity, however, such as the omission of a letter normally used or the use of one not normally used or

---

[1] i. e. there is only *one* signature signed U *or* V, or in lower-case u *or* v.

one of the extra-alphabetical signs, we must indicate this, e. g. B–C⁶, E–M⁶, or A–W–Z⁶, or A–Z⁶, &⁶. If certain gatherings have an abnormal number of leaves this also must, of course, be shown, e. g. A–D⁶, E⁴, F–Z⁶, and so on.[1]

(c) When, as sometimes happens, the first gathering consists of two [or more] leaves, none of which is signed, we may use square brackets, e.g. [ ]², A–Z⁶, or, which is, I think, more convenient and much less unsightly, we may adopt some purely conventional ' signature ' which cannot be confused with a real one. For this purpose I have suggested the use of the Greek letter π, which perhaps never, and certainly very seldom, occurs as an actual signature of preliminaries, and which, as being already used for something else to which no exact value can be assigned, and being easily recalled by the p of ' preliminary ', seems specially suitable. I may mention that the suggestion has already been adopted by Mr. Madan and Dr. Greg.

When there is apparently a single leaf unsigned at the beginning it is usual to write ' One leaf unsigned, A–Z⁶, &c.'. In most cases of this sort either the first leaf was blank and has been lost, or the leaf now first really belongs to the last gathering (see below).

(d) When a final gathering consists of an uneven number of leaves it is usual to regard it as consisting of an even number. Thus if a book normally in 6's runs to Z5, whether it is apparently complete or not, the collation would be given as A–Z⁶ with a note added ' Z6 wanting '. I am not, however, convinced that this is a sound practice. From what is said below (pp. 158–60) it will be apparent that there is always a possibility that spare leaves at the end of a book were used to print matter that was to be bound elsewhere in it, such as titles or cancels ; or even that did not belong

[1] Some bibliographers regard the commas between the groups of signatures as unnecessary. They are, but they seem to me to make a long collation somewhat less confusing.

156

to the book at all. It is therefore safer, unless we know from the evidence of other copies of the work that the ' missing ' leaves should actually exist as part of the last gathering, to ignore them and give the collation as we actually find it, e. g. in this case A–Y^6, Z^5.

It may be remarked that when the last gathering apparently consists of a smaller number of leaves than that general in the rest of the book, they should be carefully examined in order to ascertain that the gathering really consists of that smaller number, and that it is not a case of a couple of leaves being wanting at the end. Thus, if a book has the collation A–F^6, G^4, the sewing of the last gathering must be looked at. If it comes between G2 and G3 the last gathering *is* a four ; but if it comes after G3 it evidently was a six, and the two last leaves (which may have been blank) are wanting. In such a case the usual description would be ' A–G^6 (G5 and G6 wanting) '. For the reason mentioned in the last paragraph, it would, however, be safer to give it as A–F^6, G^4 adding some such note as ' an incomplete six ' or ' sewing after G3 ', which would serve as an indication of the make-up.[1]

(*e*) With regard to the preliminary leaves there is sometimes a difficulty, as these leaves may be signed by characters which are not exactly represented in modern founts of type. In such cases it will be well not to strive after too minute accuracy, but to use any fairly similar character which is available. It is always possible to add a note if any ambiguity is caused, and the use of characters specially cast or available only at the most well-furnished presses causes great inconvenience to those who have occasion to quote from the work in which they appear.[2]

[1] An alternative and perhaps better way of indicating this would be to give the last gathering as G$^{6-2}$, indicating a six from which two leaves had been removed. Other, more scientific, notations have been suggested, but a discussion of them would lead us too far.

[2] It might be useful if some sign never occurring in early books

In a paper entitled 'Bibliographical Problems with a few Solutions' in the *Papers of the Bibliographical Society of America*, vol. x, 1916, p. 128, Dr. George Watson Cole remarks that 'a collation by signatures, to be logical, should begin where the printer began his work and not with the preliminary leaves.[1] It should begin with the text, especially if that begins with a full sheet or signature-mark—a pretty conclusive indication that the work was set in type from manuscript and is not a page-for-page reprint. In the latter case the text may by chance begin anywhere else than on the first leaf of a signature. By adopting this method, instead of beginning with the preliminary leaves, when we reach the end of the book we shall find ourselves in the same position that the printer was in, and in a far better position to understand his problems and how he went about to solve them.'

This is a very important point and one which has, I think, often been overlooked. A printer naturally, at any rate if he is himself the publisher of what he prints, will always arrange his work as economically as possible. If, for example, he is printing a book which ends in such a manner as to leave two blank leaves in the last sheet, and if he has to print preliminary matter which occupies two leaves, he will as a matter of

could be adopted to stand for *any* signature. It may often be convenient to refer to certain leaves of a gathering, whether preliminary or otherwise, without needing to specify the particular signatures. Thus if $ were understood to stand for any signature whatever, we could express the fact that in a certain quarto the third and fourth leaves of every gathering were unsigned, except D which was signed throughout, by the simple formula ' $ 3, 4 unsigned except D '. Such a symbol would also be useful in many bibliographical generalizations, e. g. ' in a quarto in fours the watermark will be found divided between $ 1 and $ 4 or between $ 2 and $ 3 '.

[1] I do not understand Dr. Cole to mean that we should *print* our collations in this order, but merely that in investigating the make-up of a book we should begin where the printer did. Collations are intended to represent the bound, or finished, book, not the sheets as they came from the press.

course impose these preliminaries in the middle of his last sheet, which may therefore run, as actually printed (supposing it to be in fours), Z_1, [*], *2, Z_2, the two centre leaves being cut out to be used as preliminaries. Such a book will be described as *², A–Y⁴, Z², quite correctly.

Suppose, however, that the preliminary matter consists of only a single title-leaf, while the Z section contains three leaves of text ; the printer would be quite likely to print it Z_1, Z_2, Z_3, [*], cutting off his last leaf to form the title.[1] Now if he did this many bibliographers, following the usual custom of assuming that all leaves must be or must have been double leaves, would give the collation [*]², A–Z⁴, adding the note, ' *1 and Z_4 wanting, probably blanks ', thus inventing two blank leaves which in fact never existed. The method of considering the preliminary leaves *last* and in close conjunction with the final sheet of the book, *as the printer necessarily considered them*, is a very useful safeguard against such possibilities of error being overlooked. Of course we must not assume that a printer would in every case economize his labour and paper in this fashion : it might sometimes have been more convenient to have the two extra leaves as covers or end-papers. But if we make it our rule to follow the printer step by step in his work, considering at every point what would be the most convenient thing for him to do, and, having determined this, to investigate whether he did it or not, we shall seldom go far wrong.

The bibliographer should indeed constantly bear in his mind that as it costs practically as much to print part of a sheet as a complete one, it was always to the printer's interest to make up a complete sheet whenever

---

[1] Dr. Cole gives an interesting example of this from *The Remembrancer*, London, 1775–84, which was issued in parts. Examination of unbound copies of these parts shows that the title-pages of the volumes were issued as integral parts of the last sheets of the volumes.

he could.[1] A modern publisher when producing a set
of volumes or a series of books on similar paper will
often economize by printing parts of different books
together. Thus supposing one book ends with a sheet
containing only 12 pages of print and another with one
containing only 4 pages, he may impose a 16-page
sheet so that the 4 pages of one book come within the
12 pages of the other. After printing, the 4 pages are
of course cut out of the sheet and placed with the sheets
of the other book. Leaflets and other advertising
matter are often printed in the same way and afterwards
cut out, in order to save waste in machining. It is
quite probable that the more economical printers resorted to similar devices to save time and labour in
early days. At periods when prints of title-pages seem
to have been used as advertisements (see pp. 90–1), it
would have been an obvious economy to print an additional one or two on spare leaves and afterwards to cut
them out of the sheets. These would differ in setting
from the actual title, and if any chanced to be used to
replace damaged titles they might produce rather inex-
plicable ' variants '. But I offer this merely as a suggestion.

Unusual Collations. In general an irregular or unusual make-up is an indication of a cancel or that some
disturbance has happened to the book in the course of
production. There is, however, one class of book in
which what seems at first sight an abnormal arrangement must be regarded as regular, namely books in
which two texts such as Greek and Latin are so printed
as to face each other. In such cases the Greek text
seems often to have been printed quite separately from
the Latin one, the two being interleaved when binding.
A little reflection will show that this interleaving is not
quite a simple matter, for it will be necessary (1) to
place the Greek and Latin text alternately outside the

---

[1] Cf. pp. 194–5, as to the tendency to make up complete sheets when
reprinting.

gathering, and (2) to insert a single leaf in the middle of each gathering. If these things are not done we shall get two leaves of the same text coming together between the gatherings and in the centre of each, which of course would not do. This sometimes produces collations which appear most extraordinary. Thus there is a little collection entitled *Ex Veterum Comicorum Fabulis . . . sententiae nunc primum in sermonem Latinum conversae*, printed by G. Morelius at Paris in 1553, which has the following make-up: two leaves not signed, A^{17}, B^{19}, C^{17}, D^{12}, E^{17}, F^{19}, G^{17}, H^{11}, I^9, K^{11}. In each gathering the Greek and Latin leaves are signed separately, Arabic figures being used for the former and Roman for the latter: thus the signatures of A run (A), A, A2, Aij, A3, Aiij, &c.

In this book we have not only a single leaf inserted in the middle of each sheet but extra pairs of leaves inserted (for what reason is not quite clear) in some of the quires. It may be remarked that the fact that D contains an even number of leaves is explained by this signature including a leaf of various readings and corrections in the Greek to which there is of course no corresponding Latin.

References to Passages in Early Books

The usual present-day method of reference to a page in a printed book is of course by the pagination, for almost all modern books are paged, and paged correctly. This was, however, by no means the case with early works, and it is therefore usual, as has already been noted, to give references to books earlier than about 1650 by the signatures, instead of by the pagination. In this connexion one or two points are to be noticed.

When the signature of a leaf consists of two or more similar letters, as BB, bbb, &c. (not Bb), it is usual and convenient to give these as 2B, 3b, &c. Thus a page referred to as 3K2 would probably be actually signed

KKK 2., or KKK. 2 (no notice being taken of the punctuation).

Leaves are usually referred to by the arabic number, even when the original uses roman, e. g. BB iij would be quoted as 2B3.

Sometimes in a single work we may find a series of signatures repeated twice or even oftener. This may be due to error, to the insertion of additional matter, to division of the work between two or more printers, or to books intended originally for separate issue being brought together under one title. In such cases we sometimes find references given as 'second A2', 'first d3', and so on. Dr. Greg has recently introduced for this the convenient notation of a 'superior' numeral, thus $^2d4$ would mean d4 of the second alphabet (as distinguished from 2d4, which would mean dd4). In referring to books containing repeated alphabets it would be well to use the superior figure even for the first alphabet. Thus $^1c2$ would mean c2 of the first alphabet, and would at the same time serve as a warning that there was more than one sheet signed c.

An unsigned preliminary sheet may, as suggested on page 156, be referred to as π, a second unsigned sheet as 2π, or perhaps better, in accordance with the notation referred to in the preceding paragraph, as $^2\pi$.

Dr. Greg refers to unsigned gatherings occurring in the body of a book, when these are clearly additions and not merely items which have been left unsigned in error, by the Greek letter χ. An alternative method would be to use as a reference the preceding letter with a plus-sign, thus $D+2$ would indicate the second leaf of an unsigned gathering following D. This notation has the advantage of showing at once the exact position of the insertion.[1]

[1] Alternatively we might, as Dr. Greg suggests, indicate the *leaf* after which the unsigned leaves occur, rather than the gathering. Thus the second leaf of an unsigned gathering following D in a book in fours

When it is desired to indicate that a leaf referred to is itself unsigned, though forming part of a signed gathering, it is usual to place the signature in square brackets, thus [B8^v]. In a mere reference to a page there is, however, seldom any need for such indication.

would be ' D4+2 '. We could thus easily show the position of supernumerary leaves inserted into a signed gathering, but such abnormalities generally demand special description.

Chapter Two

THE FORMATS OF BOOKS. FOLIO, QUARTO, ETC.

THE terms folio, quarto, octavo, &c., are often taken to refer to the *size* of books, but this is hardly the correct way to regard them. It is indeed generally recognized that owing to the great variety of sizes of paper used in present-day book-printing, the mere description of a *modern* book as folio, quarto, or octavo tells us nothing about its exact dimensions. In general a 'quarto' book may be expected to have a squarer page than a folio or octavo, and a book called a 'folio' is likely to be very large ; but this is about all the information that these terms give us by themselves. If we wish to indicate the *size* we call the book for example 'crown 8vo', meaning that the leaves are one-eighth of the size of a sheet of 'crown' paper, which, originally a particular make of paper having a crown as watermark, now denotes any sheet of paper 15″ × 20″. A crown 8vo therefore measures $7\frac{1}{2}″ × 5″$ (less, if the edges are cut), the usual size for novels.[1]

Even, however, if we are dealing with earlier books, when the sizes of paper did not vary quite so much as they do now, these designations are not of much use as indications of size, for in quite early times one book might measure nearly 50 per cent. more both in height and width than another and yet they might both be 'octavo'. The terms of format are, however, so useful in other respects as indicating the way in which a book

---

[1] Other common sizes in present-day books are foolscap 8vo, measuring, when uncut, $6\frac{3}{4}×4\frac{1}{4}$, used for many 'pocket'-sized books ; demy 8vo, $8\frac{3}{4}×5\frac{5}{8}$, a common size for 'serious' works, histories, scientific text-books, &c., and royal 8vo, $10×6\frac{1}{4}$, a size which used perhaps to be commoner than it is at present for illustrated works. A very large number of 'off'-sizes are, however, used nowadays, so that for a complete description of a modern book it is usually advisable to give measurements of the page in centimetres or inches.

is made up, that they are still universally employed, at any rate in describing books prior to the quite modern period, and a description that did not say whether its subject was in folio, quarto, or what-not, would be regarded as sadly lacking from a bibliographical point of view. It is necessary then to know how the terms are to be used.

At various times there has been, even among bibliographers, some uncertainty as to the meaning to be given to these terms of format. Apart from the tendency to call any squarish book a quarto, and any rather small book a 12mo, some have described and even defined a quarto as one in which four leaves form a gathering. Among bibliographers at least the practice is now, however, quite fixed, and the terms in question are used solely with reference to the number of times the original sheet has been folded to form the leaves of the book. Thus in a book in folio the sheets have been folded once, in a quarto twice, in an octavo three times, the size of the leaves being consequently $\frac{1}{2}$, $\frac{1}{4}$, and $\frac{1}{8}$ that of the original sheets. The problem is how we are to tell, from the printed and bound book, how often the original sheet was folded.

Seeing that, as has already been said, the size of the original sheet varied considerably, we cannot, at any rate in the case of the smaller books, infer the number of foldings from the final dimensions. Nor can we go by the number of leaves in a gathering, for we have seen that in a folio we may have any number from 2 to 12, or even more, in a quarto 4 or 8, in an octavo 4, 8 or 16. How then shall we judge what the format is? The criterion now always adopted is that of the position of the watermark, taken in conjunction with the direction of the so-called ' chain-lines ' of the paper. Unfortunately even this criterion sometimes fails us, for especially in later times the position of the watermark in the original sheet is not absolutely constant, and it is a question whether in some makes of paper the chain-lines did not run lengthwise instead of, as usual, across the normal-sized sheet ; [1] but when the watermark fails to decide the question, we must confess that the format is uncertain.

To facilitate the understanding of what follows the reader is advised to take a piece of paper ruled on both sides *across* the paper (i. e. parallel to the shorter side).[2] These rulings will stand for the chain-lines. A diamond-shaped figure may then be marked, in the same place on both sides of the paper, in the centre of one-half of the sheet, to represent the watermark. If the sheet is then folded in the same way as the printed sheets of various formats are folded, it will be clear how the watermark falls in each case.[3]

In the broadside printed to be read without folding, as posters or proclamations were usually printed, the watermark will of course be in the centre of one-half of the sheet, the chain-lines being vertical or horizontal according as the print runs parallel to the longer or shorter side of the sheet.[4]

If the sheet of paper be folded once along the shorter diameter, the watermark will now be in the middle of a leaf, and the chain-lines will run up and down the page. A book in which we find this is called a folio (figure 16).

If the sheet is folded again, the watermark will be

[1] See chapter viii of Part 1 as to these points. Eighteenth-century papers frequently, and earlier ones occasionally, had two watermarks, a device placed in the normal position, and a subsidiary mark (generally the maker's initials) elsewhere.

[2] In order that when the sheet is folded the pages should be of normal shape, the sides of the paper should be in the proportion of approximately 3 to 4.

[3] Cf. Part 1, chapter iv, where the question of the various foldings is discussed from the point of view of imposition of the type. We are here considering them from that of the finished and bound book.

[4] Should we find a sheet in which the watermark was central, or was absent altogether, and the chain-lines ran in the opposite directions from those mentioned above, we should of course be dealing with a half-sheet in folio.

on its side in the centre of the inner margins of the leaves, and the chain-lines will run horizontally. A book in which this is the case is a quarto (figure 17).

If it is folded yet once more, forming an octavo, the watermark will be found upright at the top of the inner margin (normally on leaves, 1, 4, 5, 8 *or* 2, 3, 6, 7), and the chain-lines will again be vertical (figure 18).

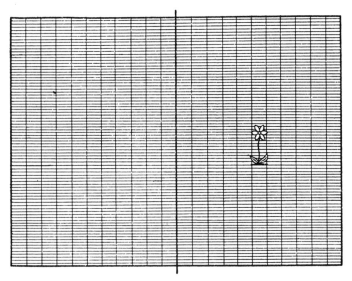

FIG. 16. Two leaves of a book in folio showing chain- and wire-lines and position of watermark.

In a 16mo the watermark will be at the outer top corners of the leaves [1] (normally leaves 9, 12, 13, 16 *or* 10, 11, 14, 15), and the chain-lines will run horizontally.[2]

In a 32mo the watermark will be at the lower outer corners of the leaves and the chain-lines will run vertically.

[1] Both in a 16mo and a 32mo the watermark is, however, often absent owing to the leaves having been cropped in binding.

[2] As to a possible 16mo folding with vertical chain-lines, see below, p. 173.

The recognition of 12mo and 24mo foldings by means of the position of the watermark alone is a matter of some difficulty, both because there were several possible methods of folding and because a comparatively small variation from the normal in the position of the watermark of the *sheet* will in all the smaller formats make much difference in its position on the *leaf*. We must therefore in all these smaller formats take into consideration the number of leaves forming the gathering. If we find a gathering of twelve leaves, and the direction of the chain-lines and the position of the watermark correspond to those of one of the usual 12mo foldings (see below), we may be reasonably sure that we are dealing with a normal 12mo. It is only in the abnormal cases that difficulty arises. There are 12mos which are sewn in gatherings of eight and four leaves alternately,[1] and it is undoubtedly possible for a book to be printed as a 12mo (i. e. for the leaf to be one-twelfth of a sheet) and yet to be sewn in 8's, though I cannot give an instance of such a thing. The proceeding would in some circumstances be quite reasonable. Suppose, for example, that a printer intending to print a small octavo wishes to use up some rather large paper. He could easily do this by cutting off one-third of each sheet and using the remainder exactly as a normal sheet for his octavo formes, making up every third gathering out of the two cut-off pieces placed one inside the other.[2] Such a book would actually have been *printed* as an octavo, but, as format

[1] e. g. *La Fable des Abeilles* (translation of B. Mandeville's *Fable of the Bees*), à Londres, chez Jean Nourse, 1750, the text of which runs A⁸, B⁴, C⁸, D⁴, &c., the evidence of chain-lines and watermarks showing clearly that the book is a 12mo. Mr. W. R. B. Prideaux tells me that he has met with a number of examples of this make-up in eighteenth-century French printing.

[2] Under early conditions there would not appear to be any great difficulty in laying two cut-offs side by side on the tympan and printing just as if they were a single sheet. Alternatively the printer might of course put the cut-offs aside for use in printing oddments.

depends on the original sheet, would have to be regarded bibliographically as a 12mo.

With this warning as to possible difficulties we may
pass to the normal 12mo foldings. Now there are

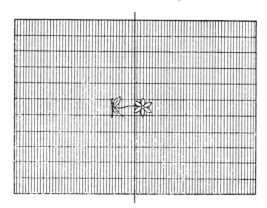

FIG. 17. Two leaves of a book in quarto.

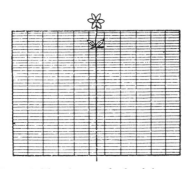

FIG. 18. Two leaves of a book in octavo.

several ways of folding a sheet of paper into twelve and
still more of folding it into twenty-four, and it seems
probable that most of these have been employed at
one time or another for producing particular shapes of
book. I have therefore added a brief note on all
possible foldings elsewhere (see Appendix v). Here,
however, we may confine ourselves to the usual and

169

regular methods, which in the case of the 12mo are two, in both of which, we may note, the chain-lines are horizontal.

(*a*) *Twelve-mo by cutting.* So far as my observation extends, this was the normal, and practically the only, method of producing a 12mo used by English printers of the late sixteenth and seventeenth centuries, and Mr. R. W. Chapman finds the same thing in the

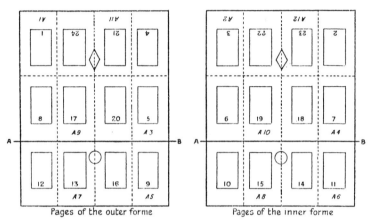

Pages of the outer forme   Pages of the inner forme

Fig. 19. A printed sheet in duodecimo imposed for cutting. The lower third to be cut off before folding. The diamond and circle indicate *alternative* positions of the watermark.

eighteenth century.[1] The arrangement will be made clear from the above scheme, which represents the printed sheet (not the forme of type).

On this scheme I have marked by a circle and a diamond the *alternative* positions of a watermark placed in the normal position in the centre of one-half of the sheet.

When this scheme is followed it is necessary after printing is completed to cut off the third of the sheet containing pages 9 to 16. The remainder of the sheet is then folded as an octavo, and the part cut off, having

[1] See *The Library*, 4th Ser., iv. 167–8.

been turned round head to foot, is folded by two vertical folds to form four leaves and placed within the larger portion.

(*b*) *Twelve-mo without cutting.* The scheme for this is as figure 20.

It will be seen that, after printing, this need not be cut. It is only necessary to fold the upper and lower thirds on the opposite sides of the central third

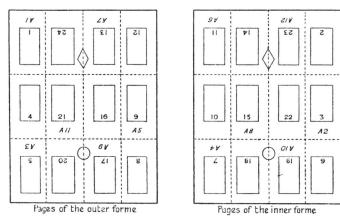

Pages of the outer forme   Pages of the inner forme

FIG. 20. A printed sheet in duodecimo imposed for folding without cutting. The diamond and circle indicate *alternative* positions of the watermark.

(z-fashion), and then to fold the long strip thus produced twice across.

This latter scheme was, I believe, quite usual during the nineteenth century (12mo has been almost given up in recent times). As will be seen, however, in certain leaves the original edge of the sheet forms the top margin. This does not matter in the case of machine-made papers having straight and even edges; but the early papers were often very irregular at the edge, and it is obvious that, unless the book were much cut down in binding, this irregularity coming at the top of the pages would be likely to detract very much from its appearance. It was probably for this reason that, as long as paper was made by hand, the method of cutting (*a*) was commonly employed, for by this the original edge of the sheet always comes at the foot of the page, where irregularities do not matter, and the top margin is as regular as in the case of a quarto or octavo.

The test by which we can determine the method followed is of course the position of the watermark. If this is normally placed on the sheet [1] we shall find it—

1. By scheme *a*, either towards the *top* of the outer margins of folios 7 and 8 (pages 13, 14, 15, 16) *or* towards the *top* of the outer margins of folios 11 and 12 (pages 21, 22, 23, 24).
2. By scheme *b*, either towards the *top* of the outer margins of folios 7 and 12 (pages 13, 14, 23, 24) *or* towards the *foot* of folios 9 and 10 (pages 17, 18, 19, 20).

It is of course quite possible that if the watermark is small, or slightly out of normal position, or if the margins have been heavily cut down, we shall only find it on one of the pairs mentioned above (e. g. on 7 alone or on 11 alone); but under scheme *a* we shall not find a watermark *divided* between, say, folios 7 and 12,[2] nor by scheme *b*, one divided between folios 7 and 8.

[1] Apart from irregularities of placing of the watermark, we must be on the look-out for a deviation from the expected position due to the fact that in printing the smaller sizes of books the printers seem sometimes to have allowed a very considerable margin round the edges of the sheet. If they had only allowed the same margin at the edge of the sheet as was necessary within the sheet, the irregularities of the paper might have cut into the page margins too far, and further the total type area of the forme might have been too large for the press. The result of this will be to make the watermark come nearer the centre of the outer margins than one would expect to find it.

[2] It might, however, exceptionally happen that, if the thirds were all cut off before folding began, and if some sheets had been laid on the press with the watermark to left and others with it to right, a gathering might contain *two* watermarks. In such a case we should no doubt under scheme *a* find parts of a watermark both on fol. 7 and fol. 12, but we ought then also to find parts on fol. 8 and fol. 11, which would show that we have not before us a *b* imposition.

This is the general principle, but as I have said, a slight irregularity in the position of the watermark in the sheet will make much difference in its position in the leaves of the printed book, and I would strongly advise those interested in the matter to work out the results of such differences of position by means of actual folded sheets such as I have suggested above. Only by this method is it possible to interpret with any certainty the results of observation.

Into the question of 24mo I cannot enter. It is obvious that a scheme similar to either *a* or *b* but with two type-pages to the leaf instead of one and the addition of a final crossways fold will give a 24mo, and that in such cases the chain-lines will be vertical. But I think that one can hardly go beyond saying that a small book gathered in 12's or 24's and with vertical chain-lines is probably a 24mo. In these small sizes, as I have said before, the position of the watermark does not help us much. Fortunately, in English books at any rate, 24mo does not seem to be a very frequent size.

As an example of the difficulties attending the 24mo format, I may mention an edition of the *Comicorum Graecorum sententiae Latinis versibus ab Henr. Stephano redditae*, printed by H. Estienne in 1569, the page of which (perhaps rather closely cut) measures $4\frac{1}{2}'' \times 2''$, being therefore exceptionally narrow for its height. This is signed and sewn in 8's, and the chain-lines are vertical. There seems to be no visible watermark. This might, I think, either be a 24mo on paper about $15'' \times 20''$, folded according to the scheme which I have numbered *c2* (see Appendix, p. 327), or it might be a 16mo printed on an unusual size of paper and folded with the final fold in the direction of, instead of, as usual, across the longest dimension of the thrice-folded sheet.

There is one other possible folding which I may mention in passing, namely 18mo, a format very common in modern French books. I have not met with it in English printing, though schemes for it are given by Johnson. In this format the chain-lines would be vertical and the watermark, if normally placed, would be central on a leaf.

There are a number of puzzles connected with format, but most of them are too complicated to be discussed here. One of the puzzles is connected with certain books of quarto shape in which the chain-marks run vertically as in an octavo. There is, for example, an edition of Hardyng's *Chronicle*, printed by Grafton with the date 1543, in which the first twelve sheets of the text are apparently on 8vo paper, i.e. the gatherings consist of eight leaves, the chain-marks run vertically, and the watermark [1] is at the top of the inner margins. The shape of the page is, however, that of an ordinary small quarto, and the rest of the book (and the prelims.) is on ordinary quarto paper, the gatherings being still of eight leaves, but there being two watermarks in each and the chain-lines running horizontally. It is not clear whether in such cases the 8vo paper was a sheet of the size of two ordinary sheets, or whether in the mould used the chain-marks for some reason or other ran the opposite way from that which was usual.[2]

[1] The watermarks are not easy to see. There seems to be not more than one in any gathering, but in some gatherings I could find none. If there is really one and only one in each gathering, we might perhaps argue that the sheets had been printed on a press of double the usual size, but this seems most unlikely at the date.

[2] Mr. Duff in his *Printers of Westminster and London*, p. 52, mentions a copy of a folio *Chronicle* of which two leaves are on quarto paper, and another book which is partly quarto and partly octavo. Dr. Greg informs me that such mixtures of 4to and 8vo are not infrequent in dramatic literature of the early seventeenth century, and Mr. R. W. Chapman has discovered a curious and puzzling example in Dodsley's *Collection of Poems by several Hands*, of which, while vols. i–iii (1748, ed. 1) are ordinary duodecimos, vol. iv (1755) is apparently 16mo in 8's, and vols. v and vi (1758) are apparently—by the evidence of the chain-lines (there are no watermarks in these volumes)—partly 16mo and partly 8vo, nevertheless all the volumes are of the same size !

Chapter Three

ON THE MEANING OF 'EDITION', 'IMPRESSION', AND 'ISSUE', AND ON DETERMINING WHETHER TWO BOOKS ARE OF THE SAME EDITION OR NOT

NO precise definition of 'issue' or 'edition' is possible, but there is among bibliographers a well-recognized difference in the use of the two words. In modern times we can define 'edition' as the whole number of copies of a book printed at any time or times from one setting-up of type (including copies printed from the stereotype or electrotype plates made from that setting-up of type), and 'impression' as the whole number of copies printed at one time, i.e. in ordinary circumstances the total number of copies printed without removing the type or plates from the press. By 'issue' is generally meant some special form of the book in which, for the most part, the original printed sheets are used but which differs from the earlier or normal form by the addition of new matter or by some difference in arrangement.[1] Thus, if to an existing book of reference were added an appendix bringing it up to date, this appendix being bound up with sheets of the original edition and a new title-page, this would properly be described as a new issue. The word is, however, very loosely used, and a 'cheap re-issue' may merely mean the old book quite unchanged, except perhaps for the substitution of a cheaper binding, but at a reduced price.

When dealing with early books, 'edition' and 'impression' as a rule are the same thing, for the early printer normally distributed his type immediately it had been printed from, though there were, as we shall see, exceptions to this; and therefore if a reprint was

[1] Parts of an impression printed on different paper are also sometimes referred to as different 'issues'.

required the whole had to be re-set and a new *edition* was created. It is thus only necessary to consider the difference between an ' edition ' and an ' issue '.

The general principle is that when we talk of a new ' edition ' of a book we mean that the type of the whole book, or at any rate of the text as distinguished from the preliminary matter, has been set up afresh ; while when we speak of a new issue, we mean that what were left of the old sheets of the text have been bound up with a new title-page [1] or with new preliminary matter.

A difficulty arises in connexion with books the edition of which was shared among several publishers, a certain number of copies of the title-sheet being printed with each publisher's name. Thus some copies of the undated edition of Chaucer's works issued about 1545 have the name of William Bonham as ' printer ', others that of Robert Toy, Richard Kele, or Thomas Petit,[2] and there are five different imprints of the 1632 folio of Shakespeare, stating that the book was printed respectively for Allot, Aspley, Hawkins, Meighen, and Smethwick. Instances of this practice are numerous. The question is, should these books be described as belonging to different issues or simply as having variant imprints ? My own feeling is that when we are dealing with books essentially the same in contents, ' issue ' implies the total number of copies put out *at one time*, and that the simultaneous publication of a book by a variety of people does not constitute separate issues ; though no doubt if a book were after a while handed over to a new publisher who published it with his name

---

[1] The mere addition of new matter *without* a new title-page, especially if the addition only consists of a dedication or an epistle to the reader, is not generally regarded as constituting a new issue.

[2] They can hardly all have been the actual *printers* of the book, and we must assume therefore that each paid a share of the cost and took a certain number of copies. When we find an early work described as ' printed by ' a certain person, we cannot by any means always assume that it was actually the work of a press owned by him. It often means no more than ' printed for '.

substituted for that of the original one, this *would* constitute a separate issue, as in the case of Barker's books mentioned below. The practice among bibliographers seems, however, not to be uniform.

The occasions of such reissues in early times were generally either : (1) for the purpose of indicating a change in the publishing arrangements, as when in 1578 Christopher Barker, on being appointed Queen's Printer, was ordered to supply new endings and titles for books printed by the former Queen's Printer (*Acts of the Privy Council*, n.s., x. 287–8) ; or (2) in order to add new preliminary matter, as in the case of the reissue of Thomas Nashe's *Christ's Tears over Jerusalem*, 1593, with a long new preface in 1594 ; (3) in order to make an old book appear a new one, as in the case of Lodge's *Scillaes Metamorphosis*, 1589, the sheets of which were reissued in 1610 with a new title as *A moste pleasant Historie of Glaucus and Scilla* ; or (4) in order to make some correction or alteration in the preliminary matter which was thought desirable, as in the well-known case of the second issue of *Troilus and Cressida*. In this last group it is often questionable whether we ought to regard those copies with altered preliminary matter as a separate ' issue ' or to consider the new matter merely as a cancel. Which we do should depend on whether the main intention seems to be to *correct* something (in which case it is a cancel) or to give a new life to the old sheets (in which case it is a reissue).

There are of course intermediate possibilities between the new ' edition ' as defined and the new ' issue ' consisting of old sheets with new title and preliminaries, and it is in the description of these that difficulties arise. For example, sometimes after the original publication of a book a lengthy addition or continuation—occasionally, indeed, as long as the original book—was printed and bound up with a new title and what remained of the original sheets. Is this a new edition or a new issue? It is often called a new edition, but it is, I think, much preferable to call it ' a new issue with additional matter '; for it is clear that there is no new edition of what was originally printed, since we have merely the remainder of the old sheets; nor can it be a new edition of the added part, for that never appeared before. In fact all that can properly be said to be of a new edition is the title-page, which is not part of the book itself but merely, as we have seen elsewhere, a kind of label, the copy for which was sometimes—if not generally—furnished by the publisher.

Occasionally even before the printing of a book was finished, or immediately on publication and before the final sheets were distributed, it became apparent to the publisher that the demand was greater than he had anticipated. In such a case the best plan would obviously be to print additional copies of sheets still in type and re-set those which had been distributed. We may then get two issues (or editions), part of which is from the same setting-up of type and part from different settings; a state of affairs which gives rise to problems somewhat similar to those which we shall have to consider presently in connexion with books set in duplicate. An interesting example of this has been discussed in Part I, chap. vi, when we saw that the duplicate settings of certain pages of a Valerius Maximus of 1471 gave us valuable information as to a detail of the printer's technique. Another will be found in the two editions of Jasper Heywood's translation of Seneca's *Troas*, printed by Richard Tottel in 1559 in octavo; which are from different settings as far as the end of sheet C. In the final sheets, however, we find that the inner forme of sheet D, with the exception of D1^v, all of sheet E except E3 and E4, and all of sheet F (three leaves only) except apparently F2^v and the colophon on F3^v, are from the same setting in the two editions.[1] The pages seem, however,

---

[1] See de Vocht's edition in Bang's *Materialien*, pp. xxxix–xliii. The editor regards D1^v as identical in the two editions. Possibly in

178

to have been unlocked from the formes, as there are differences in the position of the headline and in other minor points of arrangement. It may be noted that the amount of type needed to keep so many pages standing at one time is not so great as might be supposed, as owing to the short lines of the verse there is unusually little to the page.

Several other examples of the same sort of thing might be instanced, but in principle all are much the same, and a single one may suffice. This is the case of Marston's *Parasitaster*, 1606, of which there are two editions in the same year, the second being corrected by the author. Dr. Greg points out to me the remarkable fact that large portions of the text scattered throughout the play, as well as two whole sheets (D and I), are from the same setting in both, the rest being re-set. It is difficult to imagine how this curious state of affairs can have come about.[1]

In all such cases as these, I think we may quite fairly speak of separate *editions*, in spite of the fact that parts of the book are really only separate *impressions*. Even in those cases in which the printer may have decided that additional copies would be required before the final sheets were printed, and therefore printed the whole higher number at once so that *these* sheets in the second edition might properly be described as reissued, it seems, when there is really any considerable bulk of re-set matter, somewhat pedantic to insist on this aspect of them. From the printer's and publisher's point of view the increased number was a new enterprise not contemplated at the start of the work, and this seems of more importance than the fact that they

a few cases the apparent differences may be due to letters falling out and being replaced when the pages were re-imposed.

[1] J. P. Collier in his *Bibliographical Account*, i. 291, states that there were two issues of H. C.'s *Forest of Fancy*, both dated 1579, one consisting of 58 and the other of 80 leaves, and that part of the type was from the same setting in the two issues. I have had no opportunity of verifying this, and give the statement for what it is worth.

were able to save a few shillings by using an old setting of part of the book.

The most difficult cases to decide are those—fortunately few in number—where the printer has rearranged his type, but not re-composed it. For example, in one of the editions of the *Articles* printed by Grafton, a portion of text referring to the duties of bishops was omitted from its proper place and was added at the end under the heading, ' More for the Byshop '. This was apparently found unsatisfactory, and the formes were unlocked and the type reimposed with the addition correctly placed.[1] In Grafton's days such a thing as this could hardly happen save in the case of an official publication such as the *Articles*, of which large numbers would be printed and which only consists of six leaves (a sheet and a half in quarto), for ordinary books would, in the usual course, be distributed sheet by sheet as worked off. There are also in later times a few books such as Jasper Mayne's *City Match*, 1658–9,[2] which were issued both in quarto and, with the same type rearranged to a shorter page, in octavo. In some, at least, of such cases the two formats were probably worked simultaneously, each sheet as printed being reimposed for the other size, so that we need not suppose that the whole book was in type at the same time.

In all cases of such extensive alterations as these, we should, I think, be justified in speaking of different ' editions ', in spite of the fact that strict adherence to our definitions would seem to constitute them different ' impressions ' of the same edition.

The following hints on how to determine whether two copies of a book belong to the same edition, i.e. are from the same setting-up of type, may be of use to junior students. There is, of course, seldom any diffi-

---

[1] We can see that it is the original setting of the type by the broken letters and other peculiarities.

[2] Greg, *List of English Plays and Masques*, cxxvi and xii.

culty when we can compare the books, or even photo-graphs of a few pages, side by side. This, however, is often impossible, and we may have to rely entirely on notes : it is well to know what can be most pro-fitably noted.

First, of course, there is the ' collation ' of the book. If one copy runs to, say, F4, and the other to G4 (both being perfect copies), they evidently belong to different editions, and the only thing left to make sure about it is that sheet G is not simply an extra sheet containing an appendix or other additional matter.

Assuming that the collation of the copies is the same, notes of the following points, or of some of them, will generally settle whether they belong to the same edition or not :

(1) The catchwords on certain pages. It is well to note the first catchword on each sheet and perhaps one or two others here and there, preferably towards the middle of the sheets. There is, however, little or no use in noting the final catchwords of the sheets, as in the very common case of a reprint being divided among two or more compositors to set up they will be bound to work so that the sheets shall each end with the same word as the original which they are following, for otherwise of course the sheets of the reprint would not follow one another properly.

(2) The last words of some dozen lines on one or two pages taken at random in different parts of the book. Even when a book is set up ' line for line ' from another it often happens that the lines do not exactly correspond throughout. Slight differences in the founts used, especially the presence or absence of contractions, may cause a compositor sometimes to turn over a word into the next line. It is safer to take such line-endings from near the middle of a page, where the compositor generally allowed himself rather more freedom in this respect than elsewhere.

(3) The position of the signatures, i.e. how they

stand with respect to the words in the last line of print, may be noted on a certain number of pages.[1]

(4) The size and design of any large ornamental initials used at the head of chapters or sections may be noted.

(5) It is worth while to look for punctuation marks belonging to wrong founts, e.g. italic or black-letter queries or colons in a Roman text. These are quite unlikely to be corrected at press, and the chance of their occurring in the same place in two separate editions is of course negligible.

(6) Most founts of italic types had two forms of capital letters, a plain form and one with flourished projections (the latter form being called ' swash letters '). These were generally used indiscriminately, and consequently the use of the one form or the other in particular words is often a good test as to the edition to which a particular copy of a book belongs.

(7) Broken letters may be looked for in the text and the place in which they occur noted. Broken letters are, however, not a very satisfactory means of identifying editions. In the first place, they may get broken during the actual printing and may therefore only print as broken in certain copies. Secondly, it is not always easy to distinguish between a broken letter and one that, for some reason or other, has failed to print properly. An example will illustrate the danger of relying too much on their evidence. Some years ago, wishing to decide whether two copies of a book, one at Oxford and the other at London, belonged to the same edition, I noted down certain peculiarities, including the fact that in a certain word, let us say ' sunne ', the second limb of the first n failed to print and seemed to be imperfect. I had, I may say, made sure that other n's on the page printed correctly. The other copy showed exactly the same imperfection, but when I came to examine the other points noted, I saw that the editions

[1] For an example of the use of this method, see Bond's *Lyly*, vol. i, pp. 89, 94, 96.

were clearly different. Thinking that this was odd, I looked further and found that, though single n's printed correctly, in nearly *every case* of two n's coming together the second limb of the first one failed to take the ink. What had happened was evident. The matrix from which the letter was cast had not been struck perfectly true [1] and consequently one limb of all the n's of the fount was slightly higher than the other. In ordinary cases the difference of height was not enough to prevent the lower one from being inked and printing properly ; but when two n's came together the unusually high first limb of the second n came against the unusually low second limb of the first n, and so prevented it from printing. We must therefore remember that such apparent faults of printing may sometimes be faults of the whole fount of type used, and be on our guard against taking these as faults of a particular impression.

(8) If these tests fail to satisfy us, there is one other that we may try. I have used it several times and have never known it fail to give a clear answer one way or the other. It is this : Take any page of the book and find in it two full stops at a distance of some ten or a dozen lines apart (if possible the lines should be towards the centre of the page). Note of course the page and the words before the stops so as to identify them. Now lay a ruler on the page from one of these stops to the other and note the letters or parts of letters that it cuts. If a rule placed in a similar position in the other copy cuts the same letters, the chances are many hundreds to one that the two pages were printed from the same setting-up of type ; for however carefully a compositor followed his original, the irregularity in the casting of type and spaces would almost inevitably prevent the two prints corresponding in this respect.

---

[1] In type-founding the type is first cut on the end of a steel punch. From this a matrix is made by striking it into a piece of copper. The matrix is then fixed in a type-mould.

Chapter Four

ON BIBLIOGRAPHICAL EVIDENCE AS TO THE ORDER OF
EDITIONS

WE may as a general rule assume that the hand-
somest edition of a book is the first.[1] The
tendency of reprints has at all times been toward the
saving of expense in production, for when the reputation of a book is once established, its appearance
becomes a less important factor in its sale ; while if
it can be sold at a cheaper rate it may fairly be expected
that a new public will be reached and a larger number
of copies disposed of. Accordingly we sometimes find
that books originally issued in folio or quarto are
reprinted in a smaller size, in quarto, octavo, or even
twelvemo ; or when the original size is retained, paper
is saved by the matter being compressed into a smaller
number of sheets, while occasionally the paper itself
is of a cheaper make. The actual quality of the workmanship is not by itself a safe guide, for in this respect
so much depended upon the particular house from
which the book issued.

In cases which form an exception to this rule it will
generally be found that there is some special reason
for the inferiority of the first edition. Either it is more
or less surreptitious, a matter to which we shall have
to refer later, or was issued in haste, or it was desired
for some reason to produce it as cheaply as possible.

Handsomeness of ' get-up ' is as a general rule much
better evidence of priority than correctness of text, if
by ' correctness ' we mean the reproduction of what

[1] Unless, of course, in its later form it was part of a ' collected
edition ', or was intended to range with some handsomely produced
edition of another work, or there was some other special reason for
setting it out in a more luxurious manner.

184

the author intended. On the other hand, a handsome edition is as a rule carefully produced and is comparatively free from *literal* errors. The words in it will as a rule be real words correctly spelt; but they may not be the correct words. Whether they are so or not would depend less on the care taken by the printer than on the correctness of the MS. (if a copy and not the original), on its legibility, and on whether the author read the proofs.

And here it is to be noted that there is a very important difference between errors of wording and errors of printing (which alone are properly called ' misprints '), and that the two kinds of errors vary quite independently of one another. A most carelessly printed book, absolutely swarming with literals, may contain important corrections, and from an editor's point of view give us the best text. Indeed if we may imagine an author making improvements from time to time in his own copy of his work (presumably a copy of the original edition) and sending lists of these to the printer to be inserted in reprints, or even inserting them in proofs himself, and if these reprints were in other respects not more carefully supervised than the general run of such things, we might have a series of editions steadily degenerating in correctness of printing and at the same time steadily improving in ' readings '. It was insufficient attention to this point that in the early days of editing led to the general assumption that the first edition of a work was necessarily the best to take as the basis of a modern edition, which we now see to be not by any means always the case.[1] We can indeed only assume it to be the case when we can be

---

[1] To prevent misunderstanding, I should perhaps say that I refer to those modern editions the purpose of which is simply to reproduce an author's work as literature, and especially to editions in modern spelling. The literatim reprint is a different matter. When we have to choose a single edition to reproduce, and there is no question of an eclectic text, the earliest (provided that it was not printed from an obviously corrupt MS.) will as a rule be preferable to any other.

reasonably certain that the author had nothing to do with the later editions. In using ' correctness ' as evidence of priority of issue we must therefore be careful to confine our attention to *mechanical* correctness, i.e. the absence of misprints, alone.

To turn now to the more special kinds of evidence as to priority which may be deduced from the comparison of editions of a book. The most conclusive evidence as to the order of editions and as to which was printed from which is often to be obtained by a comparison of readings, but this is a lengthy business, and even if in the end we find it necessary to undertake it, much time may generally be saved if we can first arrive at an approximate or *probable* order before we proceed to the actual collation of the texts.

It seems clear that in the great majority of cases a new edition of a book was printed from an earlier one, and not from the original MS.[1] or from a copy of it. In the first place it is easier for the compositor to read, and hence he could presumably work quicker. Even at present, the composition rates are 8 to 10 per cent. less for exact reprinting from a work already in type than for composition from a MS. In the second place, if it was intended to reprint page for page, as was usually done unless there was some special reason

---

[1] It has been held, I know not on what grounds, that the MS. of a book when once printed from was destroyed. This seems unlikely, as it would in most cases bear the signature of the licenser, and it would therefore be important to preserve it for a time in case any question should arise as to the book having been duly passed by the authorities. The only piece of evidence bearing on the matter which is known to me is Jaggard's epistle in Vincent's *Discovery of Errors*, referred to on p. 206, where the printer states that the original MS. of the work against which Vincent was writing was extant, and it could therefore be proved that the errors in the printed book were not due to the printer's carelessness. The small number of extant MSS. which appear to have passed through the hands of a printer is easily explained by the very slight value which in an unsentimental age would be attached to them when their practical utility was exhausted, and by the destruction caused by the Great Fire.

against it, the book could conveniently be divided among two or more compositors, who could work simultaneously.[1]

It may then generally be *assumed* that a later edition is printed from an earlier one unless there is clear evidence to the contrary; but one can often get direct evidence of the fact. For example, if two editions of a work in prose correspond line for line they must be of the same series (i.e. the later one must have been printed from the earlier or from one which itself was derived from the earlier). No two compositors working independently from a MS. would set line for line the same, even if they followed the spelling of the MS., which they probably seldom or never troubled to do, unless in the case of a few authors who made a special point of spelling, such as Churchyard, Stanyhurst, or Ben Jonson. The proof is as good if, as we sometimes find, the texts do not agree line for line throughout, but are brought to agreement at the end of each page so that the catchword is the same, for this could only be done by a compositor who had a printed page to work from.

In the case of verse, the lines of which do not as a rule occupy the full breadth of the page, the line-for-line test is of course useless, but the identity of catchwords is usually evidence enough that one printed text was set up from another; for even if by chance the second printer had determined to use the same number of lines to the page as the first, he would be almost sure to make some variation in the space between stanzas, or in turn-overs or at the head of sections or elsewhere, and this after a few pages would throw the correspondence out.

It need hardly be said that the more unthinkingly

---

[1] I do not mean to say that a MS. was never divided up among several compositors, for this was no doubt done when there was special haste (cf. pp. 128–30); but it would be much *easier* to arrange it when exactly reprinting a book already in type.

and mechanically a compositor reproduces what is before him, the easier it is to show that he was following it. For example, in plays we occasionally find light thrown upon the relation of editions by a curiously stupid trick of compositors, who when a piece of prose is found among verse will sometimes when reprinting it treat each line as if it were a line of verse, not being careful to fill the lines out by spacing or, when necessary, bringing up part of the next line, but allowing them to remain short when differences in the fount of type used chance to make them so. Similarly in a reprint we sometimes find words carried over to another line, or stage-directions misplaced, because in the original edition there was no room for them where they belonged, even though the reprinter might easily have found space for them. Points like these, however, will easily be noticed. It is sufficient to warn an editor that whenever he comes across anything abnormal in the typographical arrangement of a text it will generally pay him to consider whether this may be due to the blind following of an earlier edition, in which perhaps the arrangement was for some reason or other quite justifiable.

Important evidence as to the order of editions can sometimes be obtained from a consideration of the signatures.

When a book is set up from MS., it is in most cases convenient to begin composition not with the title-page or preliminary matter, but with the commencement of the work itself. There are several reasons for this. It may be required that the preliminary leaves shall include a list of contents, with page-references ; and these page-references cannot of course be inserted until the text of the book is in type. Further, an author often wishes to leave his preface or dedication until the last. Corrections also are often given in the preliminaries. Hence it was a general, though not a universal, rule in earlier times, and is practically a universal rule at the present day, to begin with the beginning of the text.

A printer setting up a book in this way would do one of two things. Either he would sign the first sheet of the text A, intending when he came to the preliminaries to sign these with an asterisk, or with letters of another fount; or he would begin the text with B, keeping A for the preliminaries. The second is the usual method at present, though indeed A is not now as a rule actually printed in the preliminaries, it being evident to the binder that these are to come first. In Elizabethan printing there seems to have been no definite rule. It probably varied with the printing-house, but the question has not, I think, been investigated.

The *safest* method was evidently to begin with A, for if the author afterwards came along with preliminary matter extending to several sheets, it was easy enough to find arbitrary signs such as *, **, ***, &c., for them, or to use letters of the lower-case alphabet. On the other hand, if the printer had begun the text with B, he had only A to go before it, and if the preliminaries needed more than one sheet a difficulty arose as to how he should sign those after the first.

Now let us consider a few possible cases of signatures. It will seem at first sight that the points raised are matters of very small importance, but I hope to show that they may sometimes give us useful information.

(1) Suppose the preliminary matter occupies one sheet signed A, the text beginning on B—what does this tell us? The answer is, nothing at all. The preliminaries may have been printed either before or after the text.

(2) But suppose the preliminaries only occupy three leaves and the text begins on the fourth leaf of the sheet (A4). This gives us the information that the preliminaries, including the title-page, were set up first.

Hence the printer had the whole of his matter in hand before beginning composition. Hence there is a considerable chance that the book is a reprint.

(3) So also if we find very long preliminaries signed A, B, or A, B, C, and the text begins on C or D, it is likely, though not certain, that the book is a reprint.

(4) Suppose that the preliminaries consist of two sheets signed A and a, and the text then begins on B. We should at once guess that the printer began with the text, and that when the preliminary matter came in he found it unexpectedly long. Having only left one signature for it, he found two were required and had to add ' a '. If he had been reprinting, beginning from A, he would naturally have signed the second sheet B, and so on. Hence in this case the book was probably printed straight from MS. and is likely to be a first edition.[1]

From these considerations, we can deduce the general rule that an edition in which the signatures are all of one alphabet, beginning with A and proceeding regularly, is likely to be later than an edition in which the preliminary leaves have a separate signature.[2]

In the above cases we are only dealing with probabilities. The signatures give us a hint, which we must, if we can, turn into certainty by other evidence. But sometimes we can at least be certain that a book is a reprint.

For example, suppose that the preliminaries contain remarks by the author about the printer's haste or slowness, skill or carelessness ; or corrections or additions ; or a list of contents in which page-numbers are

---

[1] Provided that sheet a runs on from A. If not, the second sheet may be a later addition, as in Richard Harvey's *Lamb of God,* where sheet a contains an Epistle only found in a few copies.

[2] Excellent use of this point was made by Miss Henrietta C. Bartlett in her paper on ' Quarto Editions of Julius Cæsar ' in *The Library,* 3rd Ser., iv. 128.

given ; it is evident that the preliminary matter dates from after the book was originally put in type.

Now suppose also that the signatures are regular, beginning with A, but the text does not begin at the beginning of a sheet, but, say, on A4 or on B2, we see at once that the printing must have begun with the title-page and gone straight forward, and hence our book cannot be a first edition, but must be a reprint. More than this, if in the preliminaries there are references to pages of the book, it must be a page-for-page reprint from an earlier edition.[1]

One or two examples may make things clearer. To the second edition of Thomas Nashe's *Pierce Penilesse* is prefixed a letter from the author to the printer, in which Nashe says that he hears that the book is ' hasting to the second impression ' and that if the printer ' had not been so forward in the republishing of it ' he would have added something. He also asks him to shorten the title, which in the first edition had been too long. This the printer did. He had evidently begun printing with the text, which is signed A ; the title and the above-mentioned Epistle, which we may assume not to have been written until the book was, at least partly, in type, being signed by a paragraph-mark.

In the third edition the arrangement of signatures is similar ; but in the fourth the title-sheet is A, the epistle being on A2 and the text beginning on A3. Here then the Epistle was evidently set up *before* the text. Hence, even if the second and third edition had completely disappeared, we could have inferred the existence of one of them in which this letter was printed.

A still better example of what may be learnt from

---

[1] It is perhaps necessary to say that this would not be a valid inference in the case of modern books, where the whole might be standing in type at once ; but such was not the custom with the earlier printers.

signatures is to be found in the two undated editions
of George Chapman's *Memorable Masque of the Two
Honourable Houses or Inns of Court* [*c.* 1613]. The
arrangement of the two editions is as follows:

1. Printed by G. Eld for George Norton.

Quarto. ¶², A⁴, a⁴, B–E⁴, F².

(¶1) Title, verso blank. ¶2 Dedication. A1—a2ᵛ
'The Maske of the Gentlemen' (a general account of the
performance). a3—3ᵛ 'To answer certaine insolent obiections made against the length of my speeches, . . .' (a4) 'The
aplicable argument of the Maske' and Errata (in which errors
are referred to by the signatures of the text); verso blank.
B1—Fiᵛ The Names of the Speakers, followed by the text
of the Masque.

2. Printed by F. K. for George Norton.

Quarto. A–G⁴.

(A1) wanting, probably blank. (A2) Title, verso blank.
A3—3ᵛ Dedication. (A4)—C1ᵛ 'The Masque of the
Gentlemen.' C2—2ᵛ 'To answer certaine insolent obiec-
tions.' C3 'The applicable argument, . . .' verso blank.
(C4)—G3ᵛ The Names of the Speakers, followed by the
text of the Masque.

In this edition the List of errata does not occur, but only
one or two of them, and those the most obvious, have been
corrected.[1]

Now even from the make-up alone we might guess
that Ed. 1 is the earlier, for the work itself begins on
B1 and this is preceded by A and a, the latter signature strongly suggesting that the preliminary matter
was more than the printer had expected and allowed
for. But we have what amounts to absolute proof, for
on a1ᵛ, in the middle of the description of the masque,
we find the following passage:

These following [i. e. certain descriptions of the setting and
action of the masque] should in duty haue had their proper

---

[1] It may be noted that in this edition D1 is missigned B, perhaps
owing to the fact that the corresponding leaf in Eld's edition had
been B2.

places, after euery fitted speech of the Actors; but being preuented by the vnexpected haste of the Printer, which he neuer let me know, and neuer sending me a proofe, till he had past those speeches; I had no reason to imagine hee could haue been so forward.'

Now it is of course evident that this could not have been written until much of the play was in type; and therefore the preliminary matter must have been set up *after* the text. In Ed. 1 this, as we have seen, is possible; the arrangement even strongly suggests it. But consider the arrangement of Ed. 2. Here the passage just quoted is on sigs. B4^v and C1, and the masque itself begins on the last leaf of sheet C. It is therefore impossible that the text should have been set up before the preliminaries, and this edition *must* be a reprint.

Hence we cannot reasonably doubt that the edition printed by G. Eld preceded that by F. K.

Occasionally of course an author might deliver all the prefatory matter to the printer with the beginning of the work, and he might then begin composition with the title-page. We get an instance of this in another work by Nashe, *Strange News*, 1592, where as the text begins on B4 we might reasonably suspect that we have, not the original, but a reprint. Fortunately, however, the author settles the question by referring in sheet I to the word ' Gentleman ' which the printer had added to his name on the title-page (without his consent or privity), thus showing that the title was already printed and that he had seen it, and incidentally informing us that he was sending his copy to the printer in batches, as he wrote it. In this book the corrigenda come of course at the end, and it is interesting to observe that, though Nashe appears to have been in the Isle of Wight at the time when the book was being printed, he was able to include in his list of corrigenda (in sheet M) errors in sheet K, which must therefore have been already printed off and a copy forwarded to him.

I have referred to the fact that in certain circumstances errors in signatures may afford us information as to the order of editions of a book. It frequently happens that a reprint follows the original page for page but that the signatures differ. Thus the original may have been signed *, A, B, &c., and the reprint A, B, C, &c. Hence sheet B in Ed. 1 will be sheet C in Ed. 2. Now we sometimes find that the compositor in setting up the reprint forgets that he has to alter the signature. A mistake of this kind is almost invariably corrected in the first leaf of a gathering,[1] because it is important to the binder that these first signatures be correct, but it is sometimes left uncorrected in the later leaves of the gathering. Thus we may find a gathering signed B1, B2, B3 in Ed. 1, and C1, B2, B3 in Ed. 2. We at once guess that our Ed. 2 was printed from an edition in which this particular gathering was signed B, hence in the present case from Ed. 1 or an edition similarly arranged. And suppose we have also an Ed. 3 page for page the same, but this gathering correctly signed C1, C2, C3, we shall be fairly safe in assuming that it was later than Ed. 2, or at any rate was not intermediate between Ed. 1 and Ed. 2.[2]

Other points that it is well to be on the watch for are the following :

The manner in which the editions end, i.e. whether they do or do not fill an exact number of sheets. Odd leaves, not forming a complete sheet, whether at the beginning or end of a book, are naturally disliked by any one who has to pay for the printing of a book, as they involve a waste of labour in machining.[3] In a first

[1] But cf. p. 192, note.

[2] It may of course have been independently printed from Ed. 1.

[3] A half-sheet or even a single leaf takes of course as much time and labour to machine as a full sheet. Evidence of the avoidance of these waste blanks may be found in the occasional addition of odd fragments of matter having little or no connexion with the book itself, which we sometimes find at the end. Thus Hake's *News out of Paul's Church-*

edition, set up from MS., it may be impossible or not worth while so exactly to calculate the length that, using a particular size of page, it will fill an exact number of sheets. In reprinting, however, it is quite an easy matter to do this, and when a reprinter does not follow his original page for page it will generally be found that he adjusts his size of page to give this result.[1] Hence, if of two editions of a book one has a collation, say, $*^4$, A–L^4, M^2 (or M^4, M4 being blank) and the other $*^4$, A–L^4 only, both containing the same matter and being complete, we may be almost certain that the second one represents an attempt to save costs by getting the matter into an exact number of sheets, and is the later.

Differences in paragraph division. If these are only occasional and do not seem to have been dictated by any purpose of lengthening or shortening the matter,[2]

yard [1579] has on sigs. H3–H8 a ' letter written by the Author to his friende lying at the point of death ' inserted ' for the fillinge vp of emptie pages '. Another instance of this filling up of waste space, though not at the end of the book, is to be found in _The Generall Historie of Virginia_ by John Smith, 1624. The setting of the book was evidently divided between two compositors, one taking Books 1–3, the other Books 4–6. The second compositor began his work at page 105 (sig. P1), but either some of the first man's material was withdrawn or a miscalculation had occurred, for his matter came to an end on page 94 (N3^v). On page 95 (N4) we therefore find the heading ' _Now seeing there is thus much Paper here to spare, that you should not be altogether cloyed with Prose ; such Verses as my worthy Friends bestowed upon_ New England, _I here present you, because with honestie I can neither reiect, nor omit their courtesies_ '. Then follow verses to fill the two pages. There is no signature O. I am indebted for my knowledge of this book to Miss Albright's _Dramatic Publication_, p. 344.

[1] For an example of the readjustment of matter to save space, compare East's edition of Baldwin's _Moral Philosophy_ referred to on p. 78, and, for saving by imposing oddments together, see pp. 158–60.

[2] A curious instance of difference in paragraphing may be found in the two editions of Nashe's _Unfortunate Traveller_. Here, perhaps with a view to the saving of time, the reprint seems to have been divided between two printers, and, it being apparently desired to get the book

it is worth noting whether in cases of running-on in one edition (A), it happens that the last line of the preceding paragraph in the other edition (B) is a full one. If this is so, it is probable that the compositor did not notice that a new paragraph was intended. The occurrence of several cases of the kind would strongly suggest that A was printed from B.

Evidence from superfluous hyphens. When a word in one edition happens to be divided at the end of a line, a printer setting up from this text, and not following it line for line, will sometimes carelessly repeat the hyphen when it is no longer required. Thus in the three editions of Nashe's *Pierce Penilesse* printed in 1592, we have in one place :

Ed. A. frantick (the word midway in a line).

Ed. B. fran-tick (the word divided at the end of a line and correctly hyphened).

Ed. C. fran-tick (the word midway in a line and the hyphen incorrectly retained).

Knowing, as we do, that A is the first edition, we can see that it is highly probable that B was printed from A, and C from B.

Thus far we have been dealing mainly with editions which do not correspond line for line. In the case of exact reprints of this kind it may seem at first sight especially difficult to determine the order. There is, however, one consideration which will often help us greatly, namely the fact that unless a book is reprinted by the original printer within a very short time of its first appearance, the reprinter seldom has available all the original varieties of type, initial letters, ornaments, &c. The consequence often is that when he comes to an abnormal passage, a long heading in large type, or

into a smaller number of sheets, the page arrangement was not kept. It happened that one printer had rather more than the other to get into the same space, and consequently one tended to run his paragraphs together, the other to make new ones wherever he could (see my edition of Nashe, ii. 189–96).

a note or other passage in small type, or when he has to reprint a page containing an initial letter or ornament, he may have to substitute type, initials or ornaments of larger or smaller size than those in the copy. Now as his text runs page for page, at least, with the original, he must in his reprint make the matter occupy just the same space as it formerly did, either by crowding it or spacing it out. As the original printer was under no such compulsion, his text would be set in a perfectly normal fashion, and comparison of two such pages side by side will often show at once which was the original setting and which the copy. In dealing with line-for-line or page-for-page reprints, therefore, it is generally well to begin by looking for differences in the size of headings, &c., in the editions under consideration, and, if any are found, considering them from the point of view of normality or awkwardness of arrangement.

Lastly, we may sometimes require to decide which of two *issues* of a book is the earlier, e.g. when new introductory matter has been substituted for what was originally printed, the rest of the sheets being the same. Such substitutions are generally to be regarded as cancels (see chap. ix, below), but it may be said in passing that the best evidence of priority is often the watermark. If we find that in one issue the watermark of the introductory matter is identical with that of the paper of the text, while in the other issue it is different, we may be practically certain that the former is the original issue.

It will of course be recognized that evidence derived from points such as these, though often useful, is mainly of cumulative value. The relationship of editions can sometimes be most conclusively *proved* by full collation and comparison of readings, and with this I have nothing to do here. It may, however, be remarked in passing that the most satisfactory evidence in this respect is often to be obtained from wrong attempts at correction on the part of a compositor or proof-reader. I may give a single example from a marginal note in *Pierce Penilesse* where a corrector has produced a reading which is really rather ingenious. Here the first three editions have correctly ' The confutation of Citizens obiections against Players '. The fourth edition accidentally drops the word ' obiections ', producing ' The confutation of Citizens against Players '. This evidently puzzled the proof-reader of the fifth edition and he altered it to ' The coniuration of Citizens against Players ' [1]

But any careful student of works of the Elizabethan period will have come across numerous examples of this transformation of sense by the attempt to correct mistakes, and it is unnecessary to say more about the matter here. One rather curious instance of a difference in editions susceptible of what may be called a ' bibliographical ' explanation, may, however, be given, as it throws some light on the casual methods of the Elizabethan printer.

It occurs in a translation from a French summary, by Pierre de Changi, of notable facts out of Pliny's *Historia Naturalis*. This was first published in English as *A Summarie of the Antiquities, and wonders of the worlde* [c. 1565], and again in 1585 as *The Secrets and wonders of the world*. The first edition is in 8vo, running to H8^v, the second in quarto, running to I1^v.[2] Now the two editions are, with the exception of certain changes in the preliminary matter, practically the same save for the ending, which is altogether different. The earlier edition has, beginning at the foot

---

[1] Miss Albright in her *Dramatic Publication*, p. 375, notes other instances of progressive corruption from *The Bloody Brother*, ii. i (*B. & F.* ed. Dyce, x. 392), and *Richard III*, v. iii. 182.

[2] This is, by the way, a curious instance of a reprint both being larger in size and ending more irregularly (on the first leaf of a sheet) than the original. Had neither book been dated and had we no other evidence to go on we might reasonably guess that the 1585 edition was the earlier.

of the last leaf but one (H7^v–8), a passage about a certain tree as follows : ' The *Ciper* tree is slowe in growing with-¹/[H8] out fruit, hauing bitter leaues, violent smell, and naughty shadow.' This is followed by a page and a half more about various kinds of trees, and the book then ends.

In the edition of 1585, however, there is a remarkable difference in the information that is given about the ' *Ciper* tree '. There we read [I1^v] ' The *Ciper* tree is slowe in growing without the ground be fat and fertile, then it spreadeth very large and long.' There is nothing more about trees. The page proceeds, ' And thus to conclude, I finish this abstract ', and ends with a few words of praise to God for ' these his benefites and giftes geuen for the vse of mankinde '.

It is of course obvious what has happened. The printer was working from a copy of the earlier edition which lacked the last leaf. He came to the words ' The *Ciper* tree is slowe in growing without '—and there it ended. Did he trouble to find another copy, or to get some one to look up in Pliny what was said about the ' *Ciper* tree '? Not he : it was much simpler to set his brains to work and guess what was missing !²

¹ Catchword ' out '.

² In this he was less honest than the printer of Thomas Scot's *Philomythie*, 1616, who having lost part of the copy and ' the Author being far from London ' left a blank for it (on p. 126), promising to supply the defect in the next impression (Collier, *Bibliographical Account*, ii. 327). The missing passage, 64 lines, was duly added in another edition, printed in the same year.

Chapter Five

ON DATING UNDATED EDITIONS AND ON FALSE DATES

IT is one thing to determine, by bibliographical methods, the *order* of undated editions of a book, and another, often much harder, task to assign to an undated edition even an approximate date. It is indeed probably the most difficult that an expert bibliographer can undertake, and the more carelessly the book is printed the less chance is there of success. Even when the printer is known, the date can generally be inferred only by the investigation of a large number of examples of his work; while if he is unknown the task is almost hopeless. It may, however, be well to caution young students against blindly accepting the conjectural dates given in the catalogues of libraries. Sometimes they are probably right, but often they are wrong or at least very doubtful. Librarians have better opportunities than most people of settling such points correctly, but they are not infallible, and besides we seldom know in using their catalogues *who* it was that guessed the date, or upon what evidence he relied. In some cases conjectural dates have simply been taken over from authorities such as Collier, whose knowledge of early printing was by no means extensive.

Apart from such external evidence as entries in the Stationers' Register, which of course seldom tell us more than that *one* edition, which may or may not be the one in question, was published or was intended to be published at or about a certain date, we have the following points to guide us:

1. We may be able to place the book between two other dated editions.[1]

2. We may be able on the evidence of the signatures to infer that the particular edition was probably the first, or was not the first.[2]

[1] See pp. 114 and 196–8 above.   [2] See pp. 188–94 above.

Neither of these considerations, however, will give us an exact date, and the only way in which we can obtain this is by comparing the book with dated books printed by the same printer at about the time when it seems likely that the one in question appeared. Chronological lists of books issued from 1500 to 1557, arranged under their printers, together with information as to the libraries in which copies are to be found, are given in the Bibliographical Society's *Hand-lists of London Printers*. For books after 1557 there are no lists approaching the same completeness,[1] but partial ones can be constructed from Herbert's edition of Ames's *Typographical Antiquities* (to 1600 only), Sayle's *Catalogue of English Books at Cambridge*, and Mr. Gray's Index to Hazlitt's *Handbook* and *Collections*. The index to the 3-vol. Catalogue of English books to 1640 in the British Museum is also useful, but in order to find the books published in the neighbourhood of the date required, it is necessary to look up *all* the references under the printer, as these are not in chronological order. From 1640 onwards almost the only help is to be found in the Term Catalogues and in the few existing accounts of the work of particular printers.

Having before us some books in the neighbourhood of the probable date of the book in question, we must proceed to derive from them such evidence as we can—often there is very little. If the work under investigation contains a woodcut border or woodcut ornaments, and if we can find these in other books, it is often very helpful, as it may be possible to discover the order in which the books were printed from the condition of the blocks. See Part I, chap. ix, pp. 113–19.

If there are no title borders or large blocks in the book in question, evidence of a similar kind can sometimes, though rarely, be derived from the initial letters.

---

[1] It may be hoped that the Indexes to Pollard and Redgrave's *Short-Title Catalogue of English Books 1475–1540* will, when issued, supply at least in great measure this want for the period with which it deals.

Occasionally something can be learnt from the type used,[1] but this generally necessitates an investigation of the whole of a printer's work, as it is quite possible for him to abandon the use of a particular fount for a time and afterwards to employ it again.

Lastly it is sometimes worth while to examine the watermark of the paper carefully. If the same paper can be found in a dated book, it is *probable* that the two were printed within a short time of each other. We have, however, always to take account of the possibility of oddments of old paper being used up.

The question of false dates is one that has of late been brought into prominence by the brilliant investigations of Professor Pollard, Dr. Greg, and Mr. Neidig on the dates of certain Shakespeare quartos. False dates are probably common in some classes of books.

1. A large number of official religious books, volumes of statutes, &c., seem to have been reprinted with the original date, apparently as an indication that they were exact reprints of the work as authorized. Thus at least seven editions of the 1547 *Injunctions* were issued with the date 31 July, 1547. Seeing that no editions are known with dates for many years afterwards, it is not necessary to suppose that they were all issued together. The date may simply mean that they are the *Injunctions* promulgated in that year. Five edi-

---

[1] A point which may be worth noticing is the appearance of new type. Especially about the period when the capital J and U were coming into use, the date at which a printer began to use these letters may be worth investigation. A little later, during the second and third quarter of the seventeenth century, we find printers gradually substituting the rounded form of U for the U similar to the lower-case letter (cf. pp. 311–12). This replacement often occurred at different times in different sizes of type. At earlier periods it may be worth while to watch a printer's purchases of new type (often of slightly different face) in order to supplement his existing founts. An interesting example of an argument based on the purchase by a printer of an additional supply of capitals to eke out an old fount may be found in Professor Pollard's *Shakespeare Folios and Quartos*, p. 95.

tions of the *Homilies* bear the same date as the *Injunctions*. Seven editions of the *Statutes* of 1 Edward VI are dated 1548. Seven editions of the *Statutes* of 5 and 6 Edward VI are dated 1552, and so on. In all books of this class the date must often be taken as that of the *first* edition, not necessarily that of all those in which it appears. The same repetition of the original date may be found in many unofficial publications. Thus all three editions of the Caxton *Dicts and Sayings* are dated 1477, though the last two were probably printed about 1480 and 1490 respectively. Professor Pollard also instances Middleton's reprint of a volume of Pynson's *Froissart* and the reissue of Hobbes's *Leviathan* [1651, reissued with the same date about 1680].[1]

2. Books seem sometimes to have been dated falsely simply in order to create the impression that they were not a new edition. They were presumably piratically printed by some one who had no right to print them, and sold to booksellers more or less surreptitiously. It was probably for some such reason as this that the quartos of Shakespeare's plays, now believed to have been printed in 1619, bear the dates of the earlier editions. We may perhaps explain in a similar way the existence of two editions of Thomas Heywood's *Love's Mistress*, both called ' the Second Impression ' and dated 1640 though the later was probably printed about 1660.

3. We sometimes find a *colophon* containing a date reprinted from an earlier edition without change. This is perhaps due to simple carelessness. For this reason dates in colophons should be regarded as of little weight, if other evidence tends to show that they are incorrect. An engraved title-page was also sometimes reprinted without alteration of the original date, presumably because of the trouble involved in changing it.

[1] *Shakespeare Folios and Quartos*, p. 102.

Chapter Six

ON VARIATIONS IN DIFFERENT COPIES OF THE SAME
EDITION

IT has long been recognized that different copies of
the same edition [1] of early, and indeed even comparatively modern, books may present differences of
reading, a fact which has been the cause of much
trouble and a certain amount of perplexity to many
editors. The whole matter is, however, perfectly
simple when regarded from the point of view of early
methods of printing, but its importance in textual
criticism necessitates that we should discuss it with
some care.

There are two kinds of variation. Accidental variation owing to displacement of type during the actual
machining; and intentional variation due to the type
being corrected after the process of printing was
begun.

As regards the former, it need only be said that the
method of inking by dabbing the type with ink-balls
was especially likely to draw out loose type. When
a printer noticed that a type was thus drawn out, he
would no doubt as a rule replace it. Unfortunately
he seems not always to have troubled to replace the
right letter, but to have put in any type he could find.
We may suppose that when drawn out of the forme
the type was sometimes jerked by the ink-ball on to the
floor, where other type may have been lying, and
a careless workman might easily pick up the wrong
one. Certainly we can find errors in some copies of

---

[1] i. e. printed as a whole from the same setting-up of type. The
variants referred to occur in books printed at all periods, but they seem
especially common, or have been especially observed, in books of the
sixteenth and seventeenth centuries.

books which we can prove not to have been in the forme as originally placed on the bed of the press.

Accidental variations such as these are, however, for the most part matters of a single letter, and, once the possibility of their occurrence is recognized, present little difficulty to an editor. Far more important is the correction of the type during the process of printing.

Of all matters connected with the book-trade in the Elizabethan times, the one of which we know least is probably the relation of the author to the publisher or printer. We have indeed one scene in a play between an author and John Danter the printer-bookseller,[1] a scene to which Danter's declaration that he had lost money by the author's last book gives the stamp of realism, but which otherwise tells us little ; and we have one dialogue between an author and the printer William Hoskins,[2] but this, being concerned entirely with the doings of Dame Fortune, is of even less practical value. One thing we may, however, infer from incidental references as well as from the evidence of the texts themselves, is that it was usual, or at any rate not uncommon, for an author to attend in person at the printing-house in order to revise proofs. Nashe, for example, in the Epistle before *Lenten Stuff*, 1599, speaks of the ' faults of the presse, that escaped in my absence from the Printing-house ',[3] and in a letter of

[1] See *The Return from Parnassus*, I. iii.

[2] See Ulpian Fulwell's *First part of the eight (sic) liberall science*, 1575, sig. B1 *et seq.* ' The first Dialogue betwene the Author and the printer.'

[3] Cf. the Preface to Jasper Heywood's translation of *Thyestes*, 1560 (ed. de Vocht, p. 105), where the author says that he corrected the proofs of the first edition of his *Troas*, but when he was gone the printer ' renewed ' the print (i. e. presumably, printed a second edition) and ' corrupted all ' ; also the first edition of Nashe's *Unfortunate Traveller* (sig. A3) ; the second edition of Marston's *Parasitaster* (title) ; R. Turner's *Nosce Te*, 1607 (sig. F4) ; and H[enry] P[arrot]'s *Mastive*, 1615 (sig. I4). In George Gascoigne's *Drum of Doomsday* (1576) the author makes similar excuses, stating that being ill he was ' unable himselfe to attend the dayly proofes ', and appointed a servant to oversee them in his place ; and in a concluding epistle to his *Palladine*

the printer William Jaggard, prefixed to Augustine Vincent's *Discouerie of Errours in the first Edition of the Catalogue of Nobility published by Raphe Brooke*, we find a passage which for the light which it throws on the methods of the time deserves quotation in full.

It must be explained that Ralph Brooke, York Herald, published in 1619 a *Catalogue and Succession of the Kings, Princes, Dukes, etc., of England since the Norman Conquest.* This work proved to contain numerous errors, and in 1622 Augustine Vincent published the above-mentioned criticism of it. In the meantime, however, Brooke, hearing of Vincent's work, rushed out a second, corrected, edition of his own, in the preface of which he attributed the faults of the earlier edition to the printer, William Jaggard, who had foisted them in while he, Brooke, was away ill. As Jaggard was also printing Vincent's criticism, he took the opportunity of replying to Brooke in a letter prefixed to Vincent's work. He tells us incidentally that of Brooke's earlier edition 500 copies were printed, of which almost 200 still remained ' rotting by the walles ' (sig. ¶ 5ᵛ), and that in order to get out his revised edition before Vincent's criticism, Brooke had made his printers work day and night (sig. ¶ 5ᵛ, 6). The most important passage of Jaggard's letter is as follows :

' Seeing then we haue with much inquirie sifted out, what

of England, 1588, Anthony Munday says that the many errors were caused ' partly by want of my attendance to read the proues, being called away by matters of greater importance, and whereto I am bound by dutie of mine office '. As late as 1785 Boswell ' hastened to the printing-house ' to make a correction in a sheet of his *Journal of a Tour to the Hebrides*, cf. Mr. Chapman's edition of Johnson's *Journey*, &c., 1924, p. 324 ; but this is hardly the same thing as the regular attendance which seems to have been customary in earlier times. A number of other passages showing that authors of the sixteenth and seventeenth centuries were in the habit of either attending at the printer's to correct proofs or having proofs sent to them are given by Miss Albright in her *Dramatic Publication*, pp. 350–4. Cf. also the important article by Mr. Percy Simpson on ' Proof-reading by English Authors of the 16th and 17th Centuries ' referred to on p. 218 note 1.

tares they were, which the Printer sowed in Master *Yorkes* booke, it remaines, that we take notice of the time pickt out to sow these tares, which is a point of especiall consequence. And to say truth, what time could it possibly bee, but in Master *Yorkes* absence from the Presse, occasioned by his vnfortunate sicknesse ? Who all the time before, while hee stood sentinell at the Presse, kept such strict and diligent guard there, as a letter could not passe out of his due ranke, but was instantly checkt and reduced into order; but his sicknesse, confining him to his chamber, and *absenting him from the Presse,* then was the time, that the Printer tooke, to bring in that *Troiane horse* of *Barbarismes,* and literall errours, which ouer-runne the whole volume of his Catalogue. Neither makes it to the purpose, that in the time of this his vnhappy sicknesse, though hee came not in person to ouer-looke the Presse, yet the *Proofe,* and *Reuiewes* duly attended him, and he perused them (as is well to be iustifyed) in the maner he did before. For let that be true, say he viewed, reuiewed, directed, corrected, or whatsoeuer els, yet what is all this to the presence of an olde Herauld at a Presse, one that were likely to blaze out any mans disgrace, and print it (for a neede) in the fore-head of a Booke, that should commit the least literall fault ? No, I must confesse, that the sight alone of such a reuerend man in a Printing-house, like an old Fencer vpon a Stage, would do more good for keeping the presse in order, then the view, and reuiew of twentie proofes by himselfe with all his Latine, and other learning, he being in the meane time personally absent from the Presse.' (sig. ¶ 6ᵛ).

Besides the fact that Brooke attended at Jaggard's press to correct proofs and that during his illness they were sent to him, we may note the interesting point that revises, or as Jaggard calls them ' reviews ', were seen by him, as well as the original proofs.

But it appears that corrections made by the author at the printing-house were not limited to proofs, and that alterations, sometimes of great importance, were made in the formes after printing-off had begun. Variations between copies of the same edition are too frequently found for us to suppose that the uncorrected sheets are proofs accidentally bound up with the others, and indeed such a theory would, for reasons which will be clear later, lead us into further difficulties.[1]

Perhaps in the case of important books, or of books by important authors, a printer did not proceed to work off a sheet until the author had finally passed the proof for press ; but in the case of those in which correctness was merely desirable without being essential, we must, I think, suppose that if the author did not turn up when a sheet was ready for printing, the printer did not wait for him, but proceeded to work it off as passed by his press-reader. If the author came in later and, picking up a sheet fresh from the press, found mistakes in it, the printer seems to have been willing to stop the press and let them be corrected. Making-ready was doubtless a less elaborate process in Elizabethan days, and the disturbance of the type a matter of little importance.

How extensive the alterations made during printing-off might be can be seen, for example, in Barnabe Barnes's play *The Devil's Charter*, where out of five copies in the British Museum, the Bodleian, and Cambridge University Library, two have on sig. B4 a couple of lines which are absent from the other three. As those copies with the additional lines have on pages B3ᵛ and B4 one line more of print than on other pages, and no catchwords, it is clear that these represent the corrected state of the forme, and that the lines had been omitted by accident.

Besides these added lines, *The Devil's Charter* exhibits a very large number of striking variants in different copies, some being mere corrections of literal errors, others important alterations in wording. The following are a few examples. In each case the earlier reading

---

[1] If they were proofs we should expect them to exhibit both formes in an uncorrected state, whereas it is at least equally common for one to be correct and the other incorrect. Besides, why in any case should a printer print so many proofs that they had to be used up by treating them as perfect sheets ?

is given first. It may be noted that in the second and last cases the ' correction ' is itself incorrect.

suspect. : suspect vs.	rewarde. : rewarde of sinne.
baudes and : beastly *Bardes*, and	Wounds both of : Wounds of
sheere : sweete	falce liers : familiers
of home : horne	slepe : steps
Plegmatist : stigmatist	hags : darkensse

One or two of these variants might be conjectures of an unusually intelligent press-reader, but others seem hardly likely to be due to any one save the author.

Some idea of the frequency of this habit of correcting while at press may be obtained from the fact that of twenty plays published by the Malone Society up to the end of 1912, in the preparation of which two or more copies of the same edition were collated, variant readings were found in no less than fifteen. In all but three or four of these fifteen the variants are such as an editor would be bound to notice. In fact we may say that in any early book the probability of finding such variants is very great and cannot be neglected by any careful editor.

Now there are several things to say about these variations. In the first place it cannot be supposed that the binder, when gathering the sheets for binding, would trouble himself as to whether they represented the final corrections or not; he would take them as they happened to come. It is therefore quite un-scientific to speak of a more or less corrected *copy* of a book—unless indeed it only consists of a single sheet, or, indeed, as we shall see later, of a single forme.

I do not deny that it is possible that a few sheets in the most correct state might be selected to be made up into presentation copies for the author's friends; for the MS. corrections occasionally met with in presentation copies show that trouble was sometimes taken to render them as correct as possible; but I have certainly never come across any evidence of such a practice, nor does it seem at all likely.[1] There are of course copies of books all the sheets of which are in the most corrected state, but in all such cases known to me the number of sheets existing in two states bears a small proportion to the whole number in the book, and the result might therefore easily come about by chance.

But we must go further. Though to a binder the sheet is the unit, yet it is not the unit for our purpose at present. When we consider the process of printing, this is sufficiently obvious ; for the two sides of a sheet are printed at different times and there may be a considerable interval between the two printings. Let us see what the result of this will be. Suppose that a printer is engaged in printing the inner forme of a certain sheet and that this inner forme is the first to be printed. When he has printed a certain number of copies, the author comes in, picks up a sheet, and finds some errors. He points them out to the printer, who stops the press and corrects them. The rest of the sheets are then printed on one side with the corrections inserted. As they are printed they are hung up to dry, a process the duration of which depends on the ink used, the state of the atmosphere, and other considerations, but which will always take an appreciable time. If the printer is only using one press he will not begin to perfect the sheets by printing the other side until the whole number are worked off. If, however, he is using two, he may begin to perfect as soon as the earlier sheets printed on one side are dry : or perhaps he may begin working off the two formes

---

[1] It is of course quite possible that copies might be made up of sheets specially selected as perfect from the printer's point of view, clean impressions free from flaws in the paper and other technical imperfections, but this is another matter. The ' picked copies ' occasionally heard of in later times were, I think, generally selected from this point of view. For a record of one such copy see Mr. Chapman's note in the *Review of English Studies*, iii. 79.

simultaneously, printing half his sheets from one and half from the other. The exact arrangements are a matter of the convenience of the moment. It results from this that the order in which the sheets are perfected is undetermined, and that if during printing, corrections are made in the *outer* forme, as they were in the *inner*, there is no reason for assuming that the sheets which were printed from the uncorrected inner forme will be perfected from the outer forme while that also is in its incorrect state.

This may be seen more clearly by taking figures. Let us suppose a sheet of which 1,000 copies in all are to be printed. Suppose one press to be used, and corrections to be made in the inner forme when 200 copies have been printed. There will then be 200 incorrect + 800 correct. Suppose the printer begins to perfect in precisely the same order in which the sheets were originally printed, but that the author comes in rather earlier during the operation—say, when 100 sheets are printed—stops the press, and has corrections made, this time in the outer forme. There will then of the perfected sheets be 100 incorrect on both sides, 100 incorrect on the inner forme but correct on the outer, and 800 correct on both. Suppose, however, that the printer had begun to perfect from the *last* sheet printed on the one side, we should then have 200 incorrect on the inner but correct on the outer, 100 incorrect on the outer but correct on the inner, and 700 correct on both. If, lastly, he had collected the dried sheets for perfecting more or less at haphazard, as is indeed most probable, the result would be a mere matter of chance.[1]

---

[1] I have of course assumed the usual early method of working one forme at a time. If this method of correction during printing off were ever used in conjunction with 'half-sheet' imposition (see pp. 66–70), it is obvious that of any one signature we might, besides 'mixed' sheets, have *either* sheets corrected in both formes (if the corrections were made before perfecting began), or sheets uncorrected in both

It is thus quite clear that we cannot assume that because we find corrections in a page belonging to the outer forme (pages 1, 4, 5, 8 of a quarto sheet), the pages belonging to the inner forme (pages 2, 3, 6, 7) will also be corrected; but it does follow—and this is most important for textual criticism—that if on two pages of one forme (suppose on pages 1 and 4 of a sheet) we find variants, and if it is clear that in a certain copy the variants on page 1 are corrections, then those on page 4 in the same copy must also be corrections,[1] and if we follow the readings of that copy on one of these pages we must also follow them on the other. On the other hand, our following the readings of this copy on pages 1 and 4 does *not* oblige us to follow them on pages 2 and 3, as these belong to the other forme.

When we reprint an early book, we as a rule wish to reprint it in its most correct state. We must therefore, if we find variants in two or more copies, print from those *formes* in the copies which are most correct, neglecting the bound books, and also neglecting the sheets as such. It is only thus that we can reproduce the book as its author meant it to appear.

It is perhaps hardly necessary to add that correction during working-off was not by any means limited to the sixteenth and early seventeenth centuries, though it was probably more common then than it was later. Mr. Chapman, in his edition of Johnson's *Journey to the Western Highlands* and Boswell's *Journal of a Tour*, 1924, p. 481, points out that alterations were made in

---

formes (if the corrections were made after perfecting began), but not *both*. Also exactly half of the ' mixed ' sheets must be uncorrected in one forme and half in the other.

[1] ' Corrections ', not necessarily ' correct ', for it sometimes happened that in carrying out the corrections a printer made fresh—and even worse—blunders. We must of course also allow for the possibility of entirely new errors being caused by the accidental disturbance of the type of other words when making a correction, but these can seldom be mistaken for intentional changes.

the latter while at press,[1] and one may even find instances of the practice in quite modern books. Nowadays, however, if an alteration required were sufficiently serious for it to be worth while to stop the press, it would usually be thought desirable to reprint the peccant sheet or leaf.

[1] See also p. 206, note to p. 205, above.

Chapter Seven

ON BOOKS SET IN DUPLICATE

IT being now, I hope, clear that from the textual point of view the forme, not the sheet, is the unit, we may deal with a matter that is fortunately of theoretical rather than of practical interest to the majority of those who edit our early literature, for it affects chiefly a class of books that are seldom reprinted. In order to divide the work of the printing-houses fairly between compositors and pressmen, it was at one time customary not to print more than a limited number of copies of a book from one setting-up of type.[1] Books of which a large number of copies were required, such as service books and other official publications, were therefore sometimes set up in duplicate. Now of course if the printer had simply set up the book twice and printed from the two settings as if he were printing two independent works, he would merely have produced two editions.[2] The binder would indeed prob-

---

[1] The limit in the case of most books was 1,250 or 1,500 (see Arber's *Transcript*, ii. 43, 883, and v. liii). It is difficult to make out when this rule or custom began to be observed. In 1576 we find the edition of a certain book limited to 1,500 copies (ibid., ii. 307), and the entry and the conditions attached seem to indicate that the limitation is a special one and that no rule in the matter then existed. The first definite regulation seems to date from about 1587, but I think that we may suppose the existence of some equivalent custom by that date or there would have been traces of dissent or discussion ; probably indeed as a custom the limitation may have been very much older though it may never have been precisely formulated. In the case of a very short book of which a large number of copies were required for immediate sale, the printer might perhaps set up in duplicate for another reason, i.e. to save time in working off. I doubt, however, whether as a rule there would have been any gain in doing this on account of the small number of presses owned by most of the printers.

[2] An example of this kind of duplication may probably be found in

ably have mixed the sheets ; we might find copies of the book made up of sheets of A setting and of B setting indiscriminately, but we should still say that two editions of the book were printed. To the confounding of bibliographers, however, the printer did not by any means always do this. If he printed the outer forme from setting A he might print the inner either from setting A or from setting B as chance directed him, and thus of each sheet he would make four varieties, the outer and inner formes being respectively A A, A B, B A, B B. Many examples of this kind of confusion are found in books printed by Richard Grafton.

A still more troublesome variety is where even the pages of the forme are not kept together. We may suppose that after printing a certain number of copies of the book the printer, perhaps needing the chases or the furniture, would unlock the pages of type, tie them round with string, and put them aside for future use ; [1] there being two (or possibly in some cases more) of each. When he wished to print further copies of the book he would take one page 1, one page 4, and so on, for the outer forme, and one page 2 and one page 3, &c., for the inner, but it would be a matter of complete indifference to him whether those pages 4 and 3 had originally been used with the same pages 1 and 2 or not. Examples of this reimposition and mixing of the original pages will be found in the

Tottel's Miscellany, of which there exist two editions dated 31 July 1557. These differ throughout and in the few copies known the sheets do not appear to have been mixed, but it seems reasonable to suppose that they were set up and printed at the same time and at the same house in order to supply an exceptional demand. See the article on 'Tottel's Miscellany' by W. W. Greg in *The Library*, 2nd Ser., v. 113–33.

[1] It may be thought that this contradicts what I have said elsewhere about the general custom being for a printer to distribute his type as he went along. This is true, but such work in duplicate would in any case only be found in very large firms or very small books.

Statutes of 3 and 4 Edward VI, printed by Grafton with the date 1549, and the *Return of Pasquil*, printed by Charlewood in 1589.[1]

Occasionally also we find this duplicate setting in part of a book alone, and for a different reason. It sometimes chances that a book ends in such a way that there is a single leaf or two of print beyond a certain number of sheets. Under such circumstances a printer who had to print, say, 1,000 copies of the book might find it cheaper to set up the last leaf or so *twice*, and print 500 copies of this, afterwards of course cutting the sheets in half, rather than to set it up once and print 1,000 half-sheets. This probably explains the fact that Richard Harvey's *Astrological Discourse* of 1583 (8vo) is found with two settings of sig. F (two leaves), though all the rest of the book was apparently only set up once.[2]

[1] See *The Library*, 2nd series, iv. 384 ff. (November 1903).

[2] A later example of this duplicate setting has been noted in vol. ii of Mandeville's *Fable of the Bees*, 1755. See the *Fable*, ed. Kaye, ii. 396, Dr. A. E. Case's note. Duplicate settings of this sort must of course be distinguished from the partial re-setting sometimes resorted to when, after part of a book had been printed and distributed, it was decided to increase the size of the edition, or when a reprint was called for before the whole of the type of the first issue was distributed, cf. pp. 59–60, 178–9.

Chapter Eight

ON AUTHOR'S COPY, PROOFS, AND PROOF CORRECTIONS

THE subjects of this chapter are unfortunately among those on which we have, at any rate until comparatively late in the seventeenth century, very little knowledge. It would be of the greatest value to us if, of even a few important books of the first two centuries of printing, we had the MSS. actually used by the printers and could see not only how closely they were followed in such matters as spelling and punctuation, but how much ' editing ' was done upon them in the printing-house in the way of cutting the matter up into paragraphs or chapters, and adding chapter-headings and side-notes, tables of contents, index, and the like.

Perhaps for the reasons suggested in the note on page 186, the existing MSS. that appear to have passed through an English printing-house before *c.* 1700 are very few indeed. I can only learn of one certain example, the MS., unfortunately incomplete, of Harington's translation of *Orlando Furioso* (printed by Richard Field in 1591), which was described by Dr. W. W. Greg in *The Library*, 4th series, iv. 102 ff., under the title of ' An Elizabethan Printer and his Copy '. This is in many ways of very great interest as showing that in *some* cases at any rate the printer paid very little attention to his author's spelling and punctuation, and at the same time that some authors took a very considerable amount of interest in the way in which their work was printed. Harington specifies the type which he requires (by reference to the *Arte of Poesie* which Field had recently printed), states where he wants a blank leaf or page, and even in one place demands ' some prety knotte ' as a tail-piece, which Field duly supplied. Unfortunately, however, we dare not take this MS. alone as representative. Field was a more than usually careful printer, and Harington was a man of forceful personality who was, I think, more likely than many authors to know what he wanted and to see that he got it. One would imagine that the average writer would be likely to think that his duty in the matter began and ended with reading through the proofs.

There exist also a few MSS. which may have been prepared for the printer though not actually used. For example, in the MS. of R. Carew's *Excellency of the English Tongue* now in Brit. Mus. Cotton Julius F. xi certain passages are underlined which in the printed text are in italics (see facsimiles of a passage in an article on 'The Arte of English Poesie' by B. M. Ward, *R. E. S.* i. 290–1). There appears no indication, however, that the MS. was actually printed from, and there is some slight evidence that it was not. Other MSS. which have been described as prepared for press, on the ground that the title is set out as in a printed book, may be simply fair copies.

Proofs are even less likely to be preserved than original MSS. The following are the only corrected proofs from English presses that I can hear of up to the end of the seventeenth century.[1]

1. Proofs of two broadsides in the possession of the Society of Antiquaries, namely, *A Spectacle for Periurers*, 1589, and *A Table shewing all the distances betweene all the Cities and Shire Townes of England*, by John Norden [?c. 1620] (nos. 90 and 255 in R. Lemon's *Catalogue*). Both these are corrected in much the same way as is now usual, but unfortunately most of the marginal corrections have been cut off.[2]

2. A portion of Milton's *Lycidas*, 1638, namely

---

[1] But see the article by Mr. Percy Simpson in *Oxford Bibl. Soc. Proceedings*, II. i (1928), pp. 5–14, for some important additions to this list.

[2] It may be remarked that No. 250 in the same collection, which is also described by Lemon as 'proof sheets', is printed on one side of the paper only but bears no corrections.

lines 23–35, reproduced facing page 89 of the type-facsimile of Milton's *Poems*, 1645, issued by the Clarendon Press in 1924. The corrections appear to be those of a printer's reader and refer solely to such matters as missing hyphens, letters failing to print, &c.

3. Corrected proofs of parts of sheets A and I of Cartwright's *Royal Slave*, 1639 (first edition).[1] I am indebted to Dr. Greg for sending me rotographs which show that the corrections were indicated in much the same way as at present. Unfortunately, however, the fragments are mutilated and several of the corrections are cut off. It is interesting to note that the proofs were printed on both sides of the paper, evidently without any trouble being taken about the register.

In addition to these there exist a certain number of fragments printed on one side only, but without corrections. These may perhaps be proofs, but in most cases I suspect that they are merely printers' waste, either rough pulls taken during making ready in order to see that the type was duly levelled and no further under-laying or overlaying was necessary in order to get a proper impression, or else sheets which had, by the not uncommon accident of two sheets sticking together, failed to be perfected. When they are rough pulls taken from a forme before correction they may of course exhibit variants from the accepted text, but they contribute little, if anything, to our knowledge of typographical methods.

When, much later, we do find proof sheets which have been preserved, as those of Boswell's *Life of Johnson*,[2] we find that the methods of correction were practically the same as at the present day, and that

---

[1] In one of the Bodleian collections of fragments.

[2] See *Reproduction of some of the Original Proof-sheets of Boswell's 'Life of Johnson'*, printed by R. B. Adam for his Friends, Buffalo, N.Y., 1923, in which some 70 pages are reproduced in full-size facsimile. Also Mr. Chapman's articles on 'Boswell's Proof Sheets' in *The London Mercury* for Nov. and Dec. 1926.

Boswell marked his proofs 'For Press' or 'Send another revise' just as is now done.

It is occasionally possible to find evidence whether a reprinted text has been set up from an altered copy of an earlier one or whether such differences as it exhibits from that earlier one are due to correction in proof. The point may be of importance in deciding on which edition to base a reprint.

Most editors will, I think, agree that the text which embodies the author's latest corrections should, as a general rule, be given decisive weight in questions of reading,[1] and it is commonly part of an editor's task to determine which this is likely to be. It sometimes happens that the text which appears to give the best readings is one that appeared after the author's death, when it is obvious that he could not have made corrections in proof. In such a case it is some satisfaction to an editor if he can show that the alterations were probably in the copy from which the compositor worked, as this will undoubtedly increase the likelihood of their being the author's.

No one, I hope, who has followed me thus far will need or expect to be given precise instructions how this may be determined. Obviously the point cannot *always* be decided, but it is at least worth while to look for such evidence as there may be, and this will be found in the spacing of the lines in which the new readings occur.

In a book printed with not more than the usual amount of care we shall generally find that when a correction in proof involves the substitution of a longer

---

[1] Provided that on comparison with earlier editions the variant readings appear to be genuine and intentional changes and not explicable as printers' errors. They must in every case be judged on their merits, for too slavish following of a 'last' edition is as bad as too slavish following of a 'first'. Indeed the tendency to gradual degeneration in minor details, referred to at p. 185, above, frequently renders it advisable to make an early edition the basis of a reprint, while incorporating in it the alterations of a later one.

or shorter phrase than that originally in type, a certain amount of irregularity will be caused in the spacing of the line in which it occurs. If the inserted phrase is longer, we may find the line, and perhaps one or two others before and after it, unusually crowded, or we may find an unusual number of contracted forms or short spellings (-nes, y, a, &c., for -neffe, ie, au, &c.), or finally, if the addition is a long one, an extra line or two in the page. The reverse will of course be the case if the substituted phrase is shorter than the original.[1] Needless to say, such irregularities are most likely to occur in careless workmanship, but then reprints of popular literature were seldom among the best examples of the printer's art.

[1] Considerations of this kind will frequently enable us to decide at once, in the case of texts which have been corrected while on the machine, which is the original and which the corrected version. It may be noted that a similar argument, derived from the abnormal spacing of certain lines, was used in recent times in a copyright case concerning the *Letters of Dorothy Osborne* in order to show that the volume under discussion had been set up from an uncorrected copy of another edition and that corrections had then been made in the proof (*A Report of the Facts of the Copyright Action brought by E. A. Parry*, 1903, p. 14).

Chapter Nine

ON CANCELS, AND ON ADDITIONS TO SHEETS ALREADY PRINTED

A CANCEL is any part of a book substituted for what was originally printed.[1] It may be of any size from a tiny scrap of paper bearing one or two letters, pasted on over those first printed, to several sheets replacing the original ones. The most common form of cancel is perhaps a single leaf inserted in place of the original leaf.[2]

Cancels have been common at all times in the history of printing. Mr. Chapman has found them very frequent in the eighteenth century; and they are still not infrequent to-day. For technical reasons, however, it is now generally easier and cheaper, if anything has gone wrong, to reprint the four-page fold (two conjugate leaves), or even sometimes the whole of the faulty sheet rather than to insert separate leaves.[3]

It is convenient to have a means of distinguishing clearly between the original sheet or portion of a sheet

[1] See Mr. R. W. Chapman's valuable paper entitled 'Notes on Cancel Leaves' in *The Library*, 4th Ser., v. 248-58. This is concerned primarily with cancels in eighteenth-century books, but much of what is said is applicable to work of all periods. I have taken hints from this and from Mr. Chapman's paper, 'Notes on Eighteenth-Century Bookbuilding', in *The Library*, 4th Ser., iv. 165-77.

[2] It may be remarked that these cancel leaves were not always printed separately from the book. Indeed, if the need for them became apparent before the printing of the book was completed, they were normally worked as part of the last sheet or of the preliminaries, it being left to the binder to cut them out and insert them in their proper place. Thus the cancel leaf for the second issue of Nashe's *Christ's Tears*, 1594, was printed (with the signature X3) as the fourth leaf of the second preliminary sheet.

[3] When this is done before any copies of the book are issued, the reprinted portion is hardly a cancel in the bibliographical sense. It will in any case generally be impossible to detect it.

which is intended to be cancelled and what is intended to replace it. We may call the former the *cancellandum* [1] or ' cancelland ', the latter the *cancellans* or simply ' cancel '.

Into the purpose of these cancels we need not enter. There may have been in the original print something so grossly incorrect that it was too much for even the easy-going printer of the day—or for the author ; [2] or, as often in early times, there may have been something that the authorities found objectionable. The point at present is the aid that bibliography gives us in detecting them.

Of course if the book with which we are dealing happens to be unbound or but loosely cased, and if we are permitted to pull it about a little (with discretion), there is generally no difficulty in discovering whether any leaves are cancels, for if they are, we can see where they are stuck on. As a rule, when it was desired to cancel a leaf, this was cut out, leaving a stub of paper to which the new leaf could be pasted. When this stub is at all wide the cancel will often be at once detected on turning the leaves, for the thickness at the back will cause it to bend differently as we turn it over. If, however, the stub is narrow or the original leaf has been removed without leaving one at all, and, as is often the case, the book is substantially bound, a cancel may be exceedingly difficult to detect. We must then rely on other indications.

A cancel should always be suspected if : ˙

1. The type or manner of setting, either of the

---

[1] The Latin terms are used by Mr. Chapman in *The Library*, iv. 173.

[2] An instance of cancellation on account of a serious error is noted by Collier (*Bibliographical Account*, i. 65) in George Best's *True Discourse of the late voyages of discouerie*, H. Bynneman, 1578, where certain sentences in the dedication were first printed in the wrong order. Fols. a4 and b1 were therefore reprinted—apparently as conjugate leaves. Cf. B.M., C. 13. a. 9 (original), and G. 6527 (cancel).

headline, pagination, signature (if there is one), or of the text, is different from that of the rest of the book.

2. There is a larger or smaller number of lines to the page than elsewhere, or if the lines are longer or shorter.

3. If the leaf is signed when other leaves in similar positions in a gathering are not signed. Thus, supposing in an octavo book in which as a rule only the first four or five leaves of each gathering were signed we found one signed F7, we might at once guess that it was a cancel.

4. If the paper appears to be different.

5. If in books which have volume- or part-signatures [1] such a signature occurs on any leaf other than the first of a gathering, the leaf is almost certainly a cancel, for such an indication is particularly necessary in the case of a cancel and would in other cases be quite useless.

6. In books printed 'with figures',[2] the presence of two *different* figures in what should be the same forme would indicate a cancel.[3]

If we notice any of these points we must examine the leaf more closely. If the book is a quarto, the first thing to observe is the horizontal chain-lines of the paper. Compare these with the lines of the leaf which should correspond to and be part of the leaf in question: i.e. if the gatherings are of four leaves, compare the first with the fourth, the second with the third; if of eight leaves, the first with the eighth, the second with the seventh, and so on. Are the chain-lines the same distance apart?[4] If not, one of the two leaves must be a cancel. Determine which by comparing other leaves. If they are the same distance apart, do they

---

[1] See Part i, chap. vii, p. 81.   [2] Ibid., pp. 81–2.

[3] I owe the last two points to Mr. Chapman's article in *The Library* u.s., v. 252.

[4] Allowing for their not being always quite parallel or straight.

meet the chain-lines of the corresponding leaf? If not, examine the position of the type on the two leaves with respect to the chain-lines. If it is different on the two, one is a cancel. If it is the same, we may be dealing with a leaf that has at some time been loose, and in rebinding has been stuck in at a wrong level (cf. fig. 21).

Examine also whether there is a watermark. If so, does it correspond in position with that on the corre-

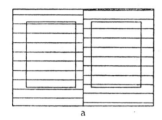 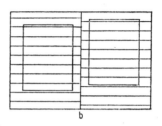

a   b

Fig. 21. Pairs of leaves of a quarto book which should be conjugate. In *a* one of the leaves is probably a cancel; in *b* one of them was probably at one time loose and has been refixed carelessly.

sponding leaf? If there is part of a watermark on one leaf,[1] and it is not continued on the other, one is a cancel. Similarly, if there is the same part of the watermark on both leaves.[2]

Examine the surfaces of the paper. If one leaf has the smooth surface on the inner side and the other on the outer side, one is a cancel.[3]

If none of these methods gives a satisfactory answer, it will be necessary to refer to other copies of the book.

Cancels consisting of a whole sheet or of several

[1] We must of course allow for the binding. In a tightly bound quarto a considerable portion of the watermark may be invisible in the fold. When dealing with smaller formats the tracing of watermarks from one leaf to another is often impossible owing to the amount trimmed away by the binder.

[2] This point is excellently dealt with in Mr. Chapman's paper on Cancels referred to above.

[3] In the case of many kinds of paper it is, however, almost impossible to detect any difference between the two sides.

sheets cannot of course be detected in this manner. Fortunately, however, it seldom happens that the substituted matter is of exactly the same length as the original, and the irregularity of the number of leaves in the gathering comes to our assistance.

As a rule a book may be expected to have an equal number of leaves in each gathering (not counting preliminaries or final leaves), and any irregularity should lead us to suspect a cancel or something added. For example, if in a quarto one gathering consists of six leaves or of two, while the others have four each, there has almost certainly been something added or omitted.[1]

Thus a tract of Gabriel Harvey's, the *Gratulationes Valdinenses*, 1578, runs A–C⁴, D⁶, E–L⁴ + one leaf of errata. The leaves signed D5 and D6, which are conjugate, contain a poem evidently added after the rest was in type.

Sometimes such irregularities merely indicate some accident of the printing. For example, sheet C of Nashe's *Summer's Last Will* has only two leaves, C1 and C2, the other gatherings having four each. As C1 and C2 do not belong together (are separate leaves), it is evident that C3 and C4 were printed and for some reason cancelled. As, however, D1 follows correctly from C2ᵛ, we may infer that the error, whatever it may have been, which led to the cancellation of these leaves was discovered before the next sheet was printed.[2]

---

[1] A similar irregularity in the gatherings may, however, be produced by division of the work between printers, cf. p. 129 above.

[2] An almost exactly similar thing occurs in T. Churchyard's *Misery of Flanders*, 1579, where sheet C has only three leaves but the text runs on without a break to D1 (G. W. Cole, ' Bibliographical Problems ', in *Papers of the Bibliographical Society of America*, x. 135). I am indebted to Dr. Greg for calling my attention to another parallel in Nat Lee's *Princess of Cleve*, 1689, where C4 was cancelled and reprinted with alterations as D1, so that a copy perfect so far as the text is concerned has only three leaves in sig. C. One copy at the British Museum (839. h. 41) has the leaf in both forms.

An interesting example of a large cancel is to be found in ed. 1 of T. Cooper's *Admonition to the People of England*, which appeared in 1589 shortly after the beginning of the famous Marprelate Controversy. It contains a reply to Marprelate's *Epistle* and has been regarded as having been written as the official answer to him. The book is a quarto and runs A–I⁴, K–L⁸ (less L8 wanting), M–Y⁴, Aa–Kk⁴, Ll².[1]

The presence of two sheets of eight leaves in a quarto is very suspicious, and when on examining the pagination we find that the *leaves* alone of these two sheets are numbered [2] whereas the rest is numbered by *pages*, an evident device to cause the pagination to run on correctly to what follows, it becomes clear that the two sheets are a cancel. The interesting point is that we are able to infer from this that the reply to the Martinists which the book contains was not part of the work as originally printed, but was added at the last moment.[3]

Another interesting cancel occurs in a book by Henry Howard, Earl of Northampton, *A Defensative against the Poison of Supposed Prophesies*, 1583, which was supposed to contain treasonable matter.[4] No one, I believe, has ever been able to discover anything

[1] Sig. M1 follows on from L7ᵛ; sig. L8, which was cut out leaving a stub, was evidently blank. The omission of Z from the signatures is of no significance; see p. 76, above.

[2] Except L7, which is numbered on both sides.

[3] The first edition of the *Admonition* has also two small paste-on cancels, on F4ᵛ and S3. These are ridiculed in *Hay any Work for Cooper* (ed. Petheram, p. 63), the author of which refers to the ' two patches ' which ' this patch T. C. ' has used ' to couer his patcherie '.

[4] The writer of Howard's life in the *D.N.B.* appears to assume that Howard's imprisonment in the Fleet in 1583 was in consequence of this book. This, however, seems to be, at least, doubtful. The charge on which he was imprisoned ostensibly concerned a quite different matter (cf. Nott's *Works of Surrey and Wyatt*, 1815, i. 435), and there is no mention of the book in the answers to the interrogatory preserved in Cotton MS. Caligula C. VII, fols. 260–1 (modern fol. 349–50).

treasonable in the book as it stands, and the reason of the charges is a mystery. The probability is, however, that the treasonable passage was suppressed. In all copies that I have been able to see—some half-dozen—one leaf, sig. E4, has been cancelled. In one case the leaf has been simply cut out, but in all the others it is replaced by a cancel-leaf. We may surmise that it was on the original E4 that the passage occurred to which objection was taken, and it would be interesting if a copy of the book could be found in which this leaf remained.

Another case of cancel occurs in the first edition of Robert Greene's *Quip for an Upstart Courtier*, by which the passage containing the attack upon the Harveys which led in part to the famous Harvey-Nashe quarrel was suppressed. In the *Gentleman's Magazine* for February 1908, when no copy of the book containing the attack was known to exist, I argued on ' bibliographical ' grounds that this passage began near the foot of E3^v in the original issue of the edition represented by the Bodleian copy, which now has cancels replacing the original E3 and E4. In 1919 a copy of the book as originally issued turned up in the Christie-Miller sale. As the attack contained twenty-two lines instead of, as Nashe said, about seven or eight, it began fourteen lines from the foot of E3^v instead of four or five as I expected.

These few examples will, I think, serve to show that there is often a good deal of interest attaching to cancels, and that they are worth attention on account of the light that they may throw on obscure points of literary history, but I cannot leave the subject without calling attention to a most remarkable book which was altered by cancels to an extent which could hardly be believed without seeing it. This is James Dymocke's book of characters in French entitled *Le Vice Ridicule*, P. Sassenus, Louvain, 1671.[1] With two exceptions

[1] See Miss G. Murphy's full description in her *Bibliography of English Character Books*, 1925, pp. 78–82.

every sheet of this book contains one or more cancels, and in addition there are a number of small cancels pasted on here and there. There seems no rational explanation of an amount of alteration which must surely have been more costly and troublesome than to reprint the whole book.[1]

A sort of subdivision of cancels seems to require a word or two, cases, namely, in which something is added to a printed page after publication, the addition being sometimes perhaps stamped on by hand and sometimes printed by passing the sheets again through the press. These are of course not properly cancels, as a cancel implies the omission of something, whereas in the present case there is merely something added.

Most of such additions are quite honestly made; for example, the earliest known use of Caxton's device, which was almost certainly cut in England, is in a book printed for him in France. The device was most probably stamped in after receipt of the books from abroad. One of Pynson's devices may have been added to certain books in a similar way. Additions of this kind can sometimes be detected by differences in the colour of the ink from that of the rest of the book, but the most satisfactory proof would be the comparison of several copies of the book. If the device, or whatever else the addition may be, is found to differ markedly in the various copies in its position with regard to

---

[1] Many other examples of books containing cancels could easily be given. A particularly interesting example is the second volume (1640) of the Ben Jonson Folio, of which an account was given by Dr. Greg in the Introduction to his *List of Masques*, 1902. Another is *Coryats Crambe*, signature D of which is quite abnormal, being an eight-leaf gathering running D1, D2, two leaves unsigned, D3, D4, two leaves unsigned, whereas the normal gatherings of the book are fours. Something evidently went very wrong and D must have been reprinted. The make-up of this book differs in different copies (cf. the description of the Capell copy at T. C. C. in Greg's *Catalogue*, pp. 25–6), and it presents some pretty bibliographical problems which, so far as I am aware, have not yet been fully worked out.

the rest of the type, it is almost certainly stamped in
by hand.

In a few cases, however, such additions were made
with more or less fraudulent intent. For example, certain copies of the 1599 quarto of *Soliman and Perseda*
have ' Newly corrected and amended ' stamped on the
title-page. The sheets are identical with those of the
1599 edition without these words, and it seems most
likely that they were added in order to encourage the
sale. It may be remarked that in the copy at the
British Museum (161. b. 4) the words are closer to
the central ornament than would have been possible if
they had been printed at the same time with it. In
cases where an addition of this sort is suspected, it is
always worth while to consider whether the words in
question come too close to other print on the page.
If, for example, the descenders of one line overlap the
ascenders of the line below, it is impossible, save in
the case of a few fancy types, for the two lines to have
been printed simultaneously. It may also be noted
that lines stamped in by hand are often not parallel
with the rest of the print.

There are a fair number of books, especially, it
would seem, plays, of which some copies are anony-
mous and others have the author's name, or of which
some are dated and others not.[1] We also find dedications or preliminary epistles signed in some copies of
a book, unsigned in others. In some of these it seems
probable that the name or date was stamped in after
the original printing, while in others the change may
have been made in the forme during the original
printing. Which of the alternatives is the correct
explanation in a particular case can as a rule only be
settled by the comparison of several copies.

[1] I refer of course only to those in which the rest of the title is from
the same setting-up of type, and not to distinct title-pages.

Chapter Ten

ON FAKES AND FACSIMILES

THE subject of faked copies of early books is one which may be at times of great importance to an editor, and it seems therefore necessary to say something about them here, although it may with some reason be argued that it is really the duty of a librarian to discover the fakes in the library under his charge and to warn readers against them ; not of the readers to discover them for themselves. It is indeed, as a rule, only a person familiar with large numbers of early printed books who will readily detect a good fake, and he will do it more by a sort of instinct than by any knowledge that can be formulated. It is thus very difficult to say anything about them which will be of much use to those for whom these pages are primarily intended, and some general warnings must suffice.

Fakes are of many kinds. There are in the first place complete reprints of early books which appear to be original editions. There must surely be very few of these, for it is difficult to see how it can have paid any one to attempt such a deception ; but there is one notorious example, namely an edition of the play *Soliman and Perseda*, purporting to have been printed by E. Allde for E. White in 1599, but actually printed about 1815.[1] I believe that nothing is known of the

[1] On the back of the title some copies have an imprint (? stamped in) : ' J. Smeeton, Printer, St. Martin's Lane.' In others this imprint has perhaps been erased. The book is a page-for-page reprint of the genuine quarto dated 1599, the ornaments of which have been somewhat roughly reproduced (one being reversed). Smeeton also printed [in 1807 ?] in apparent facsimile [Luke Shepherd's ?] *John Bon and Mast Person*, 1548. On a separate leaf there is a note by Richard Forster, from whose copy the reprint was made, and this bears Smeeton's name and address, but the four leaves of text bear no indication that they are not the original edition, for which indeed they might easily be taken by any one unfamiliar with early printing.

circumstances in which it was printed, whether it was intended to be passed off as an original edition, or whether it was merely an honest ' facsimile reprint '. When once it is suspected, it is easy to see that it is not a genuine sixteenth-century print ; the type is too regular and the paper is evidently of much later date ; but it has deceived very competent scholars in the past and will in all probability deceive others whenever it turns up in circumstances which prevent it from being placed side by side with a genuine old edition.

I know of no other English book of the period that has been completely reprinted in such a way that it could be taken for an original by any one with an elementary knowledge of early work,[1] but it is quite possible that the *Soliman and Perseda* does not stand alone, and any ' original ' of suspiciously modern appearance, either in type, ornaments, or workmanship, should be carefully scrutinized with this example in mind.

The most numerous class of faked copies consists of those which, having been at one time imperfect, have been ' perfected ' by the insertion of leaves or of parts of leaves, either in facsimile or from another genuine copy—sometimes, unfortunately, from another edition.

When such insertion takes the form of an honest and unconcealed facsimile from another copy of the same edition, it is a clear gain, for none but the most uncompromising of bibliographical purists would prefer an imperfect copy of a book to one so made-up. When such facsimiles are photographic, they may often serve an editor as well as originals, provided of course

[1] We learn from Sir Sidney Lee's introduction to the Clarendon Press facsimile of the First Folio of Shakespeare that several possessors of the 1807 reprint have mistaken it for an original, in spite of the modern imprints at the back of the title and at the end, and of the date 1806 in the watermark of the paper. Some of the facsimile reprints of the Shelley Society have also, I understand, been mistaken in the same way. There are fraudulent editions of a few early foreign books such as the *Letters of Columbus*.

that he is certain that they *are* taken from the correct edition. It is indeed only when there is a question of variant readings in different copies that difficulties will arise. A genuine leaf from another copy of the same edition is of course, in all save this matter of variants, as good for editorial purposes as the original one.

It is, however, quite a different affair when a leaf has been inserted from another edition, and it is the possibility of this which makes it so important to examine all inserted leaves with the utmost care. I need hardly say that I am not referring to the cruder sort of made-up copies that one often finds in the second-hand market.[1] Many of these are made up of editions which, though usually corresponding page for page, are so obviously different that they would not deceive a child. There were, however, a number of books which passed through two or more editions identical in general appearance and in signatures, and the insertion of a leaf or two from one of these into another may be exceedingly difficult to detect.[2]

The best guide in discovering inserted leaves, whether in facsimile or genuine old ones from other copies, is generally the paper. In a facsimile the paper seldom corresponds exactly with that of the other leaves, save in the rare cases in which a blank leaf from the book itself has been used. In a genuine old leaf the paper may be identical in quality, and so far as this is concerned our only guide may be that want of proper correspondence in chain-lines, watermarks, &c., which, as we have already seen, may aid us in the detection of cancels.

In the case of fakes we have, however, as a rule, far

---

[1] There seems to have been a good deal of very clumsy making-up of copies in the early part of last century—to judge at least from the apparent date of bindings.

[2] Those who wish to get some idea of the extent of this practice of ' making-up ', and the difficulty of dealing with it, may profitably glance at Francis Fry's *Description of the Great Bible*, 1865.

better means of detection than we had in the case of cancels. Cancels have generally been in their place in the book from the date of the original binding, but facsimiles or leaves from other copies have been inserted in modern times, since the book came to possess a certain value. Now a book that requires to be perfected has of necessity been subject at some time or other to neglect or ill-usage. In nine cases out of ten it has suffered from damp or from the ravages of insects, and it is likely to have suffered most in those parts which have to be made good. Any reasonably competent faker who inserts a leaf into a book will of course take care that if there happen to be worm-holes in the adjacent leaves there shall be holes to correspond in the inserted leaf, for this is a simple matter; but if the inserted leaf is one from another old copy, or a facsimile on old paper, there may be worm-holes in *that*. In such cases an attempt is generally made to fill them up, but it is very difficult to do this well and they may usually be detected on careful examination, especially if the leaf be held up to the light.

Best of all, however, is the evidence to be derived from water-stains, rust-spots, and dirt-marks. Water-stains generally go through a number of leaves, or through the entire book, often increasing so regularly in size and intensity to a maximum at the point where the damp has entered, that if the leaves of the book were loose they could be rearranged in almost perfect sequence by the stain alone. If then, in a part of the book which is water-stained, we come across a leaf in which the stains (if any) do not correspond with those on the adjacent leaves, we may be quite sure that that leaf is in some way or other a fake. The correct imitation of a stain is fortunately a task that seems to puzzle even the most expert fakers, though no doubt it can be done. Rust or grease-spots and dirt-marks of various kinds will often run through several leaves and may afford us useful evidence of a similar kind.

The books in which faking is most difficult to detect are those which have been taken to pieces, washed, mended, and re-bound. Washing, especially if followed, as usual, by re-sizing, so alters the appearance of the paper and print, that it may be most difficult to tell what is genuine and what is not. In general, then, a washed book should be regarded with even more than usual suspicion.

Sometimes only part of a leaf is in facsimile. There may have been a hole in it or a corner may have been lost. Some of these patchings are very well done and when they are small are sometimes by no means easily noticed. The edges of the paper at the join are pared thin and attached by a minute quantity of gum, so that on the surface it may be impossible to see that there is any join at all. In most cases, however, this may be perceived as a darker line in the paper on holding the leaf up to the light.

Facsimiles can as a rule be more easily detected by such incidental evidence as that of the paper, the stains, &c., than by an examination of the letterpress itself.[1] Forgers are as a rule people of considerable skill, and though one may perceive that a page of brush- or pen-work does not look exactly like a page of print, it is generally hard to say wherein the difference lies. Pen-work may sometimes be detected on examination with a high-power magnifying glass, as the edges of the letters tend to be too even and to be free from the minute *angular* indentations, caused apparently by the fibrous nature of the paper, which are usually to be seen in print. There is, however, some facsimile work which it is extremely difficult to detect at all.

Lastly there is one peculiar kind of fake to which

[1] There are several different ways of executing these facsimiles, from direct brush or pen work to photographic methods. Some of the best are, I believe, produced by a process of lithography, but the details are probably a ' trade secret '.

reference must be made here, though one hopes that it is rare. That, namely, in which what *purports* to be a facsimile is not a facsimile at all, but the mere invention of the man who made it. Such are those unique copies of books wanting title-pages which have been provided with a title-page ' in facsimile '. At first sight one is of course tempted to suppose that there are other copies in existence, though at present unknown, and that the ' facsimile ' has been made from one of these, but in some instances it seems that this is not so. We must remember that the invention of a title-page from the half-title, head-line, and colophon, if there is one, together perhaps with the entry in the Stationers' Register or an early mention of the book is by no means a difficult task.

Such a fake-facsimile occurs in a copy at the British Museum (C. 57, b. 43) of an entertainment to Queen Elizabeth at Woodstock, in 1575. To this is prefixed a title-page, ' The Queenes Maiesties Entertainement at Woodstock [ornament] At London, Printed for *Thomas Cadman*. 1585.' The title at first sight appears to be in facsimile, but its arrangement and general appearance are suspicious, and when we find that the wording is made up from the head-line and the colophon (the imprint, even to the full stop after the printer's name, being derived from the latter, from which also the ornament is copied), it becomes practically certain that it is false.

An even more dangerous species of fake consists in the insertion into a defective copy of parts apparently in facsimile but really made by transcribing the text of another edition in the type and style of the one to be completed. Thus in an account of the lithographer John Harris, one of the most skilled of (honest) facsimilists, in R. Cowtan's *Memories of the British Museum*, p. 335, the author tells us, on Harris's own authority, that ' he supplied on one occasion the 97th folio of a rare edition of the " Spanish Chronicle of

Don Rinaldu's ",[1] where he had no perfect copy to make it from, but parcelled out the words from a later edition of the work '. He was paid, it appears, £12 for the leaf. This is indeed a most insidious kind of fake, and it is fortunate that there have probably been few men sufficiently skilled to engage in such work.

The faking which we have had under consideration has for its object the making good of a defective or damaged copy of a book, but a word must be said as to an even more objectionable procedure which seems to have been much practised in recent times since the cult of collecting first issues of modern authors found so many and such wealthy followers, and which has for its purpose the transformation of an ordinary and comparatively valueless copy of a book into one belonging to a much rarer issue.

There are a number of modern books in which alterations were made after a few copies were bound up; sometimes the wording of the title-page or the date on it was changed, sometimes a dedication was added or revised, sometimes even alterations were made in the text itself, the original leaf or leaves being suppressed and new ones substituted. These first few copies were in certain cases not intended for sale to the public, but were merely advance copies for the author and the publisher, and should therefore rank rather with proofs than as an actual issue ; but, nevertheless, they are regarded by collectors as the original issue and may command a high price. As the difference between the copies in question and the regular issue is often limited to one or two leaves, and similar type and paper to that used in modern books is generally obtainable with little difficulty, it may be profitable to print in facsimile the leaves characteristic of such ' first issues ' for insertion

---

[1] I must confess my inability to identify the book referred to, unless it is the *Libro del noble . . . cauallero Renaldos de Montaluan* (B. J. Gallardo, *Biblioteca Española,* No. 1074), but it does not seem even to have been called a ' Crónica '.

into ordinary copies, and these leaves may be almost indistinguishable from the original ones even by the expert. It goes without saying that the fraud can only be worth attempting when there is a considerable demand for the rare issue and when a reasonable number of copies of the commoner one are available for transformation.

Fakes of this sort can sometimes be detected by the existence in them of slight deviations from the original in spelling or in punctuation, but direct comparison with a genuine examplar is frequently necessary. It is sometimes easier to detect a fake after a few years than when it was first made, as paper which at one time matched that of the original perfectly may so change with age as to be quite different from it.

PART THREE

Chapter One

THE EXTENT TO WHICH THE COMPOSITOR ATTEMPTED TO FOLLOW HIS COPY. THE QUESTION OF SETTING FROM DICTATION

ALL that has been written hitherto in this book has been, or should have been, directed, immediately or remotely, to the elucidation of the single problem of the relation between the text of a printed book and the original MS. of its author. We may seem indeed at times to have wandered very far from the subject, but such wanderings have, I hope, been justified by the fact that in order to understand modern methods in the study of textual problems, a very thorough knowledge of all that affects the mechanical side of book-production is desirable, indeed indispensable, and that in comparatively unexplored fields of investigation such as are now being opened up the wider his outlook the better chance has the pathfinder. We must, however, now come to somewhat closer grips with the problem itself, and consider first how nearly we should expect the printed book to reproduce the author's MS., and secondly the chief causes which may prevent the reproduction from coming up to our reasonable expectation.

Leaving out of account those causes of departure from an author's intention which produce their effect before ever the MS. reaches the printing-house, such causes I mean as the intervention of revisers, or the mistakes of copyists,[1] we may say without fear of con-

---

[1] Or of the original scribe in the case of the MS. having been first written from an author's dictation (as *Paradise Lost*) and not by his own hand.

tradiction that the most important link in the transmission series is in the vast majority of cases the
compositor. Let us, then, first consider to what extent
the compositor is likely to have *tried* to reproduce the
exact form of a MS. before him. Then, having got
as clear as we can as to his intentions, we shall be in
a better position to consider the nature and causes of
errors which result in his work falling below—often very
far below—the ideal. Lastly, we will consider those
causes of error, as a rule of little real importance,
though their effects may be sometimes startling at first
sight, which are due not to the compositor but to those
processes in book-production which come later.

For the purpose of our inquiry we may consider the
actual compositor and the master-printer as one. It
is probable that when a MS. came into the printing-
house, the master-printer or some one of the type of
an editor or ' corrector of the press ' would run through
it before it was actually given out to the compositor,
and would settle not only the size and kind of type to
be used, but any such matters of arrangement, division
into chapters or books, emphasis or subordination of
particular sections and the like by the use of larger or
smaller type, italic, &c., on which the author has failed
to make his intentions clear. It is quite possible that
a conscientious or officious printer or editor would add
such chapter or section headings as seemed to him
necessary or desirable, and indeed much more extensive
tampering with the text is quite possible, though we
cannot regard this as part of the normal procedure of
the printing-house. Unfortunately, as has been mentioned above,[1] though there exist MSS. which seem to
have been prepared for press, only a single piece of
early MS. which has certainly been used by an English
printer is at present known, namely, part of Sir John
Harington's translation of the *Orlando Furioso*, and the
printer of this, Richard Field, seems to have contented

[1] See p. 217.

himself with carrying out the author's rather minute instructions. We shall have occasion to return to this MS. later.

Assuming, then, the MS. to have been made ready for the compositor and handed over to him with all such general directions as were necessary, how closely are we to expect him to follow it in such matters as spelling, punctuation, use of italics for proper names, expansion of contractions, and the like? It is an important question and we cannot get away from some attempt to answer it, but unfortunately the evidence on which we have to rely is extremely scanty.

In the first place a word must be said as to the suggestion that has sometimes been made that the early compositors worked from *dictation*, for of course if this was done the MS. spelling could have no influence whatever on the printed text, whatever might be the case with punctuation, italics, &c. The reason for this suggestion is presumably the existence of a certain number of errors in sixteenth- and seventeenth-century books which are more easily explained as due to mishearing than to misreading of the MS.[1] I give the three most striking examples of this which are known to me.

1. In Marston's *Malcontent*, I, iii. 28–30, there are some remarkable variations in the readings of copies of the second quarto (sig. C 4).[2] One of the copies in the British Museum reads, evidently correctly: 'as your knight courtes your Citty widow with jingling of his guilt spurres, aduauncing his bush colored beard, and taking Tabacco ', the other copy, however, has instead: 'as your knight courtes your Citty widow

---

[1] Reference should be made to the full and careful discussion of this question of dictation in Miss Albright's *Dramatic Publication in England, 1580–1640*, pp. 326–34, which appeared when the present book was already in proof. Miss Albright comes to much the same conclusions as I have done.

[2] The scene in question is not in the first quarto at all.

with something of his guilt : some aduauncing his high colured beard ', &c. Now, neglecting the other errors, we have here the word ' something ' where there should be ' jingling '. It seems quite impossible that this should be in the ordinary sense a misreading, for the two words have no resemblance in any script. Is it not, however, possible that a reader trying to decipher a bad MS., and coming to a word he could not make out, should hesitatingly fill the gap with ' something ' as we often do nowadays when trying to puzzle out a difficult script, intending doubtless to go back to it when he had got the drift of the passage? A compositor *seeing* an illegible word in a MS. would probably fill the space with quads, leaving the corrector to insert the right one. He would hardly go to the trouble of setting up a word which was obviously wrong. If, however, the passage was read out to him he would be likely to set up what he heard without bothering his head as to whether it was sense or not.

2. In Sir John Harington's *Epigrams*, ed. 1618, bk. ii, epigram 23 is headed :

To Bassifie, *his wiues mother, when shee was angry.*

On reading the poem it becomes quite evident that the title should run ' *To pacify his wiues mother . . .* ', as indeed it is printed in the edition of 1633 appended to Harington's translation of the *Orlando Furioso*.[1] Now this is, of course, not a simple *misprint*, for the type of ' Bassifie ', as well as the comma after it, shows that the printer undoubtedly took it for a proper name. We can easily imagine such an error arising through the title being set up from the dictation of a man with a heavy cold in the nose : it is hard indeed to see how it could arise from misreading a MS.[2]

---

[1] The epigram in question is not in the earlier editions, which only contain Book IV.

[2] I am indebted for this very pretty example of apparent dictation to Professor Moore Smith.

3. In Fletcher's play of *The Elder Brother* the first four lines of III. iii, in Q I (and substantially in all other early editions), run :

What noise is in this house, my head is broken,
Within a Parenthesis, in every corner
As if the earth were shaken with some strange Collect,[1]
There are stirres and motions, What Planet rules this house ?

It is quite evident that the words ' Within a Parenthesis ' merely mean that ' my head is broken ' should be printed within parentheses, or round brackets, and an early MS. of the play bears this out by omitting the words and marking the close of a parenthesis after ' broken ', though the scribe has forgotten to begin it before ' my '.[2] Now the text as printed in Q I is just as it would be *dictated*, whereas surely no compositor would be so foolish as to omit parentheses which he saw in the MS. before him, and then set up the words ' within a parenthesis ' in their place. On the other hand it must be admitted that this error might possibly arise from a misunderstood correction in proof, the corrector having written the words in the margin instead of using the ordinary sign for parentheses to be inserted.[3]

So much must suffice for the internal evidence in favour of setting-up from dictation. Of external evidence there seems to be very little save the statement of John Conrad Zeltner in his book entitled *C. D. Correctorum in Typographiis eruditorum centuria speciminis loco collecta*, 1716, pp. 408–9. Though late, the passage is sufficiently important to be quoted in full. It occurs in the account of the Swiss historian Henri Pantaleo, 1522–95, and runs as follows :

Posthaec . . . aliquamdiu in *Isengrinii* officina lectorem egit.

[1] i.e. colic.

[2] See Dr. Greg's edition of the play in A. H. Bullen's *Beaumont and Fletcher*, vol. ii.

[3] But, if so, must we not assume that the author, or at any rate some one not a regular reader to the press, corrected this quarto in proof ?

Olim enim diverso a nostris more prae ceteris unus eligebatur, qui sonora voce praelegeret e Manuscripto Typothetis, quae imprimenda essent. Quo facto promti erant, qui verba ex ore recitantis excepta componebant, idque ex tribus vel quatuor schedis tot etiam praelegebatur compositoribus. Nostro vera aevo, ut nemini ignotum est, is, qui munus componendi elementa sibi impositum habet, Schedam Manuscriptam ante oculos positam inspicere solet. Qui modus haud dubie propter ignorantiam Typographorum mutatus, cum temporis rationem habeat, et halluciationibus minus est obnoxius, maxime mihi arridet.[1]

This, indeed, is definite enough, so far as it goes, but there seems a curious absence of confirmatory evidence, in that not one of the early pictures of compositors at work gives any indication of the practice, while on the other hand several of them distinctly show the copy supported on a stand in front of the compositor.[2] We must also remember that dictation would generally have meant the employment of an extra man or boy for each compositor, an expense which we should certainly not expect the average sixteenth- or seventeenth-century printer to have incurred if he could help it, whatever might have been the case in earlier

---

[1] Attention was, I think, first drawn to this passage by J. P. A. Madden in his *Lettres d'un Bibliographe*, Paris, 1868 (1st Ser.), p. 11, in connexion with an argument that three editions of the letter of Pius II to Mahomet II, printed by Ulrich Zell *c.* 1463, were set up from dictation.

[2] See in this connexion Professor A. W. Pollard's introduction to the facsimile of Mr. A. W. White's unique quarto of *Richard II*, 1916, p. 35, where he discusses this question of dictation in connexion with an intrusive 'Ah' appearing in some copies of the play before the line 'But ere I last receiude the Sacrament' (i. i. 139). As he says, this is 'one of the few really probable cases of a compositor having had his text read out to him', for the 'Ah' 'could hardly have crept in from any other cause than our English habit of making strange noises, now generally "Er", between our sentences'. Nevertheless, his conclusion is that dictation cannot have been employed except perhaps occasionally and in quite exceptional circumstances. Cf. also Professor Pollard's *Shakespeare Folios and Quartos*, p. 132.

times; and there is further, I think, a still stronger
reason for rejecting the theory when we consider the
actual process of composition. As has already been
explained, a line must end with a complete word or
syllable. A skilled compositor acquires a very exact
sense of the letters which he can get into the space
available and will, as he comes towards the end of
a line, modify his spacing (or in early times would have
modified his spellings) accordingly, and thus save himself much trouble in justifying the lines by altering
spaces or spellings afterwards. But such adjustment
in advance is only possible if he knows or can refer to
the words to be set as far as the end of the line or
a little further. With the MS. before him he can of
course read as much or as little at a time as suits his
convenience, but if it is being dictated to him he is at
the mercy of the reader, who will read the words in
groups—probably according to their grammatical construction—without any regard to how they fall in the
lines of type. I believe that in practice this would be
a very real hindrance to rapid work.

My own belief in the matter, which I give as a mere
guess, is that dictation was never customary but that
it may sometimes have been resorted to. There are
two things which one must always remember in connexion with the handicrafts of former days: first, that
long hours were worked and that artificial light was
very bad, with the result that even in such composing-
rooms as had a good allowance of window there must
have been at times a real difficulty in getting sufficient
light to read a crabbed MS. by. In such circumstances
it seems to me far from improbable that the master-
printer, or perhaps another workman, would take the
MS. to the light and read it aloud so as to enable
the compositor to continue. Secondly, a large number
of craftsmen must have found their eyesight fail long
before the skill of their hands, and spectacles, though
of course known, seem not to have been common and

were probably expensive.[1] Compositors so afflicted may well have employed a boy to read the MS. to them. Thus I think we must admit the *possibility* of setting from dictation, though we must beware of assuming it without evidence in any particular case.

Having so far cleared the ground we must return to the question of how closely a compositor would be likely to follow what he saw before him. In view of the trend of much modern textual work the important point is whether he would be likely to follow the *spelling* of the MS. or not. Evidence has recently been brought forward to show that in some cases he did,[2] but before we can accept this as anything approaching a general rule, much more investigation seems to be required.

In the first place we know for certain that, in the sixteenth century at any rate, variation of spelling was resorted to for the purpose of justifying the lines, and though this would not be inconsistent with a certain degree of following the MS., it makes exact following impossible. In the second place, any attempt to reproduce exactly an unfamiliar spelling would make composition far more laborious, without so far as one can see the slightest compensating advantage. No one who has ever either copied or collated an early text in which it was necessary to preserve the original spelling will have any doubt as to the extra trouble involved, and it may be added that at the present time the composition rates for old spelling texts are some 10 per cent. above the normal rate. In the third place, any reason there might be for keeping the spelling of a MS. would surely act with equal force in the case of books re-

---

[1] Spectacles seem first to have been used at Florence shortly before 1300, but in any case only spherical lenses were known. The correction of astigmatism, the effects of which often become more troublesome with age, was not understood until the nineteenth century.

[2] See the paper by Miss Byrne referred to below.

printed from a printed copy, unless at so long an interval that the customary spelling had changed,[1] and though I do not profess to have made any minute investigation of the point, I have certainly seen little or no evidence that this was ever done. When a reprint follows the spelling of its original closely, this seems generally due to the spelling of both being ' normal ' for the time. There were, of course, a few authors who for one reason or another wished their spelling to be reproduced exactly, such as Churchyard, Stanihurst, the phoneticians such as Bullokar, and perhaps Ben Jonson, and no doubt a special attempt could be made to carry out their wishes, but I see not the slightest reason to suppose that in the case of the average author there was any conscious attempt at exact reproduction. In the Harington MS. referred to above there seems very little evidence that the printer was influenced by the author's spelling, save that Harington's constant use of y in such words as ' myndes ', ' devysed ', ' vyle ', &c., perhaps led him to use a few more y's than is quite normal. On the other hand he seems never to follow Harington's use of w in words like ' chawnge ', ' stownge ', ' townge ', ' discowrce ', &c., printing the usual ' chaunge ', ' stoung ', ' toung ', ' discourse '. For ' slawnder ', which occurs twice in the pages printed by Dr. Greg, he prints once ' slaunder ' and once ' sclander '. For ' sell ' he substitutes ' cell ', and for ' strayt ' (meaning narrow) ' straight '.

To take another example. We know something of Gabriel Harvey's spelling from his *Letter-Book*. Among many other peculiarities he had the habit of using i in many places where y or e is normal, as in ' mi ', ' dai ', ' Inglish ', ' standith ', ' offendid ', ' callid ', and so on, and of omitting g in such words as night, might. In his printed works there is hardly a trace

---

[1] One might have supposed that there would indeed have been some definite advantage in following the original spelling in a line-for-line reprint as saving trouble in justification.

of such peculiarities.[1] Of course it is possible that Harvey's pamphlets were printed from copies and not from his own MSS., but the circumstances of their production and publication render this unlikely, at any rate in the case of the *Four Letters*.[2]

The point can perhaps only be settled by a careful examination of the output of several printing-houses and of several authors, choosing those whose works were printed by a variety of printers, with a view to discovering whether peculiarities of spelling tend to follow the printer or the author ; but the investigation would be a tedious one and perhaps would yield no certain result. An excellent beginning has indeed been made in a paper by Miss M. St. Clare Byrne on ' Anthony Munday's Spelling as a Literary Clue ' in *The Library*, 4th series, iv. 9 ff. Munday's MSS. show that he had a habit of doubling the o in such words as ' looue ' and ' woorthy ', and Miss Byrne finds these peculiarities reproduced consistently in those of his books which were printed in 1580–90, less consistently in those between 1590 and 1600, and not at all in those after 1600 ; and further, that in other books printed by the printer of the early group there is no general tendency to the use of these oo forms, though they appear occasionally. The evidence is striking and I think that, so far as the spellings with which Miss Byrne deals are concerned, it can hardly be doubted that the compositors of Munday's earlier books followed his MS. At the same time it must be remembered that these particular spellings were common between 1580 and 1590 and were probably quite well recognized forms. It seems to me that a compositor might easily be influenced by the MS. before him to

---

[1] ' inough ' is so spelt a few times, but not always, and this was in any case hardly an unusual form.

[2] These, save the first letter, which is not Harvey's, seem to have been written for immediate issue and while Harvey was actually living in the printer's house.

the use of one of two equivalent and equally common spellings, without there being any conscious attempt to follow the spelling of the MS. throughout. Such a case as the representation of MS. ' slawnder ' by ' slaunder ' and ' sclander ' within the space of a few lines in the *Orlando Furioso* shows how erratic a printer's spellings might be.

Though, however, both *a priori* probability and such evidence as there is seem to point to the compositor making as a rule little or no consistent attempt to follow the spelling of the MS. before him, there are certain cases in which this may have been done. It is natural to assume that in the case of any word which was unfamiliar to the compositor or was not understood by him he would follow the spelling of the MS. as nearly as he could, for (1) he would have paid special attention to it, and (2) he would have no alternative spelling in his mind.[1] We may thus regard it as a general rule—for what it is worth—that in common words and in words misread as common words, the compositor would follow his own spelling; in rare ones, or words which are not words at all, the spelling of the MS. or what he believed to be its spelling.[2]

---

[1] It is for this reason somewhat more probable that the *ductus litterarum* of the MS. will be more closely followed in unintelligible or very rare words than in common ones. Thus, supposing we find a common word like ' manie ' which is evidently incorrect in its context, we have no means of knowing whether the word in the MS. which the printer misread *looked* to him like ' manie ' or like ' many '. If, however, the word printed were a non-existent word like ' mame ', or like the ' perttaunt ' of *Love's Labour's Lost*, v. ii. 67, or the mysterious ' fircug ' of *Wit without Money*, ii. ii. 37, it is more probable that the word in the MS. actually looked *something* like this.

[2] There is, I think, no doubt that in later times—from the late seventeenth century onward—the compositors generally normalized the spelling of their copy. Many writers used peculiar spellings. Mr. Chapman tells me that in Johnson's letters printed from his MSS. in 1788 and 1791 nearly all his (not infrequent) odd spellings are normalized, and that Jane Austen *always* wrote ' beleive ', ' neice ', and even ' veiw ', but, save in the first edition of *Mansfield Park*,

A few words will suffice for the other three points in which a compositor was likely to diverge from his MS. So far as punctuation is concerned, there seems very little evidence that many authors exercised any care about it whatever. After all, even at present, few authors trouble to punctuate their MSS. with any care or consistency. Such punctuation as is to be found in ordinary MSS. of the sixteenth and seventeenth centuries is indeed most erratic and seldom goes beyond full stops at the end of most of the sentences and some indication of the cæsura in lines of verse. Harington was probably more learned in linguistic matters than most of his contemporaries, and yet his punctuation in the *Orlando Furioso* MS. is beneath contempt and evidently was thoroughly revised by the printer. The subject of punctuation has only recently begun to attract attention, and there is still much work to be done on it, but so far the evidence seems to be that such rules as there were existed chiefly among the printers, and it is quite possible that they varied from house to house, as indeed they do still.

The question of contracted forms—I mean the significant contractions of verbs, &c., not such things as ẇ for ' with '—is more difficult. It is, I think, probable that in poetry the MS. would be followed in this respect, for authors clearly used these contractions with intention and would have insisted that they were kept.

which is very badly printed, hardly any trace of such spellings survives in her novels. Of course this does not apply to the rather numerous writers who used abnormal spellings of set purpose, such as Edward Capell, who omitted the e of the -ed termination wherever not pronounced, writing ' produc'd ', ' advanc'd ', &c., as well as the more usual ' desir'd ' ; Joseph Ritson, who on the contrary objecting to the suppression of e's, wrote ' romanceës ', ' translateëd ', ' writeër ', &c. ; or William Herbert the bibliographer, whose modesty caused him to use a lower-case ' i ' for the pronoun of the first person, though only when the ' i ' was himself and not in quoting the remarks of others. Such peculiarities as these they would naturally insist on their printers retaining.

Whether, however, this applies to plays is another matter. The author of a play was not writing primarily for print but for an actor whose business it was to know how to speak verse, and who probably, if it did not scan already, would have *made* it do so, using full or contracted forms as he thought good. It seems therefore quite possible that neither the author nor the printer of a play would have bothered much about which form stood in the text and that we are entitled to exercise our own judgement in its interpretation.

Lastly, italics. In the later years of the sixteenth century it seems to have been a common practice, though to what extent it was the usual one I cannot say, in MSS. written in the English hand to insert proper names and foreign quotations in an Italian hand; this practice of course corresponding to that of printing such things in italic type in a roman text. The question therefore arises to what extent italics are likely to represent words in an Italian hand and thus to have MS. authority, a point which is sometimes of importance in textual criticism.[1] On the whole it seems improbable that many MSS. were careful or consistent in the use of the Italian hand, and therefore we may, I think, assume that printers probably followed their own practice as regards the use of italics without regard, or with little regard, for the MS. from which they were setting. Thus in the Carew MS. mentioned on p. 218, the writer has been very erratic in his use of the Italian hand, while the printer simply follows his ordinary rule. It may be remarked that certain passages of this MS. (written in an English hand) are underlined, and these are printed in italic; so we may perhaps assume that underlining was a customary indication that this was to be done, as it is at present.

[1] If italics in a printed book are likely to have authority, we must be careful how we emend an italicized word to one that would not normally be italicized or vice versa.

Chapter Two

ERRORS OF THE COMPOSITOR DUE TO MISREADING THE
MS., FOUL CASE, ETC. ERRORS DUE TO FAULTY COR-
RECTION. ERRORS IN IMPOSITION, PERFECTING, AND
FOLDING

WE may now pass from the question of what
a compositor aimed at doing to what he actually
did and consider those departures from the MS. which
were unintentional and hence are properly called errors.
We may, I think, class these, so far as they are due to
the compositor alone and appear in the type before the
proof stage, as (1) errors due to misreading of MSS.
(including mishearing when and if the compositor set
from dictation), (2) errors due to failure of memory,
(3) muscular errors, those in which the fingers do not
visit the intended division of the type-case, as when
one strikes a wrong key in typewriting, (4) those due
to 'foul case', i.e. to wrong types being in the divisions.

Into the question of errors caused by misreading the
author's MS., either on the part of the compositor (or
dictator) or of an intermediate copyist, I cannot enter.[1]
A full discussion of the matter would involve us in an
inquiry as to the history of English handwriting and
would require a knowledge of palaeography which is
not part of the usual equipment of a student of printed
books. A general warning may, however, be given
against forgetting the difference between the forms of
the Elizabethan and earlier scripts and the modern,
and that from about 1550 to 1630 two forms of script

---

[1] An excellent example of an error evidently due to misreading the
MS. was recently noticed by Mr. H. J. Byrom in *Tottel's Miscellany*,
where the first edition has 'the R. fo depe can auoyde' the second
correcting to 'the Rodopeian maide' (ed. Arber, p. 200). The MS.
probably had the 'Rhodopeian mayde'.

were in current use together. Generally speaking, the bulk of an Elizabethan MS. intended for the press [1] would have been in the so-called ' English ' hand, while proper names and citations in Latin or in modern foreign languages would be in ' Italian ' hand. The latter is practically the same as ' copy-book ' writing of the present day; the former, however, differed in the shapes of certain letters, especially c, e, h, p, and t and some of the capitals. Long ſ was of course commonly used in both in all positions except at the end of words.[2]

The result of these differences in the English hand is that certain words which in print, or when written in a modern hand, seem very similar, could not possibly be confused when occurring in an Elizabethan MS., while others which are quite different in modern script might in an English MS. easily be mistaken for one another. Thus, supposing in a printed book we have the word ' challinge ' in an obscure passage about sun-dials, it might seem a reasonable conjecture that the word intended was ' diallinge ', for in the writing with which we are now familiar, the difference consists in little more than a slight lateral displacement of the first upstroke. In Elizabethan ' English ' hands, however, the words have no resemblance at all, and the replacement of one by the other could not be due to a simple misreading on the part of a compositor.

On the other hand, in a proper name or in foreign

---

[1] Not a legal MS., and perhaps not a MS. written by a professional scribe.

[2] For a brief introduction to Elizabethan handwriting, see Appendix 8. Much which bears on the subject will also be found in Dr. Leon Kellner's *Restoring Shakespeare*, 1925, an elaborate investigation of those errors in the text of Shakespeare which may be due to misreading of the MSS. Dr. Kellner is perhaps inclined to refer too many errors to this cause, but his book contains much that is valuable and deserves careful study. Much also will be found in the writings of Sir E. Maunde Thompson, Dr. Greg, Professor A. W. Pollard, and others on the MS. of the play of *Sir Thomas More*.

words, which would probably be in Italian hand in a MS., this very confusion of ' ch ' and ' di ' is quite a possible one. Thus *Adian* might easily be a misreading for *Achan*, if the latter name were required to give sense, or *die* for *che*.

Conversely, in Elizabethan hands letters might be confused which are now perfectly distinct, as, for example, d and e, p and x. Further, in *certain* hands a final st was but little different from a final se, and words like ' case ' and ' cast ', which we hardly think of as similar in appearance, might easily be confused by a printer.[1] It is, however, quite unsafe to guess at misreadings of this kind, unless we know or can somehow infer the character of the hand of the original.

No rules can be laid down for the guidance of a student in interpreting errors due to misreading of Elizabethan MSS. He should familiarize himself with the more usual forms of Elizabethan writing and then trust to his common sense.

The second important cause of error is failure of memory on the part of the compositor. As Blades says, ' Every compositor when at work reads over a few words of his copy, and retains them in his mind until his fingers have picked up the various types belonging to them. While the memory is thus repeating to itself a phrase, it is by no means unnatural, nor in practice is it uncommon, for some word or words to become unwittingly supplanted in the mind by others which are similar in sound.'[2] Had Blades added that the word or words might also be supplanted by others which are similar in *sense*, his statement of one of the most fruitful causes of typographical error would have been complete.

The third cause, which I have called ' muscular error ', is when, although the compositor knows quite

[1] Errors might perhaps also arise occasionally from misunderstanding contractions ; see Appendix, p. 323.

[2] *Shakspere and Typography*, p. 72.

well which division of the case his fingers should visit, they automatically take up a type from the wrong one. It need hardly be said that no reasonably skilled compositor can be in any doubt as to the division of the case in which any letter is to be found, but this does not mean that even if the case is perfectly free from incorrectly assorted type there will be no errors in his work owing to the insertion of wrong letters. The human body is not a perfect machine, and it is within the experience of every one who has worked at any long-continued mechanical task, such as sorting index slips or typing, that after a time, though one *knows* perfectly well where each letter of one's index should be placed or which key of the typewriter one ought to strike, one's muscles cease to follow one's intentions perfectly and errors begin to occur, which, unless rest is taken, tend to increase rapidly in number. In the case of typing, the common mistakes besides the substitution of a wrong letter are the dropping of letters and (with some people the earliest to appear) inversions, so that ' hwen ' or ' won ' is written for ' when ' or ' own '. Similar errors due to fatigue or mental failure of one kind or another naturally appear in the work of compositors also, and it is, I think, on the whole probable that these causes account for a larger percentage of errors than ' foul case ' does.

' Foul case ', the last of our four causes of error, means the presence, in the divisions of the case, of letters which should not rightly be there, and is generally due to carelessness in distributing type used for previous work. In distribution a word or two is picked up at a time between the finger and thumb and, the word having been read, the letters are released one by one over the division to which they belong. It is very easy, especially if the types stick together a little, to drop two by mistake for one or to drop a type a fraction of a second too early, so that it falls into the wrong division, and, even if this is noticed, it may be so difficult to pick it out again that it is not regarded as worth the trouble. Irregularity of spelling must have added to the difficulty of distributing, for it laid a much greater strain on the memory unless the compositor resorted to the very tedious method of looking at each type separately. In passing it may be said that each compositor probably distributed the type which he himself had set up into cases which he himself used and which were under his own care. It would thus be to his interest to keep the case as clean as possible, for he would presumably be responsible for the correction of errors due to foul case in his own time and without extra pay.

Besides careless distribution there is another possible cause of 'foul case' which should be mentioned, namely, over-filling the divisions, or some of them, with the result that types may slip from one division into another. There is a discussion of this possible cause of error in William Blades' *Shakspere and Typography*, 1872, pp. 73–8, in which he argues that letters would be most likely to slip into the division which is next below that in which they ought to be.[1] Thus an o out of place would probably be among the a's, a d might be among the n's, an e among the h's. This is an interesting suggestion, but it must not be pressed too far, for we must remember that if the printer picked up a letter much thicker or thinner than the one intended, he would instantly recognize the error; thus, although the m-box is below the c's, a c occurring in the m-box could hardly be placed in the stick in mistake for that letter. Similarly the i's are above the o's, but the thinness of an i would prevent it from being mistaken for an o.

In connexion with errors due to foul case, Blades draws attention to the importance of remembering the

[1] Moxon's diagram of the arrangement or 'lay' of the case (see fig. 2) is given by Blades. He assumes that this was the same as that of Shakespeare's time.

existence of ligatures.[1] Thus the word ' light ' cannot
be an error for ' fight ' due simply to the presence of
an l in the f box, for in setting up the word ' fight '
the compositor would have used the fi ligature, not the
simple f. Nor must we, if we come across John
Partridge's lines in *Plasidas*,

> Thus ended they their mortall race
> their file was at an ende,

hastily assume that ' file ' should be ' life ', even if we
do not know that ' file ' was used for the ' thread of
life '. Similarly, if we find such an obviously erroneous
combination of letters as ' ift ', we must not suppose
that we have merely a transposition of i and f, and
emend it to ' fit ' ; for in that word the separate letters
f and i would not have been used at all. The point
has not infrequently been overlooked by editors un-
acquainted with typography.

One of the most puzzling errors is the frequency
of ' turned ' letters used for the letter which, when
inverted, they resemble, especially u for n and n for u.
It is very hard to explain these as due to foul case, for
to produce them a *double* error seems to be required :
first, that in distribution they should be misread—not
easy to understand if the compositor read a word at
a time, for in English at least the number of pairs of
words in which u or n stand in the same position is
very small ;[2] and secondly, that when picking up the
mis-distributed letter the compositor should place it in
his stick the wrong way up—a very unlikely thing, for
the presence of the notch on the underside of the type,
of which the compositor is constantly aware, would
normally prevent this. There seem to be two possible

---

[1] See p. 312, below.

[2] They *may*, however, be due to inversion-errors, the very frequent
combination ' un ' being treated as ' nu '. This, by the way, seems
a particularly common inversion in typewriting. As in distributing
type the faces of the letters are (and presumably always were) seen
inverted, the error would perhaps be a particularly easy one to commit.

explanations. One is that the errors *are* due to foul case, that the wrong letter was set the right way up by the compositor, producing, say, ' uow ' for ' now ', and that in correcting he simply turned the letter to save trouble, instead of replacing it by the right one ; the other is that mistakes were made in casting, an inverted u-matrix being used for an n, and vice versa. Neither of these explanations is very satisfactory, but I can suggest no better one.

We may note that errors due to foul case or to the compositor unconsciously taking a type from the wrong division of the case will generally result in the production of meaningless words or of nonsense ; those due to misreading the MS. may or may not do this ; but those which arise from failure of memory will always produce a real word and generally some sort of sense, though neither the word nor the sense is what was intended by the author.

But the compositor is not the only cause of faulty text. A considerable number of serious mistakes seem to arise from careless correction of an evident error, by which a slight slip which if left alone could have been easily put right is made into something which is far harder to emend. An illustration may make matters clearer, though in this particular case emendation is easy : in the *Interlude of Impatient Poverty*, 1560, l. 794, we have the word ' obserued ' where the sense evidently requires ' obscured ', and in the original print the cross-bar of the first ' e ' of the word is broken so that the letter might be taken for a ' c '. Now the error may of course be a simple misreading ; but on the other hand it may have arisen thus : in distribution of earlier matter the ' e ', looking like a ' c ', may have been placed in the c box, and so have been used for c in printing the line in question. The proof-reader finds the word ' obseured '. Without pausing to reflect on the meaning of the passage, he assumes that he has the very common mistake of the transposition of

258

two adjacent letters and that the ' ur ' should be ' ru '.
He alters them and the word becomes ' obserued '.
A more complicated case of the same kind will be
found in the side-note of the fifth edition of Nashe's
Pierce Penilesse, quoted on page 198. If no earlier
edition of the book had survived it would, I think,
have been quite impossible to guess how the note had
originally stood.

It is well to remember the possibility of this form
of wrongly emended error, as it may sometimes serve
to justify, or at least render plausible, an emendation
which at first sight seems very daring. For my own
part I may say that I believe that a large number of
the greatest puzzles in early dramatic texts are due not
to the compositor but to correctors who have forcibly
wrested to an impossible sort of half-sense passages
which in the beginning probably contained merely one
or two literal errors which reference to the MS. or even
a little thought would have sufficed to put right.

It remains to say something as to disturbances of
text which may occur in books independently of the
work of the compositor and corrector by means of
wrong imposition of the pages of type or wrong folding
of the printed sheets. These seldom are of much concern to an editor or to a literary student save in so far
as they may render a copy of a book defective by
causing certain pages to be duplicated and others
omitted ; but it is sometimes useful to be able to
describe briefly what has gone wrong, and it is in any
case of interest to see how simply what appear at first
sight to be extraordinary confusions in the arrangement
of pages in a book may occur.

We may, I think, say that the wrong arrangement
of pages of type in a forme is, in ordinary work,
extremely rare. The correct imposition for the various
sizes of books is so elementary a part of a printer's
training that such an error could hardly occur save by
most extraordinary carelessness or misunderstanding ;

and if it did, it would almost certainly be corrected in proof. In work, however, which for any reason is somewhat out of the common, wrong imposition may occasionally be met with. For example, in his reprint of Heywood's translation of *Hercules Furens* (Bang's *Materialien*, xli, p. xlvi), Prof. de Vocht points out that in the edition printed by Sutton in 1561, in octavo, the recto pages of D 4 and D 6 have been interchanged. The imposition was in this case somewhat complicated by the fact that the Latin text of the play is on the verso pages throughout, faced by the translation on the rectos, and the catchwords of the two texts run independently, i.e. the catchword of a Latin page refers to the next Latin page, not to the English page immediately following. It may be noted that the pages interchanged belong to the same forme. Another example occurs in J. Hooper's *Declaration of the Ten Commandments*, R. Jugge, 1550 (B.M. 697, A. 14), of which the final gathering, O, has the last four pages (part of the ' Table ') arranged O 7, O 8, O 7^v, O 8^v, pages O 7^v and O 8 having been interchanged. Here also the pages interchanged belong to the same forme. A few other examples can, I think, be found, but they are very rare in straightforward work, at any rate of the Elizabethan period.

There is, however, a fault sometimes found in the arrangement of pages which should be mentioned here, as it may at first sight seem to be due to an error in imposition, though a little reflection will show that the true cause is quite different. This is the fault by which the pages, instead of running 1, 2, 3, 4, &c., as they should, run, in a quarto, 1, 6, 7, 4, 5, 2, 3, 8, or in an octavo, 1, 6, 7, 4, 5, 2, 3, 8, 9, 14, 15, 12, 13, 10, 11, 16.

This may seem a strange muddle, but it is due to a very simple cause, namely, to the sheets, after being printed on one side, having been turned the wrong way round when being perfected ; or, alternatively, to the second forme printed having been placed the wrong way round on the bed of the press. Experiment with a piece of folded paper, as before suggested, will show clearly how this error occurs. Let the type-pages be numbered as before, but the paper be turned round before numbering those at the back, so that the back of page 1 is numbered 6.[1]

An even greater confusion than this can occur, for it is possible that a sheet may be perfected from a wrong forme, so that the pages would run, say, B 1, C 1^v, C 2, B 2^v, and so on. This is a most unlikely accident to happen in the ordinary course, for it would necessitate two sheets being worked off simultaneously and in such an unmethodical way that the partly printed sheets could get mixed. When, however, that system of half-sheet imposition is followed in which formes of two consecutive sheets are on the bed together, this strange confusion may easily arise as the result of the same error in laying the paper which, as we have just seen, with a single forme will cause the pages of a sheet to run 1, 6, 7, 4, and so on. Examples of this have been already given on pages 68–70 in discussing half-sheet imposition, and need not be repeated here.

Other examples of confusion in page-order could easily be given, but once the general principles of imposition are understood, it is easy to deal with any cases that arise. The simplest way is, indeed, to fold a sheet of paper as it is in the book, mark the pages on it as they there occur, and then open the sheet out flat. Remembering the ' looking-glass ' correspon-

[1] Gordon Duff, in his *Westminster and London Printers*, 1906, p. 50, mentions an error in a book printed by Machlinia, *The Revelation of St. Nicholas*, which he attributes, doubtless correctly, to this cause. The book is a quarto in eights and the pages of the third gathering, as printed, run, 1, 14, 15, 4 . . . 13, 2, 3, 16 (not as Duff states 1, 14, 16, 4, an arrangement which could not possibly have come about in this manner, for 14 and 16 would belong to different formes). The error occurs in both copies of the book known and has in each case been corrected by pasting correct pages over the erroneous ones.

dence between the printed sheets and the forme, we shall at once see how the pages were arranged in the latter, when the cause of the error will generally be apparent.

The faults that occur during the actual printing are, so far as they affect the text of a book, limited to the shifting of letters due to the lines not being properly justified or the furniture not being sufficiently tightly locked up ; or to the loss of letters altogether by their being drawn out by the ink-ball during inking. This last is sometimes a cause of variant readings in different copies of a book.[1]

The only fault that can occur in the folding of the printed sheets is that of folding them wrong way round so that the pages of a quarto run 5, 6, 7, 8, 1, 2, 3, 4, or 3, 4, 1, 2, 7, 8, 5, 6, or 7, 8, 5, 6, 3, 4, 1, 2. As a matter of fact, however, in the text of a book provided with signatures in the usual way, such an error would be practically impossible, as the presence of a wrong signature on the front leaf, or the absence of a signature altogether, would at once reveal the mistake. It may, however, and does occur in books consisting of illustrations, and more frequently in pairs of pages inserted as a cancel, or to contain something which it was not originally intended to include.[2] The matter is, however, of little practical importance, as the cause of errors of this kind is generally obvious.

To conclude this section an example may be given

[1] See p. 204.

[2] Thus it seems possible that the two added leaves in the prelims of the First Folio of Shakespeare—those with the verses by Digges and the names of the actors, about the proper place of which there has been much discussion—were really meant to come in the middle of the gathering, as they do in some copies, and have simply been folded the wrong way round. Folded the other way the List of the Actors follows Heming & Condell's address to the Reader, then come all the verses together, those of Digges with their large-type heading first. But I do not propose this as a better arrangement than others— merely as a possible one which seems to have been overlooked.

of a complication arising both from wrong perfecting and wrong folding. This is found, as Dr. Greg pointed out to me, in the Dyce copy of Greene's *James IV*, 4to, 1598, where the pages of sheet K run as follows: 1, 6, 3, 8, 5, 2, 7, 4, an arrangement which it seems at first sight difficult to achieve by anything less than completely erroneous imp ition. Consideration shows, however, that the *pairs* of pages (i.e. those printed on the back of each other) are the same as in an ordinary case of wrong perfecting—only they are differently arranged. What has evidently happened is that the binder, or re-binder, of the book, the original top fold of the sheet having been cut so as to make two pairs of conjunct leaves, has attempted to do the best he could with the sheet by getting the *recto* pages in order, neglecting the versos. To do this he has sewn the sheet as two twos instead of as one four, turning the second pair of leaves inside out. If this is difficult to follow, an experiment with a sheet of paper folded in quarto will make all clear. Mark the pages in the order which follows from simple wrong perfecting, 1, 6, 7, 4, 5, 2, 3, 8. Then cut the top fold, rearrange to get the rectos in order, and see what results.

APPENDIX ONE

THE purpose of this appendix is not to attempt
even the sketchiest history of printing, for it is
obvious that nothing useful on so wide a subject could
be said in the space at my disposal, but merely to give
such few outstanding facts about it as should, it seems
to me, necessarily be familiar to students of literature
in general. I shall therefore first deal in the briefest
possible manner with the introduction of printing into
the various countries of Europe and then say something of each of the dozen or so printing-houses of the
sixteenth and seventeenth centuries which most notably
contributed to the advancement of learning, leaving
out of account entirely those printers whose contributions were of interest mainly for their artistic merit.
To the student of printing as an art such men as
Erhard Ratdolt, Geoffroi Tory, Claude Garamond, or
the two Fourniers are of the first importance; to the
student of literature they matter hardly at all. Those,
however, who wish to make a further study of one of
the most interesting and amusing of arts or crafts will,
I think, find ample material in the authorities which
I shall have occasion to mention.[1]

[1] In spite of the large number of books and articles which have been
published in recent years on various aspects of the history of printing
and on particular printers and books, there is an almost complete lack
of successful attempts to deal with the subject as a whole. The best
account of fifteenth-century printing is to be found in E. Gordon Duff's
Early Printed Books, 1893, but this attempts to give so much information that it is not very readable. A good attempt to summarize the
story to 1600 has been recently made by Mr. G. P. Winship in his
Gutenberg to Plantin, 1926. Here in less than 100 pages the student
can get a general account which, though necessarily far less detailed

264

The actual beginnings of the art of printing form an obscure subject and one full of controversy, owing partly to the fact that so much of the early work is undated, partly to the vagueness of the external records, and partly perhaps to the intentional secrecy which seems to have surrounded the doings of the first printers. Fortunately, however, in its broad outlines the story is clear enough, and these are all with which we need concern ourselves here.

The invention of printing was of course essentially the invention of movable type. It would be difficult if not impossible to find a definite beginning for the impression of images or even of lettering from a carved block, though as a matter of fact there seems to be no trace of any design or picture printed on paper, parchment or similar material in Europe earlier than the fourteenth century, while the earliest print with an unquestioned date, the picture of St. Christopher [1] now in the John Rylands Library, Manchester, belongs to the year 1423. In China, however, the printing of letter-press from wooden blocks is said to have been

than Duff's, deals with the subject in a much more interesting and human fashion. It seems well also to mention the British Museum's *Guide to the Exhibition in the King's Library, illustrating the History of Printing*, &c., 1926, price 1s. This is of course limited in its scope to the books exhibited, but the various sections are headed by excellent historical summaries and in the descriptions of the various exhibits, which form a most representative collection, the particular features which give them their historical interest are carefully indicated. There are facsimiles from the more important works. There is, I think, no recent general history of printing, but the aesthetic side is dealt with in Prof. A. W. Pollard's *Fine Books*, 1912, which contains an excellent general account of the early development of printing and many facsimiles, and in Mr. Stanley Morison's *Four Centuries of Fine Printing*, 1924, which may be mentioned as containing a large and valuable series of collotype reproductions of titles, type-pages, &c. In the same author's *Art of the Printer*, 1925, a selection of 250 of these are reproduced in half-tone.

[1] Reproduced in facsimile in *Woodcuts of the Fifteenth Century in the John Rylands Library, Manchester*, with an Introduction and Notes by Campbell Dodgson, 1915.

practised from much earlier times. Japanese block-prints exist which date from A. D. 770, and ' there is evidence that the art had been brought from China and had already before this date had a certain amount of development on the mainland '.[1] Between 1041 and 1049 a method was devised of printing from movable types. These types were cut in clay and afterwards baked. For printing they were attached with a layer of wax to an iron plate. After use the wax was softened with heat and the type removed for use again. Later than this, but some time before 1314, type were cast in tin.[2] Later still they were cut in wood, being set up for printing in a kind of wooden chase in which they were fixed by wedges consisting of strips of bamboo. This seems by 1314 to have developed into quite a practical method, though there is no evidence as to the extent of its use. Metal type cast from a mould seems to have been used in Korea from 1392 or earlier, and there are detailed records of the casting of founts of type in 1403–9, 1420, and 1434. The great number of different characters necessary for printing languages employing the Chinese script [3] seem, however, to have militated against the employment of movable type and, in spite of its having been first used in these countries, it was never widely employed until within quite recent years when more efficient methods of casting made it economically possible. Even now it has by no means

[1] See the excellent article by Professor T. F. Carter of Columbia University, entitled ' The Chinese Origins of Movable Types ', in *Ars Typographica*, vol. ii, 1925, pp. 3 ff., which completely supersedes all earlier accounts of the matter.

[2] It is remarkable that these are described as being ' strung on an iron wire, and thus made fast in the columns of the forme, in order to print books with them ', Carter, u.s., p. 10.

[3] The smallest fount of Chinese characters generally sold contains 6,000 different types, and this would only suffice for the most ordinary kind of work. A well-equipped press would require founts of some 10,000. The number of characters recognized in the larger dictionaries is upwards of 40,000.

altogether superseded the method of printing from woodcut blocks.

The primitive woodcuts were printed by laying the paper down upon the block and rubbing the back of it with a pad or frotton, exactly as Chinese and Japanese woodblock books are now printed, the ink being of a watery rather than of an oily nature ; the paper could therefore only be printed on one side.[1]

From the production of single illustrations to that of books of such illustrations with or without a certain amount of descriptive lettering cut on the blocks the step is a small one. Unfortunately there is much doubt as to the dates of the early block books. While it seems reasonable to suppose that some at least preceded the invention of movable type, there seems no actual proof of their existence earlier than 1460, while the majority of those now extant appear to date from after 1470. Block books continued to be produced until the early years of the sixteenth century, and these later ones were naturally influenced by the methods of the book-printers ; some were printed on a press with ordinary printing-ink and on both sides of the paper, and occasionally the text was printed from movable type, either at the same time as the pictures or separately.[2] In such cases there is no clear line of demarcation between block books and ordinary illustrated books.

The date and place of the invention of printing from movable types in Europe is still a matter of controversy. The chief point of debate is the interpretation of an obscure passage in the *Cologne Chronicle* of 1499.[3] This passage refers to a prefiguration (vurbyldung) of the

---

[1] Not because the surface first printed would be damaged in printing the other, for this could easily be avoided by laying a sheet of paper over it, to protect it, but because watery inks necessitate absorbent paper and the colour comes through.

[2] Duff, *Early Printed Books*, pp. 13–14.

[3] *Die Cronica van . . . Coellē*, fol. 312 (sig. 2g2).

invention of printing in Holland before the invention itself, which is assigned to Mainz,[1] and there exists a group of very roughly printed books which correspond sufficiently well with the indications of the *Chronicle* for some writers to regard them as the products of the 'vurbyldung' referred to, and thus as the earliest known printed books.

However this may be, the first piece of printed matter showing an efficient use of the invention of movable types which can be dated with certainty is a printed form of *Indulgence* of Nicholas V to such as should contribute money to aid the King of Cyprus against the Turks. A copy of this bears in MS. a contributor's name and the date 12 November 1454.[2]

It is certain that some time before 15 August 1456 the great Vulgate Bible called the Mazarine or 42-line Bible had been finished, and this is the earliest date that can be positively assigned to any printed book. It has been claimed that both this Bible and the 36-line Bible which was set up, at least in part, from it were actually printed two or more years earlier.[3]

We have very little definite knowledge as to the details of early printing, but so far as the type is concerned it seems probable that it was in all essential points very similar to the type of a hundred years later.[4] Several theories to the contrary have been based on the vague and probably ignorant allusions to the discovery in early chronicles and the like, but there is

---

[1] The 'vurbyldung' is by a doubtful tradition connected with the name of Lourens Janszoon Coster of Haarlem.

[2] Duff, *Early Printed Books*, p. 21, and *B.M. Facsimiles*, note on Nos. 3 and 4. Three persons, Johann Gutenberg, Johann Fust, and Peter Schoeffer, are known to have been connected with the early Mainz printing, but their relative shares in it are too obscure to be discussed here.

[3] Duff, *Early Printed Books*, pp. 25–6. There is a facsimile of a page of the 42-line Bible in *B.M. Facsimiles* (No. 5).

[4] It may be mentioned that De Vinne (*Invention of Printing*, 1876, pp. 66–8) and Updike (*Printing Types*, p. 5) regard the Mainz invention as essentially that of casting type accurately and in large quantities.

THEORIES ABOUT EARLY TYPE

little reason for attributing to the writers any more exact knowledge of the craft of printing than the average author has at the present day. At any rate, until fresh evidence is produced, we may dismiss from our minds such theories as that the types were made of wood, that they were cut on the ends of cast metal bodies, and that when composed in a forme they were threaded together with wire or string, the most improbable of all suggestions.[1] There seems every reason for thinking that they were cast in some sort of mould, not very different in essentials from that used until comparatively modern times, that they were made of lead or an alloy consisting mainly of lead, and that the face was formed in a matrix made by striking or pressing a punch engraved in hard metal into soft copper. Type can be made, and actually has been made experimentally, from wooden punches by using matrices of sand or clay, and from copper punches by using matrices of hard lead,[2] but it is to be remembered that the people of the Middle Ages were skilled workers in metal, and I think that the difficulty of their cutting punches in steel has been much exaggerated. What hampered the Middle Ages in metal-work was not any want of skill in the handling of small objects but their inability to work a large level surface in metal and the consequent extreme difficulty in constructing of metal any machine with heavy sliding parts.

The obvious variation in the type used in some of the early printed books, which has been used as an argument against the type having been cast, may be

[1] See T. B. Reed, *Letter Foundries*, pp. 3–6. All the same, it is but fair to mention that within recent years Japanese printers employed engravers who could rapidly cut wooden types of such of the rarer characters as were not included in the regular founts of cast type. As to the stringing together of type, cf. note 2 on p. 266, above. The suggestions that have been made as to the early practices of European printers are therefore perhaps not so impossible as some have supposed.

[2] See T. B. Reed, u.s., p. 15.

explained as due to want of skill in casting.[1]   It is to be remembered that pure lead shrinks considerably when cast, and that the exact composition of the alloy, probably lead and tin,[2] best for the purpose, would only be discovered after a good deal of experiment.   It is also possible that imperfect types were touched up with the graver after casting.

Once having made a start, the art of printing spread rapidly, Bamberg and Strassburg being probably the first two German towns, after Mainz, at which it was practised.   In both of these printers seem to have been at work in or before 1460.   It reached Cologne by 1466, Augsburg by 1468, and from that date onwards it is found in many other towns of Germany.

The second country to receive the new art, as indeed we might expect from the keenness of the Italian scholars of the time, was Italy.   By 1465 two Germans, Conrad Sweynheym and Arnold Pannartz, had established a press in the monastery of Saint Scholastica at Subiaco, about thirty-three miles east of Rome, and these printed, with type in which an Italian intention struggles somewhat ineffectively against a Gothic predisposition, a *Donatus* of which no copy is now known, an undated Cicero *de Oratore*, which disputes with another work of Cicero printed at Mainz the honour of being the first printed classic, and a *Lactantius* which bears the date 29 October 1465, and is noteworthy as containing occasional Greek words, the first to be printed.   In 1467 these printers moved to Rome, where they printed until 1473, Pannartz continuing by himself until three years later.   By 1472 they had printed

[1] Certain peculiar twists and jerks of the hand holding the type mould were necessary to cause the metal to flow properly into the hollows of the matrix, and as these differed more or less according to the letter which was being cast, they were only acquired by much practice (see T. B. Reed, u.s., p. 18).

[2] The type-metal now used generally consists of lead, antimony, and tin with sometimes a small percentage of copper.   Iron, bismuth, and several other metals have been tried in the alloy at different times.

twenty-eight books, generally issuing 275 copies of each.[1]

By 1469 printing had begun at Venice, perhaps the most interesting centre of the art in early times, and by the following year Nicholas Jenson had established himself there. According to the commonly accepted story, Jenson was a Frenchman who in 1458 had been sent by Charles VII to learn printing at Mainz, but having learnt it had found his patron dead, and decided that Italy offered a better field for the practice of his art than France. His work is of course mainly remarkable for the beauty of the roman type used in his earlier books.

Printing reached France in 1470. There is indeed a mysterious story about printing at Avignon as early as 1444, but all that can be said about this at present is that records in the archives of that place certainly seem to imply the practice there at that date of some form of printing by means of movable types. What was printed is not clear; it is by no means certain that it was books at all, and no fragment of it has come to light. Should it ever do so, the honour of having originated the art of printing may pass from Germany to France, but in the meantime we must date the beginning of French printing in 1470, when a press was set up in Paris at the Sorbonne by three Germans, Martin Cranz, Ulrich Gering, and Michael Friburger, who in that year and the next printed thirteen books. Printing at Paris in the fifteenth century has some importance to us on account of its close connexion with this country both in the matter of personnel and material and because a number of liturgical and other books were there printed for the English market, but in itself the early Paris printing is, in spite of some noteworthy illustrated books of Antoine Vérard, rather it seems a publisher than a printer, less important than

[1] Duff, *Early Printed Books*, p. 62, from a list in one of their books dated 1472.

either the German or Italian work of the period. The art spread to Lyons soon after 1470, and to Toulouse in 1476.

In later times two Swiss towns, namely Basel and Geneva, became very important centres of printing. It is known to have begun at the former by 1468 at latest, though no extant work bears a date earlier than 1470.

If we ignore the mysterious 'Coster' books already referred to, the Low Countries would seem to have been less prompt in taking up the invention of printing than their later activity in the art would have led us to expect. The first known dated book belongs to 1473, in which year printing was in progress both at Utrecht and Alost. It reached Louvain in 1474 and Bruges in 1475.

The press of Colard Mansion at Bruges is of especial interest to us, for it was in collaboration with Mansion that Caxton printed the earliest books generally assigned to him, namely, *The Recuyell of the hystoryes of Troye, The game and playe of the Chesse, Les quatre derrenieres choses,* and probably the French *Recueil.* One other Dutch printer also deserves special mention, namely, Gerard Leeu of Gouda, who was at work from 1480 to 1493. He not only printed a very large number of books, but seven of them, printed between 1486 and 1493, were in English.[1]

We need not trouble ourselves with the further spread of printing on the Continent except to note that the art reached Spain (Valentia) in 1474, Denmark in 1482, Portugal in 1489, and Sweden in 1495.

The story of the introduction of printing into England has so often been told that the briefest possible account of it will suffice. It is essentially the story of the life of William Caxton, who, after many years spent in commerce, suddenly, in what the fifteenth century regarded as old age, set to work to learn a new

---

[1] For his remarkable anticipation of the modern use of u and v see p. 310–11.

art and earned enduring fame by introducing it to his
fellow-countrymen.[1] Caxton was born probably about
1420, of a Kentish family, and in youth was apprenticed
to a London mercer. He seems almost at once to have
been sent abroad, apparently as an agent of some sort,
for ·by 1469 he had been for some thirty years in the
countries of Brabant, Flanders, Holland, and Zeeland,
acting for the later part of the time as governor of the
English merchants at Bruges. In 1469 or 1470 he
gave up his commercial pursuits and entered the service
—in what capacity is unknown—of Margaret, Duchess
of Burgundy, sister of Edward IV, devoting his leisure
time to literary work, including the translation into
English of the *Recueil des Histoires de Troye* from the
French of Raoul le Fèvre. On 17 July 1471 he visited
Cologne, where he remained until the end of 1472,
and probably learnt the art of printing in the house
of a printer who was then engaged in an edition of
Bartholomeus de proprietatibus rerum. Later, from 1475
to early in 1477, he worked with Colard Mansion [2] at
Bruges, where, as already mentioned, his translation
of the *Recueil* was printed. In 1476, however, his
patroness, Margaret, had been compelled by political
changes to retire into private life, and Caxton presumably could no longer count on her assistance. He
therefore left Bruges and set up his press at Westminster, where in 1477 he printed the *Dictes and
Sayings of the Philosophers*. From that time onwards
his press was constantly active. In the first three years
of work he is known to have produced at least thirty
books, and although many were small, several were

[1] The standard authority on Caxton is the *Life* by William Blades
(here cited from the one-volume edition of 1882). See also Duff,
Printers of Westminster and London, 1906, pp. 1–23.

[2] The relation between the two men is not clear. It seems generally
to be assumed that they were in partnership, but, as Mr. Pollard has
pointed out to me, there is no evidence that Mansion was not simply
employed as manager or foreman.

quite serious undertakings. It must also be remembered that a number of Caxton's books are only known by fragments or single copies and that no small part of his production may have disappeared altogether. The most important of his early books was his edition of *The Canterbury Tales* (372 leaves in folio, ? 1478).

Caxton's early work was typographically crude, but the appearance of a rival printer, John Lettou, in 1480, seems to have spurred him to improvement, and he introduced a new and neater type and such modern features as signatures and woodcuts. Later he introduced other types, the total number being (according to Duff) eight, of which two exist in re-cast or altered forms. His most active period was during 1483–5, when he produced twenty-two books, including some of his most important works. The total of his productions known to us is at present just 100.

Caxton died in 1491 and his materials passed to Wynkyn de Worde, his assistant, a most industrious printer who until his death in 1534 or 1535 poured out a constant stream of books, though one might guess that he was intellectually a very different sort of person from his master and that his aims throughout were more commercial than literary.

We must now turn again for a time to the Continent, where at the beginning of the sixteenth century we find several presses of the greatest importance in the history of learning, namely, the Aldine press at Venice, that of Jodocus Badius Ascensius at Paris, and that of Johann Froben at Basel.

Aldus Manutius (Aldo Manuzio) seems to have set up his printing-house at Venice in 1494 primarily with the idea of printing satisfactory texts of Greek authors, a project in which he was greatly aided by the large number of learned Greeks who had settled at Venice after the taking of Constantinople in 1453 and had made that town more than any other in Italy a centre of Greek study. From the first he gathered around him, as editors, press-correctors, and assistants in general, a band of scholars some of whom at least seem to have dwelt in his house and to have been permanently maintained in his employ. Important, however, as was his work in the larger volumes of his earlier years, his fame now rests chiefly on the series of classical and Italian authors in small volumes printed in italic type, which was begun by the *Vergil* of 1501. As Mr. Updike has pointed out, though these volumes are now valued for their typography, they were introduced as handy and cheap volumes, in fact ' a sort of Venetian Everyman's Library ' (Updike, i. 127). Among the scholars enthusiastic over the work of Aldus was Erasmus, who visited him in 1508 and had an enlarged edition of his *Adagia* printed by him ; in the preface of this he testifies to the assistance rendered to him in the work by Aldus and his friends and fellow-scholars.

Aldus senior died in 1515, leaving, it seems, a great reputation and a well-established printing-house, but little in the way of worldly goods. The press was carried on by his father-in-law until in 1533 one of his sons, Paolo, who had been an infant of three years old at the time of his father's death, took the direction of it. Paolo, in spite of difficulties due to ill health, want of means, and family quarrels, carried on the press at Venice besides taking part in the establishment of presses at Bologna in the name of his brother Antonio, and at Rome. He seems to have been primarily a scholar, a Ciceronian by inclination rather than a Greek scholar like his father ; and perhaps rather by fortune than by choice a wanderer. He died at Rome in 1574.

The third of the family, Aldus junior, was born at Venice in 1547. After the death of his father Paolo he carried on the press at Venice,[1] but apparently with less

[1] Aldo seems to have been actually in charge of this press during the later years of his father's life.

close attention to business than his predecessors. His literary reputation was very great and led to his being called to occupy the chair of eloquence at Bologna, Pisa, and at Rome. He eventually left Venice altogether and spent his last years as director of the printing-house of the Vatican, the Venetian house passing to other hands.

Another important Italian family of printers was that of the Giunti or Junta, who are first heard of as printers at Venice in 1482. The more important branch of the family was that established at Florence, where Philippo printed from 1497 to 1517, his press being carried on by his descendants until early in the seventeenth century. The Venetian branch lasted still longer, until 1642, and there was a third branch at Lyons which printed from 1520 to 1592. The Giunti were, however, far from being on the same level of scholarship as the house of Aldus, and though Philippo has to his credit the first Greek edition of Plutarch's *Lives* (1517), the greater part of their output was merely good sound work without any special pretensions.

In France the most noteworthy of the early scholar printers was Jodocus Badius, called Ascensius, from his birthplace at Aasche near Brussels, who studied printing in Italy, then resided for a time at Lyons, and coming to Paris in 1499 established there the ' Prelum Ascensianum ', from which he issued a long series of annotated editions of the Latin classics, acquiring also great fame as an author by his satiric writings. Among his claims to the remembrance of posterity was his use of a reasonably accurate drawing of the printing-press as a device. He died in 1535.

More important than Badius was the Basel printer, Johann Froben, a German, who set up a press at Basel in 1491. In 1513 he printed the *Adagia* of Erasmus in a type modelled on the Aldine italic. In the following year Erasmus visited Basel, and in 1516 Froben printed his edition of the *Greek New Testament*, with Erasmus's Latin translation, this being the first edition of the New Testament in Greek. From 1521 Erasmus settled at Basel, living at first in Froben's house. Froben's work is remarkable for the correctness of his texts and the general care given to execution. He was assisted by several of the foremost scholars of his time as correctors, including Oecolampadius and Wolfgang Musculus. He was associated with Holbein, who designed numerous title-page borders and other embellishments for his books from 1515 onwards. Froben died in 1527.

Perhaps the most important of the great printer families of the sixteenth century is that of the Estiennes, which began with Henri Estienne (1460–1520).[1] He started a press at Paris in association with Wolfgang Hopyl, in 1500, and printed about 120 books, some of considerable excellence; but his fame and that of his immediate successors, François and Charles, has been overshadowed by that of the later members of the family, Robert I and the second Henri. Robert (1503–59), who was the first to use the famous Estienne device of the man plucking olives with the motto *Noli altum sapere*, was remarkable for his numerous editions of the Bible, in Latin, Hebrew, Greek, and French, and for the number of Greek authors of which he printed the first editions, including Eusebius, Dionysius of Halicarnassus, Dion Cassius, and Appian, as well as for the great *Thesaurus Linguae Latinae* (1532 and, much enlarged, 1543), in the compilation of which he took the principal part. Estienne was interested not only in the higher kinds of scholarship but in the elements thereof, especially as applied to instruction, and published a large number of editions of various Latin grammars for school use. These were of excellent correctness and workmanship, and were issued at

[1] He and his successors more commonly used the latinized form of the name ' Stephanus '.

a very low price. He made also a study of the French language and printed a French grammar and a number of subsidiary treatises of his own composition.

Estienne's Bibles, with their new readings and their clearings up of many dark passages dear to a certain type of theologian, had caused great trouble at the Sorbonne, in spite of the approval bestowed on them by some of the more learned professors, and he was subjected from the very beginning of his career to the most violent attacks on the ground of heresy. So long as K. Francis I lived he was able, thanks to the king's constant support, to bear up against his adversaries, but after the accession of K. Henry II in 1547 his position became more and more difficult, and he at length decided definitely to adopt the reformed religion, to which for many years he had had strong inclinations, and to leave Paris for Geneva. He did this in the autumn of 1550 and at once established a press there which was active until the time of his death in 1559, the earliest of its productions being an edition of the New Testament in which for the first time the text was divided into verses.[1] His press at Paris came later into the possession of his second son, Robert II, who remained in the Catholic faith, and on returning from Geneva after a short sojourn there was allowed to enter into possession of his father's property. His work was, however, of comparatively little importance, much less than that of his elder brother the second Henri, who remained at Geneva.

The latter was, in his way, quite as notable a man as his father, but his fame rests rather on his scholarship than on his printing, in spite of the importance and very large number of works that came from his press. In accordance with the wishes of his father he established in 1557 a press at Geneva which was at first independent, but after the death of Robert I in 1559 the two presses were united. It would appear, how-

[1] The Psalms had been so divided by his father Henry in 1509.

ever, that the rigid protestant atmosphere of Geneva was never really congenial to him, and he spent much of his life in travel, frequently visiting Paris, where he seems to have felt most at home. The very numerous editions of classical authors which he printed were for the most part either edited by Estienne himself or published under his close supervision, and the benefit conferred by them upon scholarship was enormous. His most important work was, however, the *Thesaurus Graecae Linguae*, for which a part of the material had been collected by his father. This great work in five folio volumes appeared in 1572, and the expense seems to have made inroads upon his capital from which he never entirely recovered, so that in spite of the energy with which he continued to edit and print he died a poor man. His death occurred at Lyons in 1598, after which date, though members of the family carried on his press and produced some good work, the Estiennes cease to be of any great importance in the history of printing.

The outstanding Dutch printing-house of the sixteenth century was that of Christophe Plantin at Antwerp. Plantin was a Frenchman born near Tours about 1520, and he began to print at Antwerp in 1555, at first using local material. In 1563, however, he established a foundry of his own and began a business which constantly grew in importance until his death in 1589. His earlier work was on French models, and he made large use throughout his career of French types, but his later work has a solidity and indeed heaviness that was later more characteristic of Dutch printing. Much of his output—and probably the most remunerative part—consisted of missals, breviaries, and other liturgical works, for which he had special and exclusive privileges from the Spanish court, but besides these he printed a number of large and important volumes, including atlases and botanical and other scientific works, and several emblem books. His most impor-

tant work was his polyglot Bible of 1572, which like
most polyglots produced more fame than money. To
some extent the press of Plantin is a sort of parallel
to that of the Estiennes at Paris in its importance in
the history of learning, but while the Estiennes concerned themselves mainly with the classics of antiquity,
Plantin's chief work was the printing of the science
of his own day. He was succeeded by his son-in-law
Moretus, and the family continued as printers for
many generations.

If we take the early period, say the first 150 years,
of printing as a whole, we may sum up the story by
saying that the centre of gravity which was in about
1465 in the neighbourhood of Mainz and Cologne
had, by the end of the century, shifted to Venice. Then
for a time the most important centre was Basel; next,
for some years preceding 1550, Paris, until with the
establishment of Robert Estienne at Geneva in 1551 this
latter town took the first place. Finally, towards the
end of the century, we find the Antwerp and Frankfurt
presses among the most important, though at this
period no one town or country takes a very definite
lead.

The publication of the first editions of the Greek
and Latin classical authors is in early times not a bad
indication of the relative energy of the various presses.
Reference to the very useful tables given by Sandys [1]
shows that of sixty-four *editiones principes* of Latin
authors which appeared up to 1500, all save six were
printed in Italy, the exceptions being two, among the
very first productions of the press, which appeared at
Mainz and Cologne in 1465-6, two printed at Strassburg *c.* 1470, one at Paris in 1471, and one at Nuremberg in 1472. From 1478 onwards about sixty-two
editiones principes of Greek authors appeared in Italy
before a single one appeared elsewhere, this being
Polybius, printed at Hagenau in 1530. Then from

[1] *History of Classical Scholarship,* ii. 103-5.

1532 to 1544 we find seven at Basel against two in Italy, and from 1545 to 1557 six in Italy, eight at Paris, one at Basel, and one at Zurich.

When we turn from the presses of such scholars as Aldo and Paolo Manuzio, Johann Froben, and the Estiennes to consider the work of our own countrymen we find, naturally enough, a very different level of accomplishment. At the same time, however, we may fairly claim that the earlier English printers did not do so badly considering the relatively small market that they could have for their publications, the inaccessibility of manuscript sources, and the distance from all really important intellectual centres of the time; for there is no use in trying to disguise the fact that though in the first half of the sixteenth century there were scholars here of eminence and keenness who made as good use of their opportunities as the greatest continental scholars did of theirs, the number of them was small and their difficulties were many. With the possible exception of John Day there was, I think, no single printer in England during the sixteenth century who can be said to have contributed in any perceptible degree either to the progress of knowledge in the wider sense or to that of his own art.

This is not to deny that many of our early printers were very worthy fellows and of great interest to us, but it would be, I think, misleading to deal, however briefly, with such men as de Worde, Pynson, Berthelet, Grafton, Bynneman, Denham, and John Wolfe, to name a few of the more prominent, in such a brief general statement as is attempted here. Their work can only be properly considered in an account of English printing as such, and to the books on this subject I must refer readers desirous of detailed information.[1]

[1] For the early period of English printing, see E. G. Duff, *The Printers, Stationers, &c. of Westminster and London from 1476 to 1535*, 1906. The only modern general account is H. R. Plomer's *Short*

Of Day, however, a few words may appropriately be said. He was born in 1522 and began to print as early as 1546. Soon after Queen Mary came to the throne he seems to have been imprisoned ; at any rate he disappears from view until 1557. It has been said by some that he went abroad, but there is no certain evidence of this. With the accession of Elizabeth in 1558 he resumed printing on a much larger scale, and from this date until his death in 1584 he was one of the chief English printers in the size of his business, and certainly the chief in enterprise. He was greatly befriended by Archbishop Parker, and it was perhaps as much due to Parker's initiative as to his own that he produced his most important work. The excellent founts of roman and italic type which he cut about 1572 are mentioned elsewhere, as also the Anglo-Saxon fount which was used in printing one of Ælfric's homilies in Parker's *Testimony of Antiquity*, 1567, and in *Alfredi Res Gestae*.[1] Among his notable books were William Cunningham's *Cosmographical Glass*, 1559, Sleidan's *Chronicle*, 1560, Foxe's *Acts and Monuments*, 1563, the first English translation of *Euclid*, 1570, Latimer's *Sermons*, 1571 (and frequently), Parker's *de Antiquitate Britannicae Ecclesiae*, 1572, and the writings of Tyndale, Frith, and Barnes, and many others of the more serious and learned works of the period.

Besides John Day we should perhaps mention Christopher Barker, the chief part of whose work consisted of Bibles and certain official publications, for which he had a patent from 1578, and the important combina-

---

History of English Printing, 1476–1898, 1900. The *Century of the English Book Trade* by Duff, and the 'Dictionaries' of printers, &c., issued by the Bibliographical Society, contain notices of all known printers, publishers, and others associated with the book trade from 1457 to 1725.

[1] This, though printed in Saxon characters, is in Latin (facs. in Reed's *Letter Foundries*, facing p. 96).

tion known as the Eliot's Court Press,[1] which turned
out a large quantity of sound but uninspired printing,
and was indeed responsible for a considerable proportion of the output of the more 'solid' literature
between 1585 and 1609.

We must now turn again to the Continent, where
we shall find almost everywhere a steady decline in the
personnel of the presses, and consequently in the work
that they turned out. Almost everywhere the printers
were becoming mere men of commerce, and the time
of the scholar-printers was over. There was, indeed,
one family of printers in Holland, namely, the Elzevirs,
who kept up a high standard of work until well past the
middle of the century. They were, however, printers,
not scholars, attending diligently to the correctness of
the books which they printed, but not themselves
writers or editors. The first of the family to engage
in printing was Louis, who printed in Leyden from
1592 to 1617. It was, however, under his youngest
son Bonaventura, who worked at Leyden from 1626
to 1652 in association with Abraham, Bonaventura's
nephew, that the Officina Elzeviriana distinguished
itself for the small volumes of Latin authors which
made its fame, and have since been especially known
as 'Elzevirs'.

In 1638 an Elzevir printing-house was set up at
Amsterdam by Louis III, a nephew of Bonaventura,
who printed there alone until 1654, and afterwards in
association with his cousin Daniel, son of Bonaventura.
Louis retired about 1664, Daniel continuing alone
until his death in 1680. This Amsterdam house produced between 1655 and 1680 a very large number
of works of importance and of typographical excellence,
and indeed was perhaps in reality the more important
of the Elzevir presses, though their work was never
sought by collectors as were the small Leyden volumes.

[1] See an article on this press by H. R. Plomer in *The Library*,
4th Ser., iii.)ł ff.

Members of the family continued to print at Leyden until into the next century, but their work was of little importance.

It may be mentioned that according to the figures given in the *Nouvelle Biographie Générale* about 80 per cent. of Elzevir books were Latin, about 10 per cent. French, and less than 4 per cent. Greek, the remaining 6 per cent. being divided between Flemish, German, Italian, and Oriental languages.

The seventeenth century was, throughout Europe as well as in this country, the worst period for printing. With very few exceptions the printers were merely more or less honest tradesmen whose work was purely commercial and had no relation to scholarship. In England there seems to have been no press deserving of mention with the exception of the Oxford University Press, which by the efforts of a number of benefactors, of whom the most important were Dr. John Fell, who in 1667 presented a complete type-foundry, and Francis Junius, who made a similar present of type and matrices ten years later, was placed in a position to undertake all kinds of learned publications. In spite, however, of producing some valuable books the Oxford Press did not at this period show any remarkable activity. The output during the second half of the seventeenth century never averaged more than thirty-two books per annum, and even this number fell off to a yearly average of sixteen in the period 1731–40.[1]

During the eighteenth and nineteenth centuries the printer as a factor in the spread of culture gave place to the publisher. The printer was no longer a scholar who edited the books that he printed like the Estiennes, nor did he even finance them and organize their sale like the Elzevirs. These latter functions had passed to the publisher, and the printer merely executed the work for which he was paid. This does not mean that

[1] See F. Madan, *Chart of Oxford Printing*, p. 48.

printers of the period might not be of importance from the artistic or technical side, for several printing-houses were noteworthy on these accounts, but this is not our present concern. It will be best therefore to close this chapter by a brief mention of two or three of the chief English booksellers or publishers of these later times.

The most noteworthy member of the trade at the end of the seventeenth century was Jacob Tonson, who may, I think, be regarded as the first in this country to develop a really considerable publishing business by his own enterprise. He opened a bookseller's shop in 1677 and at once began to purchase the copyrights of such authors as Dryden, Otway, and Tate. In 1684 he issued a volume of ' Miscellany Poems ' edited by Dryden, which was a great success and became the first of a series. From this time onwards he was constantly associated with Dryden, though not always harmoni- ously, as well as with almost all the noteworthy authors of the time, whose acquaintance he assiduously cultivated. He published Pope's earliest work in his sixth miscellany in 1709, and in 1725 his nephew, also Jacob, his uncle having more or less retired from business in 1720, published Pope's edition of Shakespeare. Jacob Ton- son the elder died in 1736, his nephew having pre- deceased him, and the business was carried on by two grand-nephews until the death of the younger in 1772. For nearly a century the Tonson family occupied a prominent place in all literary ventures which, allowing for the different interests of the periods, can be not unfairly compared with that of the scholar-printers of earlier times.

In his later years Tonson had a rival in Bernard Lintot (1675–1736) who, though he never attained to Tonson's eminence, published much for Pope, Gay, Steele, and other writers of the period. In several ventures he was associated with Tonson.

As an example of a prominent publisher of a different class may be mentioned the famous Edmund Curll

(1675–1747), who is perhaps now best remembered for the fierce attacks made upon him by Pope in the *Dunciad* and elsewhere. He was an enterprising person with more brains than scruples, and would seem to have been ready to publish anything by which he could make a profit, but we need not take too literally all that has been said against him. It was not altogether a dishonour to be reviled by Pope, and some at least of Pope's attacks on him have been proved to be groundless or worse. He undoubtedly published a number of important books, including some biographical and antiquarian works of great value.

In the second half of the eighteenth century there seems to be no one to compare with such men as Tonson or Lintot, at any rate in their importance in the literary world. Important publishing ventures were as a rule financed by a number of booksellers of whom each would take a definite share in the risks and profits, and whose interest in the works seems to have been almost entirely commercial. In fact a change seems to have come over the publishing business very similar to that which came over that of printing towards the end of the sixteenth century. Perhaps, however, Robert Dodsley (1703–1764) deserves to be named, though indeed his activities as poet, dramatist, and miscellaneous compiler rather overshadow his actual publishing. This, however, includes Johnson's *Vanity of Human Wishes* and *Rasselas*, as well as shares in other works. His *Select Collection of Old Plays* gives him a title to the gratitude of all students of English literature, and the *Annual Register* which he founded in 1758 still survives.

John Nichols (1745–1826) should also perhaps be mentioned. He was for the first part of his life a printer, but his interests throughout seem to have been mainly those of an antiquary, and he has left work in this kind which is of enduring value. He seems, in connexion with his printing, to have undertaken a certain amount of publishing, but a great part of this business consisted of his own works, which were numerous.

Towards the end of the eighteenth century we find the name of Longman as one of the sharers in most works of importance. This firm had been founded in 1724 by Thomas Longman (1699–1755), who became one of the shareholders in Chambers's *Cyclopaedia*, a very valuable property, and in Johnson's *Dictionary*. The business increased in the hands of his nephew (also named Thomas) and of the son of the latter (1771–1842), and by the beginning of the nineteenth century the firm, which from time to time took in new partners, occupied the leading position in the London book trade. We here, however, approach modern times, and this hasty survey must be brought to a close.

APPENDIX TWO

PRINTING TYPES. GENERAL SKETCH OF THEIR EARLY
DEVELOPMENT. THE TYPES IN ENGLAND. THE SIZES
OF TYPE-BODIES. THE EM

Type faces.

As was only natural, the style of letter adopted by
the early printers was based, with such modifications
as were necessitated by the process to be employed in
making the type, on what were regarded as the best
MSS. of the time and place at which they worked;
the first types to be cut followed therefore the hand-
writings current in Western Germany in the middle
of the fifteenth century.[1] These were those developments of the Carolingian minuscule which came to be
called gothic, and the type based thereon is called
gothic [2] or black-letter.

[1] Much valuable material for the study of English printing types
is to be found in Talbot Baines Reed's *History of the Old English Letter
Foundries*, 1887, but all earlier general accounts of the history of type-
forms have been superseded by D. B. Updike's *Printing Types*, Harvard
University Press, 1922, 2 vols., which covers the whole subject of
European and American types down to the present day and is illustrated
by a most valuable series of 367 facsimiles. These facsimiles (line-
blocks) are excellent, but for the early types the student should, when
possible, consult collotypes, which, especially when the original press-
work is not of the first class, often reproduce more faithfully the general
effect. The portfolio of collotype *Facsimiles from Early Printed Books
in the British Museum*, 1897, will be found useful, though it is limited
in its scope, having very few examples after 1500. Facsimiles of all
types used in the fifteenth century in England will be found in Gordon
Duff's *Early English Printing*, 1896, and his *English Fifteenth-Century
Printed Books* (Bibliographical Society, 1917); the former are in collotype, the latter in line. Many other series of facsimiles will be found
mentioned in Mr. Updike's book, but unfortunately most of them
are, on account of their price and the limited number issued, not
available to those junior students to whom we must look for future
bibliographical work.

[2] This use of ' gothic ' to designate the earliest of the great families

From the very earliest days of printing three main kinds of gothic type can be distinguished, namely, the so-called ' lettre de forme ', ' lettre de somme ', and ' lettre bâtarde '. The first of these, the *lettre de forme*, was derived from the most formal script, which was used especially in the writing of liturgical books, and is in general of a rather narrow and pointed character, tending everywhere to angularity. This came to be, though not the earliest, the usual form of English black-letter, towards the middle of the sixteenth century to the virtual exclusion of both the others. The *lettre de somme* shows little difference in the form of the individual letters, but the type as a whole is broader and less angular, and represents a somewhat less formal handwriting. It is not at all easy to draw a definite line between the *lettre de forme* and the *lettre de somme*, and Updike apparently does not admit any of the types used in England to the second group. The distinction is perhaps hardly worth attempting when intermediate forms are so numerous, but certain of the smaller sizes used by Wynkyn de Worde and Grafton, and such types as Berthelet's Nos. 5 and 6 (Greg in *B. S. Trans.*, vol. viii, with facsimiles)—to take a few examples at random—seem very definitely to have that feeling of breadth and openness which is characteristic of the *lettre de somme.*

The *lettre bâtarde* represents the cursive hand of its time, and in several respects differs from the other groups. Among its characteristics may be noted that the f and long f are prolonged to a point below the base line and slope slightly, instead of being rigidly upright ; the short s is closed on the left hand, being somewhat like a b of which the top has been battered downwards ; lastly, the final n and m usually, but not

---

of type-faces (gothic, roman and italic) is convenient provided that it is not confused with the so-called ' gothic ' of the modern type-founder, where, as Updike says, it is purely an arbitrary name, ' unless it hints at the artistic abilities of its inventor '.

always, end with a tail below the base-line. Certain
characteristics of the *lettre bâtarde* appear as early as in
the 30-line *Indulgence* of 1455, the 31-line one being
in *lettre de somme*, and Caxton's earlier types are also
of this group. Later the *lettre bâtarde* was characteristic of French printing. It never attained to any
great vogue in England, though it crops up here and
there as in Berthelet's type 4 (Greg in *B. S. Trans.*,
viii. 190, with facs.).

It is, of course, to be understood that these three
groups of gothic letter represent merely tendencies ;
it must not be expected that all varieties of type can
be definitely assigned to one or other of the groups,
for there exist all degrees of transition between them
as well as many founts which must be regarded as more
or less mixed. Some bibliographers on this account
object to the use of these terms altogether,[1] but they
are well recognized and have at least the advantage of
enabling us to give in a phrase some rough indication
of the general character of a page of type.

Besides the ' gothic ' hand used generally in northern
Europe in the fifteenth century there existed in Italy
another derivative of the Carolingian minuscule of a
less angular character.[2] It is unnecessary to describe
it, for on it was ultimately based the ordinary ' roman '
type of to-day. To what extent this hand was used in
fifteenth-century Germany I cannot say, but it must
have been familiar to many classical scholars of the
north who were in touch with the more active spirits
of the Italian renaissance.[3] In any case we find as
early as 1460 a rounded gothic used by Gutenberg at
Mainz and one used by Menthelin at Strassburg

---

[1] Professor A. W. Pollard, for example, tells me that he regards
them as a mere nuisance.

[2] Actually an imitation of the later (twelfth century) Carolingian
writing by the Italian scribes of the Renaissance.

[3] It may be noted that roman type was in Germany specially associated with the classics and is still called ' antiqua ' in German.

(Updike, figs. 17 and 21) which, while still distinctly gothic, have a marked tendency towards the simpler and more legible roman character; and some four years later, *c.* 1464, we find a definitely roman [1] type used by the so-called R-printer, now identified with Adolph Rusch at Strassburg (Updike, fig. 22). Later we find a good deal of roman type in use in Germany, but it never took the hold in Germany that it did in Italy, where it represented the favourite script of the time.

When in 1465 Sweynheim and Pannartz set up the first press in Italy in a Benedictine monastery at Subiaco it was natural that, instead of using the gothic type of their northern fellows, they should attempt to follow the script of the locality in which they had established themselves. The first fount which they produced, though certainly to be classed as roman, or at least transitional, had marked gothic features, especially in the slight angularity of the ' round ' letters such as e, c, o, and is indeed less roman than the type used by Rusch at Strassburg in all probability several months earlier (Updike, fig. 24). Altogether it is too thick and clumsy to be called a success, and their second type used at Rome at the end of 1467, though much more roman in character, is hardly better in this respect. A curious feature of books printed in this type is the use of long ſ in all positions, finally as well as medially, a practice which may perhaps have been imitated from Neapolitan MSS. of the period (cf. *Brit. Mus. Reproductions from Illuminated MSS.*, Ser. 3, plates xxxviii, xl).[2]

[1] The most convenient point at which to make the division between ' semi-gothic ' and ' roman ' is perhaps at the stage where the short diagonal stroke over the i, like an acute accent, becomes the round dot. We must, however, take other characteristics into consideration, for we may find exceptional gothic founts with the round dot and roman ones with the stroke.

[2] It should, however, be remarked that other printers sometimes followed the same usage in roman type ; thus, the first printer at Paris

Shortly after this, however, in 1469, we find a genuine roman type in the work of Wendelin of Speyer, the first printer at Venice. This is quite a respectable letter, but its effect is spoiled by bad justification of the matrices, so that the letters in certain combinations appear too close together, in others too far apart (Updike, fig. 26). With the advent of Nicholas Jenson, however, who began to print at Venice in 1470, we reach at a stride what is perhaps the perfection of roman type, a letter of such excellence that though it has been constantly imitated and ' improved upon ' it has, in the opinion of some, never been surpassed.

The fortunes of roman type varied considerably in the various countries. In Germany it never took any great hold as a text type, and, indeed, from 1500 until quite modern times it was decidedly unusual except as a ' differentiation ' type.[1] In Swiss printing, however, generally classed with German, it was common from the beginning of the sixteenth century. Both in France and Spain the earliest books were in roman, but there succeeded a period of gothic which lasted in France until somewhere about the second decade of the sixteenth century, when roman again came into favour; the change of fashion in Spain coming perhaps a little later. In the Netherlands the earliest printing is gothic, then there is a period in which both this and roman were used, but from early in the sixteenth century the great bulk of the better-class printing seems to have been in roman. In Italy, as might be expected, though Ratdolt and a few others of the earliest printers used gothic type of a modified form, by far the majority of books were either roman or

(1470–2) frequently though not invariably used long f finally. See B.M. Facs. from E. P. B., plate xvii, and Claudin's First Paris Press, facsimiles on pp. 91–2, 97.

[1] i.e. for printing quotations—as we now use italic—for prefaces, &c., and in cases where two things printed parallel, e.g. a Latin text and a translation, require to be differentiated.

italic. In England roman type was introduced com-
·paratively late, and a very long period elapsed before
its final triumph, much longer than in any of the
countries with which we have been dealing save Germany, but of this I shall have more to say later.

The third of the great families of type, the italic,[1]
was introduced by Aldus Manutius at Venice in 1501.
It used to be said that it was based by him on the
handwriting of Petrarch, but this is perhaps due to
a mere misinterpretation of a phrase used in the 1501
edition of Petrarch's *Cose Volgari*, ' tolto . . . dallo
scritto di mano medesima del Poeta ' (Updike, i. 128).
It is no doubt actually derived from one of the forms
of the Humanistic hand of which there are many
examples at the time, and of which Aldus probably
liked the appearance, while at the same time he doubtless knew the value of originality in book production.
The Aldine italic is a genuine attempt to produce an
appearance of script, and for this purpose contains
some sixty-five ligatures (Updike, i. 129), such as *c*,
m, *n*, *t*, with each of the vowels following, as well as
the more usual *um*, *ct*, and the ordinary *f* and long *ſ*
ligatures, the latter including some unusual combination such as *ſp*. Oddly enough, however, *is* and *us*,
so common later, do not seem to be used. It was
solely a lower-case fount and was used by Aldus in
conjunction with small roman capitals which are much
less tall than the ascenders, and are, in addition, at the
beginning of lines of verse, always separated from the
word to which they belong by more or less space.
These peculiarities, both the roman capitals and the
space after them, will also be found in MSS. of the
period, and were doubtless taken over from them by
Aldus as a matter of course ; and though to us who
are used to the modern forms these apparently wrong-
fount capitals may be at first somewhat disconcerting,
they were quite in accord with the taste of the time,

[1] Called by the Italians ' Aldino ', by others Italic or Kursiv (Ger.).

and Updike even claims that they are artistically correct, as they give the page ' an agreeable perpendicular movement which italic capitals do not supply '.

The Aldine character found immediate favour with book-buyers, and was soon widely imitated in Italy and elsewhere, especially at Lyons, though the imitations are of varying degrees of closeness.[1]   It is not necessary to discuss the complicated story of the development of italics, but one point of importance may be referred to which has recently been brought out in an excellent article by A. F. Johnson and Stanley Morison in *The Fleuron*, No. 3, which supplements and to some extent corrects Updike.   In this they show that, parallel with the Aldine italic, there existed from 1524 onwards an altogether different italic face, originated by the writing-master and printer, Ludovico degli Arrighi of Vicenza.   This family of italic can be most briefly characterized as more flowing and script-like than that of Aldus : the tail of the g is brought round in one sweep to the left (as in the modern written g), instead of being zig-zagged to left and then round to the right again as in the usual italic and roman g ; the ascenders are curved over to the right, and the descenders to the left in a manner that seems suggested by the *f*, instead of being straight, and the h has a more marked bow.

The development of the small upright capitals used by Aldus with his italics into the sloping capitals of modern founts, of equal height with the ascenders, was slow and hesitating.   The early users of italic, indeed, such as Froben at Basel, Simon de Colines at Paris,

---

[1] A badly cut italic type used by Denis Roce at Paris in 1513 in the *Viridarium Illustrium Poetarum* (the work which became later the *Flores Poetarum* of the Elizabethans) is remarkable for the fact that certain letters, including b, g, h, r, p, q, v, though italic in general character, are quite upright, while others, d, f, i, l, ʃ, s, t, &c., have the usual slope, the result being an odd irregularity.   An interesting example of almost upright italic is reproduced in *The Fleuron*, iii. 38, as used by G. A. Castiglione at Milan in 1541.

and others, only departed from their model in giving a very slight cant to their capitals, which remain roman in form, and in letting them be slightly larger than in the Aldine books, though they still do not reach to the height of the ascenders (cf. Updike, figures 81, 101, 139, 141). Examples of this practice can be found until 1580 at least, and probably much later. As early, however, as 1538, in the work of Sebastian Gryphius at Lyons, we find definitely sloped italic capitals of a modern form, inclined at the same angle as the lower-case ascenders and of an equal height with them,[1] and by the middle of the century many printers in Italy at least were using capitals of the form which became the normal tradition of italic down to the present day.

Alongside these normal sloped italic capitals there existed in most founts a more script-like or ' swash ' form, ornamented with a certain amount of flourish. Thus we have A and $\mathcal{A}$, B and $\mathcal{B}$, C and $\mathcal{C}$, I and $\mathcal{J}$.[2] These ' swash ' letters seem to have been taken over from the non-Aldine group, for they are first found in Arrighi's italics of 1524, and though he afterwards abandoned them, they reappear in founts based on his which were used by Colines at Paris in 1528 and by Francesco Marcolini da Forli at Venice in 1536.[3] By the middle of the century they were in general use with a lower-case of the Aldine form.[4] Curiously enough there seems never to have been a complete alphabet of ' swash ' letters, or, if there was one, certain characters never came into general use. There are, for example, no swash forms, so far at least as I can ascertain, of F, L, O, S, W, X in any of the italic

[1] See p. 48, fig. 18 of the *Fleuron* article already mentioned. Oddly enough the matrices seem to have been so justified that the letters are more upright than the designer intended, with the result that in such a letter as M the left-hand limb comes noticeably lower than the right. One suspects that the overhang was found inconveniently great.

[2] The ' swash ' forms of I and V ($\mathcal{J}$, $\mathcal{V}$) came later to be used for J and U.

[3] *Fleuron*, iii. 24, 34, 44.   [4] e. g. by Gabriel Giolito at Venice

founts in ordinary use in England in the earlier periods, nor can I point to a swash H, though forms with the first or second upright curled outwards occur in certain foreign founts.[1] These swash letters, whatever may have been their original purpose, seem to have been used at all times absolutely interchangeably with the plain letters in all positions, with the result that, though sometimes useful to the bibliographer,[2] they can hardly be said to add to the beauty of the work in which they appear.

It should be noted that italic was originally intended as a body-type for general purposes and was therefore not at first cut to range with gothic and roman. Books entirely composed in italic are very frequent in Italian printing of the sixteenth century, and there are examples of the same thing in other countries. Its main use, however, save in Italy, was as a differentiation type.

It only remains to mention the ' script ' types which were intended to imitate as closely as possible current handwriting, and few words will suffice for these, as they are of no practical importance. The most famous and apparently the earliest of these types were the so-called *caractères de civilité* [3] introduced at Lyons by Robert Granjon of Paris about 1557. They are an imitation of ' a gothic cursive handwriting which was in vogue at the time '.[4] A somewhat similar attempt was made in certain cursive type used by Froschouer at Zurich in 1567 (Updike, fig. 77), and a few founts of this kind were cast in England, but they were never much used.[5]

[1] *Fleuron,* iii. 34, and in books printed by Giolito in 1554.

[2] See p. 182.

[3] Thus named because they were early employed in two educational works entitled respectively *La Civilité Puérile* and *Civile Honesteté pour les Enfants* (Updike, i. 201).   [4] Updike, u. s.

[5] For some examples see Updike, fig. 254. The specimen gives us strong reason for suspecting that the compositor who set it up found the type difficult to read. Cf. also T. B. Reed, *Letter Foundries,* pp. 56, 289.

The types in England.

The earliest type-faces used here were of course of black-letter or 'gothic' character, roman type being first used as a text type by Pynson in 1518 in Richard Pace's *Oratio in Pace nuperrima composita*,[1] and italic not until 1524, when it is found in Wakefield's *Oratio de laudibus trium linguarum*, printed by Wynkyn de Worde, a book which also contains the first Arabic and Hebrew printing in England, though these are from woodblocks, not type. Until about the middle of the sixteenth century black letter remained the normal character for all purposes, though a certain number of Latin books were printed in roman, this being especially used for the Latin text of books printed in English and Latin. It is also commonly found in head-lines, chapter headings, &c. Early in the reign of Elizabeth roman began to be more popular, and by about 1580 the use of black letter in plays and the higher kinds of English verse,[2] as well as in Latin books, had almost ceased, and there seems to have been a tendency to abandon it in scientific and theological literature also. Popular prose and ballads, however, continued to be printed in black letter until well on in the seventeenth century, and law-books were still in this character in the eighteenth. Even in black-letter books, however, the preliminary matter (dedications, and epistles to the reader) were from about 1580 generally in roman or italic. The printers of this time seem seldom to have possessed any black letter type of a larger size than that used for the text of their books, and commonly used roman or italic for their title-pages, headings, &c. There are, however, a fair number of exceptions to the general rule.

Soon after the introduction of roman and italic type

[1] According to Updike, ii. 89, it was actually first used in Pynson's *Sermo fratris Hieronymi de Ferraria*, 1509.

[2] I suspect that the use of black letter in the *Shepherd's Calendar* of 1579 was an intentional bit of antiquarianism.

these began to be used for the purpose of differentiation. Thus, in a black letter text, proper names are
often in roman, quotations from foreign languages
generally in italic,[1] while in a roman text italic is
generally used both for proper names and for quotations.

It is not of any importance to our subject that we
should try to follow the course of type-designing or
type-founding in England. Those desirous of full
information on the subject should consult the work of
Talbot Baines Reed, already frequently referred to, or
that of Mr. Updike, which, although on account of
its wider scope it goes into less detail concerning
English work, supplements Reed in many important
particulars. A few more or less random notes may,
however, be not without interest.

The most important English printer of the sixteenth
century, from our present point of view, was John Day,
who about 1572 cast some excellent founts of roman
and italic. He is stated to have been the first English
printer to cast the two forms on similar bodies so that
they would range properly with one another when used
together. He was a man of great enterprise and was
lucky also in his patron Archbishop Parker, for whom
he cut the first fount of Anglo-Saxon, used in 1567.
He also had a Greek fount which was superior to those
hitherto in use in this country.

There is little to say concerning English type-faces
from the time of Day for more than a century. During
the whole period, although no doubt there were many
type-founders at work in England—indeed several of
the chief presses apparently had their own foundries

---

[1] In roman reprints of black-letter texts editors desiring to keep the
distinction of the three types have sometimes used small capitals for
original roman, using italic only for original italics (e.g. in the Hunterian
Club reprints of Lodge, Rowlands, &c.). This gives rather an odd
appearance to the text, and it is now, I think, more usual to ignore
the distinction of original roman and italic, representing both by italic.

—the matrices or punches seem to have been imported, as a rule, from abroad, particularly from Holland, or at least to have been cut according to foreign patterns. From 1637 to 1640, and again from 1662 to 1693, the number of type-founders was officially limited to four, but there is no means of determining to what extent the restriction was effective. There was a fairly constant dissatisfaction during the seventeenth century with the type used in this country and attempts were made to remedy the state of affairs, notably by the famous Dr. John Fell, who in 1667 presented to the University of Oxford a complete type-foundry containing punches and matrices of a very large assortment of founts. The importance of Fell's gift has, however, I think, been somewhat misunderstood. It consisted rather in its extent, especially in the variety of 'learned' founts, Arabic, Syriac, Coptic, &c., than in any peculiar excellence of design in the roman and italics. These were doubtless the best that Fell could procure from Holland at the time, and there was a very useful range of sizes, but I venture to think that in spite of its present vogue, the 'Fell' roman type, though excellent for giving a pleasant flavour of antiquity to reprints of sixteenth- and seventeenth-century books, is not in itself particularly beautiful, and that the italic, mainly on account of the irregular slope of some of the characters and its appearance of being smaller than the roman to which it belongs, is, when used with roman, positively ugly, though it is by no means unpleasing, especially in the larger sizes, when standing alone.

Those who wish to form an idea of the dependence of the English printers of the pre-Caslon period on the Dutch type-founders [1] should read the amusing account given by Reed of the adventures of Thomas James, one of the chief English type-founders of the

---

[1] Moxon in 1683 wrote in high praise of the Dutch letters, which he liked for their ' commodious Fatness ', rendering them more legible than any others (*Mech. Ex.*, p. 15).

early eighteenth century, who visited Holland in 1710 in search of matrices (apparently no offer would induce the Dutch founders to sell their punches). One is glad to know that he was successful in obtaining several good founts and prospered as the result, even though towards the end of his life he seems to have been badly hit by the superior productions of the Caslon foundry.

The most important English letter-founder since Day, namely, William Caslon, was born in 1692 and was first apprenticed to an engraver of gun-locks and barrels. His earliest work in the direction of type appears to have been the designing of tools for book-binders, and his first actual printing type an Arabic fount which he cut in 1720. In the same year or shortly after he cut the first of his roman and italic founts, and from this time to his death in 1766 he produced a great number of founts of very varied kinds.

Caslon's roman and italic were at once accepted as far superior to any others, and were even purchased by foreign printers. In England they were in very general use until the end of the eighteenth century, when for a time they went out of fashion.[1]

After Caslon the most notable type-designer of the eighteenth century was probably John Baskerville

[1] It may perhaps be well to warn the reader that ' Caslon ' as applied to type has not an absolutely precise connotation. Though, for example, the founts of different sizes cut by Caslon himself are all in the same general style, the forms of the letters do not correspond with mathematical exactness. Further, of some sizes Caslon cut two or more separate founts slightly differing in form (cf. Updike, ii. 104, note). When it is added that ' Caslon ' founts have been repeatedly cut in modern times, it will be evident that we must be prepared for a certain range of variety.

The Caslon foundry itself produced, towards the end of the eighteenth century, type-faces more in accordance with the current demand for greater lightness and regularity. Indeed, their specimen of 1798 (Updike, figure 279) shows a roman and italic type more resembling a weakened and slightly condensed Baskerville than ' Caslon '. In 1805 they ceased to show the original types cut by the first William Caslon (Updike, ii. 196, note).

(1706–75), who was successively footman, writing-master, cutter of monumental inscriptions, and japan-ner. In this last business he prospered sufficiently to enable him, from about 1750, to experiment in printing, to which he seems to have been originally attracted by his interest in lettering. Baskerville's ideal was not, however, the production of a perfect type, but of a per-fect book ; he was concerned as much with the correct-ness of the text that he printed and with the excellence of paper, ink, and press-work as with the design of the type itself. This last, however, was of necessity specially cut to harmonize with Baskerville's preference for a somewhat open appearance, wide spacing, and leading between the lines. His lower-case letters are for the most part very similar to Caslon's in form, but are slightly wider, the chief difference being apparently in the greater width of body of some of them. The truth is, if I am not mistaken, that Caslon justified his type for Latin and Baskerville for English. The original Caslon type has a better appearance, at least in my opinion, in Latin than it ever has in English, which, I think, cannot be said of Baskerville types. In italic the difference is, however, far more noticeable. The Caslon italic retained something of the angu-larity of the current script, especially in the upper curves of such letters as *n* and the lower curves of *t* and *d*, the type of Baskerville being everywhere much more rounded. It is perhaps in this that his influence on later designers was most marked. The design of his type had, however, less to do with the effect produced by his books than his method of pressing the sheets, immediately after printing, between hot plates of cop-per. This gave a brilliant gloss both to the paper and the ink, which was no doubt very pleasing to those who liked it. Others, however, condemned the effect as too dazzling, as would most people at present.

Baskerville's work attracted a great deal of attention in his day, but he met with strong opposition from the

301

established type-founders and printers, and his press
was by no means a financial success. After his death
his types were sold in France where they were in use
for some time. Eventually they seem to have been
dispersed and the whereabouts of the punches and
matrices is not known.[1] But in spite of this appearance
of failure Baskerville's work exercised a marked influence in the direction of a greater neatness and lightness of character, as may be seen especially in the type
of Alexander Wilson used by the brothers Foulis at
Glasgow in the last quarter of the eighteenth century
(cf. Updike, ii. 117–18, and Wilson's specimen in
fig. 275) and in some of the later type of the Caslon
foundry itself.

Towards the end of the century we find, however,
a reaction from the rather weak and grey descendants
of Caslon plus Baskerville, and a change begins which
was to end in the production of the so-called ' modern-
face ' type. Essentially this change was due to the
attempt to attain greater brilliancy of effect by increasing the differentiation between the heavy and light
portions of the letters. It is best represented in the
work of William Martin (*fl.* 1786-1815), whose types
were used in the ' Shakespeare Press ' established by
Messrs. Boydell & Nicol in 1790, at which were
printed the folio Shakespeare edited by George
Steevens in nine volumes, 1792–1802, a three-volume
Milton, and many other ' fine ' books of the day.

The earliest type found by Mr. Updike which he
would call actually ' modern face ' is in 1804 (fig. 330),
but my impression is that it was not in common use
until about 1815. The greater differentiation between
thick and thin strokes which accompanied and indeed
led to the modern-face design [2] increased until it re-

---

[1] Cf., however, Updike, ii. 114. It appears that some of the types
have recently come to light in French printing-houses.

[2] The two things are not the same but tend to go together, for in
many of the Caslon types any considerable thickening of the strokes

sulted in the production of some forms of extraordinary ugliness. Hansard's *Typographia*, 1825, quoted by Updike, ii. 195–6, says: 'Caslon's fonts rarely occur in modern use, but they have too frequently been superseded by others which can claim no excellence over them. In fact the book-printing of the present day is disgraced by a mixture of fat, lean, and heterogeneous types, which to the eye of taste is truly disgusting.'

The period 1815–44 was perhaps the worst of all from the point of view of type-design, though at the same time it was one of the most prolific of novelties, and though the press-work is generally, and the layout occasionally, excellent. It was at this time that many of the fancy display types and ornaments so dear to the jobbing printer of the nineteenth century were introduced, and, if one can judge by their design, most of the conventional head- and tail-pieces of which even recent type-founders' specimen-books are full; but we need waste no time over them.

But the original Caslon founts were still remembered by a few persons of somewhat antiquarian tastes, and in 1840 we find them being used at the Chiswick Press in titles and half-titles of books printed for the well-known publisher William Pickering.[1] It is thus hardly correct to date the revival as beginning with the printing of *The Diary of Lady Willoughby* in great primer Caslon in 1844, though there can be little doubt that the success of this book led to the wider use of Caslon in other works of antiquarian character. It was used by Pickering in a number of publications from 1844 onwards, and appears also in Payne Collier's five-volume edition of Spenser, 1862, and in the eight-volume Milton and in other books printed at the

---

would necessarily render the counter, or hollow, liable to become choked with ink.

[1] See *William Pickering, Publisher*, by Geoffrey Keynes, 1924, pp. 25–6.

Chiswick Press. According, however, to Mr. Jacobi, 'the excellent design of these different founts [of Caslon] was not generally appreciated until about the year 1888, when the Arts and Crafts Exhibition Society first came into existence, and Mr. Emery Walker was perhaps more responsible than any one else for making known this series of type-faces '. [1]

A brief reference should perhaps be made to the so-called ' revived old style ', a type which is said (Updike, ii. 201, 232) to have been cut about 1850 and has been much used for reprints of our older literature, such as, for example, the Ben Jonson printed at the Chiswick Press in 1875. It is a somewhat colourless attempt to combine the general characteristics of a Caslon type with a slightly more open and more regular face, and like most modern types exists in a variety of slightly different cuttings.

Modern type-faces, however, are not our affair, whether the more elaborate and fanciful ones designed for private presses or those intended for general use in book-printing, and this is fortunate, for the subject is an intricate one and cannot be dealt with briefly. Studies of the best of them may be found in Mr. Stanley Morison's useful monograph, *On Type Faces*, 1923.

A brief note may be useful on some characteristics of the three styles last mentioned. The progress from Caslon, via Revived Old Style, to Modern Face— taking them in order of similarity, not in order of date —is accompanied by the descent of the cross-bar of the e, which in Caslon is very close to the top, with the resulting inconvenience of easily becoming choked with ink, in the modern face practically half-way up, the ' old style ' being intermediate between the two. A sloping bar to the e is characteristic of many ' antique ' founts. The Caslon s is considerably narrower than

[1] *A Note on the Caslon Old-Faced Printing Types* (Design and Industries Association), 31 March 1920—a four-page leaflet with specimen of Caslon types on the fourth page.

in either of the other faces. The thick strokes of ' old style ' are on the whole thinner than in Caslon, with the result that there is less differentiation between heavy and light strokes. In modern face there is more. The serifs of the ascenders of practically all the older founts are wedge-shaped, the lower line being level and the upper inclining downward to meet it; the serif of the modern face is thin and perfectly horizontal. These few indications will aid greatly in the classification of ordinary type of the eighteenth and nineteenth centuries, but when we come to quite modern times there is far too much mixture of styles for them to be of any use, and one has to depend on ' specimens '.

It should be mentioned that the use of modern type-setting or casting machines in which the presence of kerned letters is impossible or at least most inconvenient has led to the narrowing of f and j so as to bring the curve entirely on the body of the type. The early attempts at a sickle-form f, in which the curve was bent back, have, I think, been abandoned, and well it is, for they were very ugly; but the narrow f that we now meet so commonly is likely to be permanent, and no doubt in the course of time we shall get used to it. After all it is but a matter of habit. One generally finds that in examining a new type, what one dislikes is just whatever is new, and with all respect to our modern typographical experts on such matters there is a great deal of truth in what Thomas James wrote from Rotterdam in July 1710 when he was on his famous type-hunt in Holland: ' The beauty of letter, like that of faces, is as people opine.'

The sizes of type-bodies.

The sizes of type-bodies used by the earliest English printers were somewhat various.[1] Gradually, however, they settled down to three for ordinary bookwork,

---

[1] The first type used in England (Caxton's No. 2) was about equivalent to two lines of long primer (10 lines = *c.* 65 mm.).

namely, english, pica, and long primer. Brevier was occasionally used for side-notes.[1] Small pica, such a usual size at present, was not introduced until towards the end of the seventeenth century,[2] and bourgeois, which is intermediate between long primer and brevier,

[1] Until comparatively recent times type-bodies, as cast by various founders, were far from uniform. Towards the end of the sixteenth century we find the measurement of ten lines of type (measuring from the base-line of one line to the base-line of the eleventh line above or below) to be approximately as follows : in english, 45–47 mm. ; in pica, 41–42 mm. ; in long primer, 31–33 mm. ; in brevier, about 27 mm. It is well to remember that pica has always been *about* six lines to the inch. If it were accurately this, ten lines would measure 42·3 mm. Moxon gives the sizes of english as 66 lines to the foot; pica 75, long primer 92, and brevier 112, the equivalent of these measurements being respectively, 10 lines = 46·2 ; 40·6 ; 33·1 ; 27·2 mm.

Many incunabulists take *twenty* lines as the unit of measurement and there is an unfortunate want of uniformity in the way in which the measurement of these twenty lines is taken. Proctor's measurement was 'from the top of the short letters in line 1 to the bottom of the short letters in line 20, no account being taken of the tails of the longer letters ', *Index of Early Printed Books in the British Museum*, 1898, p. 13. Others appear to measure from the top of an ascender in line 1 to the bottom of a descender in line 20. This of course gives a measurement nearer to that of 20 lines of actual type than Proctor's, but both are more or less short. The only way which can possibly give an accurate measurement of 20 lines of type, and one from which that of any other number of lines can be deduced, is to measure from any point in one line to the *corresponding* point in the 21st line above or below. Further, it is only by measuring in this way that we can calculate the measure of our unit number from actual measurement of a smaller number of lines, a thing which it may very often be necessary to do when the type with which we are concerned is not the text type of the book.

In any case I submit that 20 lines is a less natural and less convenient unit than 10, if only because it complicates calculations. There is also the practical consideration that it is much harder to count 20 lines quickly and accurately than 10 (or 11), and that an error in the count is far more likely to be overlooked.

[2] It is mentioned by Moxon as ' sometimes used ' (*Mech. Ex.*, 1683, p. 13), but he disapproves of it as too near to pica and likely to get mixed with it.

did not appear until about 1748.[1] It may be noted that Elizabethan black-letter occupied, as a rule, a much smaller space on the body than the black-letter of most modern founts. Thus a modern small pica black-letter is almost identical in size of face with the early pica, and a modern pica with early english—a fact which gives rise to much trouble when one attempts a facsimile reprint in modern type of an old book containing both black-letter and roman.

It is hardly necessary that I should refer to the modern 'point' system of standard type-faces, as this can be found described in any recent book on printing. Briefly, in the American and English systems the standard is pica, which is made exactly $\frac{1}{6}$ of an inch and is regarded as measuring 12 'points'—the 'point' thus being $\frac{1}{72}$ of an inch. English is 14-point, small pica 11, long primer 10, bourgeois 9, brevier 8, and so on. The point system was originally introduced in France in 1737 by Fournier the younger, whose system was modified later as the 'Didot' point system, the unit of which is slightly larger than the American point.

The em.

In certain early founts of type the letter M was apparently cast on a square body[2] and thus formed a convenient measure of the amount of work done by a compositor, for though the area of type corresponding to a certain piece of copy will naturally vary according to the size of the type used, the amount measured in 'ems', i.e. squares of the type itself, will remain approximately constant. Compositors' wages came therefore to be reckoned on the basis of the number of 'ems' composed, and the system still continues

[1] Reed, *The Old English Letter Foundries*, p. 39.
[2] The 'em' is sometimes said to be derived from the lower-case m, but I doubt if in any normally proportioned type this has ever been cast on a square body. Actually in ordinary roman founts the M also is narrower than its height and, I believe, always has been.

save that the actual measure in use in England [1] is now the thousand ' ens ', the ' en ' being half an ' em '. The em is also used as a measure of the length of the line, though in this case, in order to avoid the inconvenience of having to keep a multiplicity of rules, ornaments, &c., of a fixed number of ems of all the different sizes of type, the pica em (now ⅙ of an inch) is taken as the standard in all cases, a line of 3½ inches of whatever size of type being known as a line of 21 ems.

As a measure for calculating the work done by compositors the em is said to have been in use from the fifteenth century, but I have found no certain evidence of this. That it was of very early date can, however, perhaps be inferred from its name, for it must have been instituted at a time when the body of the M was actually square. Nor have I been able to trace when the em came into use as a measure of length of line. If in a page of pica set solid (i. e. without leads between the lines) we find that dividers set to the length of the lines will also measure exactly any whole number of lines of type,[2] it is at least possible that the printer was working to an em-standard of length. I have, however, measured a number of English books of the sixteenth century without detecting any such general correspondence, though it must be confessed that a comparatively slight irregularity in the casting would serve to disguise the use of any standard of this kind. Indeed, although we often find books from the same printing-house and of near dates set to the same length of line, there seem no traces of any standard measures of length as between one printing-house and another.

---

[1] The unit in America is still, I believe, the ' em '. It must of course be understood that the actual rate of pay varies to some extent according to the type used, small type and very narrow type involving more work and being paid at a higher rate.

[2] Measuring from the base of the type in one line to the base of the type in another line, neglecting the descenders.

APPENDIX THREE

The letters ſ and s. From the beginning of printing until towards the end of the eighteenth century ſ was used initially and medially [1] and s finally, following of course the practice of the MSS. The first book to discard ſ is said to have been Joseph Ames's *Typographical Antiquities* of 1749, but this was regarded as an eccentricity, and the normal ſ is used in Herbert's edition of 1785–90.[2] The effective introduction of the reform has been credited to John Bell who in his *British Theatre* of 1791 used s throughout,[3] the same practice being followed in the Boydell *Shakespeare*, of which vol. i appeared in 1792.[4]

In London printing the reform was adopted very rapidly and, save in work of an intentionally antiquarian character, we do not find much use of ſ in the better kind of printing after 1800.[5] The provincial presses

---

[1] There were certain exceptions to this; see pp. 291, 314–15.

[2] Herbert introduced his own eccentricity of spelling the pronoun of the first person with a lower-case i.

[3] See Johnson, *Typographia*, ii. 24, and T. B. Reed, *Letter Foundries*, p. 52, note. The plays forming the *British Theatre* were published at various dates from 1791 onwards, being collected into volumes in 1797.

[4] See facsimile No. 297 in Updike, *Printing Types*, vol. ii. It is perhaps worth noting that Capell in his *Prolusions*, 1760, had attempted a modification of the usual practice. He there uses s medially for a z-sound, retaining ſ for an s-sound, thus: easily, visible, rais'd, &c., but verſes, purſuit, ſatiſſy. I cannot find that he comments upon the innovation, which, considering the nature of the work, is strange. It was printed by Dryden Leach and published by J. and R. Tonson.

[5] The ſ was used in the *Post Office London Directory* until 1824, but one would perhaps expect survivals in publications of this sort.

seem, however, to have retained it somewhat longer, and it is said to have been used at Oxford until 1824.[1]

The letters i, j, u, v. As a general rule, until early in the seventeenth century there was only one capital letter, I (in roman) or 𝔍 (in black letter), for the letters now represented by I and J; and only one capital letter, V (in roman) or 𝔘 (in black letter), for the letters U and V.[2]

In lower-case most founts had i, j, u, and v, but j was only used in the combination ij (often a ligature) or in numerals, as xiij, while v and u were differentiated according to position, not according to pronunciation; v being always used at the beginning of a word and u always medially. Thus the following are the normal spellings: iudge, inijcere or iniicere (= *lat.* injicere), vse, euent, vua (= *lat.* uva). Certain printers varied the practice in a few books, but the rule followed by most was absolutely rigid. It is quite incorrect to say that the letters were used indifferently, or that the sixteenth-century usage was the converse of the modern.

I have discussed elsewhere at some length the history of these four letters in sixteenth-century printing,[3] and a few notes on the matter will be sufficient here.

Apart from the use of j (to represent a guttural aspirate) in certain Spanish books dating from 1485 to 1487, the earliest instance known to me of the distinction between i and j, u and v, being made according to pronunciation is in the *Dyalogus between Salomon*

---

[1] Reed, *Letter Foundries*, p. 52, note.

[2] As was once pointed out by F. W. Bourdillon, this has in early French books the odd result that a *libraire juré* is liable to appear in capitals as ' IVRE '. When reprinting a black letter text in roman it seems logical to represent these by I and V in all cases, though some editors have preferred to use J and U, perhaps because the black letter forms approximate rather more closely to these letters in shape.

[3] See *The Library*, 3rd Ser., i. 239–59. Rimes and puns show that the Elizabethans *called* V by the name we now give to U (hence W is called double-u). I have failed to discover the originator of the modern name ' ve '

and Marcolphus printed at Antwerp by Gerard Leeu about 1492, where *medial* u and v are distinguished as in modern practice, and in the latter part of the book a somewhat ineffectual attempt is made to distinguish initial i and j (Leeu has ' is ', ' juftyce ', ' japyng ', but 'iudas' and 'iugeth'). Medial j (by pronunciation) does not seem to occur, so we do not know how the printer would have treated it.

A serious attempt to distinguish u and v according to the modern practice was made by Giangiorgio Trissino, Italian poet and spelling-reformer, in his books printed in 1524. Not much came of Trissino's attempt, however, and the reform was next taken up by Pierre de la Ramée or Ramus, whose *Grammatica* of 1559 distinguishes i and j, u and v according to the modern system throughout, both in capitals and lower-case. Ramus does not, however, claim the innovation as his own, but mentions it with approval as due to the printers, so it may perhaps be found somewhat earlier. Be this as it may, it was probably the great authority of Ramus that led to its adoption.

In England no example of the distinction seems to have been found earlier than J. Banister's *History of Man*, printed by John Day in 1578. The new method is followed in a few other books of Day, and in 1579–80 we find it followed by Henry Middleton in reprinting a Latin Bible from a Frankfurt edition in which the distinction had been made. From that time onwards to the end of the century we find a certain number of books following the new system either completely or with certain modifications, and thereafter the number gradually increased until between 1620 and 1630 it became the general rule.

It may be mentioned that the majuscule U at first employed was of the general design of the lower-case u with a small tail or serif at the foot.[1] The modern

---

[1] i. e. U. This has been revived in some modern founts.

U begins to come into use in English printing [1] about the middle of the seventeenth century. It occurs in the heading of page 1 of Gayton's *Festivous Notes upon Don Quixot*, 1654, but as late as the 1692 Ben Jonson Folio we find many examples of the tailed form.

As regards j we may note that in some of the early black letter founts the only separate form of the letter is one with two dots over it, used in roman numerals. In these founts it also occurs, with a single dot, in the ligature ij.

The letter w. In early founts this is often represented by vv. In later times the same is often found in founts of extra large size (presumably of foreign origin), and in ordinary founts when there happened to be a run on the w and the compositor had not enough.

It may be noted that in the capitals of certain large-sized founts used for titles, especially between about 1590 and 1640, the left-hand side of the second V of two used to form a W is filed or cut away so as to allow the two letters to come closer together and form a more regular W. [2] In a bibliography or facsimile reprint it is a question whether we should represent this by two V's or by a W. [3]

Ligatures. Two or more letters joined together, or differing in design from the separate letters, and cast on one type-body, such as ſt or ffi, are called a ligature. There were two reasons for their being so cast, custom and convenience. In the early founts the great majority of the ligatures were due to custom alone and represented a following of scribal practice which commonly joined together certain pairs of letters. Thus in the fount used by Caxton in the *Dictes and Sayings of the Philosophers* we find such ligatures as ad, be, ce, ch, co,

---

[1] It seems to have been somewhat earlier used in Dutch printing, but I have failed to discover by whom or where it was first introduced.

[2] Less frequently the right-hand side of the first V is cut away, or the adjacent sides of both.

[3] Cf. p. 153.

de, en, in, ll, pa, pe, po, pp, re, ro, te, &c., all of which owe their existence solely to imitation of MSS. of the time. Many of these customary ligatures persisted throughout the sixteenth century, and even later, in black letter founts, where we commonly find ee,[1] oo, ch, ph, pp, wh, and others, while a few have combinations with certain capitals such as Ch, Sh, Th, Wh.[2] Even in roman founts we find ct, oo, &c., of which ct has persisted until modern times. In italic founts we also find *es*, *us*, *st*, and others.[3]

When a letter part of which overhangs the body of the type, such as f or ſ, happens to be followed by such an upright letter as l or h, or by an i, the overhanging part or ' kern ' of the first letter comes in contact with the top of the second, and either the two types do not fit together properly or the kern of the first letter gets broken off. To avoid this, most founts even at present have ligatures of f with l, i, and another f (the end of the curve of the first letter or the dot of the i being suppressed), and of ff with l and i. In early times these ligatures for convenience included also a set with ſ. The f and ſ ligatures are also presumably copied from the MSS., where they frequently occur, though not in all hands. In MSS., however, especially in those hands which do not dot the i, there is little or no difference between the letters written close together, and so written as to touch and practically form a single character. For the sake of avoiding an ugly gap the scribe would naturally place an i under the beak of the ſ or bring up an l to touch it.[4] Thus it does not seem to have occurred to all the early printers to cut these f and ſ ligatures ; and although some of the early

---

[1] There is also a ligature ée, the origin and purpose of which have not been explained.

[2] e.g. in the fount used in the 1587 edition of Holinshed's *Chronicles*.

[3] The original Aldine italic had many more, see p. 293.

[4] In some Italian MSS. of the second half of the fifteenth century the ſi and ſt have exactly the form of the ligatures in roman type.

founts contain them, others do not.[1] As in the MSS.,
however, so in some of the early printed books, it is
difficult to be certain whether ligatures or the separate
letters were used.

In the earliest type used by Caxton in England we
find no f or ſ ligatures with the exception of ff, ſh, and
ſſ,[2] and indeed the shape of the type-faces did not
render them necessary. Others of his types have fl and
ſt, but no one fount seems to have the whole series as
used in later times, though most of them have a variety
of other ligatures. The complete series included fi, fl,
ff, ffi, ffl, ſi, ſl, ſh, ſt, ſſ, ſſi, ſſl,[3] and we find these in most
founts of roman, italic, and black letter throughout
the sixteenth, seventeenth, and eighteenth centuries.[4]
There were, however, certain rarer combinations of ſ
with upright letters, namely, b and k, for which in
early times no ligatures seem to have been cut. In
words in which these combinations occur it was customary in roman and italic type to use a short s, thus
' husband, Catesby, ask, skill ', the same practice being
followed when the s preceded an apostrophe or an f,
thus : ' vs'd, aduis'd, ſatisfie,[5] transform, misfortune,
ſuccefsful ', &c. In black letter founts the ſ does not
seem to overhang the body quite so much, and we
generally find ' huſband, aſk ', &c., though it is indeed

---

[1] The combinations ff and ſſ seem to be more frequent than the
others.

[2] Possibly there was an ſi ligature, but the i is dotted.

[3] So far as I can discover, no ft ligature was ever cast, though one
would have supposed that it was at least as much needed as ſt.

[4] In a certain number of Elizabethan founts there seem to have
been no ligatures of ff or ſſ with i or l, and even when these existed
they were not always used. One may find ' possible ' printed with
ffi, ſſi and ſſi in adjacent lines.

[5] Alternatively we sometimes find ' ſatiſ-fie ', &c., a hyphen being
used to keep the letters apart (which hyphen should perhaps not be
retained in a reprint which does not use long ſ). It may be remarked
that in French printing the accents cause similar trouble. Momoro,
in his *Traité Elémentaire*, p. 165, says that a thin space must be placed
between f and î and in certain other sequences of letters.

sometimes evident that the types are not flush against one another.

This practice of using s instead of ſ before b, k, f, and ' continued until early in the eighteenth century. By the date of Strype's edition of Stowe's *London*, however, 1720, an ſk had been cut, though the compositor apparently did not always remember its existence, for we find ' skilful ' (Bk. I, p. 64ᵃ, l. 14), but 'Baſkets' (I, 110ᵃ, 11 from foot); but I have failed to find an ſb. This, however, occurs regularly, as well as ſk, in the second edition of the *Letters of Lady Mary Wortley Montague* in 1763,[1] and from that date onwards until the long ſ was discontinued. Short s is, however, still used before f.

Finally it may be remarked that when ſ was followed in black letter printing by w the same difficulty arose, but in an exaggerated form, on account of the curl of the w, which was kerned to the left. It was therefore usual to put a thin space between the two letters, and when this space happens to be rather large such a word as ' anſwer ' may appear to be broken in two. In reprinting a text it is usual to ignore this break.

Punctuation marks.

/ In quite early founts this sign is used for the comma, or perhaps we should rather say to indicate any short pause in reading. A form in which the line slopes in the opposite direction is occasionally found (see Ames, *Typographical Antiquities*, ed. Herbert, pp. 491–2). The modern comma seems to have been introduced into England about 1521 (in roman type) and 1535 (in black letter) (ibid., pp. 268, 348). It occurs in Venetian printing before 1500.

---

[1] No doubt this was not the first book in which ſb was used, but I leave it to historians of typography to say which was. The only usual word (apart from proper names) in which the combination occurs is ' husband ', and it is surprising how rare this word is when one is looking for it.

? The query mark seems to have been used in England from about 1521 (*Typ. Antiq.*, p. 268).

': In black letter books printed in England about 1580–90, but not, so far as I am aware, much earlier or later, we sometimes find a curious query-mark resembling an acute accent followed by a colon. I have been unable to discover the origin of this mark.

; The semicolon seems to have been first used in England about 1569 (*Typ. Antiq.*, p. 858), but was not common until 1580 or thereabouts (ibid., p. 782). Herbert remarks that Henry Denham was the first to use this mark with propriety (p. 942). A mark of similar form had, we may note, been used from much earlier times as part of ' q;', the contraction for ' que ', but this was not a punctuation mark.

The full stop was commonly used *before* as well as *after* roman, and sometimes also arabic, numerals until about 1580.[1] Thus ' .xii. '. It was also used before and after i (.i. = id est) and f (.f. = scilicet), and I have found it once with q = cue : ' as though his .q. was then to speake '.[2]

' and ' were used indifferently in such abbreviations as th' or th' for ' the '. It may be noted that ' t'is ' or ' t'is ' (instead of ' 'tis ') for ' it is ' was so common in the Elizabethan period that it should perhaps be regarded as normal.

" Inverted commas were, until late in the seventeenth century, frequently used at the beginnings of lines to call attention to sententious remarks.[3] Modern

---

[1] It is probable that full stops before and after roman numerals could be found in occasional use much later. The practice was for a long period very irregular. In the late sixteenth century we sometimes find a full stop used after arabic numerals but not before ; the stop after roman numerals persisted for a long time and is still used by some printers.

[2] U. Fulwell, *First part of the eight liberall science*, 1576, fol. 40.

[3] Johnson, in his *Typographia*, ii. 58, first note, seems to admit the use of single inverted commas at the beginning of lines for the purpose

editors have occasionally regarded such passages as *quotations* and completed the quotes, which is generally wrong. So far as I have observed they were not especially associated with quotations until the eighteenth century, although, owing to their use for calling especial attention to a passage, they often appear in passages which are actually quoted.

Even after they become clearly used to mark quotations they generally appear at the beginning of the passage and at the beginning of every line, but not always at the *end*. The practice of closing the quotation with two apostrophes seems to be comparatively modern.[1]

Inverted commas, as well as many other signs, Greek letters (sometimes inverted), &c., were used in sixteenth- and seventeenth-century printing as reference marks directing to side- or foot-notes.

( ) were often used in the sixteenth century where we now use quotation marks, and were indeed the general way of indicating a *short* quotation, e. g. :

' in eo vico qui dicitur vulgariter (flete strete) '.[2]

' she was neuer heard to giue any the lie, nor so much as to (thou) any in anger.' [3]

' To win worship I would be right glad,
Therefore (willing to win worship) is my name.'

' I fayth to shew thee what luck we haue had,
By (Willing to win Worship) that lusty lad.' [4]

' take (had I wist) for an excuse ' [5]

of emphasis even in the first quarter of the nineteenth century, but they were surely uncommon then.

[1] I have found it in the middle of the eighteenth century, but it does not seem to have been regularly observed until much later.

[2] Colophon of a 1519 book printed by W. de Worde (Herbert, *Typ. Antiq.*, p. 161).

[3] Stubbes, *Christal Glasse*, 1591, A 2^v.

[4] *The Tide Tarrieth No Man* in *Sh. Jahrbuch*, vol. xliii, ll. 596–7, 1002–3. In the second quotation we should now rather use hyphens than quotation marks.   [5] Greene, ed. Grosart, iii. 186.

' In one place of the booke the meanes of saluation was attributed to the worde preached : and what did he thinke you ? he blotted out the word (preached) and would not haue that word printed.' [1]

They also seem sometimes to be used merely for emphasis, e. g. :

' Qui alios, (seipsum) docet.' [2]
' What yesterday was (*Greene*) now's seare and dry.' [3]

[ ] Square brackets are common in some Elizabethan founts, being used as we now use round ones. They were also sometimes used instead of round ones for the purposes mentioned above ; e. g. :

' πάλαι, which is as much as [of olde] or [in times past].' [4]

[1] Marprelate's *Epistle*, ed. Arber, p. 31.
[2] Wilkins, *Miseries of Enforced Marriage*, 1607, title.
[3] Cooke, *Greene's Tu Quoque*, 1614, sig. A 2ᵛ. I am indebted for the last two examples to Dr. Greg.
[4] Plutarch, *Morals*, 1603, p. 672.

APPENDIX FOUR

ABBREVIATIONS AND CONTRACTIONS IN EARLY PRINTED BOOKS

THE numerous abbreviations which we find in books of the fifteenth and sixteenth centuries, especially those in Latin and Greek, are perhaps rather a nuisance than a serious difficulty, for saving in the case of legal works (where they occur in extraordinary profusion, so that sometimes almost every word seems to be abbreviated), a sufficient knowledge of the language in which the book is written will, with a little practice, enable them to be read easily enough.[1] Nevertheless, a general knowledge of the more common Latin[2] contractions is often useful, and it may at times save errors of interpretation.

Seeing that the use of abbreviations in printed books is of course derived from the MS. practice,[3] the best method of approach is doubtless by way of the MSS., though this is perhaps hardly necessary. In any case, however, the student will find it useful to consult the sections dealing with abbreviations in *English Court Hand A.D. 1066-1500*, by C. Johnson and Hilary Jenkinson, 1915, pp. xxii–xxxv, though the usage in printed books, which is indeed far from uniform, does not correspond exactly with that of the MSS.

[1] A good example of a much-contracted text will be found in the *Questiones super Physica Aristotelis* printed at St. Albans in 1481, of which a page is reproduced by Duff, *E. E. P.*, Pl. XXXIII.

[2] The Greek contractions are too complicated to be dealt with here. A convenient list of those most commonly found in printed books is given in Johnson's *Typographia*, ii. 291–3. Or they can of course be studied as derived from the contractions of the MSS., details of which will be found in the standard palaeographical works.

[3] For the principles governing the MS. practice cf. Madan, *Books in Manuscript*, 1920, pp. 33–9 and *Mediaeval England*, ed. H. W. C. Davis, 1924, pp. 466–8.

The following are the chief types of abbreviation which will be met with in printed books : [1]

1. Vowel contractions, as ã, ẽ, ĩ, õ, ũ, made by placing a straight mark or a double curve (the Spanish *tilde*) over the vowel.[2] These indicate in later times merely the omission of a following n or m (e. g. mẽ = men) and are almost the only contractions except those for the English words *the*, *that*, *with*, and *which*, persisting into the Shakespearian period. In the earlier texts, however, their use is much wider than this. They indicate not merely the omission of a following nasal (tribulãt = tribulant, quoniã = quoniam), but also that of a preceding nasal (eĩm = enim, huĩliter = humiliter).[3] Further, they may apparently stand for almost any combination of nasals with a vowel, thus ĩ, besides in, im, ni, mi, can stand for

nim, e. g. aĩa = anima.
min, e. g. hoĩes = homines ; noĩe = nomine.
mni, e. g. oĩs = omnis.
mnin, e. g. oĩo = omnino.

But besides this, abbreviations in this form are used to stand, apparently quite arbitrarily, for parts of a large number of common words, thus ẽ = est, eẽ = esse, mõ = modo, orõnẽ = orationem, spũs = spiritus, &c., &c.[4] A list of some of the commonest words thus abbreviated will be found below.

The ~, indicating the omission of a nasal, is found

---

[1] Besides the special signs standing for certain groups of letters such as ꝯ = con, ꝶ = rum, &c., abbreviations consist mainly of ' suspensions ', i. e. the omission of letters at the end of a word, and ' contractions ', i. e. the omission of letters within a word.

[2] It should be noted that ‾ and ~ are used quite indifferently. Some founts of type had one and some the other. This applies also to the strokes over consonants.

[3] It seems to be almost a general rule in early practice that contractions are reversible.

[4] The use of õ for ion in such words as ĩnouatõe = innovatione seems especially frequent.

also over m in oм̃es for omnes, &c., and perhaps we should class with this dñs for dominus.

2. g-contractions. A g with a superscript e is sometimes found, e. g. reġdi = regredi.

3. l-contractions. An l with a cross-mark or curl, ł or ɫ, is used to indicate a number of contractions or suspensions, e. g. ałr = aliter, Hercuł = Herculis.

4. p-contractions, of which four were in common use :[1]

p standing for per in such words as opa = opera, opire = operire, supos = superos ; for par in pte = parte, for peri in pculosus = periculosus ; for por in corpibus = corporibus. Abnormally in tpe = tempore. It is occasionally used in English, e. g. psones = persones.

p̄ standing for pre in p̄dicti = predicti. Abnormally in ip̄oꝝ = ipsorum.

ꝓ = pro, as in ꝓuidentia = providentia, ꝓfecto = profecto, ꝓpe = prope, ꝓpter = propter, ꝓces = proces (Engl.).

p̓ (apparently p with a superscript r) = pri, as in p̓oris = prioris, p̓mus = primus ; also rip in fcp̓fit = scripsit.

5. q-contractions. These vary greatly in form in different founts.

q̦, q̇, q̓ = qui, as qd = quid, qs or q̇s = quis, eloq = eloqui, aqloni = aquiloni.

q̃ = quæ, as in q̃runt = quaerunt, q̃dã = quaedam.

q̈, q̈, or q̈ = quam, as tanq̈ = tanquam, q̈q̈ = quamquam.

q̦ = quod, also for English ' quod ' = quoth.

q̈̃ = quum, as antiq̈̃ = antiquuum.

ꝗ = que, as atꝗ = atque. In later use often replaced by q; (q followed by a semicolon [2]).

---

[1] The first two, at least, of these seem often to be confused.

[2] In reprinting texts containing this abbreviation care must be taken to prevent the insertion of a space after the q.

6. r-contractions.

r̃ = re in difcer̃ = discere, r̃nafcẽt̃ = renascentur.
This form also occurs in a number of words
where t is omitted, e. g. igr̃ = igitur; gr̃as =
gratias; pr̃ = pater, pr̃is = patris.

7. t-contractions.

t̃ = tur, e. g. colit̃ = colitur, ĩduẽt̃ = induentur,
noct̃na = nocturna.

8. w-contractions (in English).

ẇ = with.
ẇ = which.

9. y-contractions (in English).[1]

ẏ = the.
ẏ = that.

10. Special forms.

ꝛ or ꝗ = con,[2] e. g. ab om̄ib3 pct̃is tuis ꝺtritis
ꝺfeffis & oblitis = ab omnibus peccatis tuis
contritis confessis et oblitis. ꝗa = contra.
Used also, but rarely, for the con-prefix in English words.

ꝩ, ꝶ = rum. quoꝶ = quorum, integꝶ = integrum.

3 or ⁹ = us, e. g. infirm⁹ = infirmus, crimib3 = cri-
minibus, v⁹ = quintus. The 3 is also used in
English books for final -es. In MS. usage it
stood for -et in such words as liq3 = liquet, and
came to indicate other groups of letters in
which -et- or similar combinations occurred,
thus v3 = videlicet, f3 = sed. It also not un-
commonly stood for a final m.

[1] It should be superfluous to remind any possible reader of this book
that in these abbreviations the y is the OE. þ, and that it is only in
quite modern times that any one has had the strange notion of pro-
nouncing 'the' as 'ye'. In reprints in which these abbreviations
are not expanded a *superior* e or t should always be used, either above
the y or following it as 'yᵉ' 'yᵗ'. It is incorrect to print 'ye' or
'yt', which were at no period used as abbreviations in printed books.

[2] In some black letter founts (cf. Duff, *E. E. P.*, Pl. XII a) this contraction is almost like an arabic 2 with a hook at the lower left corner.

The ⁹ is properly a small curl above the line, but occasionally the Arabic figure 9 or the letter q was used, with the result that misunderstandings were liable to occur, both on the part of printers and of modern editors. Thus in Gascoigne's *Steele Glas* [1576], sig. F3ᵛ, is a marginal note ' Auguſt. 9. '. This refers to ' That worthy Emperour ' Augustus, and should evidently have been printed ' Auguſt⁹ ' if the abbreviation was not to be expanded. It is difficult to believe that the form found in the text is other than a mere misprint due to misunderstanding the contraction. This 9, which came sometimes to be printed as the letter q, has often been misinterpreted in modern times. In a letter from Rowland Whyte to Sir Robert Sydney dealing with Lord Essex's Entertainment to Queen Elizabeth in November 1595 occurs a phrase which, as printed in Arthur Collins's *Letters and Memorials of State*, 1746, pt. ii, p. 362, runs : ' Thold Man was he, that in *Cambridg* plaied Giraldy, . . . and he that plaied Pedantiq, was the Soldior.' The form ' Pedantiq ' seems to have been retained by all of the numerous writers who have quoted the passage, but it is quite evident that it should be Pedanti*us*, as was, I think, first suggested by Professor Moore Smith in his edition of the play of *Laelia*, p. xiii. The same scholar has also pointed out to me a different misinterpretation of the ⁹ contraction in the *Works of Randolph*, ed. Hazlitt (vol. ii), p. 673, where in a side-note to the ' Oratio Praevaricatoria ', printed from MS., occurs the form ' Jesuanque ', the original having evidently had Jesuan⁹, i. e. Jesuan*us*.

A list of some common contracted forms.

Abbreviated nouns and verbs are given in the inflexional form in which I happen to have noted them. Other forms will of course as a rule follow the same model, but it seemed safer not to assume this, as the whole use of these abbreviations was so much a matter of custom rather than of rule. It is not of course pretended that this list gives more than a selection even of the commonest abbreviations, but I think that most types are represented and that a knowledge of the forms given will enable a student to guess most abbreviations that he will meet with in non-legal books.

aliqñ = aliquando.
ałr = aliter.
añ = ante.
apłice = apostolice.
apłoꝯ = apostolorum.
bñ = bene.
cãm = causam.
corpibus = corporibus.
dc̃m = dictum.
dño = domino.
dñs = dominus.
ds̃ = Deus.
ẽ = est.
eẽ = esse.
eẽt = esset.
em̃ = enim.
ẽt = etiam.
etem̃ = etenim.
fr̃em = fratrem.
g̊ = ergo
gr̃a = gratia.
hẽant̃ = habeantur.
hẽat = habeat.
.i. = id est.
igr̃, ig̃r, g̊ = igitur.
ip̃ius = ipsius.
ip̃oꝯ = ipsorum.
ĩr (perhaps for ir̃) = ire.
lrãs, lrĩs = litteras,
   litteris.
mõ = modo.

mr̃is = matris.
.n. = enim.
nr̃ = noster.
nr̃is = nostris.
oẽs = omnes.
oĩm = omnium.
or̃o = oratio.
orõẽ = orationem.
pñtes = praesentes.
p̄t = potest.
pp = propter.
pr̃ = pater.
pr̃is = patris.
qđ = quod.
qm̃ = quoniam.
rõ = ratio.
r̃furr̃ctõem = resurrectionem.
.ſ. = scilicet.
ſc̃us = sanctus.
ſñĩa = sententia.
ſp = semper.
ſpm̃ = spiritum.
ſpũs = spiritus.
ſt̃e = sancte.
tm̃ = tantum.
tñ = tamen.
tp̃a = tempora.
tpe = tempore.
tp̃s = tempus.
uñ = unde.
xp̃s = Christus.

APPENDIX FIVE

ON FOLDING IN 12mo AND 24mo

O N pages 169–72 I have described what I believe to be by far the most usual methods of imposing the type and folding the sheet for 12mo, but there are other possible methods of folding about which it seems well to say something though they are, so far as my observation extends, of rather theoretical than practical importance.

There are evidently several ways of folding a sheet of paper into twelve, and more of folding it into twenty-four. Most of these will, of course, give different shapes of page, and whether or not they are practical ways will depend in every case on the proportions of the sheet of paper which is folded, and this as we know might differ considerably in different makes. Further, a printer wishing for any reason to turn out a book of a particular size might be willing to sacrifice a small part of the paper by cutting it off after the book was finished. It may therefore be exceedingly difficult in these formats to infer from the bound volume what was the size of the original sheet or how it was folded.

For the sake of simplicity let us take a sheet 15″×20″, as this will represent sufficiently closely what seem to have been the usual proportions of a sheet of sixteenth- and seventeenth-century printing paper, and see what happens when we fold it.

Let us begin by considering a sheet folded into six, though the size is one that would seldom if ever be used for book-work. There are obviously two possible ways of folding it: we may either fold it in three lengthways, afterwards doubling it, or into three short-ways, afterwards doubling it. The important thing to notice is that in *all* cases of folding, the final fold must be a doubling, as otherwise the sheet cannot be sewn.

With our sheet 15″×20″ we shall, according to which of the ways of folding we choose, get a page 6⅔″×7½″ or 5″×10″. In both cases the breadth is more than the height and the format therefore could not be used for ordinary book-work, though it might for a book containing maps or pictures or for music.

To pass now to 12mo. We have evidently to fold the sheet once into three and twice into two, and so long as the last fold is into two, the direction or order of the other folds does not matter, except so far as it will give us differently shaped pages. Let us take our first kind of sexto folding. We may fold again in either direction. In one case (*a*) we have a book 7½″×3⅓″, in the other (*b*) we have one 6⅔″×3¾″. The second is evidently a better proportioned page than the first, and this way of folding may indeed be reckoned as the normal one for a 12mo.[1] Our other sexto will, according as we fold it, make (*c*) a page 5″×5″, which is possible but not very likely; or (*d*) 10″×2½″, an impossible shape.

The direction of the chain-lines and place of the watermark will be as follows. I place an asterisk against the more likely formats :

   (*a*) Chain-lines vertical : watermark in middle of
        top margin.
 * (*b*) Chain-lines horizontal : watermark towards
        top or bottom of outer margin.[2]

[1] It may be pointed out that if our sheet of paper, instead of measuring 20″ × 15″, measured 22½″ × 13⅓″, not by any means an impossible departure from the normal proportions, the results of folding by methods *a* and *b* would be interchanged, so that *a* would now give us a page 6⅔″ × 3¾″ while *b* gives us the awkwardly shaped 7½″ × 3⅓″. It is thus apparent that a comparatively small difference in the proportions of the sheet may make now one method of folding, and now another, practicable or impossible.

[2] This is the normal 12mo folding fully described on pp. 169–72.

* (c) Chain-lines vertical : watermark in middle of inner margin.

A 24mo can evidently be produced by folding any of the above 12mos again in either direction, but several of the foldings would give us quite useless shapes for book-work and may therefore be passed over without mention. We see that our a, if folded again, would give us $3\frac{1}{3}'' \times 3\frac{3}{4}''$, an oblong shape that could only be used if the fore-edge was cut, while b will give the same dimensions but interchanged, $3\frac{3}{4}'' \times 3\frac{1}{3}''$, a squarish but quite possible shape, c would give us pages $5'' \times 2\frac{1}{2}''$ in either of *two* ways of folding, while d would only give us an oblong $2\frac{1}{2}'' \times 5''$.

The position of the chain-lines and watermarks would be :

(a) Chain-lines horizontal : watermark in middle of outer margin.

* (b) Chain-lines vertical : watermark in middle of lower margin.

* (c) 1. Chain-lines horizontal : watermark at top of inner margin.

(c) 2. Chain-lines vertical : watermark in middle of outer margin.

(d) Chain-lines vertical : watermark at top of inner margin.

Nothing more need be said about the imposition of the pages for these various arrangements.[1] It must depend on the order of the foldings; on whether in folding into three we bring both ends to the same side of the centre piece (as we ordinarily do in folding a letter into three), or whether we bring one to one side and the other to the other (Z-ways); on whether the whole sheet is meant to be folded in a piece, or, as was commonly done, a third is meant to be cut off and folded as a quarto (in the 12mo format), to be placed

[1] Typical schemes for 12mo have been given on pp. 170, 171, above.

within the rest folded as an octavo ; lastly, on whether the book is intended to be *sewn* as a 12mo or 24mo or as an 8vo or 16mo, which is also a possible way of proceeding.[1]   Once the manner of folding is determined, however, the arrangement of the pages in the formes can easily be arrived at by experiment.

[1] Cf. p. 168.

APPENDIX SIX

ON PRINTING IN TWO OR MORE COLOURS

FOR the sake of simplicity we will refer to the colours to be used as ' black ' and ' red '. It evidently makes no difference what the actual colours are, while the use of three or more inks instead of two merely means, as a rule, a further development of whatever process is employed.

At the present time the usual method of printing in two colours is to use two formes, the portions to be printed in black being in one forme, and those to be in red in another, and the paper being passed through the press twice. Under modern conditions, type and furniture being made very exactly to size, there is no difficulty in causing the type for the two colours to occupy the correct positions in the two formes and, especially now that paper is ordinarily printed dry, it is, or should be, quite easy to obtain perfect register.

In early times, however, such a method as this must have presented serious difficulties when dealing with anything more complicated than a few lines of large type on a title-page, or a heading well separated from a block of text. In the first place, if as we may suppose the furniture was mainly wood, and was liable to vary more or less in size according as it happened to be dry or damp or in consequence of wear, it must have been a troublesome matter to get the portions of type in two formes to register perfectly, and even if the formes themselves were correct, any slight difference in the dampness of the paper at the moment of printing the two colours would throw the register out. It is probably for reasons such as these that the early printers seem to have relied chiefly on other methods.

There is a good deal of doubt about how some of

329

the early printing in colours was managed. The very remarkable large two-colour initials [1] in the Mainz *Psalter* of 1457, in which the letter itself is in one colour while within or without it there are elaborate ornamentations of another, were, according to one theory, printed not in a press but by placing the blocks face downwards upon the paper and striking them with a mallet. There seem to have been three blocks for each initial, the outer and inner ornamentation, though printed in the same colour, being on separate blocks, and the letter itself of course on a third.[2] It must, I think, at any rate be admitted that it is difficult to believe that such perfect register as we find in this *Psalter* could have been obtained by double printing in a press, while there is more than one obvious method of ensuring good register in handwork on the lines suggested.[3]

This method of stamping in initials and also short passages of text, headings, &c., which were probably set up in a small holder, seems to have been common in early work. There is an undoubted instance of it in the *Valerius Maximus* printed by Schoeffer in 1471. In one copy (Brit. Mus., IB. 158) the text of the first page is much askew, as occasionally happens in this book, part at least of which seems to have been printed page by page.[4] On this first page there are two rubrics, the upper one a general heading, the lower the heading to a list of the sections of the first book, ' Tituli primi libri '. Now the first of these rubrics is printed *straight*, i. e. parallel with the edges of the paper and conse-

[1] There are also numerous plain red initials, perhaps printed by being set up in a different forme. See on the whole question Haebler, *Inkunabelkunde*, p. 105.

[2] Duff, *E. P. B.*, pp. 27–9 ; but cf. Haebler, u. s. Facsimile in *B.M. Facs.*, Pl. 6.

[3] No one who knows how Japanese colour-prints are executed can doubt the possibility of obtaining perfect register by the most primitive methods in combination with highly skilled craftsmanship.

[4] See pp. 59–60, above.

quently at an angle to the lines of print, while the second is parallel to the lines of print. It is thus clear that the two rubrics were printed separately. Presumably they were both stamped in,[1] but certainly one of them must have been. The upper rubric overlaps the black text slightly in places and it is possible to see quite plainly that the red ink is on the top of the black. It may be noted that there is also a printed rubric on the next page, but no more throughout the rest of the book. It was probably intended that they should be inserted in MS., which has been done in some copies.

It should as a general rule be quite easy to discover whether a rubric has been printed at the machine as part of a forme or stamped in by hand, if we have an opportunity of placing several copies of a book side by side. The evidence is especially good if there are two or more rubrics on a page, for if these are part of a forme their *relative* positions will remain constant (however they may register with the black type), while if they are independently stamped in by hand their relative positions will vary in different copies of the book. Even when there is only one rubric on a page we can sometimes find similar evidence, but we must be careful that the shifts of position are not due to the paper not having been properly laid.

This stamping in of rubrics and initials by hand was a very primitive method, and in the case of a book with any considerable number of rubrics would be exceedingly laborious. It is highly probable that at a very early date attempts were made to improve upon it. One of the most curious methods was, according to Blades, used by Colard Mansion at Bruges, and as it was thus presumably known to Caxton it is worth

[1] It might possibly be argued that the first (that parallel to the sides of the paper) might have been a second printing at machine, and only the second stamped in ; but the difference of position in different copies seems against such a view.

a passing mention, though it does not seem to have found favour with other printers. If Blades correctly interpreted the evidence, both the colours were printed with the same pull of the press, the method being first to ink the whole forme with black ink, then to wipe off the ink from the portion to be printed in red, and to re-ink this in red with a very small pad or with the finger. This procedure resulted in a very dirty colour in the red portion, as it was impossible to remove the whole of the black ink.[1]

Another method of printing in two colours which, according to Haebler,[2] was usual in the fifteenth century, was by differential inking of one forme by the use of masks. Two masks of strong paper were prepared, in one of which holes were cut corresponding to the red portions, in the other holes corresponding to the black. These were laid successively on the forme, which was inked first with red, then with black ;

---

[1] *Caxton*, 1882, p. 52. I give this method, as I believe that Blades's view has been accepted, and he says that he has tried it and found it give the required results, but I cannot help doubting whether, unless done with extraordinary care and uniformity, one would get quite the even dirtiness of ink which is sometimes found. I should have expected the wiping to leave little particles of black ink in the hollows of the letters, which would show in the impression. The occasional accidental printing of the edges of neighbouring lines might equally well be explained by a second printing with the use of a cut-out frisket which was either slightly displaced or in which the holes cut out were slightly too large. By Blades's theory one would have apparently to assume that the black ink was accidentally wiped off portions of the adjacent lines and that exactly these same portions were afterwards inked with red ink—a coincidence that I think would be impossible, unless indeed some kind of mask was used. Otherwise we should expect to find some edges not printing at all and others printing with an equal mixture of black ink and red. The colour of the ink may possibly, I think, be explained by a chemical change. One can find similar cases of red ink turning blackish in modern books—especially those printed early in the nineteenth century. On the other hand, if Colard Mansion's register is always as perfect as Blades states, this is a point strongly in favour of a single printing.

[2] *Inkunabelkunde*, p. 109.

one impression sufficing to print the two colours, which were necessarily in perfect register. If the masks were not quite correctly cut or were slightly out of position during the inking, one would expect to find red ink on the edges of some of the black portions and black ink on the edges of some of the red ones. The method would, I think, have been quite workable provided there was nothing in either colour detached from the margin of the page, but I do not see how one would have dealt with islands of red in a black text or vice versa. Even had one tried to lay down separate paper patches—an impossibly tedious method—they would surely have been caught up by the ink-balls.

In England during the sixteenth and early seventeenth centuries two methods of red-printing were, I believe, in regular use.

(a) Printing from two separate formes, as is commonly done nowadays, seems to have been occasionally resorted to when it was merely necessary to print a word or two in red in a title. When the type is large and widely spaced it would of course, in spite of the difficulties in the way of exact register which I have mentioned above, be quite possible to get the words to fall near enough to their proper places.[1] Such a method has the advantage that no part of the black printing will be found duplicated in, or edged with, red. Difficulties in getting the two formes to correspond exactly would, however, render this method impracticable when there were many red words scattered about among the black. In such cases the second method (b) would be used.

(b) This, which was, I think, the normal method in the sixteenth century, at least in England, was as follows. The whole forme, including all that was to be printed, both in black and in red, was first proved.

---

[1] In the case of a few woodcut borders separate black and red blocks seem to have been cut. Cf., for example, Device No. 218 in my *Printers' and Publishers' Devices*.

A frisket was then cut out so as to allow only those parts to print which were to be in red. These parts were inked and the sheets were printed. The frisket prevented, or should have prevented adjacent type (although inked) from printing. Actually, as may be seen from inspection of any calendar before a Bible printed in red and black, it was common for parts of rules, &c., bordering the red printing to print in red.[1] The type was then washed down, the red portions removed, and the spaces left filled up with quads. The frisket having been replaced by one so cut as to allow the whole page to print, the forme was now inked in black and the sheets were passed through again.[2]

It is essential for this method that there should not be in any forme islands of red surrounded by black and *also* islands of black surrounded by red. If these exist in any books some other method must have been used, such as dissection, but I have sought for them in vain in English work of the period.

A curious habit of the English printers during the sixteenth century may be referred to here—I think it was rare in continental printing—in connexion with woodblocks. This was to print certain portions *both* in black and red. The register being seldom, if ever, absolutely perfect, the result was that every black line in such double-printed portions was edged by a red

[1] As one cannot raise *part* of a rule by underlaying, this seems to show that the red portions were not brought up above the level of the black, as was done later : see below.

[2] Note that in such things as the calendars mentioned above, while some of the intended black is duplicated in red, the intended red is never duplicated in black; showing that the intended black portions of the forme were present during the red printing, but the intended red were not present during the black printing. I may perhaps be allowed to refer for further details to an article of mine in *The Library*, 3rd Ser., vol. ii (July 1911), pp. 323–7. This was a reply to an article by Mr. Horace Hart in the previous issue on ' The Red Printing in the 1611 Bible ', in which he put forward a theory which, however ingenious, seems to me most improbable.

334

one, which the printers presumably regarded as an embellishment. This was evidently done by the same method of cut-out friskets as I have just described, though of course as there was in this case nothing to be removed it did not matter which printing came first. Where there was in the same forme letterpress to be printed in red alone, they would of course normally print the red first, but otherwise I think they tended to print the black first. This form of embellishment was especially common in the title-page borders of the almanacs of the early seventeenth century, a great nuisance when one desires to photograph them! The earliest instance of this double printing that I have noticed is in a device at the end of Musculus's *Commonplaces of Christian Religion* printed by R. Wolfe in 1563.[1]

The method explained on pp. 333–4 had, however, the disadvantage that adjacent parts of the ' black ' tended to get duplicated in red, giving a messy appearance to the page, and a better one was devised. This is described by Moxon, in his *Mechanick Exercises*, and seems still to have been in use in the time of Johnson.[2] The procedure was as follows. As before, the whole forme was proved, black and red together, and a frisket was cut out to allow the red alone to print. This frisket was, however, then laid aside. The red portions were removed from the forme, being replaced by quads, a frisket allowing the whole page to print was cut out, and the forme inked and printed in black, the places for the red words being now of course blank. After the black printing, the quads were removed, slips of card were inserted in their places, and the ' red ' types replaced upon these slips so that they were raised a sixteenth of an inch or so above the general level of the forme. The ' red ' frisket was then placed in position, the forme inked with red, and the paper passed

[1] *Printers' and Publishers' Devices*, 1913, No. 146.
[2] Moxon, *Mech. Ex.*, pp. 328–30; Johnson, *Typographia*, ii. 532–3.

through again. Care had to be taken to give only a light pull to the bar of the press as the printing surface was at a slightly higher level than before. On account of this there was little or no chance of any of the ' black ' portions printing, even if they had chanced to get inked or were insufficiently masked out by the frisket.

Substantially the difference in the processes is no more than the underlaying of the red and the printing of the black first. Why they should not have under-layed the red at once and printed it first, thus saving themselves the trouble of inserting it a second time, I do not understand, but they seem not to have done so.[1]

---

[1] There was probably some technical difficulty. I can only suggest that it may have been found that if the red was printed first, red ink tended to accumulate on neighbouring ' black ' portions of the forme, necessitating this being washed down before the black printing.

APPENDIX SEVEN

A SHORT LIST OF SOME DIFFICULT LATIN PLACE-NAMES

THE indications of place of printing found in books of the fifteenth and sixteenth centuries are often somewhat puzzling to students who have not at hand a bibliographical reference library, on account of the strange forms in which the names of many of the important continental towns appear. A very full list of these is given in Henry Cotton's *Typographical Gazetteer* (second edition, 1831), and shorter lists can be found in other bibliographical works of reference.[1] It may, however, be useful to give a few of the more difficult names which are likely to be met with. It is to be understood that forms of obvious meaning, like Amstelaedamum, Amstelodamum, or Amstelredamum for Amsterdam, Antwerpia for Antwerp, &c., are omitted; and that minor variations are common, e. g. Davantria and Daventria, Thaurinum and Taurinum.

The form in which the name appears in an imprint is usually the genitive case if the word is of the first or second declension and of singular number; otherwise the ablative. Thus we have Basileae (generally spelt Basilee), Duaci, Lovanii, &c., but Andreapoli, Barchinone, Senis, Parisiis (a curious form ' Parisius ' also frequently occurs as a locative in the fifteenth century). Adjectival forms are of course also used, e. g. in urbe Parisiensi. Some Dutch and German towns commonly keep the vernacular form, e. g. ' Delf impressum ', ' in oppido Hagenaw '.[2]

[1] The *Orbis latinus* of J. G. Th. Graesse, ed. F. Benedict, Berlin, 1909, though not especially concerned with names found in imprints, is also of great value in this connexion.

[2] I am indebted to Mr. Victor Scholderer for kindly looking through the list which follows and sending me some valuable corrections and additions. It must be remembered that the form of Latin place-names was far from being fixed, and that, especially in the sixteenth century, some were used which seem to have been intentionally fanciful.

Andreapolis = St. Andrews.
Argentina = Strassburg.
Argentoratum = Strassburg.
Audomaropolis *or* Audomarum = St. Omer.
Augusta = Augsburg.
Augusta Trebocorum = Strassburg.
Augusta Treverorum = Treves.
Augusta Trinobantum = London.
Augusta Vangionum = Worms.
Augusta Vindelicorum = Augsburg.
Augustoritum (Pictonum) = Limoges.
Aurelia Allobrogum = Geneva.
Aurelia, Aureliacum, *or* Aureliani = Orleans.

Babenberga = Bamberg.
Barchino = Barcelona.
Basilea = Basle.
Bellovacum = Beauvais.
Bellovisum = Bellevue (part of Paris).
Bononia = Bologna.
Borbetomagus = Worms.
Brixia = Brescia.

Caesaraugusta = Saragossa.
Caesarodunum Turonum = Tours.
Civitas Austriae = Cividale del Friuli
Colonia (Agrippina) = Cologne.
Colonia Allobrogum = Geneva.
Colonia Claudia = Cologne.
Colonia Munatiana = Basle.
Colonia Ubiorum = Cologne.
Condivincum Nannetum = Nantes.
Cracovia = Cracow.

Daventria = Deventer.
Delphi = Delft.
Divio = Dijon.
Dordracum = Dordrecht.
Duacum = Douay.

Eblana = Dublin.
Eboracum = York.
Erfordia = Erfurt.

Genabum = Orleans.
Gravionarium = Bamberg.

Hafnia = Copenhagen.
Haga Comitum = The Hague.
Herbipolis = Würzburg.
Hispalis = Seville.

Leida = Leyden.
Lemovicense Castrum = Limoges.
Lipsia = Leipzig.
Lovanium = Louvain.
Lugdunum = Lyons.
Lugdunum Batavorum = Leyden.
Lutetia = Paris.

Mantua Carpetanorum = Madrid.
Matritum = Madrid.
Mediolanum = Milan.
Moguntia *or* Moguntiacum = Mainz.
Monachium = Munich.
Monasterium = Münster.
Mons Regalis = Mondovi (*or* Monreale).
Mutina = Modena.

Nannetae *or* Nannetum = Nantes.
Neocomum = Neufchâtel.
Norimberga = Nuremberg.
Noviomagus = Nimeguen.

Olyssipo = Lisbon.

Panormum = Palermo.
Papia = Pavia.
Parisii = Paris.
Parthenope = Naples.
Parthenopolis = Magdeburg.
Patavium = Padua.

Perusia *or* Augusta Perusia = Perugia.
Pictavia *or* -ium (*loc.* Pictavis) = Poitiers
Pisae = Pisa.

Regiomontium = Königsberg.
Rhedones = Rennes.
Rothomagum = Rouen.
Rupella = La Rochelle.

Salmantica = Salamanca.
Senae = Sienna.
Spira = Speyer (Spires, Palatinate).

Tarvisium = Treviso.
Taurinum = Turin.
Tholosa = Toulouse.
Trajectum ad Rhenum = Utrecht.
Trecae = Troyes.
Tricasses = Troyes.
Tridentum = Trent.
Turonum *or* -ium = Tours.

Ultrajectum = Utrecht.
Ulyssipo = Lisbon.

Venetiae = Venice.
Vienna = Vienne.
Vindobona = Vienna.
Vormatia = Worms.

APPENDIX EIGHT

A NOTE ON ELIZABETHAN HANDWRITING

IT is, I think, generally with the writing of the period between 1500 and 1650 that the literary student finds most difficulty, and until quite recently there has been for this period hardly any help available.[1] The majority of Old English and Medieval MSS. that he is likely to come across, being in the more or less careful and practised hands of professional scribes, are when once the forms of the letters are known, easy enough to decipher with a little practice, or if they are difficult the difficulty is due to the condition of the MS. rather than to the writing itself. Such help as is needed will be found in W. W. Skeat's *Twelve Facsimiles of Old English Manuscripts* and Dr. W. W. Greg's *Facsimiles of Twelve Early English Manuscripts in the Library of Trinity College, Cambridge*, and a student who works through these should have little difficulty with most other literary MSS. up to the fifteenth century. Charters and other documents written in legal hands are another matter. For these the best guide is *English Court Hand A.D. 1066 to 1500*, by C. Johnson and Hilary Jenkinson, with the invaluable portfolio of facsimiles which accompanies it. The deciphering of legal documents of any period is, it may be remarked, very largely a matter of knowing what the writer is likely to have intended to convey, for common formulae are often so much abbreviated that without a knowledge of them it is impossible to read them correctly.

[1] I know of no elementary introduction to the subject except Miss M. St. Clare Byrne's very useful article entitled ' Elizabethan Handwriting for Beginners ' in *The Review of English Studies*, i. 198 ff. Students would be well advised to read this article, to which I am indebted for several points in the pages which follow.

The student who concerns himself with such things must therefore begin by familiarizing himself with the formulae used in other documents of the same kind by reference to works in which these are printed at length.

When we come to the sixteenth century, and especially to the later years of the century, we find a much larger number of literary documents which, not being the work of professional scribes, are in cursive hands of various degrees of informality and carelessness, and some of these are by no means easy to read.[1] The only way in which the student can learn to make them out is by practice, and he should be warned that however much he practises he must not expect to be able to read every unfamiliar hand at a glance. The most skilled palaeographer may find the first few lines of a new manuscript somewhat puzzling.

The best way of acquiring a sufficient knowledge of the matter for ordinary purposes is, I think, to take some facsimile of a good and clear Elizabethan hand such as Kyd's letter to the Lord Keeper Puckering, which forms the frontispiece of Dr. Boas's edition of Kyd,[2] and having read it through two or three times with the transcript printed in the book, to proceed to *imitate* it, taking first single words and then passages of two or three lines together, writing them over and over again until he has the ' feel ' of the letters and working from the transcript can produce something which he is certain that Puckering could have read with ease. The essential thing is that he should be very careful to make all the strokes in the right order

[1] For a sketch of the history of handwriting during the Elizabethan period the student may be referred to Sir E. Maunde Thompson's chapter on the subject in *Shakespeare's England,* vol. i. The subject will be fully dealt with in a work on Elizabethan Handwriting which Mr. Hilary Jenkinson has now in preparation.

[2] I suggest this, not as being an absolutely typical hand, for it is in some respects rather legal, but as including all the normal characteristics of the English hand and as showing, more clearly than most, the way in which the letters were formed.

342

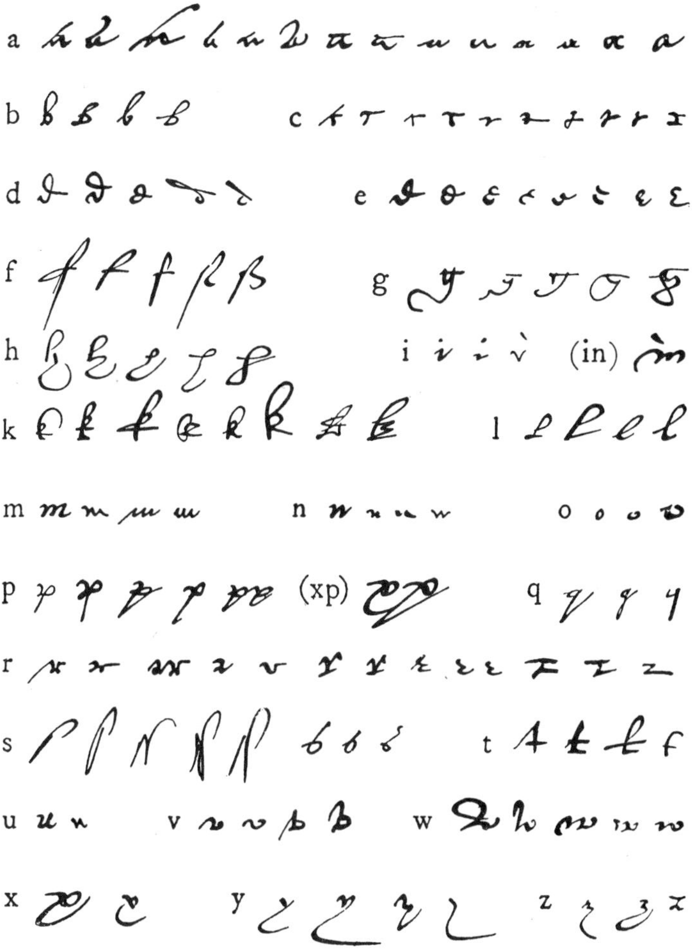

Fig. 22. Elizabethan Handwriting. Typical forms of
the minuscules.

and direction, especially in the case of such letters as c, e, f and p (see the notes on pages 345–8). When he can produce a fair imitation of any one Elizabethan hand he should proceed to work through a collection of facsimiles such as the series of *English Literary Autographs*, 1550–1650, edited by Dr. W. W. Greg.[1] In a first reading of these he would be wise to begin with the easier pieces, leaving the more difficult and all short scraps (generally somewhat puzzling) until later. Before beginning to read a MS. he should always take a general glance at it and note whether the hand is Italian or English or mixed. The habit of keeping the two styles distinct in his mind may often save him from mistakes.

As has been stated on page 253 above, there were two forms of handwriting in regular use during the Elizabethan period, the ' English ', or ' Secretary ', hand, which had developed naturally out of the current hands in use in earlier times in this country, and the imported ' Italian ' hand, which from about 1580 was gradually replacing it. About the Italian hand there is no difficulty whatever, except such as may be due to the carelessness of the writer, for the formation of the letters is practically that of the ' copy-book ' hand of to-day. The notes which follow are therefore confined to the current ' English ' style.

The following general tendencies may be noted in English hands :

1. The downstrokes are as a rule more nearly vertical than in modern writing.

2. Uprights ending on the line often have a small spur to the left, the pen being carried horizontally along the line first to left and then again to the right so as to form a kind of foot (as in a printed letter).

3. If we call a curve starting downwards on the right then moving from right to left and so upwards

[1] Part I (Dramatic), issued 1925. To be completed in three parts, containing in all about 100 facsimiles.

to the left ' clockwise ', we may describe the sixteenth-
century English hand as having a more anti-clockwise
tendency than the handwriting of to-day. Especially
is this the case with tailed letters, such as h, y, x,
which are often brought round in such a large left-to-
right sweep that a word may seem to be divided into
two. In the Italian hand the tails of g and y are
generally made clockwise and crossed as at present.

It is quite impossible to describe adequately the
formation of a written letter. The following notes
must therefore be read in close conjunction with the
outlines of letters here given. These have been chosen
from a variety of documents of the period, written in
widely differing styles, and are believed to represent
the chief forms which will be commonly met with.

A roman letter (a, b, &c.) stands for the letter in
the English hand, an italic letter (*a*, *b*, &c.) for a
written letter in the customary ' copy-book ' hand of
to-day.

a. Often like *a*. Sometimes, however, written more
   like *u*, the top being afterwards closed by a short
   horizontal stroke similar to that which closes the
   top of g (see below). Sometimes, again, the letter
   is left open at the top, in which case it may resemble
   u or *ir*. There is also a form, especially of initial
   a, which begins with a large curve brought down
   to the line and slightly spurred; the whole may
   then look like a loosely written 2 followed by
   a minim.[1]

b. Differs from *b* in that the upstroke instead of
   being looped to form a forward link is simply
   brought round towards the downstroke. The
   downstroke is generally looped, and in upright
   hands often has a small spur to the left on the line.

c. Quite different from *c*. Generally a simple short

---

[1] A ' minim ' is the single stroke of which three form an m—like
a ' hanger ', but in Elizabethan hands generally more angular.

345

downstroke, with a thin cross-stroke at the head, which may form a forward link. Not unlike the lower part of an upright *t*.

d. Occasionally as *d*, but more often resembling a *c* through the top point of which is a heavy straight dash, much back-sloped. In such cases there is no forward link. Another common form is written without raising the pen. If this is carried round in a bow to the right the letter may resemble the older form of the Greek θ (ϑ) and may then be similar to a rather large e.

e. The important point to remember is that the lower part of this letter is always made first. It may be considered as an ε begun and ended in the centre and formed of two almost similar curves: the upper is often continued forward from the centre to form a link with the next letter. When written without raising the pen so that the lower and upper strokes are connected by a bow on the right it may much resemble a loosely written small d.

f. The tail is written first, as a straight downstroke, then from the top of this a loop is made sloping to the right and ending in a small tick across the downstroke. In some hands this tick is a horizontal dash at the end of the loop, not touching the downstroke: the letter may then be very similar to ſt or even ft.

ff is often written with two tails diverging slightly and but one loop (cf. ſſ in fig. 22).

g. The usual form of this is like a rather angular *y* closed at the top by a cross-stroke. This cross-stroke is sometimes formed by bringing up the tail of the *y*, but more often it is separate.

h. The common form is quite different from modern *h*. It consists of a small loop at the head of a short vertical stroke which is continued in a wide sweep to the left and up again to join the following letter.

In many hands the lower curve of the sweep is the heaviest part of the letter. Occasionally the lower curve is made in a clockwise direction and crosses the downstroke; the letter may then be not unlike a rather wide Italian *f*, as in the last form shown.

i. As *i*, but tending to be more upright and angular, as is the case with minims generally. If not linked to the preceding letter it may begin with a long thin upstroke. It may be written with a minim exactly like those of n, so that ' in ' and ' m ' may be indistinguishable save by the dot.

k. Generally formed like an l crossed by a small *z* or 2, the lower portion of which is continued as a forward link. Sometimes the *z* is continuous with the end of the upstroke, in which case it may degenerate into a small loop which may or may not cross or touch the upright. If it does not, the letter may resemble a modern *b* (not, however, an English b, for this normally has no forward link).

l. As *l*, but in upright hands the downstroke instead of being curved round to the right is sometimes terminated by a small spur to the left. This also applies to the upright of k.

m, n. As *m*, *n*, but in many Elizabethan hands the minims are all exactly similar, and there seems less sense of the individuality of the letter than in modern writing; thus mn may be written as five similar and equally spaced minims, with the result that the count sometimes goes wrong and there are one too many or too few.

o. As *o*, but in careless writing sometimes not closed at the top.

p. Quite differently written from *p*. It begins with a stroke like a 2. The end of this is continued upwards in a loop until it touches the bow of the 2 and then brought downwards in a straight stroke or anti-clockwise curve. In some hands, not very distinct from y; in others, resembling x, from

347

which, however, it should be distinguishable by
the form of the tail.

q. As *q*, but sometimes ends in an anti-clockwise
curve.

r. There are several forms, perhaps the commonest
being one which survived until recently, I believe,
in copy-books, but not elsewhere. It can most
simply be described as a 2 with the end brought
up and looped, the loop being carried forward as
a link. Sometimes there is a little cusp in the
middle of the lower stroke so that it resembles a *w*
with the middle point only slightly indicated. In
some forms r might be confused with v, only that
the latter has no forward link.

s. The long ſ is as f but without the tick across the
downstroke. ſſ, like ff, often has two tails and but
one loop. Occasionally a form in one stroke,
beginning with the upper loop, similar to the
Italian ſ, is found in conjunction with an English
hand.

Final s is a clockwise loop ending generally in
a blob or thickened tail above the letter. The little
anti-clockwise loop or curl properly standing for
final -es or -is is also found for simple final s.
There is also a form resembling a much elongated
roman S.

t. An upright, generally looped, with a cross-bar,
very like one modern form of *t*. Occasionally has
a spur or foot like *l*.

u. Generally like *u*, but sometimes consisting of two
similar minims and then indistinguishable from n.

v. Resembles the form of r described above, except
that the 2 is simply carried upwards in a curve to
the left without being looped. It consequently
does not link with a following letter.

w. A v preceded by a minim or an n with the last
stroke brought up in a curve to the left.

x. This is generally formed by writing a roman v

348

Fig. 23. Elizabethan Handwriting. Capitals.

(downward and upward) and continuing the top of
the second limb in an anti-clockwise curve crossing
the centre of the first limb and returning in an
upward sweep to link with the letter following.

y. Like *y*, but the tail usually anti-clockwise and not
crossed.

z. Generally much like *z*, nearly always tailed.

&. The forms of this are so various that it seemed
useless to attempt to give them; one of the commoner resembles a reversed 3 ; another is like the
-es contraction, i. e. an anti-clockwise curl beginning in a small loop.

Capitals. The forms of these vary so much that it
is difficult.to say anything useful about them. They
frequently resemble, more or less vaguely, the usual
black letter printed capitals, and fortunately it is
generally possible to guess what they are meant to be.
One or two hints may be given : occasionally a capital,
especially B, H, M, and P, is very wide, so that it may
at first sight appear to be two, or even more, separate
letters ; certain letters, especially L, are often practically the same as the small letter, only written slightly
larger ; F is two small f's ; a capital I or J carelessly
written may resemble *g* or *y* (with clockwise crossed
tail) ; and an unrecognizable letter consisting of several
interlacing curves is likely to be either C, E, or G.

Some of the commoner forms of capitals are given
in the accompanying figure. A slightly larger selection, together with notes on the formation of the letters,
will be found in a short article on ' The Capital Letters
in Elizabethan Handwriting ' in *The Review of English
Studies*, iii. 28–36.

INDEX

INDEX

INDEX

'galley', 13; long galleys not used in early printing, 14; first use of, 65, 66 *n.*; the page galley, 63–6.

'gatherings', 25, 28; for folio, 30; need for whole gathering to be in type at once, 31–4.

Ged, William, and stereotyping, 72.

Gentleman's Magazine, The, book-lists in, 139.

Gering, U., printer, 271.

Giunti, printers at Venice, 276.

Grafton, R., duplicate settings in his work, 215–16.

Greene, R., cancel in his *Quip,* 228; wrong perfecting in his *James IV,* 263.

Greg, Dr. W. W., 19 *n.*, 58 *n.*, 81 *n.*, 95 *n.*, 129 *n.*, 131, 156, 162, 174 *n.*, 179, 217, 219, 226 *n.*, 229 *n.*, 253 *n.*, 263, 344, &c.

Gresham, Sir T., his paper-mill, 99.

Haebler, Dr. Konrad, 130, 332; his *Inkunabelkunde* cited 75 *n.* and frequently.

half-sheets, imposition by, 66–70; effect of on variants, 211 *n.*

handwriting, Elizabethan, 253–4; 341–50.

Hansard, T. C., on early 19th-cent. types, 303.

Harington, Sir John, MS. of his *Orlando Furioso,* 217, 240–1, 247; his *Epigrams* possibly set from dictation, 242.

Harris, John, facsimilist, 236.

Hart, Horace, on the printing of the First Folio, 58 *n.*; on red printing, 334 *n.*

Harvey, G., his *Gratulationes Valdinenses,* 226; his spellings not followed by the compositor, 247.

'head' of the press, 48.

'head-line', 26.

'head-ornament', or 'head-piece', 26.

Herbert, W., used i for I, 250 *n.*

Hogarth, W., book illustrations by, 112, 113 *n.*

Holbein, 277.

'hose' of the press, 49–50.

Hoskins, W., printer, imaginary dialogue with, 205.

Howard, Henry, cancel in his *Defensative,* 227.

hyphens, evidence of order of editions from, 196.

I and J (i and j), 152, 295 *n.*, 310–12; in signatures, 75.

illustrations in books, 111–13; transference of, 111.

'imposition', 14; for 4to sheet, 15–18; for other sizes, folio, 8vo, &c., 29–36; rule for checking, 36; imposition by half-sheets, 66–70; modern impositions, 70–1; errors in, 259–60.

'impression', meaning of, 175; partial re-impressions, 179.

Indulgences, early, 268; line arrangement in, 55.

initials, ornamental, 26, 117.

inking of type, 20; type drawn out during inking, 204.

'issue', meaning of, 175–6; or 'edition', 177–9; evidence of order of issues, 197.

italic type, development of, 293–6; capitals, 294–6; whether representing Italian hand in copy, 251; how indicated in copy, 251.

Italy, first printing in, 270.

J, evidence of date from use of, 202 *n.*; *see* I and J.

Jacobi, C. T., 64 *n.*, 66 *n.*, 304.

Jaggard, W., on printers' errors, 206–7.

James, Thomas, typefounder, 299, 305.

Jenkins, Rhys, on paper, 97 *n.*, 98.

Jenkinson, Hilary, 342 *n.*

Jenson, Nicholas, 271; his roman type, 292; irregular lining in his work, 56.

Johnson, A. F., 294.

Johnson, John, his *Typographia* cited, 42, 61–2, 65, and frequently.

Johnson, S., his spellings, 249 *n.*

354

INDEX

INDEX

ornaments, 26; as evidence of date, &c., 114–17; how measured, 151–2.

Oxford University Press, 284, 299.

pages, made up as composed, 65; printing by single pages, 57–63.

pagination, 85–6.

Pannartz, A., *see* Sweynheym.

paper, 97–108; laid and wove, 28, 105; manufacture of, 100; machine-made, 104; modern book papers, 105–6; printed damp, 116 *n.*; shrinkage after printing, 151 *n.*; sizes of, 102–6; names of sizes, 103; use of ' double ' (and ' quad ') sizes, 69, 104; weights of, 106; calculation of quantity required, 106–7; quire, ream, &c., 106; *see also* watermark.

paper-mills, early English, 98–100.

paragraphing, evidence of order of editions from, 195–6.

Parker, Archbishop, patron of printing, 282.

' peel ', for hanging up printed sheets, 40.

' perfecting ', 21–2; errors in, 69, 70 *n.*, 260–1.

pica, size of, 306 *n.*, 307; as standard for measuring leads and page-width, 148, 308.

picked copies, 210 *n.*

Pickering, W., and Caslon type, 303.

place-names, Latin, 337–40.

' plank ' of the press, 44.

Plantin, Christophe, 279–80.

' platen ' of the press, 19, 50; small size of early platen, 61–3.

Plomer, H. R., 46 *n.*, 281 *n.*

' points ', used to obtain register, 22, 23 *n.*

point-system in measuring type, 307.

Pollard, Prof. A. W., 13 *n.*, 27 *n.*, 59–60, 88–89, 140–1, 202 *n.*, 203, 244 *n.*, 253 *n.*, 273 *n.*, 290 *n.*

preliminaries, unsigned leaves in, 156, 162.

presentation copies specially corrected, 209–10.

press, the early printing-press, 19–20; 38–52; use of several presses in early printing, 59.

' press-numbers ', 81–2.

' press-stone ', 44.

prices of books, *see* book-prices.

Prideaux, W. R. B., 168 *n.*

' printed by ' may mean ' printed for ', 176 *n.*

printers, distinctive bindings of early, 122; division of work between, 128–30; casualness of Elizabethan printers, 199.

printing, a note on, 264–87; general continuity of methods from early times, 6; changes in, 53–72; succession of chief localities of, 280.

printing-press, *see* press.

Proctor, R., his method of measuring type, 306 *n.*

proofs, authors' attendance at press to correct, 205–7; few surviving early proofs, 218–19.

Prynne, W., on the paper of Shakespeare's plays, 103.

publication, ascertainment of date of, 137–40.

punctuation, whether followed by compositor, 250; notes on some punctuation-marks, 315–18.

Pynson, R., signatures in quartos, 77–8; catchwords, 83; pagination, 86; device sometimes added after printing, 229; use of roman type, 297.

' quad ' sheet of paper, 69, 70.

' quads ', 13.

quarto, imposition in, 15–17; position of watermark in, 166–7, 169.

quaternus, or quaternion, sometimes equivalent to gathering, 87.

' quires ', 25 *n.*

' quoins ', 17.

Ramée, Pierre de la, and u, v, 311.

red, printing in, 329–36.

Reed, T. B., his *Old English Letter Foundries* cited, 72 *n.*, 269 *n.*, and frequently.

356